THE AGE OF JUSTINIAN

THE AGE OF
JUSTINIAN

The circumstances of imperial power

J. A. S. Evans

London and New York

DF568
.E83
1996

First published 1996
by Routledge
11 New Fetter Lane, London EC4P 4EE

Simultaneously published in the USA and Canada
by Routledge
29 West 35th Street, New York, NY 10001

© 1996 J.A.S. Evans

Routledge is an International Thomson Publishing company

Typeset in Garamond by Florencetype Ltd, Stoodleigh, Devon
Printed and bound in Great Britain by Mackays of Chatham PLC,
Chatham, Kent

British Library Cataloguing in Publication Data
A catalogue record for this book is available from the British Library

Library of Congress Cataloguing in Publication Data
Evans, J.A.S. (James Allan Stewart), 1931–
    The age of Justinian : the circumstances of imperial power /
J.A.S. Evans.
        p.   cm.
    Includes bibliographical references and index.
    1. Byzantine Empire–History–Justinian I, 527–565.   2. Justinian
I, Emperor of the East, 483?–565.   I. Title.
    DF568.E83   1996
    949.5′01–dc20

                                                            95–36732
                                                            CIP

ISBN 0–415–02209–6

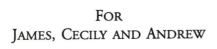

FOR
JAMES, CECILY AND ANDREW

CONTENTS

CONTENTS

PREFACE

Over the long gestation period that produced this book, I enjoyed the assistance of a number of institutions and granting agencies, which I want gratefully to acknowledge. I started work on the Syriac sources in the Bibliothèque Nationale in Paris, supported by a grant from the Social Sciences and Research Council of Canada. From there I migrated to the Dumbarton Oaks Center for Byzantine Studies in Washington D.C., where I encountered the gracious hospitality of Giles Constable, who was director at that time. My university gave me a year's administrative leave in 1993–94 when I retired as head of the Department of Classics, and a portion of it was spent at the Institute for Advanced Study at Princeton, N.J. I want to acknowledge the kindness of old and new friends there, particularly Homer Thompson, Glen Bowersock and the late Alison Frantz, who introduced me to the architecture of the Byzantine world many years ago at the American School of Classical Studies in Athens. I must acknowledge, too, the patient help of the Interlibrary Loan section of the University of British Columbia Library. The librarians there have done much to smooth out the rocky path of my research. I owe thanks, too, to my successor as head of the University of British Columbia Department of Classics, Anthony Barrett, whose yoke has been very easy. Last but by no means least, I acknowledge a debt of gratitude to Richard Stoneman, senior editor at Routledge, who has waited out this book's gestation period with patience.

My son, Andrew, has given me invaluable assistance with the maps shown on pp. xi–xiii. The map on p. xi is taken from C. Mango and R. Dagron, *Constantinople and its Hinterlands* (Ashgate Publishing Co., 1955), and the map on pp. xii–xiii is derived from A.H.M. Jones, *The Decline of the Ancient World* (Longman, Green & Co., 1966), both with permission.

Finally, to my wife Eleanor, my grateful thanks. She has tolerated a husband hunched behind a computer screen for longer than I have a right to expect.

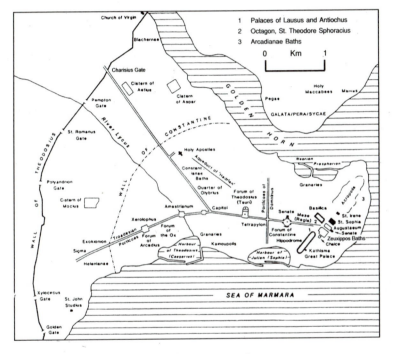

1	Palaces of Lausus and Antiochus
2	Octagon, St. Theodore Sphoracius
3	Arcadianae Baths

0   Km   1

Church of Virgin

Blachernae

Charisius Gate

Cistern of
Aetius

Cistern
of Aspar

Pempton
Gate

River Lycus

GOLDEN

HORN

Pegae

Holy
Maccabees

Mamas

GALATA/PERA/SYCAE

St. Romanus
Gate

WALL OF CONSTANTINE

Holy Apostles

Aqueduct of 'Hadrian'

Neorion

Prosphorion

WALL OF THEODOSIUS

Polyandrion
Gate

Cistern of
Mocius

Constant-
ianae
Baths

Quarter of
Olybrius

Forum of
Theodosius
(Tauri)

Porticoes of
Domninus

Granaries

Acropolis

Amastrianum

Capitol

Senate

Basilica

St. Irene

Xerolophus

Tetrapylon

Mese
(Regia)

Augustaeum

St. Sophia

Senate

Exokionion

Troadesian
Porticoes

Forum
of
the Ox

Forum
of
Arcadius

Granaries

Kainoupolis

Forum of
Constantine

Hippodrome

Zeuxippos Baths

Chalce

Sigma

Harbour
of Theodosius
(Caesarius)

Harbour of
Julian (Sophia)

Kathisma

Great Palace

Helenianae

Xylocercus
Gate

St. John
Studius

SEA OF MARMARA

Golden
Gate

Map of Constantinople

Boundaries between the praetorian prefectures of
the East, Illyricum, Italy and Africa
(QE) Provinces under the quaestor exercitus
(A) Provinces under the praetorian prefect of Africa
(Q) Sicily was directly under the quaestor of the sacred palace

0   100   200   300 miles

Map of the Roman Empire

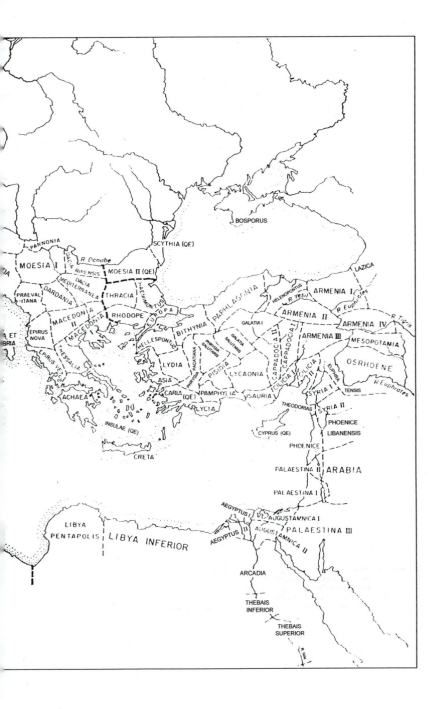

PANNONIA

MOESIA I

R. Ocnube

SCYTHIA (QE)

BOSPORUS

DACIA RIPENSIS

MOESIA II (QE)

DACIA MEDITERRANEA

LAZICA

PRAEVAL ITANA

DARDANIA

THRACIA

HELENOPONTUS

ARMENIA I

R. Yesi

PAPHLAGONIA

MACEDONIA II

RHODOPE

HAEMIMONTUS

EUROPA

BITHYNIA

ARMENIA II

R. Euphrates

R. Tigris

MACEDONIA

ET BRIA

EPIRUS NOVA

GALATIA I

ARMENIA IV

ARMENIA III

MESOPOTAMIA

THESSALIA

EPIRUS VETUS

MELLESPONTUS

HELLESPONTUS

PHRYGIA PACATIANA

GALATIA SALUTARIS

PHRYGIA SALUTARIS

CAPPADOCIA II

CAPPADOCIA I

OSRHOENE

R. Euphrates

ACHAEA

LYDIA

ASIA

PISIDIA

LYCAONIA

CILICIA II

CILICIA I

EUPHRA TENSIS

CARIA (QE)

PAMPHYLIA

ISAURIA

SYRIA I

LYCIA

THEODORIAS

SYRIA II

INSULAE (QE)

CYPRUS (QE)

PHOENICE

PHOENICE LIBANENSIS

CRETA

PALAESTINA II

ARABIA

PALAESTINA I

LIBYA PENTAPOLIS

LIBYA INFERIOR

AEGYPTUS I

AUGUSTAMNICA I

AEGYPTUS II

AUGUSTAMNICA II

PALAESTINA III

ARCADIA

THEBAIS INFERIOR

THEBAIS SUPERIOR

R. Nile

INTRODUCTION

The definitive history of Justinian has not yet been written. I am not sure that one can write a truly 'definitive history' about any figure in the historical landscape, but I have no doubt that the time is not ripe for a 'definitive history' of Justinian. A generation ago, the possibility seemed closer than it does now. Edward Gibbon's model for decline and fall was still largely accepted. Justinian's attempt to regain the lost territories of the Roman Empire could be regarded as a misguided attempt to reverse the course of history which resulted in fatal inattention to the eastern provinces. His corpus of law was a major attainment, to be sure, as Gibbon recognized, and his great church of Hagia Sophia in Istanbul stands as witness to his achievement as a builder. But even Hagia Sophia puts his personality flaws on record. Impatient, eager that his great church should exhibit his worthiness as God's vicegerent on earth, he refused the builders time for their mortar to set properly, thereby contributing to the structure's instability. Yet Hagia Sophia has lasted far better than his conquests, which began to crumble before the century was over.

Our perspective has changed. We are better equipped now to see Justinian and his empress Theodora within their own context. Late Antiquity was not a period of inevitable decline, and what was most impressive about the eastern Roman Empire and its successor state was their ability to survive a series of hammer blows as a succession of folk migrations from the 'Third World' of the Asian steppe pushed against the imperial boundaries. Within the empire too, Justinian's age saw plague, earthquakes and apprehension that the world was nearing its end. Perforce the empire changed. But change and decline are very different matters.

So perhaps the time *is* ripe to attempt a reassessment, even if the definitive history must wait. Justinian was the offspring of a Thracian

1

peasant family: a parvenu in a society which was all the more conscious of status and background because it allowed a good deal of social mobility. His wife was an actress, and actresses in contemporary Constantinople had the status of whores, with good reason. The pair made a remarkable husband-and-wife team as long as Theodora lived, and her influence did not die with her. I cannot think of a close parallel. The emperor Augustus took his wife Livia's advice very seriously, but that was as far as it went. Livia was never Augustus' loyal opposition: publicly she did not oppose him at all. Nor can I think of a good modern counterpart. Perhaps Juan and Evita Perón of Argentina come close. But the comparison cannot be pressed. Yet this imperial couple left their mark on their historical period as few rulers have.

I came to Justinian in a roundabout way. I began as a papyrologist, but my research stopped short of Late Antiquity. But Egypt led to Herodotus, and in the process I started to cast glances in the direction of the late Roman imitators of the great historians of classical Greece, not only Herodotus but his great successor, Thucydides. And so I arrived at the greatest of these, Procopius of Caesarea who, to quote an elegant phrase of Edward Gibbon, 'successively composed the history, the panegyric and the satire of his times'. Without him, we would know a great deal less about Justinian.

The vogue of classicizing history began with the literary movement known as the Second Sophistic. Lucian of Samosata satirized it in his essay on *How to Write History*. The best model was Thucydides, the proper subject was war, the Greek was Attic, and the product was not meant for the masses. It was a *ktema es aei*: a 'possession for all time'. The language of these classicizing historians was a status marker: it defined them as products of Greek *paideia*, the cultural legacy of classical Greece. When Christianity took over the empire, the style developed a mandarin quality, all the more so because the history of the church lay beyond its self-imposed limits, and Eusebius of Caesarea (ca. 260–339/40) developed a new genre, ecclesiastical history, to narrate the story of the Christian faith. Yet Procopius and his continuator, Agathias of Myrrhina, were two of the greatest heirs of this tradition which the Second Sophistic began, and taken together, within their limits, they are the fullest sources for Justinian's reign.

Averil Cameron has dealt ably with both of these historians, and the reader who wants to know more about them should turn to her books.[1] But the personality of Procopius is of importance, and so, too, is his attitude towards the Justinianic regime, which darkened as the years passed, and since a quarter-century ago I made a partial break with the conventional opinion of the dates when his several works were published, it is fair to state where I stand now. Procopius published his seven books narrating the course of Justinian's wars in 551. The first two books deal with the war on the eastern front, the next two with the war in Africa and the last three with the campaigns in Italy. There is no hint that when Procopius published his *History of the Wars*, he knew that the war in Italy would end with a decisive victory in 552, but at the same time, he brings his narrative of the wars down to the end of 550, and so 551 seems an obvious date for publication. About 557, he published a final, eighth book of his history. Its date can be fixed by a passage where Procopius reckoned the 'present time', that is, the time of writing, at eleven and a half years after 545, when Justinian's government began to pay Khusro, king of Persia, a yearly subsidy of 400 pounds of gold.[2]

It is Procopius' two other works which give difficulty. One is the *Buildings*, a panegyric on Justinian's building programme throughout the empire, with Justin's thrown in for good measure. It is a remarkable account, the like of which exists for no other Roman emperor, and it is an invaluable source. But it is an encomium, and Procopius kept in mind the advice which the author of a third-century handbook on rhetoric urged an orator to do in an oration on an emperor: 'you will have opportunity here to link up a passage on wisdom, saying that he himself was the planner, the commander, the discoverer of the moment for battle, a marvellous counsellor, champion, general and orator.'[3] Where Justinian repaired a wall, the *Buildings* claimed Justinianic reconstruction. But Procopius could report reliably enough when his sources were sound and he had no ulterior purpose: his descriptions of the Holy Apostles church in Constantinople and the 'New Church' (*Nea Ekklesia*) of the Virgin in Jerusalem are accurate enough, but his descriptions of Hagia Sophia and the great fortress of Dara on the Persian frontier are intended more as illustrations of Justinian's special relationship with God than a meticulous record. Yet he was selective and the basis for his selections is unclear: why, for instance, did he no more than mention the extensive construction which Justinian made at Nicopolis near Preveza in Greece?[4] Nicopolis had been founded by the emperor Augustus to commemorate his victory over Antony and Cleopatra at Actium in 31 BC. Was the city's historical significance unimportant to a man with Procopius' mandarin tastes? Or did his sources fail him?

The date when the panegyric was composed has been discussed by Averil Cameron, who eschews dogmatism but prefers 554 or thereabouts. However, I continue to hold the opinion which I expressed a quarter century ago, which owed a great deal to the analysis of the work by Glanville Downey.[5] It is that the first book was delivered as an encomium in Constantinople *before* the collapse of the first dome of Hagia Sophia on 7 May, 558. Procopius never hints at this collapse; on the contrary, he cites the raising of the dome as evidence of Justinian's special relationship with God![6] Historical accuracy is perhaps not a profitable characteristic for an encomiast, but neither is obvious falsehood. Panegyrics were, we know, delivered on formal occasions before a *theatron*, that is, a select audience gathered in a public space, and I cannot imagine that Procopius could present his audience with Justinian as a divinely inspired builder after the dome which demonstrated his divine inspiration had come tumbling down. It would verge on irony if he had.

But the remainder of the panegyric seems less suitable for oral delivery, and may well have been added later. At least it refers to building activity which postdates 558.[7] The work may be unfinished, for parts of it seem carelessly written and there is no reference to building in Italy. But Justinian built little there, and the omission of Italy may demonstrate authorial tact as much as incompletion. The *Buildings* is a puzzling work.

Even more puzzling is Procopius' *Anekdota*, the 'Unpublished Memoir' or, to give it its popular title, the *Secret History*. How it survived remains a mystery. The *Souda*, a lexicon dating to ca. 1000, knew it and classed it as a burlesque, but there is no earlier reference. In the early seventeenth century, a copy turned up in the Vatican Library. There were some grounds for suspecting its authenticity, for the secret historian's antipathy for the empress Theodora conformed almost too well with the rancour which contemporary Catholic historians directed at this spirited foe of the Council of Chalcedon. But scholars nowadays no longer doubt. The problem is: when was it written?

Procopius[8] himself dates it four times: thirty-two years after Justinian commenced his rule. Procopius considered Justinian the real administrator of the empire while Justin was on the throne, and if we count thirty-two years from Justin's accession, we arrive at 550.

So the *Secret History* itself asserts that it was written just as Procopius was readying his seven books on Justinian's wars for publication, in the year when Byzantine fortunes in Italy reached their nadir and Justinian's management of the state must have seemed utterly bankrupt, particularly to the refugee aristocrats from Italy who were waiting out the war in Constantinople. It claims to contain the inside information which Procopius dared not make public. It is a literary composition written in classical Greek for a phantom audience with mandarin tastes, and if we can take its claims at face value, it was intended as an underground commentary upon the seven books of the *History of the Wars*, which was on the verge of completion.

Yet it must have found some appreciative readers. Unread works do not endure. We need not be surprised that there was a disgruntled underground in Justinian's Constantinople, but it is astonishing that a contemporary pamphlet belonging to it should survive, and that it should be written by the greatest historian of the age! Its date of completion continues to puzzle me. A quarter century ago I tried to revive the date which early scholars such as Felix Dahn and W.S. Teuffel assigned to it: that is, thirty-two years after Justinian's accession in 527, which would make its composition more or less contemporary with the *Buildings*. I would be more hesitant now. Yet the *Secret History* does appear to report one item which Procopius could not have known in 550,[9] and thus it cannot have reached its present form by that year. But unpublished works do not have cut-off dates; they can always have later additions. When Procopius attacks Theodora in the *Secret History*, he displays the animosity of a person who remembered her vividly (she died in 548), but his final paragraphs seem to reflect the climate of opinion in Justinian's last years. Yet the persona which Procopius assumes is that of an alienated writer producing a malevolent commentary on his own great *History* that was on the verge of publication. Its drawback as a satisfactory source is not so much its inaccuracy as its obvious malice.

After Justinian's death, Agathias took up the tale where Procopius left off, and continued it to 559, when death (we presume) interrupted him. He was a successful lawyer and no mean poet, but as an historian, he was not Procopius' equal. His account is straightforward and without prejudice, but without much insight either. After him, Menander Protector (he was probably a palace guardsman) produced an account that began where Agathias broke off, and continued until the end of Tiberius II's reign in 582.[10] We have

more than seventy fragments of it in the *Souda,* and in an encyclopaedia (the *Eklogai* or *Excerpta*) compiled under the aegis of the
emperor Constantine VII Porphyrogenitus (945–959). He is our best
source for the negotiations leading to the treaty which ended the
war with Persia in 562. It is also from the *Excerpta* that we get
fragments of Peter the Patrician, Master of Offices under Justinian,
who wrote both a history and a treatise on protocol, which was no
doubt useful in a court where ceremony was becoming increasingly
important.

So much for the *Profanhistoriker,* to borrow a label from German
scholarship. We also have a good cache of other sources. There are
two ecclesiastical historians who add to our knowledge, Evagrius and
John of Asia. Evagrius of Epiphaneia (Hama) at the end of the sixth
century wrote a history in Greek covering the years 431 to 594.
Evagrius was a lawyer and honorary prefect who was a 6-year-old
schoolboy in 542, the year of the Great Plague, which he contracted
but recovered, though later recurrences were to kill his first wife and
various family members. Personal memories and family traditions
give his history a piquancy we cannot find in the *Profanhistoriker:*
he, for instance, relates a story his family knew of how two suffragan
bishops of Second Syria broke off communion with the Monophysite
patriarch of Antioch, Severus. They entrusted a deacon from
Evagrius' home town of Epiphaneia with a letter for Severus, calling
for his deposition. But how to deliver it? The deacon dressed as a
woman, and pretending to be a petitioner, approached the all-
powerful patriarch who was proceeding with his train through the
streets of Antioch, thrust the letter into his hand and fled!

John of Asia, or John of Ephesus (he was ordained the
Monophysite bishop of the city) was a native of Amida (*mod.*
Diyarbakir) on the border of Mesopotamia and Sophanene. He
became a friend and protégé of the empress Theodora and,
Monophysite though he was, he was sent by Justinian in 542 on a
mission to convert the remaining pagans of Asia Minor, whom John
ferreted out with immense zeal. He wrote a history in Syriac that
began with Julius Caesar, but the part that survives covers 571 to
586. Yet we can savour the lost sections at second hand through the
Chronicle of the twelfth-century Monophysite patriarch of Antioch,
Michael the Syrian. It is also to John that we owe an intimate view
of Monophysite asceticism in the Syriac-speaking East, for his *Lives
of the Eastern Saints* sketches the biographies of 58 holy men and
women whom he knew at first hand.

Chronicle writing had a long, respectable tradition behind it by the time we reach the sixth century.[11] Christianity added a fillip to the genre, not only because the chronicle allowed the biblical past to be set side by side with the classical past, but because the Christian religion preached the concept of a world that began at a precise date with Adam and Eve, and would end at a precise date. For practical reasons, Christian chronicles had to end in the chronicler's lifetime, but nonetheless the aim was to reveal God's plan as far as it could be. The best of the Justinianic chroniclers, John Malalas,[12] made a point of demonstrating that the sixth millennium after Creation had already passed by Justinian's accession, and hence God did not purpose to terminate the world after 6,000 years. People did not need to fear.

Malalas means *rhetor* or *scholastikos*: that is to say, John was a lawyer, probably in the civil service in Antioch and Constantinople, and for the period of Justinian, through which he lived, he seems attuned to official sources. This gives him a peculiar value for he represents an attitude which is the antithesis of what we find in the *Secret History*.[13] He accepts Justinian's regime at its own estimation and supplies us with a summary of the official version of events. Trivia and significant reportage are jumbled together, but they repay careful reading.

Other sources that appear in the footnotes are the *Easter Chronicle*, written probably in the 630s, and the Chronographia of Theophanes the Confessor (ca. 760–817), which covers the years 285–813. The chronicle of an Egyptian bishop of the late seventh century, John of Nikiu, survives at third hand. Written in Greek or possibly Coptic, it was translated into Arabic and from Arabic into Ethiopic, and it is the Ethiopic translation which has survived. In Latin we have Count Marcellinus, whose chronicle ran from 379 to 518, and the sequel he added later takes us as far as 534. His notice on the *Nika* riots of 532 is almost contemporary. He was Justinian's man, and uncritical, but he transmits some valuable information. Victor Tunnensis, on the other hand, was a doughty opponent of the emperor. Bishop of Tunnena in Africa Proconsularis, he clashed with Justinian in the 'Three Chapters' controversy, and paid for it with exile. Only the last part of his chronicle survives, but it adds important information: it is he alone, for instance, who informs us that Theodora died of 'cancer', which has been taken, rightly or wrongly, to be what modern medicine defines as cancer.

This was also an age of law and of poetry, and both can be mined for historical data. The *Johannid*, eight books of Latin hexameters by Flavius Cresconius Corippus, is our main source for the campaign in Africa conducted by John Troglita. Corippus was a poet and a schoolmaster, who came to Carthage and recited his epic there before the dignitaries of the city in 549, only a few months after the Berber revolt was finally crushed. The subtext of the *Johannid* is an apologia for Byzantine policy in Africa.[14] Then, after Justinian's death, Corippus resurfaced in Constantinople where he produced a panegyric in Latin hexameters on Justin II. He hoped for a reward and he deserved one, for his works are helpful to the modern historian, but what he received, we do not know. From Paul the Silentiary, who was wealthy enough to need no reward, we have a clutch of sensual epigrams and a long *ekphrasis* on Hagia Sophia with its rebuilt dome, which includes a report of the conspiracy to assassinate Justinian in November 562. As for the corpus of law, which guaranteed Justinian a good odour in history, I do not imagine that the constitutions issued under Justinian's name were from his pen, but they do express the aspirations of his reign. Percy Ure asserted that by 'collating them with the historical narratives of Procopius and Agathias and such works as that of Lydus on the administrative system we can form a truer and more vivid picture of life in the realm of Justinian than is attainable in any other way'.[15] There was, however, always a gap between the promulgation of a law and its enforcement. Justinian's laws are better evidence for what he recognized as blemishes and how he wanted to deal with them than for what was actually done.

I have left two not unimportant authors to the last. John Lydus came from Philadelphia in Asia Minor to Constantinople in 511 and found a post in the praetorian prefecture. He spent forty years in the civil service and after he retired, ca. 551, he turned to literature. His most useful work is his *On the Magistracies*, on the civil *militia*, though two other compositions are extant as well: his *On the Months* and *On Omens*. He gives us an old-line bureaucrat's view of the regime, full of complaints and much information, not all of it accurate. Cosmas Indicopleustes, a retired sea-captain in Alexandria, produced a long treatise at the height of the 'Three C7hapters' controversy, which was the foremost theological dispute of Justinian's reign. Nestorian in his sympathies, he wrote to oppose the Aristotelian philosophers like John Philoponus at Alexandria and there is a political subtext to his work. We may not regard him highly as a cosmographer, for he argued that

8

the world was shaped like the tabernacle of Moses. But he does tell us something about the trade which went back and forth between the Byzantine Empire and the East.

So much for the authors. In the last generation, archaeology has also added enormously to our knowledge of the everyday life of the period, and at least in Egypt, so has papyrology. But for this evidence I leave the reader to the tender mercies of my notes.

There are other excellent books on Justinian, such as Robert Browning's *Justinian and Theodora*, John Moorhead's recent *Justinian*, and John Barker's earlier *Justinian and the Later Roman Empire*. It is customary for authors who add to the bibliography on a well-trodden topic to produce an excuse for their deed. I have none, except that I have found Justinian's period a fascinating one, and hope my readers will as well. What I have attempted to produce is not a biography of Justinian, much less a biography of Justinian coupled with Theodora, but rather an assessment of them within their context. This book is intended as the history of an age. But in the end, it is the great emperor who matters, for he actually did change the course of history as much as any ruler can. How shall we judge him? Dante encountered his soul in the Second Sphere of Paradise, where it related to him its life on earth, and then uttered a discourse on the history of the Roman Eagle. Here, in John Ciardi's translation, is the soul of the emperor speaking of its earthly experience:

Caesar I was, Justinian I am.
By the will of the First Love, which I now feel,
I pruned the law of waste, excess, and sham.

Before my work absorbed my whole intent
I knew Christ in one nature only, not two;
and so believing, I was well content.

But Agapetus, blessed of the Lord,
he, the supreme shepherd pure in faith,
showed me the true way by his holy word.

Him I believed, and in my present view
I see the truth as clearly as you see
how a contradiction is both false and true.

As soon as I came to walk in the True Faith's way
God's grace moved all my heart to my great work;
and to it I gave myself without delay.

To my Belisarius I left my spear
and God's right hand so moved his that the omen
for me to rest from war was more than clear.[16]

In a note, Ciardi remarks, 'Another reading of history might have suggested several pits of Hell that might have claimed Justinian.'[17]

1

THE IMPERIAL
ENVIRONMENT

THE EMPIRE WHICH ANASASTIUS LEFT
BEHIND

During the night of 9 or 10 July, 518, the emperor Anastasius died
in Constantinople. A violent thunderstorm was raging, and a lightning bolt struck the imperial palace, which may have hastened the
death of the aged and heretical emperor.[1] Thus ended a remarkable
reign which had begun unexpectedly twenty-seven years earlier. The
emperor Zeno the Isaurian had died; the people gathered in the
Hippodrome and waited restively for word of his successor, and
the senate, respecting the hereditary principle, resolved to invite
Zeno's widow, Ariadne, daughter of the emperor Leo I, to make the
choice. She passed over Zeno's brother and the whole coterie of
Isaurians who had supported Zeno, and chose Anastasius, a decurion
of the court ushers with senatorial rank known as silentiaries. He
was 61 years old, and had a reputation for Monophysite leanings,
but he was an old friend of Ariadne's. The next day, 11 April, 491,
Anastasius gave the patriarch of Constantinople, Euphemius, a
written pledge to make no religious innovations, and the diadem
was placed on his head. The following month he married Ariadne.

But in 518 Ariadne had been dead for two years, and there was
no obvious successor. Anastasius had three nephews, and the most
likely of them, Hypatius, was Master of the Soldiers in the East
when the old emperor died. Distance ruled him out, for he was
probably at his headquarters in Antioch. The silentiaries reported
the emperor's death to Celer, the Master of Offices, and Justin, Count
of the Excubitors. Both these men had soldiers under their
command, Celer more than Justin, but Celer's *candidati* and regi-
ments of the Scholae (*Scholares*) were largely ornamental, whereas
Justin's Excubitors were the palace guard and could fight if need be.

11

When morning came, Celer summoned the senate, the patriarch and high officials to the palace, while the people gathered in the Hippodrome next door and waited impatiently. Celer urged a quick decision: if the senators failed to act promptly, he warned, others would make the choice for them.

Yet no quick decision was forthcoming. The Constantinople senate had never chosen an emperor before. The Excubitors put forward a nominee, but the Blues[2] in the Hippodrome would not have him. The *Scholares* put forward another, but the Excubitors would have killed him but for the intervention of Justin's nephew, Justinian. The Excubitors then tried to put forward Justinian himself, but he declined. The situation was in danger of getting out of hand. Finally all the senators, who were by now a little frightened, agreed upon Justin. Some *Scholares* objected, and in the ensuing scuffle, the future emperor got a split lip. But the army and people backed Justin, and the chamberlains sent him the imperial robes. So Justin, after the conventional show of reluctance, accepted. He entered the imperial box at the Hippodrome, and there, before the people, he was raised upon a shield; an officer of the Lancers put a gold chain on his head, and while the Excubitors screened him with their shields, he put on the purple robe and red shoes of a Byzantine emperor. Then the patriarch John crowned him, and the new emperor was exhibited to the people, who shouted in unison, 'Justinus Augustus, *tu vincas!* (you are the victor)'. Justin then spoke, promising good government and a donative to the troops, and the ceremony ended with a solemn procession to the church of Hagia Sophia, and a banquet in the palace.[3]

That, at least, is the story according to the official account, which derives from the contemporary historian, Peter the Patrician, and except for the insinuation that the future emperor Justinian was himself a possible candidate in 518 for the imperial office, it is credible enough. But we have more information from John Malalas, who was familiar with contemporary traditions. The imperial chamberlain Amantius (*praepositus sacri cubiculi*) had ambitions of his own, and since he could not himself aspire to the throne, for he was a eunuch, he schemed to put forward his domestic, the count Theocritus. He entrusted Justin with money to make the necessary bribes, and Justin distributed it. 'The army and the people' took the money, reported Malalas, but they did not choose Theocritus. Instead, 'by the will of God' they made Justin himself emperor, who began his reign by putting Amantius and his clique to death.[4]

Justin, who now at the age of about 65 became emperor, had been a Thracian peasant who migrated to Constantinople, and rose through the army ranks until he became Count of the Excubitors, well positioned to succeed the childless Anastasius. The dynasty he founded was to end the series of remarkable emperors from Illyricum that began in 268 with Claudius Gothicus, who took over a Roman Empire at the point of collapse and began the restoration. They were also the last emperors whose native tongue was Latin, and perhaps the last who genuinely felt the resonance of Rome's departed grandeur. The reign of Justinian, for which Justin's was the preface, was a period of transition, when the classical Graeco-Roman world finally died, and the Byzantine world began. Not that the sixth century itself recognized the watershed: the inhabitants of the empire called their empire *Romania* and themselves *Romaioi*, and the term 'Byzantine' which we use to describe the period is something of an anachronism, for it became common usage only in the Renaissance. The shift was probably not one that Justinian consciously willed. He saw his innovations as restoration and reform rather than a break with the past, but he accelerated change nonetheless. The regime of Justinian and his empress Theodora marked the summit of Late Antiquity. It concluded the chapter that we can entitle the proto-byzantine period, and opened a new one on the Byzantine world.

Claudius Gothicus died of plague in 270, but the recovery of the empire was already under way. Under his predecessor, Gallienus, a horde of Goths and Heruls had swept into Greece; Athens was sacked in 267, and the invaders got as far south as Sparta. But two years later, Claudius defeated a fresh invasion of Goths, and in the fifteen years after his death, the empire reemerged with its boundaries almost, but not quite, intact, for Dacia, which the emperor Trajan had added at the start of the second century, had to be evacuated. Yet the old sense of security was gone. Nothing marks its passing so visibly as the walls of Rome, which are still standing and were last put to use during the Risorgimento in 1870. For three centuries, no one had thought Rome needed walls, but now it seemed otherwise. The emperor Aurelian began their construction in 271.

Aurelian died at the hands of his officers after a five-year reign; the 75-year-old Tacitus, whom the senate nominated as his successor at the army's request, lasted only six months, and after him, Probus fell victim to a mutiny within six years. His successor Carus died in turn some ten months later on an expedition to Persia. His assassin was probably his praetorian prefect, Aper, who also disposed of Carus' younger son, Numerian, or at least suspicion pointed towards him. But Aper did not succeed to the throne, for upon discovering Numerian's death, the army acclaimed Diocles, who took the name of Diocletian and, as his first imperial act, slew Aper with his own hands.

That was on 20 November, 284. Next April, Diocletian eliminated Carus' son, Carinus, whom his father had left in charge of the western part of the empire. Fifteen years after Claudius' death, the empire found a ruler with a clear idea of how it should be reformed, and the acumen and skill to do it. He ruled for twenty-one years and abdicated of his own free will. The succession was orderly. At least, for the moment.

Diocletian's design, that the empire should be ruled by a college of emperors, was not entirely new. Emperors as early as Galba in the aftermath of Nero's death had tried to secure their positions by associating colleagues with them. But Diocletian's scheme was the most elaborate and successful. In 285, he created his old friend Maximian Caesar, and next year made him Augustus, his equal but junior partner. In early 293, deciding that two emperors were not enough, he created two Caesars, Galerius in the East, and in the West, Constantius Chlorus. When Diocletian abdicated, Maximian did likewise, though less willingly, and Galerius and Constantius Chlorus succeeded as Augusti along with two new Caesars, their appointments intentionally disregarding hereditary right which the army rank and file were always disposed to recognize. Maximian's son, Maxentius, and the son of Constantius, Constantine, were both passed over.

The plan failed in the outcome. When Constantius died, his army proclaimed Constantine as his successor, and in Italy, Maxentius led a revolt which Galerius and his Caesar, Severus, failed to suppress, for their soldiers would not follow them against Maximian's natural heir. Galerius died in 311, and his portion of the empire was divided between his fellow Augustus, Licinius, and his erstwhile Caesar, Maximin Daia. The following year, Constantine destroyed Maxentius at the Milvian Bridge outside Rome: an easy victory but one which actually did change the course of history, for Constantine chose that moment to acknowledge his Christian faith. Licinius and Constantine met the next year in Milan and patched together an alliance: the Christians, whom Galerius had persecuted savagely until just before his death, were to receive toleration and their confiscated property returned. To seal the pact, Licinius married Constantine's sister.

But as the two Augusti conferred at Milan, news came that Maximin Daia had invaded Europe, and Licinius left hurriedly to deal with him. Daia was defeated near Adrianople and pulled back into Asia Minor, but there was no hope for him: at Tarsus, he ended the contest by taking his own life. Licinius and Constantine were left to share the empire between them.

It was an uneasy accord: a Cold War between an emperor in the West whose indulgence towards the Christian church became increasingly clear, and an eastern counterpart whose suspicion of the Christians mounted in tandem. In 324, the peace broke down. Constantine attacked. His troops carried into battle the Labarum, his imperial standard bearing the Christian Chi–Rho emblem, whereas Licinius' troops fought under the signs of the pagan gods. It was a Christian battle against the unbeliever,[5] and on 8 November, 324, Licinius was defeated off Scutari on the Asian side of the Bosporus. He surrendered with the understanding that his life would be spared, but Constantine soon found a reason to put him to death.

Yet something lasted of what Diocletian's Tetrarchy achieved. Diocletian had put his stamp upon both the administrative structures of Late Antiquity and the emperor's persona. One aspect of his reform, however, had a result he would not have approved. Diocletian had divided the imperial administration between two Augusti, but he did not intend to split the empire itself. Yet the fracture took on a life of its own. Constantine, who united the empire at the cost of much toil and bloodshed, divided it at his death among his heirs. But by that time, it had undergone a change which pointed forward to Justinian's empire.

In some respects, Constantine's administrative reforms merely completed what Diocletian had begun, but two of his decisions changed the course of imperial history. First, he became a Christian. It is irrelevant to ask how profound his comprehension of the Christian faith was, though we must judge him as good a Christian as Henry VIII of England, who actually founded a church. Later tradition fostered by Constantine himself had it that his conversion resulted from a vision before the battle of the Milvian Bridge, but probably the process was less precipitate, though decisive just the same. Christianity now enjoyed official favour, and a spate of church building began which reached full flood under Justinian. But along with his new religion, Constantine inherited its theological disputes. Henceforth, finding an acceptable definition of orthodoxy would be a major concern of all emperors who sought to maintain the unity of the empire.

Second, he founded Constantinople where the city of Byzantium stood at the entrance to the Black Sea. Rome on the Tiber had long since lost its strategic importance. Diocletian had made Nicomedia his capital and Galerius Thessaloniki, but in fact, the working capitals of the late imperial period were wherever the hard-driven emperors happened to be campaigning at the time. That state of affairs would not change immediately, but by the end of the fourth century, emperors had ceased to lead their armies in person, and Constantinople had become the capital city of the eastern empire, the residence of the eastern emperors. After 476, when the last emperor in the West was deposed, it was Constantine's new Rome that survived and continued as the imperial capital and the heart of *Romania*. For fifty years Justinian never stirred more than a few kilometres from its boundaries except for a pilgrimage to a shrine near Ankara at the end of his life.

THE CONSTRUCTION OF A NEW CAPITAL

Tradition had it that Byzantium was founded in 659 BC by the Greek city-state of Megara.[6] The date is probably too early, but at any rate, by 600 BC there was a Greek settlement on the west shore of the Bosporus, with its acropolis where Hagia Sophia and Topkapi palace stand now. In the civil war which brought the emperor Septimius Severus to the throne, Byzantium supported Severus' rival, Gaius Pescennius Niger, and fell to Severus only after a siege of nearly three years. Severus sacked the city, but once peace returned, he refounded it as a Roman colony named 'Antoniniana', gave it an amphitheatre and a theatre,[7] and began the construction of the Hippodrome and perhaps the palace as well. Thus when Constantine came to Byzantium, he found a Greek city already there, with three temples on its acropolis dedicated to Aphrodite, Artemis and the sun god Helios. They were to last until the very Christian emperor Theodosius I turned them to secular uses: the Artemision became the 'Temple' casino, and Aphrodite's sanctuary was turned into the praetorian prefect's carriage house, though a reminiscence of the dispossessed goddess remained in the free housing provided nearby for indigent whores.[8] West and south of the acropolis were two open commons, the *Strategion* close by the two old harbours on the Golden Horn, and the *Tetrastoon*, a plaza surrounded by a colonnade. The latter served as an *agora*, the central feature of every Greek city, which was both marketplace and civic centre.

Byzantium had no great advantages to recommend it as a future capital. Its water supply was limited, and it had nothing like the fine *pozzuolana* which Roman builders had at their disposal: instead its architects had to use rough concrete with rubble fill to form a core which could be faced with stone, sometimes with bonding courses of brick. Moreover, in the struggle between Licinius and Constantine, Byzantium was again on the losing side. Yet the city had a strategic position and Constantine recognized it. The tetrarchs had built their palaces along the new lifeline of the empire, at Trier, Milan, Sirmium (*mod.* Sremska Mitrovica), Serdica (*mod.* Sofia), Thessaloniki, Nicomedia and Antioch, where their mobile courts settled for months or years as the case might be, never far from the frontiers, for their security engaged a major share of their energy. Byzantium's location, midway between the Rhine–Danube frontier and the Persian marches in the East, was what recommended the city to Constantine. At any rate, not two months after he crushed his rival Licinius, his new city received its ritual consecration and was given both its official name and its mystic name, *Anthousa*, a Greek translation of Rome's own mystic name, 'Flora'. Construction went forward swiftly. On 11 May, 330, the city was dedicated in a double ceremony in the Forum and in the Hippodrome.

We can only infer the plan of Constantine's city, but from the beginning, the comparison with the old capital on the Tiber was unambiguous. Like Rome, Constantinople was divided into fourteen regions, and had seven hills, which could be identified with a smidgen of imagination: a sixteenth-century traveller who visited Constantinople on a French mission to Suleyman the Magnificent remarked that, unlike the seven hills of Rome which were simple to recognize, 'it is not easy to distinguish those of Constantinople, because they are joined at the top'.[9] Like Rome too, the city also had a Golden Milestone (the *Milion*), at the north-west corner of the *Tetrastoon* from which all roads were measured.[10] Across the square from the *Milion* were the opulent Baths of Zeuxippus, constructed under Septimius Severus but embellished by Constantine, and close by it, the Hippodrome. On the east side of the square stood the senate house, which may have been built by Constantine though the emperor Julian's name is connected with it, and after fire destroyed it in 532, it was reconstructed by Justinian. West from the *Tetrastoon* ran the great central road of the city, the *Mese* (*mod.* Divanyolu) which predated Constantine's foundation, but it was he who transformed it into a splendid main street some

25 metres broad, lined with porticoes on either side. Where the west gate of the Severan city had been, Constantine built a forum which, unlike most forums, was oval rather than rectangular. The *Tetrastoon* itself took the name 'Augustaeum' from the porphyry column bearing a statue of Constantine's mother, the Augusta Helena, that dominated it. North of it was the atrium of the Hagia Sophia church, and to the south, covering the area now partly occupied by the 'Blue Mosque' of Sultan Ahmed, Constantine built his palace, the Daphne, which connected directly with the imperial box in the Hippodrome beside it.

The juxtaposition of Hippodrome and Palace was a feature taken from Rome, where the Circus Maximus flanked the *Domus Augustana* on the Palatine Hill, and a private passageway connected the palace with the imperial *loge* in the Circus. Conspicuous participation in mass entertainments was part of the theatre which surrounded the imperial persona, and the Hippodrome was the centre of the ritual of victory, the *Victoria Augusti* predestined by Heaven which was a foundation block of the imperial cult. Emperors patronized chariot races and gave their favour to one or other of the racing factions, the Blues, Reds, Whites or Greens.[11] The victory of a favourite charioteer was acclaimed as the personal triumph of the reigning prince. Chariot racing became the hallmark of imperial power to such a degree that on two occasions when the Samaritans in Palestine revolted, in 484 and again in 529, the rebel leaders staged chariot races to emphasize their claim to sovereignty.[12] Hippodromes flanking palaces were to be found in Antioch, Sirmium and Thessaloniki too, all capital cities of the Tetrarchy, and in fact, the hippodrome became part of the standard palace complex of Late Antiquity.[13]

Of Constantine's walls, nothing remains, though they were still standing when Justinian became emperor, and the last vestige did not disappear until 1509. The great Theodosian walls some 1.5 kilometres west of Constantine's defences replaced them in 413 as the main defence on the landward side, and were to protect Constantinople for more than a thousand years. They were not pierced until 1453, when the city fell at last to the Ottoman Turks.

Constantine's forum which marked the city's 'navel' has disappeared, but the stump of the porphyry column which he erected there still stands, blackened with fire and reinforced with iron bands. Its shaft once rose with nine great drums to a height of more than 35 metres. On top stood a bronze statue of Constantine with a radiate crown, which may have been Pheidias' sculpture of Apollo Parnopius from the Acropolis of Athens, now recycled with Constantine's head substituted for the original.[14] There was a tradition that the statue's left hand carried a bronze orb which contained a fragment of the True Cross, and that in the column base were placed not only Christian relics but also the Palladium, which Byzantine legend claimed that Constantine had dug up in his forum.[15] Some people in Justinian's reign believed that it was still there.[16]

The column of Constantine and the mythology that surrounded it symbolized a part of the ambivalence that underscored this emperor's break with the pagan past. He considered himself a Christian and was considered as such; of that there can be no serious doubt. But it may be that the closest parallel to his conversion can be found among the 'God-fearers' (*theosebeis*) in contemporary Jewish synagogues: Gentiles who committed themselves to Judaism without breaking completely with their ancestral gods, but nonetheless looking forward to a share in the Resurrection.[17] Nor did conversion to Christianity in the early fourth century separate the convert completely from his past. The break was real, but there was nothing revolutionary about it.

Thus, for a contemporary, even with the new ingredient of Christianity, Constantine's foundation must have appeared as part of a familiar pattern. The Tetrarchs had been great builders of imperial cities with palaces to house the elaborate courts surrounding their persons, and Constantinople was another of these. But the other tetrarchic capitals were failures while Constantinople was a success. For all that Constantine's urban planning made no single-minded effort to emphasize his new religion, what was created out of the Graeco-Roman past on the old site of Byzantium was something original. The new Rome was a Christian Rome. In retrospect we can see that its foundation marked the start of a new age.

Upon his death, Constantine again divided the empire which he had united, and after a brief hiatus and some spilling of blood, his three sons succeeded him, each ruling a portion of the empire. But the arrangement was unstable: in 340, Constantine II in the West attacked his youngest brother, Constans, whose segment lay between those of his siblings, and was defeated. Ten years later, Constans fell to a usurper, who in turn was dispatched by the remaining son, Constantius II. Once again, the empire was under a single ruler, but its direction was too much for one man. In 355, Constantius summoned the last remaining male of Constantine's dynasty, Julian, from his studies in Athens, and made him Caesar. Not five years later, Julian was in revolt, and Constantius died as he marched to suppress him.

Julian was the last pagan emperor but his 19-month reign was too short to give paganism more than a brief reprieve. Yet he left a mark on Constantinople: the senate house on the Augustaeum may have been his, perhaps also a Capitolium for the cult of Jupiter Capitolinus, and he completed a new harbour on the Sea of Marmara south and west of the Hippodrome. But he was killed on a campaign against Persia which fared badly, thanks to his own tactical blunders as well as the blistering summer heat of Mesopotamia, and since he was without heir, a 'few agitators', as a contemporary[18] put it, contrived the election of the commander of the household troops, Jovian. He extricated his army by a truce which partitioned Mesopotamia and established a border that was to last two and a half centuries. Rome evacuated the Kurdish provinces east of the Tigris, abandoned five-sixths of Armenia and handed over to Persia the loyal frontier city of Nisibis, home to a Syriac Christian school, which transferred to Edessa (*mod.* 'Urfa), as well as of a Jewish academy, which had nowhere to go.[19] Less than eight months later Jovian died, after eating a heavy meal and sleeping it off in a newly plastered room![20]

The army officers chose as the next emperor Valentinian, the son of a Pannonian peasant who had risen through the ranks. A month later, he made his younger brother Valens his colleague to rule the eastern portion of the empire. Valens has two claims to our attention. First, in 376 he accepted the Goths as immigrants, and took them into the army, at the same time ending conscription within the empire, which had become difficult, and substituting a tax instead.[21] And second, he suffered a stunning defeat by the Goths at Adrianople in the summer of 378.

By then, Valentinian was already dead, and his young son Gratian, realizing that he could not cope alone with the emergency, summoned Theodosius, whose father had been Valentinian's Master of the Horse, and proclaimed him Augustus. The crisis was severe. The Roman defeat was a signal for other barbarian tribes to move into imperial territory. Theodosius took a step which was to have grave consequences, though it was necessary at the time. He took barbarians into the army as 'federates': that is, the barbarian contingents were under the command of their own leaders, but were bound to Rome as allies by treaties, and hence they took their name from the Latin word for treaty: *foedus*. The consequence was that barbarian officers became the powers behind the imperial throne, and the emperors of the fifth century had to rely upon the support of a series of barbarian warlords, while their own military role withered away.[22]

Theodosius died in his bed in 395, a pious narrow Christian who put an end to the pagan order so far as he was able. Three years before his death, the ancient oracular oak at Dodona had been chopped down and uprooted, and the next year, the Olympic Games were held for the last time; the gold-and-ivory cult statue of Zeus by Pheidias had already been transferred from Olympia to Constantinople. Theodosius' reign marks the victory of Christianity, though paganism was still to take a long time dying. The empire was split between his sons, and remained divided until Justinian's reconquest, and although in the minds of men the unity of the empire lived on, in actuality the two sections were to work out their own destinies. In the West, Theodosius' dynasty lasted until 455, and it is fair to say that the western empire died with it, though it was two decades on before the last emperor was dethroned. In the East, the dynasty ended with Theodosius II's accidental death in 450, but by then it had acquired such an aura of legitimacy that Theodosius' aged sister Pulcheria could confer imperial power upon the next emperor, Marcian, by agreeing to become his wife, though not his bed partner. Yet Marcian's military underpinning rested on the support of the patrician Aspar, the leader of the Gothic federates in the capital.

Still, the emperors in Constantinople managed to do what their western counterparts could not. They freed themselves from the barbarian warlords who tried to control them. On Marcian's death, it appears that the senate offered Aspar the purple, but he was a barbarian and an Arian heretic, and instead he promoted Leo, an army officer from Thrace whom he considered sufficiently unassertive. In the event, he was wrong. Leo showed surprising independence.[23] He freed himself from the Goths with the help of the Isaurians, who were equally barbarian, but barbarians from within the empire. They were unruly mountaineers with a dialect of their own, who drifted over the empire from their homes in the Taurus mountain range to serve as soldiers or itinerant stonemasons. Leo married his daughter Ariadne to an Isaurian chief, Tarasis, who changed his name to Zeno and counterbalanced the Goths until at last Leo was able to liquidate Aspar and part of his family. Leo's subjects, who liked the Isaurians no more than the Goths, nick-named him *Makelles* (Butcher) to mark his exploit, but he had undercut the barbarian dominance of the army.

The throne on Leo's death passed to his 6-year old grandson, Leo II, who died within the year, after conferring the purple upon his father Zeno. Zeno's reign lasted until 491, and during it, the last emperor in the West, Romulus Augustulus, was dethroned. The year 476, when Romulus was bundled off into retirement on the Bay of Naples, serves to date the fall of the Roman Empire in the West, but the imperial façade altered only slightly. The Scirian trooper Odoacer, who dethroned Romulus, sent the imperial insignia to Constantinople along with a message to the senate that the empire no longer needed two emperors, and henceforth Zeno might serve *de iure* as emperor of both East and West. Odoacer wanted for himself the rank of patrician and recognition of his right to admin-ister Italy in the emperor's name. Zeno demurred, but he sent Odoacer a written reply wherein he addressed him as patrician, thereby giving him practical recognition.

Like the other barbarian kings who occupied parts of the western empire, Odoacer used *rex* as his official title. Yet he was not a 'king' of blood royal like his contemporaries, Euric the Visigoth whose domain stretched from southern Gaul into Spain, or Clovis, king of the Salian Franks who in 486 occupied the last pocket of Roman rule in Gaul, the 'Kingdom of Syagrius' in the area of modern Paris. Odoacer was a warlord heading a heterogeneous troop of federates who were all that the last emperors of the West had left to rely upon, for the army had faded away after the death of the last of Theodosius' dynasty, Valentinian III. The historian Procopius[24] claimed that Odoacer won the allegiance of his men by granting them one-third of the land of Italy, but it seems unlikely that the expropriations were as widespread as his statement implies. In Constantinople, Zeno's grasp on power was too insecure for him to oppose Odoacer, and in any case, he had no great interest in the West, but in 488, he commissioned Theodoric, king of the Ostrogoths, to recover Italy in his name. Not, however, out of any regard for the Italians. The Ostrogoths had been ravaging the Balkan provinces for six years, and Zeno's move rid him of a dangerous nuisance. Next year, in the spring, the Ostrogoths left the Balkans and invaded Italy.

Odoacer lost two battles and was forced back into Ravenna. Next year he attempted a sortie, failed and retreated again to Ravenna. There he held out until 493, when Theodoric enticed him out with a promise of shared rule. Once he had Odoacer securely in his hands, he killed him and purged his troops.

In the East, Zeno was by now dead, but his successor Anastasius returned to Theodoric the imperial insignia which Odoacer had sent to Constantinople. Yet Theodoric's title remained *rex*, and his status was that of a barbarian king who had settled under treaty in a Roman province. Procopius[25] wrote that he had the qualities of a true *basileus*, the Greek term that was now reserved for a Roman emperor, the Persian king and the Negus of Ethiopia, and Theodoric himself may have seen his kingship as a copy of the emperor's, but he made no claim to be the equal of Anastasius.

Meanwhile, as imperial power in the West faded, Constantinople grew to become the greatest city in the empire. Its population, at its peak before the outbreak of bubonic plague in 542, has been variously estimated. The inhabited space within the Theodosian walls took up about 1,000 hectares out of a total area of some 1,200. If we estimate 200 persons per hectare, which in a west European medieval city would be considered a dense population, we would have 200,000 persons within the city walls.[26] Yet by the standards of medieval Europe, population densities in Roman cities were high, possibly 400 per hectare or more, and in any case, outside the walled area of Constantinople were its suburbs: Sycae (Galata) across the Golden Horn, which had its own theatre and hippodrome, and was made a *polis* by Justinian,[27] and on the other side of the Bosporus, Chalcedon (*mod.* Kadikoy), whose foundation antedated Byzantium's. The eastern empire was generally stable and free of pestilence in the fifth century, and there was probably a population increase in most parts of it. In the 540s, decline set in, and there was no reverse in the trend until the mid-ninth century. But the Constantinople that acclaimed Justin in 518 was a crowded megalopolis which with its suburbs may have possessed half a million souls. By contrast no city in the medieval West could claim more than 50,000 inhabitants from the end of the fifth until the close of the tenth century.

THE NEW ROME ON THE BOSPORUS

A cicerone's cityscape

A thousand years before Justinian, Herodotus, the historian of the Persian invasion of Greece in 480 BC, underscored the contrast between Greek and Near Eastern perceptions of urbanism in the words he assigned to Cyrus, founder of the Old Persian Empire. Cyrus had received a warning from Sparta, and he reacted with contempt. 'I have never yet feared men like these, who have a designated place in the midst of their cities where they assemble to exchange oaths, and deceive one another.'[28] This space in the midst of the Greek city which aroused Cyrus' scorn was the *agora*, and the Persians had no such places, explained Herodotus. Near Eastern cities *did* have markets in the open space before the city gates, or in bazaars or *suqs* where tradesmen sold their wares, but no *agorai*; what instead marked off the Near Eastern urban pattern was the *kirhu*, the inner city made up of palace and temple, which was cut off from the rest of the urban area by its own circuit wall. We can recognize the pattern still in the Moscow Kremlin and the Forbidden City of Beijing, and it represents an urban concept which accords far better with the Holy City of the Apocalypse than does a Greek *polis*. Aristotle in his *Politics*[29] summed up the difference with precision: 'A citadel is suitable for oligarchies and monarchies; a level plain suits the character of democracy.'

In Constantinople's urban development, the Near Eastern pattern asserted itself, and the various influences and traditions that caused it to do so are too complicated to unravel here. But by 518, when Justin became emperor, the Great Palace which Constantine had begun had grown into an immense complex of pavilions, churches – at least twenty of them[30] – residential quarters and reception halls, even an indoor riding school, all enclosed within its wall, and connected by a private passageway to the imperial box in the Hippodrome. Outside the palace walls prostitutes plied their trade until the empress Theodora intervened to halt it, for in her youth she had had some first-hand acquaintance with the trade herself, and on the north edge of the Augustaeum square, opposite the palace, stood Hagia Sophia, the church of the Holy Wisdom. The timber-roofed basilica of Justin's day was the second built on the site. The first was dedicated by Constantius II in 360 and replaced Hagia Eirene as the patriarchal church. Forty-four years later it was burned to the ground by rioters protesting the banishment of the patriarch John Chrysostom.[31] Rebuilt by Theodosius II, it was to be destroyed again in the *Nika* riots of 532, and replaced by the immense domed structure erected by Justinian, which still stands in Istanbul. But that is a story which belongs to another chapter.

The column bearing the Augusta Helena's statue, which gave the Augustaeum its name, had acquired companions. Constantine had erected a column of his own, and Theodosius the Great erected a third, topped with a silver statue of himself. The emperor Arcadius' wife, Eudoxia, was honoured in 403 with a silver statue set on a pillar in the north-east corner of the Augustaeum, and emperor Leo had a column in front of the senate house. The old ruling house of Theodosius was well commemorated in the capital, better than Justinian liked, for he removed Theodosius' silver statue and melted it down. In its place, he set up an equestrian statue of himself, made of a fine bronze alloy that counterfeited gold. It commemorated two victories of the year 530: one won by his best-known general, Belisarius, over the Persians at Dara on the eastern frontier, and the other in the Balkans, where Mundo, a Gepid prince in Justinian's service, defeated the Bulgars and captured their king.[32] The column which supported the statue lasted until the mid-sixteenth century; the statue itself was recycled into Turkish cannon.[33]

An extension of the *Mese* ran east from the Golden Milestone up to the vestibule of the Great Palace, known from its massive bronze doors as the *Khalke* (Brazen House). The street separated the palace on the south from the complex of Hagia Sophia and the Augustaeum to the north. A traveller heading west from the Golden Milestone along the *Mese* would pass the Baths of Zeuxippus on his left and on his right, the Basilica, a large square enclosed on all sides with porticoes, which was used for public lectures, book shops, lawcourts and bureaux for lawyers. Within the Basilica Constantine built two small temples, one to the *Tyche* of Rome and the other to the goddess Rhea, and Julian the Apostate, who may have attended lectures there as a young student, added a library. The library soon fell victim to fire, but the Basilica itself survived even the *Nika* riot of 532 when neighbouring buildings were set ablaze.[34]

Let us imagine that our traveller continued along the *Mese*, which was lined on either side with colonnades where merchants and tradesmen built stalls. Such stalls were usually wooden structures and they were to be found everywhere filling the porticoes of the cities in Late Antiquity, but in Constantinople, by a law of the emperor Zeno, they were to have marble facing, thus adding to the elegance of the city's main street.[35] Our traveller would make his way past the Praetorium, which was the urban prefect's headquarters and housed the city gaol, and passing under a marble arch, he would enter the oval forum of Constantine. A two-storey colonnade filled with shops surrounded it and at its west end stood Pheidias' famous statue of Athena Promachos, which had been removed from Athens in the late fifth century.[36] At the north end was a second senate house, with four great porphyry pillars on its façade. Opposite it at the south end there was a monumental fountain, and in the centre stood Constantine's column, the stump of which is all that survives of what was, for contemporaries, *ho Phoros*: 'the Forum'.

The area traversed by our imaginary traveller was the commercial heart of the city. The 600 metres or so from the Augustaeum to Constantine's Forum, and the 700 metres beyond it to the Forum Tauri, looked like a bazaar, thronged on any ordinary business day with buyers and sellers. Excavations at Sardis have revealed a portrait of a commercial street in a city in Late Antiquity: in the colonnade built along the wall of the Sardis Gymnasium were twenty-nine two-storey shops, well-lighted with glass windows, which contained retail and manufacturing businesses.[37] Constantinople had similar establishments, and one of them, close by the Baths of Zeuxippus, was the famous 'House of Lamps', so called because its windows were lit at night. There our traveller would find on display the best dyed silks, which only the imperial court could use until Justinian relaxed the interdict enough to allow ordinary citizens to buy them.[38]

Closest to the Brazen House was the region where the perfumers and spice merchants sold their wares, which were considered peculiarly suitable for the palace because of their fragrance. Further along were the silversmiths and money-changers, and Constantine's forum was the centre for the fur trade. If our imaginary traveller continued westward along the *Mese* from the forum, he would go under another marble arch, and pass along a row of bakery establishments and slave-dealers until he reached the swine market at the Forum Tauri or Forum of Theodosius, which Theodosius I constructed in the 390s with Trajan's Forum in Rome as its model. Theodosius erected an equestrian statue of himself there, as well as his own version of Trajan's Column, a pillar with a scroll of relief sculpture narrating his victories in a great spiral from the bottom to the top, where he placed a silver statue of himself. The statue fell during an earthquake in 480, and a quarter of a century later, Anastasius substituted one of himself, but it probably failed to survive the riots which nearly toppled him from the throne in 512. Flanking one side of the forum, there once stood a basilica modelled on the Basilica Ulpia in Rome, but it was consumed in a great fire in 465 which destroyed eight of the city's regions. The recollection of Trajan was not unintentional: like Trajan, Theodosius came from Spain, and his dynasty claimed Trajan as an ascendant. The Forum Tauri was a monument to the legitimacy of the Theodosian House.

To the west of the Forum Tauri, at the *Philadelphion* square where the University of Istanbul is now, was the large rectangular structure called the Capitolium.[39] The name recalls the Temple of Jupiter on the Capitol in Rome, but if the building ever had pagan associations, they did not long survive. It became the seat of the University of Constantinople, which was reorganized in 425 by Theodosius II. Emperors before Theodosius had appointed professors on the recommendation of the senate, and paid their stipends. But after 425, higher education in the city became the monopoly of the university, and the professors were appointed by the urban prefect acting for the emperor. The faculty numbered thirty-one, thirteen professors of Latin and fifteen of Greek, two lawyers and a philosopher, all of whom were given senatorial rank after twenty years' service in their chairs. The rank was *spectabilis*, however, which by Justinian's reign was much diminished in status, for *illustres* alone had the right to speak in the senate.[40] Twenty of the professors were *grammatici* or secondary school teachers. As an intellectual centre, the University of Constantinople was outclassed by Alexandria, Gaza and Athens, where the foundation of the Neoplatonic Academy in the last quarter of the fourth century had revived the city's reputation as a place of learning. But it outlasted all its rivals.

At the *Philadelphion*, the *Mese* forked. The southern branch led past the Amastrianos, where the horse market was held, and to the Forum of the Ox, and eventually reached the Forum of Arcadius on the seventh hill of the city. There Arcadius erected a giant monumental column nearly forty-three metres high, topped by a statue of himself. The relief which spiralled round the column shaft commemorated an incident in July, 400, which helped save the eastern empire from going the way of its counterpart in the West: the populace of the city rose and broke the power of Gainas, the leader of a group of Ostrogothic *laeti* and federates, who was on the way towards making the emperor his puppet.[41] From there the road continued to the Golden Gate, a triple gateway flanked by two great square towers, which was the city's ceremonial entrance.

The northern branch of the *Mese* led past the church of the Holy Apostles where the Fatih mosque now stands. The church was built by Constantius II beside the imperial mausoleum where Constantine and his successors were interred until the eleventh century, and it housed the relics of St Andrew, St Luke and St Timothy.[42] Along this thoroughfare, too, stood the great church of St Polyeuktos built in the last years of Justin's reign to contain the relics of an obscure soldier martyr who died in Cappadocia, probably in 251. The builder was a wealthy scion of the House of Theodosius, Anicia Juliana. St Polyeuktos, which replaced a church built by Theodosius II's empress, Eudocia, was Anicia Juliana's own chapel attached to her enormous palace, but until Justinian rebuilt Hagia Sophia, it was the largest church in Constantinople.[43] Architecturally it was also Hagia Sophia's precursor: a domed basilica.

The road left the city by the Adrianople or Charisius Gate, and if our traveller continued along it, it would take him to Singidunum (*mod.* Belgrade). The exit by the Golden Gate would put him on the old *Via Egnatia* which would take him past Thessaloniki to Dyrrhachium on the Adriatic coast, the native city of the old emperor Anastasius. Thence to Italy, and finally, after twenty-one days on the road, he would reach Rome.

The Theodosian Walls built in 413 by the praetorian prefect Anthimius were severely damaged by a series of earthquakes in the autumn of 447, and again the following January. It was a time of peril: Attila and his Huns had penetrated Greece as far south as Thermopylae, and the citizenry restored the walls within sixty days. There was a legend that the Blue and Green factions from the Hippodrome together furnished 16,000 labourers for the task, under the direction of their demarchs. If it is true, it is an early example of the factions using their organizing skills to mobilize the able-bodied *plebs* of the capital in a moment of peril.[44] But the walls were not merely restored; they were strengthened and augmented, so that the Theodosian Walls became a great complex of ramparts protecting the landward approach to the city. When they were finally complete, they consisted of a stone-lined moat twenty metres wide and seven deep, a glacis, and an outer wall with ninety-six small towers, a second glacis and the main, inner wall with ninety-two larger towers. Except for a small extension built later to shield the church of St Mary of Blachernae, whose sacred relic, the Virgin's Robe, proved inadequate protection, the Theodosian Walls continued to protect the city on the landward side and to define the area of Constantinople until its fall to the Turks.[45]

It was on this landward side that Constantinople was vulnerable. Some five centuries before Constantine, Polybius[46] had noted the fact. In a passage which could equally well have described the succession of invaders in Late Antiquity, he told how the Byzantines were engaged in a never-ending war with the Thracians, where they could expect no decisive victory: if they overcame one tribal chief, three others appeared, and if they tried paying off one, they made enemies of the rest. So in the end, they accepted warfare with the Thracians as a customary situation. But on the seaward side, the city had compensating advantages. The current in the channel between the Black Sea and the Sea of Marmara carried ships sailing from the north into the harbour, and swept them away from Chalcedon on the opposite side of the strait, and the approach from the south was easy enough once a ship had negotiated the currents of the Hellespont. Constantinople needed to fear no threat from the sea until the Arabs built a fleet in the seventh century. However, under Theodosius II seaward walls were completed in 439 along the Golden Horn and the Sea of Marmara: they too were damaged in the earthquake of 447 and restored.[47]

Some 65 kilometres west of the city was another wall, stretching from Selymbria (Silivri) on the Sea of Marmara to the Black Sea Coast near the modern town of Karacaköy. This was the 'Anastasian Wall' and its construction may have belonged to the endeavour to buttress the landward defences in the mid-fifth century. If Anastasius was not their original builder, it may at least have been he who restored them close to 503 to ward off a horde of Bulgars who annihilated a Roman army in 499 and proceeded to ravage Thrace at will.[48] A foray of Kutrigur Bulgars swept over the Long Wall in 539 or 540, and terrified the capital; a decade later, the same wall checked a Slav incursion that had advanced down the road from Belgrade which the Orient Express now follows. In 559, the wall was forced again by the Kutrigurs, who were stopped only just outside the city by a scratch force put together by Justinian's general, Belisarius. Justinian had, it seems, left the wall in disrepair after a great earthquake in 557 which had caused enormous damage.[49]

Once the Kutrigurs were repulsed, Justinian himself saw to the rebuilding of the Long Wall,[50] and it remained an effective defence until the start of the next century. But in 619, it failed to stop the Avars from raiding the outskirts of the city, including the church at Blachernae, and seven years later, when the Avar khagan Haganos laid siege to the city, an advance guard of some 30,000 men forced the Byzantine army guarding the wall to fall back to the protection of the Theodosian Walls. Thereafter the Long Wall seems to have been no obstacle for invaders. Probably it was difficult to garrison. Anastasius put it under the control of a 'Vicar of the Long Wall' whose diocese must have been carved out of the diocese of Thrace, but the civil and military authorities at the Wall failed to cooperate, and Justinian tried to solve the problem in 535 by putting both civil and military powers under the control of a new official called the 'Justinianic Praetor of Thrace' with a salary of 300 *solidi*[51] whose jurisdiction was limited to the Long Wall district.[52] The solution seems to have been unsatisfactory. But what eventually caused the abandonment of the Long Wall was overstretched resources: its length made its defence difficult, and the soldiers were needed elsewhere.

A city in constant danger of attack can survive only with a good water supply and an ample stock of food, and Constantinople was not naturally well endowed with either. Ancient cities used water lavishly. One cubic metre per person every twenty-four hours is a modern scholar's estimate,[53] based on a selection of Roman cities, and that is ten times the volume used by Paris in 1900. What is even more remarkable is that, unlike Paris, only a small portion of the water went to industry. Rather, the chief demand was from fountains and baths, public and private.

The emperor Hadrian in the second century had built an aqueduct to bring water to the city from the forests bordering the Black Sea to the north, and when Constantine refounded the city, it already possessed at least two baths. One of them was the great Baths of Zeuxippus, which Constantine renovated and embellished with coloured marble facings, mosaics and statues taken from sites in Asia, Greece and Italy, all of which were destroyed in the *Nika* revolt of 532. Justinian rebuilt the structure, but all that remained of the statues was a poetic description, an *ekphrasis*, which was a literary genre much favoured by Byzantine versifiers. The *ekphrasis*, which is preserved in the *Greek Anthology*, was the product of the modest talent of the poet Christodoros, who lived under Anastasius, and produced his work, as far as we can guess, at the beginning of the century.[54]

Bathing was not a Christian virtue, even when the sexes ceased to bathe together, as they did after the end of the fourth century.[55] The church taught that those who were spiritually clean need have no concern about the grime on their bodies.[56] Yet the urban sub-culture which centred on the public baths still flourished, little diminished, in the cities of the empire, and the construction of bath buildings was a favourite imperial project. By the mid-fifth century, Constantinople and its suburbs had 8 public baths,[57] supplemented by an estimated 153 private ones: a respectable total though it cannot be compared with Rome's 11 public and over 830 private baths. Moreover, the great public *thermae* of Rome were vast palatial establishments; the dimensions of the surviving remains of the Baths of Caracalla, or those of Diocletian, can still awe modern visitors. Constantinople had a comparable establishment, the *Constantinianae*, begun in 345 but not completed until 429. But on the whole, Constantinople's baths were more modest in size than Rome's and more parsimonious of water.

The city must always have been comparatively short of water, and by the mid-fourth century, the situation was acute enough that the imperial government built an elaborate system of conduits and aqueducts to collect water from almost as far away as the present Bulgarian frontier, and bring it to Constantinople. The happenstances of history have given the emperor Valens credit for this, for it was under his reign that the water collected by this new system reached Constantinople, but the construction had gone on for nearly half a century before him and the water supply remained a concern up to the sixth century. In fact, one of the purposes of the Long Wall stretching from Selymbria on the Propontis to the Black Sea may have been to protect the capital's water supply.[58]

The aqueducts fed tanks and cisterns, three of which were great open reservoirs with a total capacity of some 1 million cubic metres. These were supplemented by covered cisterns of all sizes, numbering a hundred or so, where water was stored for public use, for only the wealthiest houses had water piped in. One underground reservoir, built by Justinian under the open courtyard of the Basileios Stoa, now goes by the name *Yerebatansaray* (Underground Palace), which is a tribute to its dimensions. The church of Hagia Sophia nearby had no less than three cisterns. The Great Palace had its own water tanks, fed by Hadrian's aqueduct. After the mid-sixth century, a population decline relieved the pressure on the water supply, but the reigns of Zeno and Anastasius were periods of growth which continued until the plague epidemic of 542. But no more aqueducts were built. Public bathing, except within the Great Palace complex itself, began to go out of style, and by the end of the eighth century, the great public baths had fallen into disuse. It was, in the end, conservation that solved the city's water shortage.[59]

Most of the grain that fed Constantinople came from Egypt where it was levied as a tax in kind, the *annona civica*, and the amount fixed by Justinian in 538–39 at 8 million 'units'. The unit was no doubt the *artaba*, a dry measure which unfortunately was not standard throughout the empire, but the 'unit' to which Justinian referred was probably the *artaba* of about 30 kg of wheat.[60] Thus the requisition was in the neighbourhood of 240 metric tonnes. This toll was what was called in Greek, by bureaucratic euphemism, the 'happy requisition' (*aisia embole*). If its yield was insufficient, extra supplies might be purchased.[61] The notion was generally accepted that the onus was on the state to see that the market had enough grain. Private enterprise in the pre-industrial world was not up to the task of supplying a large city, and when the large city was the imperial capital, the emperor could not let the people starve without risk to his throne. Provincial cities were less fortunate.[62] Constantine diverted the grain cargoes from Egypt to his new capital, leaving Rome to feed itself with supplies from Africa.[63] The *annona* of Justinian's day was a generous estimate of what Constantinople needed, and was the equivalent of some 11,000 pounds of gold,[64] which was Egypt's annual subsidy of the capital.

Part of the *annona* was used for the 'bread dole' in Constantinople. Constantine had introduced the dole into his new city in imitation of Rome (the first distribution dates to 18 May, 332), and set the number of recipients at 80,000,[65] which never greatly increased. At designated spots in Constantinople, usually at crossroads, there were to be found high counters with steps leading up to them. There the eligible citizens of the neighbourhood went to collect their rations of free bread which was baked in the imperial bakeries with grain from the imperial granaries. Cheating was difficult: each recipient had to produce a bread ticket (*tessera frumentaria*) to prove that he was eligible for a ration, and his name was checked against a list on a bronze tablet at each distribution centre. As in Rome, the system served less to feed the poor than as an instrument of imperial patronage[66] and in time, even that aim was perverted. Bread tickets could be sold, inherited or donated; a law of Theodosius I dating shortly before his death recognized the practice,[67] and by the end of the fifth century, a large portion of them had come into the hands of the church. Gradually the church took over the bread dole, transforming it into relief for the indigent, and after 618, when the state distribution ceased, the church continued its charitable function.[68]

It took a great fleet of transports to carry the grain cargoes from Egypt to the granaries of Constantinople, where its distribution fell within the jurisdiction of the urban prefect. It is nearly impossible to estimate the number of ships unloaded at the docks of

Constantinople each year, but 3,600 cargoes annually is a reasonable guess, and since a ship could make only three round trips during
the navigation season that stretched from 7 March to 7 November,
and that only under optimum sailing conditions, we can reckon a
grain fleet of close to 1,300 transports engaged in the yearly shipment. Constantine added no new docking facilities. The city he
refounded had two old harbours on the Golden Horn and they were
evidently adequate during his reign. But Julian built a new dock on
the Sea of Marmara, no great distance from the Hippodrome, and
further west, Theodosius added another, which gave the city some
four kilometres of quays. The Hellespont was a bottleneck, for a
southward current ran through it, and transports could navigate it
only with a good wind astern, but Justinian found a solution of
sorts. On the island of Tenedos, close by the entrance to the
Hellespont, he built a large granary that measured 90 by 280 feet
(87.4 m × 28.1 m) on the ground, and its height was 'ineffable'.[69]
There transports which could not beat up the strait were unloaded
by a small army of roustabouts, who must have been kept available
on the island during the sailing season, and then the vessels returned
under ballast to Egypt for another cargo. The grain remained stored
in the granary until sailing conditions allowed it to be brought up
the Hellespont. Spoilage must have been considerable, to say nothing
of losses to rodents. But the trade winds were beyond Justinian's
power, and in 563, near the end of his reign, we are told that the
south wind simply failed to blow in the late summer. Consequently
the grain transports could not bring their cargoes to Constantinople,
and it faced the threat of a bread shortage.[70]

The regulations governing the shipping of the *annona* and the
shipowners show the imperial government at its most bureaucratic,
making a determined effort to rule the laws of economics.[71]
Constantine pegged the freight rates for the shipowners at about the
same level as Diocletian had allowed as the commercial rate in his
Edict on Price Control. Justinian in his *Edict XIII* of 539, which
laid down rules for the grain shipment, designated 80,000 *solidi* for
the cost of transport, which does not represent a significant reduction
from Diocletian's tariff.[72] But shipowners evidently found that the
grain-carrying trade brought them a poor return on their capital,
and they had to be forced by law to remain in the business. Their
obligations were made hereditary, which was the imperial government's standard response to such situations, and one which worked
poorly. In Egypt, the 'happy' *embole* was deeply resented. Yet, in

spite of all the government's efforts, the average citizen of Constantinople was not well-fed: his staples were bread, vegetables and wine, and since food was hard to stockpile and spoiled easily, shortages were a constant danger.[73] Drought inevitably caused hardship.

In any case, a more terrible solution intervened during Justinian's reign to check the population growth. Bubonic plague struck the capital in 542 and before it ran its course, it reduced the population by about half. Immigration from the provinces probably soon made up some of the loss in Constantinople itself, but the total population of the empire suffered a marked decline. But the *embole* continued to be levied each year in Egypt, and it is worth noting that from Justinian's time until the Arab conquest, some Egyptian monasteries had the chore of gathering and transporting the wheat accruing from this unpopular assessment. The Pachomian monks who took over a temple at Canopus 27 kilometres east of Alexandria at the end of the fourth century and founded the monastery of *Metanoia* – Repentance – were celebrated for their activity as boatmen as much as for their loyalty to the creed of Chalcedon. They collected a part of the *embole* in Egypt, including the various supplements, and transported it downriver in their own boats to Alexandria, and sometimes as far as Constantinople itself, though there were few riverboats capable of a voyage on the open sea.[74]

The palace and Hippodrome

The living heart of the city was the great palace which sprawled over its south-eastern tip, taking up an area of some 100 hectares. Its vestibule, the 'Brazen House' which opened on to the Augustaeum, was almost a palace in itself, particularly after Justinian rebuilt it in the wake of the *Nika* riot. Further on, beyond the vestibule, were the quarters for the imperial guards: the splendidly uniformed *Scholares*, who were established by Constantine if not by Diocletian, and numbered 3,500 before Justinian increased the roster by 2,000, the *Excubitores*, constituted by the emperor Leo, and the forty *candidati* selected from the *scholae* to be the emperor's personal bodyguard, so called from their white uniforms.[75] Beyond the guards' quarters was the Delphax, a large courtyard, and opening on to it was the great dining room known as the Triclinium of the Nineteen Couches, where foreign ambassadors were feasted. In this area too were the Summer and Winter Consistoriums, two adjoining buildings where the emperor held the joint meetings of the senate and the consistorium known as *silentia*, where the reverent silence that was the emperor's due was enforced by thirty *silentarii* marshalled by three decurions. By law,[76] the senate should approve new legislation before it was put to the consistorium, but Justinian's senate met only in *pro forma* assemblies and, to borrow a striking image from Procopius,[77] it sat 'as if in a painting', silent though colourful, without meaningful influence.

The heart of the palace was the Daphne, which dated back to Constantine I and was made up of a series of buildings, terraces, porticoes and, no doubt, gardens. There, on New Year's Day, the senators received crowns of laurel from the emperor's hands, and from it a private passageway led to the imperial *loge* in the Hippodrome, which was more a royal *pied-à-terre* than a mere theatre box. Beside the shore of the Propontis was the Palace of Hormisdas, which served as Justinian's quarters while Justin was emperor. And on the periphery of the complex was the Magnaura where ambassadors were received with pomp and circumstance.[78]

One of the features which distinguishes the later medieval West from Early Byzantium, or for that matter, the whole classical past, is the absence of the crowd in the West as a factor in government or society. Even in seventeenth-century England, the largest crowd recorded is the army of 26,000 or 27,000 men which Oliver Cromwell commanded at the battle of Marston Moor.[79] In contrast, a conservative estimate for the seating capacity of the Circus Maximus in Rome is 150,000[80] and the Hippodrome at Constantinople may have held crowds as great as 100,000. Nor were the amphitheatres and theatres small structures: the theatre at Argos in Greece could have accommodated some 20,000. We hear of four theatres in fifth-century Constantinople, though one of them, known as the 'Greater Theatre' may have been the amphitheatre that Septimius Severus built.[81] The staple fare of the theatre was now the mime and pantomime; a performance of tragedy must have been a rare event in the sixth century. But mime dancers were stars with exuberant fans whose enthusiasm sometimes got out of hand: in 502, Anastasius, exasperated by the disorder they caused, banned pantomime performance throughout the empire, and in 520 again, dancers throughout the East were banished. But theatres continued to attract spectators even though their fabric might decay: at Thessaloniki, for example, theatrical productions were still staged at the end of the sixth century.[82] As for the amphitheatres, they still offered wild-beast fights, which were a regular part of the consular games presented in the first week of the New Year until Justinian abolished the consulship in 542.[83] Anastasius banned them in 498, but his diptychs show that he offered them in his own consular games in 517. We hear of bear keepers (the empress Theodora's father was one) and bull keepers, who tended the animals used for baiting and bull-fighting in the arena.[84]

The church disapproved, and mime actors were denied the sacraments until they were on their death-beds. There may be some significance to the fact that at Aphrodisias in the sixth century, while the theatre was still in use, a chapel was constructed in the midst of the stage building.[85] Eventually these shows in the theatres and amphitheatres of the empire were to suffer from a combination of the plague, Justinian's fiscal policies and a change in civic values, and even in Constantinople the amphitheatre's main use at the end of Justinian's reign was for the public execution of criminals. In 528, Justinian restored the theatre in Sycae when he raised this suburb of Constantinople to city status, but that is the last we hear of any imperial interest in the upkeep of these structures for public entertainment.

But life in the Hippodrome was a different matter. There the emperor came face to face with the populace of the city, or the 'demes', as they are called in contemporary sources. Public acclamations were part of the empire's political essence.[86] If complimentary, they were reassuring, and if threatening, they were cause for concern, for street violence was never far from the surface in the cities of the empire. If handled with imprudence, the crowd could get out of control, and popular demonstrations could bring down governments as surely as they did with the Communist regimes of eastern Europe in 1989.

Directly opposite the imperial box in the Hippodrome were the seats assigned to the Blues, the Reds, the Whites and the Greens. These were the colours of the chariot-racing factions, the professional organizations initially responsible for fielding the teams, though at some point in the fifth century they took charge of other public spectacles as well, and thus we can find factions even in cities which had no hippodromes.[87] In fact, the executive directors of the organizations in the early sixth century seem to have been the chief pantomime dancers of each faction.

Given its expense, chariot-racing was to be found in a surprising number of cities. We know of circuses in Antioch, Alexandria, Thessaloniki, Chalcedon, Nicomedia, Edessa, Laodicea, Apamea,

Berytus, Tyre, Caesarea in Palestine, Gerasa, Bostra, Oxyrhynchus in Egypt and even little Gortyna, the metropolis of Crete. To paraphrase Norman Baynes, the Early Byzantine period had two popular idols, the saint and the victorious charioteer.[88] Papyri from Oxyrhynchus have yielded data about chariot-racing there, including a circus programme[89] of sixth-century date, which advertised six chariot races with appropriate *entr'actes* to keep the crowd amused. The financing came from various sources: foundations, imperial subventions, municipal taxes, but in Constantinople it was the emperor who was the chief patron, and after the end of the consulship, when there were no longer any consular games, he was left as the only patron.[90] The chariot races were a manifestation of his euergetism, and his alone.

There was not a great deal else to absorb the energies of urban youth. Youth societies such as the ephebate, the so-called *neoi* or *neaniskoi*, had once existed in the Hellenistic East, particularly in Asia Minor, but they had vanished. The *neoi* associations, centring on the gymnasium, had been chiefly interested in physical training, and they provided a necessary 'rite of passage': they initiated the young male adolescent into adulthood.[91] But the Christian ideal of asceticism was antithetical to physical culture, and the largesse of the city notables who had once supported the gymnasia dwindled with the fiscal pressures of the late empire. In Athens, the ephebate ceased abruptly after the mauling the city sustained as a result of a Herul invasion of 267,[92] and at Sardis, which had a combination gymnasium and bath, it is significant that while the bath continued in use, the rest of the building complex was turned to other uses: one part of it became a synagogue in the second half of the third century.[93] The athletic festivals of the ancient world were terminated. The Olympic Games were closed down in 392; the Olympia in Antioch lasted until 521, but then it too fell victim to Christian sensibilities. The historian Menander Protector, who had enjoyed wrestling naked in the palaestra in his misspent youth, looked back on it with shame.[94] The chief outlet that remained for youthful energy was the Hippodrome, and the colour parties served as male-bonding groups for the young men who sat together in blocs and acclaimed their favourite charioteers in unison.[95] It was natural for them to develop a sense of party loyalty.

Each colour had its own party of *aficionados*, and their acclamations were orchestrated by claqueurs who like other tradesmen had their own guild. By the sixth century, we find the colour parties not only in the hippodromes of the empire but in the theatres too.[96] However, by the protobyzantine period, the Reds and Whites had fallen into a secondary position in Constantinople, and in the provincial cities we no longer hear of them. It was the Blue and Green demes whose acclamations dominated the Constantinople Hippodrome. The emperors could hardly be neutral.[97] Anastasius, who lived through a period of rising factional strife and survived it, had chosen the next best course: he supported neither of the major colours, but rather the Reds.[98] Justinian is the only emperor of Late Antiquity, as far as we know, to have been a Blue patron.[99]

'Constantinople adopted the follies, though not the virtues of ancient Rome,' wrote Edward Gibbon, 'and the same factions which had agitated the circus raged with redoubled fury in the Hippodrome.'[100] Gibbon's judgement was that what produced the 'redoubled fury' in the Hippodrome was senseless hooliganism, and even though the Blues and Greens could be politicized upon occasion, they had no coherent aims, religious or political. Gibbon's successors had alternative suggestions, the most persistent of which has been that the Blues were supporters of religious orthodoxy and the Greens of Monophysitism.[101] According to this view, the emperor Anastasius, whose Monophysitism was notorious, should have been a Green, though contemporary evidence makes him a Red. Another theory would identify the Blues as the party of the upper class and the Greens of the lower, or vice versa.[102] But we can assign no consistent political or religious policies to the Blues and Greens. Yet, massed in the Hippodrome, they provided a channel of direct communication between the emperor and his people, and their expressions of approval or discontent could not go unnoticed. But they were far removed from organized political or religious parties.

Gibbon's best editor, J. B. Bury,[103] preferred the view that the demes of Constantinople were organized divisions of the populace, behind which was a military purpose. That is to say, the 'demes' were the city militia. This theory has the virtue of being applicable not only to Constantinople but to the other cities of the empire which had hippodromes and Blue and Green parties. But the evidence is sparse and unsupportive. It is true that when the Persians captured Antioch in 540, the Blues and Greens put up a spirited fight in the streets even after the regular soldiers had fled. Most of them were unarmed, but they showered the enemy with stones, and for a time, shoved them back.[104] But the incident only demonstrates two points which we already know: first, that the citizenry of Byzantine cities were ready to muster in self-defence, and second, that among the Blues and Greens there were young men who had the muscle and the expertise for street-fighting. They staged a mini-*intifada* to defend Antioch from the Persians. But few of them had armour, which is, I think, good evidence that they were not an organized city militia; for that matter, the imperial regime would likely have regarded such a militia as a threat to order and good government.

The use of the word 'deme' (*demos*, plural: *demoi*) in this context adds to the puzzle, for it is a word which slips easily from one meaning to another, and is used indifferently in the singular and plural. In classical Athens it could mean the citizen body, or the basic political division of the citizenry in the Athenian democracy, the village or ward. But the word's meaning in sixth-century Constantinople bears no relation to its connotations in classical Athens. Romanos the Melode, hymnist of the Theotokos church in the Kyrou suburb, could sing of the *demos* of the eleven apostles, and Justinian could use *demoi* to translate the Latin word *plebs*.[105] The word clearly could denote either the people as a whole or a group of them, as the context demanded. Gibbon was not far from the truth.[106] The Blue and Green 'demes' were merely the parties who backed chariot-racing teams wearing the colours of the Blue and Green factions, and it was more or less incidentally that they upon occasion espoused political causes and articulated them in the Hippodrome. The Red and White demes were mute; we hear only of the clamour of the Blues and Greens. In the next century, they underwent a change; they were transformed into instruments of imperial ceremonial, and their role as popular spokesmen vanishes.[107]

But in the early sixth century, a new element intruded. The historian Procopius witnessed it, and his narrative is as accurate as any.

> In every city the populace (*demoi*) has for a long time been divided into the Blue and Green parties, but only recently have they spent their money and submitted their bodies to brutal torture and deemed it worthy to die a disgraceful death for the name and seats which the rival spectators occupy.

That from his published *History of the Wars*, but in his *Secret History*[108] he adds that it was a gang of young hoodlums within the Blue party that stirred up trouble, and the inevitable riposte followed from the Greens. They dressed like Huns: unshaven moustaches and beards, heads shaven at front but with hair grown long at the back, and tunics which emphasized their narrow waists and upper-body development, and their criminal behaviour made the streets of Constantinople unsafe. Life for persons of property became insecure. Some citizens thought it politic to free their slaves. Revolutionary notions must have been in the air. Procopius blamed Justinian: it was his rabid partisanship for the Blues in the early years of Justin's reign which caused the trouble. Justinian went beyond mere patronage and became an instigator. Blue hoodlums went unpunished, law and order broke down, and the emperor Justin remained oblivious to it all.

We can only guess Justinian's motives. One of them had to do with 'crowd management': favouritism for one party kept the city mob divided, and furnished Justinian with a group of devoted supporters during the period that he consolidated his power. Justinian was an upstart, and his wife even more so, and there were in the city scions both of Anastasius' family and of the Theodosian house with stronger dynastic claims than Justinian had. The Blues may also have been a smaller party than the Greens,[109] though the evidence is unimpressive, but if so, as the weaker group, they had all the more reason to value Justinian's patronage and in return lend him loyal backing. Justinian recognized who his opposition was, and the aim of his 'crowd management' may have been to foil any coalitions which senatorial cliques might form against him. To that end, he was willing to cultivate radical circles in the capital: the apprehension of the slave owners which Procopius reports is significant. It appears that the Blue agitation unnerved property owners. If the upper classes had ever patronized the Blues in the past, Justinian broke the linkage and took over as patron himself.

The Blues, however, went too far and in 523 murdered a substantial citizen in Hagia Sophia. That was too much for Justin, who took firm action; Procopius claims that Justinian was sick at the time, and could not be at the emperor's elbow to defend his Blues.[110] Thereafter the violence diminished. Justinian remained a fan of the Blues, but he followed a 'law-and-order' policy and in 527 we find him sending orders to all the cities of the empire to punish rioters with an even hand.[111] His design of keeping the mob divided by patronizing one circus party eventually backfired, for in 532, the Blues and Greens united against him in the *Nika* revolt and nearly toppled him from the throne. But that is part of another story.

THE PEOPLE OF THE EMPIRE

Who were the people who filled the streets of Constantinople? Racially, they were a mixed group, where, as one source[112] has it, all seventy-two languages known to man were represented. But they had two features in common. Their *lingua franca* was Greek and their religion Christianity. Not that paganism was dead, nor had Latin perished. Latin was Justinian's native tongue, and it was still the language of Roman law which members of the legal profession were expected to master. But the culture of Justinian's Constantinople was Greek. The secular historians who eschewed ecclesiastical history attempted to write in a Greek that would have been acceptable to an audience in classical Athens, but rather less comprehensible to *hoi polloi* in contemporary Constantinople. With Justinian, laws addressed to Greek-speaking areas of the empire began to be written in Greek as a matter of course, though according to John Lydus, it was under Theodosius II that a prefect named Cyrus had first issued decrees in Greek, an untoward event which John thought was the beginning of the prefecture's regrettable decline.[113] However, the language of Justinian's *Codex* and *Institutes* remained Latin, and it was still necessary for a lawyer to master it. But Latin literature had never aroused much interest in the Greek-speaking East, and cultural interchange was small, though it was by no means non-existent.[114]

But can we see beyond the undifferentiated urban masses? What were the professions and trades of the people?

Administrative personnel

Constantinople was a city built to be a capital, and like similar cities such as Canberra or Ottawa, the civil administration was a major employer. The palatine service was open to new men, and unlike the high offices in the western empire, it was not the preserve of the senatorial class. The palace had a huge staff, some of it decorative. The guardsmen known as the *Scholares* numbered 5,500 under Justinian, but they were distinguished by splendid uniforms more than military prowess, and the task of protecting the palace fell mainly to the Excubitors. In charge of the imperial bodyguard was the Master of Offices (*Magister Officiorum*), by and large the most important official of the central administration, and the *magistriani*, as his staff were called, were the cream of the palatine service. He was the director of the secret police, the *agentes in rebus*, who ranged through the empire and combined the duties of imperial couriers, informers and spies. By the mid-fifth century, they numbered some 1,200. Under the Master's jurisdiction, too, fell the imperial ordnance factories which manufactured all the arms which the military forces needed.[115] He directed ceremonies at court, and received foreign embassies. In the fifth and sixth centuries, his portfolio developed into a ministry of state for foreign affairs, which went hand in hand with the growth of an informal diplomatic corps made up of envoys with experience and specialist skills.[116] His tentacles stretched into the office of the praetorian prefect, whose powers he circumscribed. By the sixth century, he had taken control of the imperial post from the praetorian prefect, and the directors of both the praetorian prefect's and the urban prefect's staffs were seconded from the *magistriani*.[117] The Master of Offices was well positioned to keep an eye on the palatine bureaucracy, and he was a powerful rival of the praetorian prefect.

The 'Minister for Legislation and Propaganda'[118] (*quaestor sacri cubiculi*) was the bureaucrat who drafted the laws and countersigned them with the single word *legi* (I have read [it]). Three ministers shared the portfolio of finance. The *comes sacrarum largitionum* (count of the sacred largesses) looked after imperial revenues and expenses, while the *comes rerum privatarum* (count of the private fortune) supervised the vast income from the emperor's private estates scattered over the empire. This was the revenue that paid for the emperor's private guard, his building programme, the chariot races and the considerable running expenses of the palace. However, the power of this office was diminished by Anastasius, who created a third ministry in 509; henceforth the *comes patrimonii* (count of the patrimony) supervised imperial property, and the count of the private fortune concentrated upon cases involving forfeitures and grants, undergoing in the process a transmutation into a judicial officer.

Since the emperor was all-important, everything connected with his person was significant. The consistory, the old imperial council dating back to Diocletian and Constantine, still held *silentia*, but under Justinian, its role was largely ceremonial. It perused the new imperial enactments, received foreign ambassadors and handed out honours. The *sacrum cubiculum*, so-called from its centre of operations located in the imperial private apartments, had taken over many of the former functions of the consistory. The Grand Chamberlain (*praepositus sacri cubiculi*), who was generally a eunuch, became one of the empire's most powerful officials. The count of the private fortune lost jurisdiction over the imperial estates in Cappadocia to him before the end of the fourth century, and by the next century he held the rank of *quaestor*.[119] It was the Grand Chamberlain Amantius who tried to manipulate the election of the new emperor upon Anastasius' death, and it was a former Grand Chamberlain, Narses, whom Justinian was to send to Italy to wind up the war with the Ostrogoths.

The praetorian prefect of the East lived in Constantinople, quite overshadowing his colleague at Thessaloniki, the prefect of Illyricum,[120] who had jurisdiction only over Greece and the central Balkans, and the prefect of Africa, who was appointed to govern the former Vandal kingdom after it was organized as a prefecture in 534.[121] The praetorian prefect directed the empire's most important industry: agriculture. He determined the quotas imposed on rural districts, and he was the normal channel for instructions to provincial governors. When Justinian's *Code* and *Digest* were published, and after them, the *Novels*, it was through the prefect's office that they were promulgated to the provincials.

The prefect was a grand officer of state, but he had long since lost any military function. The Master of the Soldiers in the East with headquarters at Antioch commanded the troops in Asia; Illyricum had its own Master of the Soldiers, and in the capital, the imperial guard was under the command of the Master of Offices. Nor did the prefect exercise judicial power in Constantinople itself. Since 359, the urban prefect or eparch, as Greek-speakers called him, governed the capital and its territory up to a distance of 100 miles from the city. He judged criminal cases and received appeals from provincial courts, controlled urban trade and industry and saw to it that provisions were adequate. It was the eparch's duty to maintain order and, as chief of police, he had at his disposal a force called simply the *taxiotai*, which was woefully inadequate in the face of any major public disturbance. He presided over the meetings of the senate and he alone of the great bureaucrats still wore the toga, the ancient dress of the Roman citizen. No eunuch could hold the office. The eparch's powers were further modified in 535 by Justinian, who set up a praetor of the *demoi*, with twenty soldiers and thirty firemen under his command, whose duty was to repress crime and sedition, and observe fires in the city in order to prevent theft of property. In 539, to control the swelling immigration from the provinces to Constantinople Justinian created another office, that of *quaesitor*,[122] who, according to Procopius, was also the scourge of sodomites, adulterers and heretics.[123]

Salaries in the civil service had declined in terms of purchasing power since the early empire, but bureaucrats made up for their losses by charging fees for their services. John Lydus,[124] whose *On the Magistracies* gives a vivid glimpse of a bureaucrat's career, relates that the swarm of shorthand writers was beyond count, and their perquisites many. John's own career is illustrative. He was born into a curial family in the city of Philadelphia in Lydia, and his entry into the civil service meant escape from the fiscal burdens of his class. Aged 21, he came to Constantinople looking for an opening among the *memoriales* who served on the staff of the Master of Offices. But while he was waiting for an opening, making good use of his time by attending lectures in philosophy, one of his countrymen, Zoticus, was appointed praetorian prefect, and launched John's career by taking him on as a shorthand writer.

About 1,000 shorthand writers were enrolled each year and without influential friends advancement must have been difficult. But Zoticus took an interest in his countryman and initiated John into the standard methods of acquiring income among the palatine bureaucrats, with the result that he made a splendid profit of not less that 1,000 *solidi* in his first year. Moreover, at the end of the year, Zoticus got him an unprecedented promotion to the post of first secretary (*chartularius*) of the department of civil law suits (*ab actis*). His two fellow *chartularii*, both elderly men, had purchased their offices, which was regular practice in the bureaucratic fabric until Justinian prohibited it;[125] in fact, even clergymen might be required to pay a fee before they took up their posts.[126] Offices in the *militia* were commodities, to be bought and sold like other items of merchandise. But John's purchase fee was waived, he was proud to report. Zoticus also found him a wife, a virtuous woman who brought a dowry of 100 pounds. But Zoticus remained in office only a little more than a year, and none of his successors paid the aspiring clerk the same attention. In particular, John Lydus resented John the Cappadocian, the prefect who was dismissed during the *Nika* riots of 532, though he was soon back in office. John reached the top grade of his service before he retired, but nonetheless he left it a bitter man, less wealthy than he had anticipated.[127]

One thousand *solidi*, which John reported as his dividend for his first year in the service, was an enormous sum for a tiro, even with the prefect's favour! To put it in perspective, when Justinian reorganized the administration of Egypt in 538–539, the office of Augustal duke of Alexandria was budgeted at 4,240 *solidi*, which was to cover the stipends of the duke and his staff, and overheads.[128] At the other end of the wages scale, a stone mason who received one-sixth of a *solidus* a day was considered well paid indeed.[129] The source of John's income was *sportulae*, fees which imperial officials collected for services rendered. Officials demanded *sportulae* for every transaction, even from the taxpayer for collecting his taxes! These fees began as gratuities, and Constantine had issued a law forbidding them. 'The appearance of a governor shall not be at a price; the ears of the judge shall be open equally to the poorest as well as the rich', he fulminated.[130] But rhetoric could not stop the practice, and a couple of generations later, a law of Valens implied a degree of acceptance: now the emperor tried instead to regulate the *sportulae* so as to protect the poor. 'Innocent and peaceful rustics' were to be protected from fraud in legal proceedings; they should not have to bribe court officials to obtain justice. 'The dignity of a senator does not allow such practices', the emperor decreed.

However, officials considered *sportulae* quite in keeping with their dignity. Justinian could not abolish them, but he tried to control them by drawing up a schedule of fees and posting it in public places where it could be read. In Antioch, a schedule was affixed to the notice boards in 530, and it was written in Greek, the language which the Antiochenes could read, not in Latin which was the language of law.[131] It was the quaestor's duty to enforce the schedule.[132] The schedule itself has been lost, but it is clear that the mandarins of the civil *militia*, who had regarded their posts as solid investments, reacted with bitterness as their expectations of profit were reduced.

Nonetheless, employment in the civil service remained a reliable means of amassing a fortune, though we should not imagine a swarm of clerks blanketing the empire and draining away its Gross National Product: by modern standards, the number of professional bureaucrats drawing pay from the public purse was tiny.[133] We must also make a sharp distinction between the officials who worked in the high echelons of the service and those who served ordinary provincial governors, the *cohortales* as they were called, whose posts were so unattractive that they were made hereditary: in their case Constantine's law decreeing that a son should follow a father in his office was enforced.[134] Jews, who were barred by law from the palatine service, were welcome as *cohortales*. The empire had a relatively numerous and well-rewarded civil service in its centre, but in the outlying regions, officials were sparse, unwilling and poorly paid, and Constantinople must have been a magnet for any ambitious provincials who were anxious for advancement. For every John Lydus who migrated to the capital and found a post, there must have been many whose connections were inadequate and who failed to find an opening.

It was not merely the *sportulae* which attracted aspirants from the provinces. The palatine service was a road into the senate, and senatorial rank protected the curial class in the cities from the fiscal pressures which had been besetting it with increasing rigour since the third century. The *Theodosian Code* contains 192 laws regulating decurions from Constantine to Theodosius II, and most are designed to prevent their escape from curial obligations. The lot of the ordinary decurion was an unhappy one. On the one hand, the more powerful decurions, the *principales* and *sacerdotales*, exploited the weaker members of their class, and on the other, the curials saw the privileges they had once enjoyed curtailed. Their immunity from flogging vanished. A law[135] of 436 conceded the privilege to five *principales* from Alexandria so that they might defend the interests of their city without fear; presumably it was by then quite legal to flog the rest of Alexandria's decurions.

Constantius II's establishment of a senate in Constantinople in the 350s provided a loophole. Before he died, the senate had expanded from barely 300 to 3,000 members. Senators became citizens of the capital and hence were exempt from the curial duties of their own cities. They might still maintain residences in them if they wished, but their local patriotism vanished and along with it their traditional munificence, which had once paid for many of the amenities of urban life. Entry into the senate was expensive, but once accepted, a senator up to the end of the fifth century had few if any special financial obligations. The attraction of senatorial rank to the curial class was not entirely fiscal, however. This was a society of status, and the titles of *clarissimus*, *spectabilis* and *illustris*, with their qualifiers, brought prestige and standing in the social hierarchy.[136]

The expansion of the senatorial class was partly at the expense of the old equestrian order, which had once been the backbone of the imperial bureaucracy. The senatorial order swallowed it up. But as the numbers of senators increased, the hierarchy within the order grew more marked, and the once proud title of *clarissimus* came to designate a senator of the lowest rank. It was a title which belonged to officials such as the *consulares* and *praesides* who governed the provinces. Second rankers were *spectabiles* and the highest rank, such as the principal palatine ministers and army officers by the end of the fourth century, bore the title *clarissimi et illustres*, to which the further qualifiers of *magnificentissimi* and *gloriosissimi* might be added. Under Justinian the *illustres* alone had the right to speak in the senate, and were free of all extraordinary levies. The *clarissimi* and *spectabiles* no longer were; moreover if they were ex-decurions, they were not relieved of their curial burdens. This was an aristocracy of social station and fiscal category, and it was hereditary, at least insofar as a senator's son was a *clarissimus* by birth. But at the same time it was an open-ended class, for the higher ranks within it generally went to those who had held high office, and in the eastern empire, unlike the western, emperors regularly made high-level appointments from among new men who had distinguished themselves in the palatine service.[137]

By the sixth century, municipal councils (*curiae* or in Greek, *boulai*) were on their way out. John Lydus, noting that it was common knowledge that Roman magistrates used to wear the toga, makes the significant remark:

> I myself clearly remember that this custom prevailed not only at Rome but, indeed, even in the provinces so long as the curial councils were governing the cities; when they were done away with, the species slipped away along with the genera.[138]

Exactly what happened is not clear, except that the councils did not fade out of existence everywhere at the same time. But it should be noted that John's own career illustrated one trend that destroyed the *curiae*. The *curiales* escaped their obligations by entering the imperial militia.[139] Yet it is clear that the curial order did not vanish. Cities in the protobyzantine period still possessed élite groups, whatever they might be called. Successive emperors tried assiduously to get local notables involved again in their civic governments and urged members of the senatorial order below the rank of *illustris* to reside in their native cities: a law promulgated by Justinian as late as 539 looks forward to the curial councils flourishing again.[140] But they were beyond help. The void the councils left in municipal administration was filled by new officials, such as the city 'defender' (*defensor*), who evolved from an imperial official into a local magistrate, the 'curator', who supervised local finances, the grain buyer, the *pater tes poleos* (father of the city) in charge of civic revenues, who surfaces in the mid-fifth century in some cities that had holdings which generated revenue,[141] and the *vindex*, created under Anastasius to collect the city taxes, a function he performed without compassion.[142] Evagrius,[143] writing at the end of the century, blamed *vindices* for the demise of the Late Antique city. But in the last analysis, it was the bishops who wielded the ruling power in the cities of the sixth century, for they regularly acted as both judges and supervisors of public works, markets, and a whole range of social services which were within the province of the church. It was they who supplied the direction for the urban élite, whom our sources call the 'first men' (*protoi*), under which label we may recognize the magnates who once made up the curial class. But the evidence for *curiae* or civic magistracies outlasting Justinian's reign is at best equivocal.

We cannot leave the imperial bureaucracy without comment upon one notable feature of the palatine service: the prevalence of eunuchs. They had always existed in imperial Rome, but in Late Antiquity, their importance increased. As the emperors became hallowed figures, eunuchs acquired a special role as go-betweens, providing both a screen for the emperor's sacred person and a channel of communication for his subjects, like modern lobbyists who sell their clients access to the right officials. Castration made the eunuchs a special caste, and an unpopular one at that. They were completely dependent upon the emperor's favour, without hope of heirs and unable to assimilate into the aristocracy no matter how wealthy they might become, and many eunuchs did become very rich. By the latter half of the fourth century officers from Grand Chamberlains to Commanders of the Bodyguard were customarily eunuchs, and indeed the posts with closest access to the emperor were dominated by them.[144]

Yet deliberate castration in the empire had long been prohibited, and in his old age, Justinian, horrified at a report that of ninety boys illegally castrated, only three had survived, ordered severe punishments for those who broke the law.[145] Hence eunuchs were generally immigrants brought as slaves from regions beyond the imperial frontiers, such as Persarmenia, the part of Armenia under Persian dominion, or the regions east of the Black Sea, and they must have been a polyglot group, like the Germans and Isaurians in the imperial bodyguard. The élite might use elegant Greek and Latin, but in the palace corridors, one might have overheard many languages spoken.

The army

All imperial service, whether in the bureaucracy or the army, was termed *militia*, or in Greek, *strateia*. Soldier and clerk alike were members of the emperor's retinue, and battened on the economy without adding significantly to the Gross National Product. Conscription had been abandoned by the emperor Valens, and recruitment into the army was voluntary,[146] with most of the regular soldiers coming from areas within the empire, though it was the less civilized ethnic groups in the Balkans and Asia Minor which found military life most appealing. In the early fourth century, the legions had been reorganized into local frontier militias (*limitanei*), supported by land grants which they passed on to their sons along with the duties attached to them, and mobile field armies (*comitatenses*) billeted in the cities, and, at least in name, the division still existed in the sixth century. We find five such armies in the eastern empire by the fifth century, each under a 'Master of the Soldiers' (*magister militum*). Two, the *praesentales*, were stationed with the emperor in Constantinople, where their billeting was an irksome burden: Procopius complains that householders had to find room for some 70,000 barbarians.[147] Each of the dioceses of Illyricum and Thrace had a *magister* charged with the defence of the Danube frontier. One was stationed in the East, though in the sixth century, another *magister* was created for Armenia. Only after Justinian's death, however, do we hear of a 'Master of the Soldiers of Africa'.[148]

Within the field army one might find regular soldiers (*stratiotai*), federate troops, who were now battalions that were, it seems, raised by their commanding officers, who recruited both from within and without the empire,[149] and allies (*symmachoi*), that is contingents which were sent by barbarian tribes under their own leaders. Finally there were the *bucellarii*, the personal bodyguard of the commander. Their name, 'biscuit-men', came from the biscuit (*bucellatum*) issued to soldiers two days out of three. The *bucellarii* were all mounted troops with tassels and pennants bedecking their armour and the harness of their horses to mark them off.[150] On campaigns we find them integrated with imperial troops, providing the commander with some of his most trusted officers, but we also find them in peacetime attached to great houses like the powerful Apion family in Egypt or to palatine officers like John the Cappadocian and Belisarius. We should not regard them simply as private guardsmen. Private individuals might support them, but they were expected to perform public functions such as police duties and collecting taxes, and the emperor could remove them if he wished. The emperor's subjects who paid the costs of their support did so in the emperor's service and he had the ultimate control over the *bucellarii*.[151]

In the sixth century the name *limitanei* (frontier militia) was applied simply to soldiers serving in a frontier district (*limes*), and they were under the command of a duke of the frontier (*dux limitis*);[152] indeed the term *limes* came to designate the bailiwick of a duke.[153] After the 'Endless Peace' with Persia in 532, Justinian took away the stipends of the *limitanei* on the eastern frontier, and this has been taken to show that the *limitanei* in that sector were allowed to wither away, and their military duties shifted to Arab allies under the Ghassanid sheikh al-Harith.[154] Archaeology supplies supporting evidence from the *Limes Arabicus*: the frontier east of the Dead Sea. Fortresses there which were heavily garrisoned in the early fourth century ran down under Anastasius and Justin, and were finally abandoned about 530.[155] On the other hand, the Syrian frontier further north was strengthened, and troops who were designated *limitanei* continued to hold garrison posts and to campaign in that sector; the difference seems to be that now they were no different from the regular troops. But we should not assume that what took place on the eastern front was replicated everywhere. Along the Lower Danube, it seems that *limitanei* continued to live, tied to their land grants, but the names of their units disappear.[156] They became the hereditary garrisons of strongholds positioned along the frontier, and they were no longer assigned to a unit but rather to a fort.

We are not well informed about the prefecture of Africa, but after Justinian recovered it from the Vandals, he made an effort to reinstitute units of *limitanei* there: volunteer soldier-farmers who were to receive a regular stipend.[157] This was an effort to reduce the strain that Africa's defence put upon the empire's military resources, and it was less than a success. To keep the Berber *razzias* in check, the imperial authorities in the last half of the sixth century had to rely increasingly on paying off sheikhs or buying their services. In Egypt, however, an hereditary peasant militia outlasted Justinian's reign, and though it was less professional than the *comitatenses*, it was still a useful military unit. At Syene on the southern frontier of Egypt we find *limitanei* who were recruited from locals up to the level of centurion, but had no land grants. They may have been part-time soldiers: two of them, we know, doubled as boatmen while still in military service. Perhaps these men were *stationarii*: soldiers assigned to protect customs posts, and even collect the customs dues, particularly after Justinian phased out tax farmers and used imperial agents instead to collect tariff revenues.[158] The frontiers were always permeable, and generally people moved across them freely. But trade was another matter. Exports and imports across the frontiers were carefully controlled.[159]

The total number of the imperial troops had drifted downwards since the fourth century, and about 500, they may have numbered 200,000.[160] John Lydus[161] gives precise figures for Diocletian's reign, before the division of the empire: 389,704 for the land forces and 45,562 for the fleet, and for the same general period Agathias[162] gives a total of 645,000, whereas his total for Justinian's reign after the pandemic of bubonic plague that began in the 540s is 150,000. We do not know the bases for these figures and we need not trust them implicitly. If the imperial army ever reached 645,000, some of the units must have existed on paper only. Yet even if they have a degree of accuracy, the impression of precipitous decline which they give is a flawed picture, first, because the roster of 150,000 no doubt excludes the *limitanei*, and second, because the shrinkage was a gradual process. If Justinian's army at the mid-century stood at 150,000 men, then the decrease since the previous century was about 25 per cent.

This armed force was barely adequate for the tasks it faced. The military successes of Justinian's reign were won with small battalions. The core of the army which overthrew the Vandal kingdom in Africa consisted of only 15,000 regulars and federates and four years later there were only 5,000 troops to defend Rome against a vastly superior army of Goths.[163] The numbers continued to decline: it is estimated that when Tiberius II became emperor in 578, the imperial army in the East facing Persia had no more than 6,400 men.[164] The empire clearly faced an increasing shortage of soldiers.

For that there was no single reason. We should note that as early as 531, Justinian opened the ranks to slave recruits, which hitherto had been done only in emergencies,[165] and that should warn us not to put the blame for the shortage entirely on the pandemic of bubonic plague, which spread over the empire from Egypt where it broke out in 541. But the plague must have made enlistment much more difficult. In 542, when it reached Constantinople, Justinian issued a law setting stiff penalties for persons who lured regular soldiers or allies into private employment:[166] execution for the delinquent soldiers, property confiscation for their employers. More and more, the army had to depend upon barbarian troops for its rank and file.

To be sure, the late empire always had been hospitable to non-Romans, and names in Justinian's officer corps read like a multicultural honour roll. Mundo was a Gepid, Sittas an Armenian, Chilbudius a Slav, Bessas a Thracian-born Ostrogoth. About 530, two brothers, Aratius and Narses Kamsarakan, scions of one of the great Armenian families, deserted the Persian army, and received so cordial a welcome that their mother followed them, and a third brother, Isaac, quit the Persian army too, betraying a Persian stronghold as he did so.[167] But the short-term effects of the plague forced far greater reliance on non-Roman recruits.[168] The imperial forces of the 550s were significantly more diverse in origin than those of the 520s, and the decline in size continued unabated after Justinian's death.

Merchants and tradesmen

To turn to the commercial classes: tradesmen, craftsmen, merchants and other interest groups in the cities of the empire had long been ranged into guilds (*collegia*). There were guilds of butchers, bakers, dyers, shipowners, tanners, perfume-sellers, purple-workers, porters, market-gardeners, actors, even claqueurs in the Hippodrome: the number is immense.[169] We can flesh out the picture with evidence that dates from the tenth century, the so-called *Book of the Eparch*, which was found in a Geneva library in 1892. It sets forth rules for nineteen guilds ranging from notaries and bankers to candle-makers and fishmongers.[170] These were evidently the most esteemed guilds of tenth-century Constantinople, and the regulations of Justinian's day can hardly have been identical: for instance, the *Book of the Eparch* distinguishes the guild of jewellers and silversmiths (*argyropratai*) from the bankers' guild (*trapezitai*), whereas in sixth-century Constantinople a silversmith could make loans and take deposits if his assets and credit were good enough.[171] But these tenth-century regulations betray an attitude which had changed little over the intervening years. Each guild had its own region of the city for its workshops, in the sixth century as in the tenth. Fur-dealers concentrated in Constantine's forum, for instance, and the bakeries lined the *Mese* between Constantine's forum and the forum of Theodosius. The *argyropratai* were to do business only in their establishments along the *Mese*. They were prohibited from carrying on their commerce from their homes.

The *argyropratai* were the aristocrats of the commercial scene: generally businessmen were denied entry to the civil service, but for the *argyropratai*, Justinian made an exception, and it appears that it was every banker's ambition to purchase a palatine appointment for himself or his sons.[172] Peter Barsymes, who advanced to the office of praetorian prefect under Justinian, was a banker who acquired a post on the prefectural staff, and there caught the eye of the empress Theodora and advanced with her favour.[173] Bankers could become wealthy men in the sixth century: it was a banker of Syrian origin in Ravenna, Julius Argentarius, who paid for the church of San Vitale there with its famous mosaics of Justinian and Theodora and their courtiers.

These *collegia* were legacies from the Roman and Hellenistic cities, which had had a multitude of them: not merely trade guilds, but youth societies, and associations centred on localities or religious cults. Their members met for social and religious purposes; their seats in theatre were grouped together, and if necessary they looked after the burial of their members. The encounter of the apostles Paul and Barnabas with the silversmiths at Ephesus is an example of a guild acting to protect its commercial interests: the Christianity which the apostles preached threatened the trade in silver replicas of the cult statue of the Ephesian Artemis, and the silversmiths moved swiftly to protect their trade. Each guild occupied its own niche on the social scale: the silversmiths (*argyropratai*) were the aristocrats, bakers were a cut above cheese sellers, and cobblers and weavers were generally a humble lot.[174] They elected new members, and determined their initiation procedures and entry fees. The guilds were also responsible for various corvée duties: in Constantinople, for instance, they furnished the fire-brigades.[175] In state ceremonies, they represented the commons, and in later centuries, when the parties in the Hippodrome ceased to be vehicles for public protest, the guilds assumed their role.[176]

The last emperors in Italy had tried to maintain the urban guilds by making them hereditary and prohibiting their members from escaping into the army, the civil service or, for that matter, the church. In the East, we do not find similar legislation, and none of the guild regulations of the western emperors is reproduced in Justinian's law code. By and large, guild membership in the eastern empire seems to have been free.[177] Nonetheless, a son usually did follow his father's craft, and the craft served as his source of identity. This seems clear from a remarkable set of fifth- and sixth-century funerary inscriptions from Korykos, a prosperous little coastal town of Rough Cilicia.[178] These 456 inscriptions typify a trend that was increasing in this period, whereby the dead identified themselves not by patronymics but by office, rank and/or trade, and thus this collection yields a glimpse of the social and economic life of a small community in Justinian's period. The manufacturing sector, which produced textiles, leather, pottery, metal work, perfumes and even papyrus (two tombstones belonged to papyrus workers) take up about 35 per cent of the trades. About a quarter of the workers were employed in the 'service industry', if we include in it the clergy. Only slightly smaller was the food industry: the production and sale of food and wine. Jewellers, money-changers and bankers, if grouped together, make up about 6 per cent of occupations. The inscriptions show 4 per cent in shipping or related work, for Korykos was a port, but this is probably a meaningless statistic.

In the majority of occupations where we have evidence, sons follow in their father's footsteps. There are exceptions, but not many. What is remarkable, however, is the number of individuals who practise more than one trade. A potter might be a weaver of goat-hair as well; a flute-player might make and repair musical instruments. Minor clerics might double as craftsmen. Perhaps this was found less in the great cities than in small places like Korykos, but in a small town, the crossover between trades seems to have been not only possible but perhaps prudent for the small businessman who wanted to maintain his income.

The personnel of the church

Christian clergy made up 16.8 per cent of the 456 attested professionals and tradesmen at Korykos. Add them to the civic *militia*, and we have a quarter of the work-force involved in what I have called the 'service industry' sector. The proportion in Constantinople was probably, if anything, larger. The Great Church of Hagia Sophia had a small army of clerics, which one of Justinian's laws attempted to reduce to 525.[179] The clergy of the Great Church had exceeded that number, though before we express undue dismay, we should recall that the Great Church comprised four buildings, Hagia Sophia itself, the church of the Virgin nearby built by the empress Verina (457–79), St Theodore, built by Sporacius, consul in 452, and the old church of St Helena, all administered as a unit, and Hagia Sophia's clergy served the old patriarchal church of Hagia Eirene as well. But it is clear from Justinian's legislation that bishops augmented their clergy beyond their ability to support them from endowment income. Pressure from patrons was a major reason: two letters from Severus, whom Anastasius made patriarch of Antioch in 513, complain that his church was in debt because powerful patrons had compelled it to ordain more clergy than it could support.[180]

Justinian was aware that the attraction to a monastic life was not always without base motive, and he legislated a three-year probation period for a would-be monk, during which claims could be made against him if he turned out to be a runaway slave or a thief.[181] Monasteries arrived in Constantinople relatively late; the first was founded in the early 380s by a Syrian monk who achieved celebrity by predicting the emperor Valens' defeat at Adrianople. But by the sixth century, there were some eighty monasteries to be found in the capital or its vicinity. The most celebrated of them, notable for the militant role it played in the defence of Chalcedonian orthodoxy, was the foundation known as the Monastery of the Sleepless Monks (*Akoimetoi*), so called because with teamwork they kept up an endless doxology, day and night.[182] The *Akoimetoi* were more Chalcedonian than the pope; from their monastery on the Asian side of the Bosporus they defended the Creed of Chalcedon with such vigour that they lapsed into heresy and were excommunicated by Pope John II in 534.

Taken all together, clergy, monks, and nuns, we have an impressive total. The share they consumed of the Gross National Product was immense. Justinian himself thought that they were worth the cost. 'If [monks], with their hands pure and their souls bare, offer to God prayers for the State,' he wrote, 'it is evident that it will be well with the army, and the cities will prosper and our land will bear fruits and the sea will yield us its products.'[183] Yet a series of modern historians who are heirs of the Age of Enlightenment: G. E. M. de Ste Croix, A. H. M. Jones, J. B. Bury and back to Edward Gibbon himself, have thought otherwise, and the matter is debatable.

From a purely economic standpoint, which would have been a mode of thought foreign to a contemporary of Justinian, this throng of ecclesiastics and holy persons was a burden on the resources of an empire that was already badly stretched. A large number of the people devoted to the religious life were idle mouths who subtracted from the Gross National Product and returned nothing equivalent. Every city, by a law of the emperor Zeno, was to have its own bishop,[184] whose stipend was comparable to a provincial governor's, and a metropolitan bishop might earn no less than the prefect of Egypt. In the pagan world, with the partial exception of Egypt, there had been no comparable professional priesthood, and though some temples had been full of rich dedications, the old gods had owned only a fraction of the riches which the church had amassed by the sixth century. There were, it should be remembered, some poor churches, but others possessed enormous wealth: gold and silver vessels, vestments, land, livestock, tradesmen's workshops, even slaves.[185] The endowment of Hagia Sophia in Constantinople included 1,100 tax-exempt workshops the profits from which were sequestered to cover the funeral costs of the needy![186] Jones's verdict is worth repeating: 'Leaving monks out of account, the staffing of the church absorbed far more manpower than did the secular administration and the church's salary bill was far heavier than that of the empire.'[187]

Yet even if the church played an insufficient role in the creation of wealth, it was a major instrument for its redistribution. It attracted donations from wealthy donors, and a portion went to the needy. It supported hospitals, and orphanages, provided welfare for poor widows,[188] and at the same time took an active role in economic life and made business loans: in Alexandria, which unlike Constantinople was a manufacturing centre, the see of St Mark acted as a banker for the business community, maintained a fleet of merchantmen and took an active role in commerce.[189] The church's bill for salaries was large; indeed large enough to absorb half the church's revenues, but even the function of paying the clergy served to redistribute wealth. Moreover, we should not regard all clerics were 'idle mouths'. We find professionals and tradesmen who were part-time ecclesiastics. In the Korykos inscriptions we find two presbyters, one of them a potter and the other a money-lender, a net-maker who was a sub-deacon, another sub-deacon who made cider and a lector who was a wine-importer.

As for the monks, the contribution of the great solitaries would be hard to weigh on a profit-and-loss sheet, though there can be no doubt that they played two significant roles that had economic consequences. First, they acted as ombudsmen, shielding the weaker members of society from oppression. Second, they were magnets for pilgrims, and the pilgrimage trade brought prosperity to those villages fortunate enough to have a prominent ascetic with a number of miracles to his credit. The coenobitic monasteries, however, were well-organized economic units engaged in agriculture and trade, and they must have modified the usual economic pattern of the empire whereby the villagers sent their taxes to the cities and the cities loaned money at high interest rates to the villagers. When the crops failed and the peasants were destitute, it was to the local monasteries that they turned first.[190] Monks worked at trades, farmed and cultivated gardens; in Egypt they were a source of rural labour, and in the Jordan valley we hear of them engaged in pig breeding, to the vexation of their Jewish neighbours.[191] The Canopus monastery of *Metanoia* outside Alexandria was active in the grain-carrying trade, and was itself a large landowner.

With the surplus monasteries such as these accumulated, they helped the vulnerable members of society. They provided welfare payments for widows[192] and hospitals for the sick, and they supported guest houses for wayfarers, though not without hope of payment: the monasteries at Nitria in Egypt specified that shelter was free for only a week. Monasteries took in oblates, who in the pagan world would have been exposed to die, if they were not picked up first by slave traders. In time of danger, when barbarian raids made the countryside unsafe, we find abbots such as Shenoute of the White Monastery in Egypt, sheltering refugees behind their convent walls, or organizing whatever defence there was: in the last days of Roman Noricum, it was a monk, St Severinus, who directed the defence of the provincials after the civil government there had collapsed.[193] On the other side of the balance sheet, however, it is fair to take note of the cost to the imperial treasury of protecting ascetics who retired to the desert fringes, where security was as marginal as the climate. In Egypt, for instance, the monasteries at Scetis in the western desert were sacked by the nomad Mazices in 407–8 and again in 435.[194]

The monasteries were particularly well placed to mobilize theological zealotry. Filthy of body and bigoted of mind, the monks were Christianity's shock troops, and their targets were pagans, heretics and Jews. In a polity without an organized national police force, civil laws against paganism were hard to enforce, and the monks filled a void. They were the watchdogs of whichever doctrine they considered orthodox. The Sleepless Monks were vigorous defenders of the doctrine of Chalcedon in Constantinople, and in Palestine, it was the Great Laura of St Sabas which mobilized Chalcedonian support: even the emperor Anastasius thought it imprudent to defy St Sabas and his monks.[195] In Egypt, the monasteries, with the major exception of *Metanoia* at Canopus, were generally Monophysite citadels – the *Enaton* at the ninth milestone west of Alexandria was the chief Monophysite stronghold – and in Mesopotamia, it was the monks who were the foot soldiers of Monophysitism. The great ascetics took sides: the elder St Symeon the Stylite, whose pillar was outside Beroea (*mod.* Aleppo), was commandeered by the Monophysites, though he had in his lifetime offered more support to the Chalcedonians,[196] and so, in Justinian's reign, the younger St Symeon the Stylite, perched on his column on Mons Admirabilis overlooking the port of Antioch, became his Chalcedonian counterpart.[197] The church in Late Antiquity takes us into a realm that cannot be judged in terms of profit or loss for the Gross National Product.

THE IMPERIAL OFFICE AND ITS IDEOLOGY

The office of the emperor was the result of the evolution of two concepts. One, which derived from Roman tradition, held that he was a magistrate chosen by the senate and the army, and though the hereditary principle might in practice assert itself, the office was not hereditary. The title *imperator* (generalissimo) derived from the Roman republican past, and it was conferred on the emperor by a law, the *lex de imperio*. In Greek, the word used to translate *imperator* was *autokrator*, and so it remained in official usage until the emperor Heraclius in a law of 629 employed the term *basileus*, which had long been common parlance. The other concept was a legacy of the Hellenistic period that followed Alexander the Great. The Hellenistic kings were autocrats in our sense of the word. They were divine, though they might differ in the degree to which they insisted on their divinity. Their images shared the temples of the gods. They were the source of law for their kingdoms, and as such, they were themselves 'incarnate law': *nomos empsychos*. The king was a human being and at the same time more than human: he embodied the divine vital force that gave the laws their substance.

It was this Hellenistic notion of monarchy whereby temporal kingdoms copied the kingship of the supreme *basileus*, Zeus, that informed the ideology of the late Roman imperial office. Once the emperors adopted Christianity, the idea was denatured and recycled as the concept of Christian kingship. Eusebius, bishop of Caesarea and confidant of Constantine, served as the chief theorist. The pagan emperors before Constantine had been the objects of worship, but the imperial cult could not survive unchanged in a Christian empire. Yet it had served the emperors too well to be completely abandoned. It was Eusebius' task to adapt it to a Christian environment.

We can best grasp the ideology which he developed from two of his works. His *Life of Constantine*, written after the emperor's death, linked Constantine and Augustus: the latter founded the empire, the former elevated it to a monarchy consecrated to the new faith. But it was in the oration which Eusebius of Caesarea produced for the thirtieth anniversary of Constantine's rule that we find the presumptions that governed the Christian concept of kingship. Speaking before an audience that was still partly non-Christian, Eusebius took the familiar pagan concepts of kingship which had come to full flower in the Hellenistic period, and transformed them into a new political science.[198] He drew a parallel between the Divine Word – the *Logos* – as archetype and Constantine as the image of the *Logos*: thus on one level, the *Logos* prepared the kingdom of Heaven for the Father, and on a lower level, Constantine led all men on Earth to the *Logos*. The Christian emperor, unlike his pagan predecessors, could not himself be a god, but he could be redefined as God's vicegerent on Earth, the friend and image of the *Logos* that was the mediator between God and Creation. Thus the rule of a true emperor mirrored the reign of God in Heaven. 'The good emperor', to quote one of Julian the Apostate's politically correct panegyrics[199] on his cousin, Constantius II, 'closely imitating God' acts with wisdom and foresight. Yet, though an emperor, by virtue of his office, might stand above the law, he was no tyrant, for he submitted willingly to the rule of law. His government was an *ennomos arche*: sovereignty under law.[200]

Thus the Late Antique world assigned the emperor a superhuman role as the temporal partner of God. He was the propagator of the faith even beyond the imperial frontiers,[201] the devoted shepherd of his flock, and his acts should replicate God's philanthropy. He should display his munificence with public works, such as aqueducts, bridges and fortifications for the empire's defence, and it was his duty to assist his lowliest subjects when natural catastrophes overtook them. He lived in a sacred environment, surrounded by pomp and circumstance, and like the sun, he shed his beneficence on all who entered his presence. Everything about him shared his divinity, including the imperial estates: the papyri from Egypt show that from the fifth century on, imperial property was designated the 'divine household'.[202] On his accession, his portrait, painted or sculpted, was dispatched to all government offices in the empire so that public transactions could take place in its presence, and it was treasonous to show it disrespect.

A true *basileus* was also a man of moral stature, fit to be God's vicegerent, who at the same time represented continuity of tradition.

The Old Testament was rummaged for analogies. The emperor was another David, or another Solomon or Moses: the rod of Moses, discovered providentially in Constantine I's reign, was carried in imperial processions.[203] But popular imagination did not consider the emperor a cloistered figure: rather he was conceived as a leader in war, untiring and invincible, to whom there was granted divinely predestined victory.[204] Legends on his coins proclaimed 'VICTORIA AUGUSTI' and the imperial titulature used in official oaths styled him 'Victor over All'.[205] To be sure, after Theodosius I died and left two unready sons to succeed him, emperors ceased to lead their armies in person, but the perception of the ever-triumphant ruler endured, wedded as time passed more closely to Christian symbolism: it is not without significance that in Justinian's reign, the ancient image of Victory that had lingered on imperial coins as a last denatured relic of paganism finally gave way to the figure of an angel. When Belisarius, the conqueror of the Vandal kingdom, returned to Constantinople in 534, he was given permission to celebrate a triumph, but it contrasted sharply with the triumphs that the victorious generals of Republican Rome had once celebrated. Belisarius walked on foot from his house to the Hippodrome and there prostrated himself before Justinian and Theodora. The victory he had won belonged to the emperor alone, and Belisarius was only a subject.[206]

Justinian inherited a concept of the imperial office which was already well-developed, and pressed it to its logical conclusion. He believed in his divine appointment. He prefaced a constitution addressed to the patriarch on the ordination of bishops and other clergy with the words, 'The greatest blessings of mankind have been granted on us by the mercy on high – the priesthood and imperial authority . . . both proceed from one and the same source.'[207] The preamble to the *Digest* proclaims his divine mission: 'Governing under the authority of God our empire, which was delivered to us by the Heavenly Majesty, we both conduct wars successfully and render peace honorable, and we uphold the condition of the state.'[208] Kingship (*basileia*), after God Himself, was the common father of all.[209] It was God who entrusted His emperor with the mission of defending orthodox belief and of guarding and remaking the Roman Empire.[210] Justinian could, and did, refer to himself as 'king and priest' (*rex et sacerdos*), as had Marcian before him, though we should remember that no emperor was an ordained priest with the right to perform sacraments, and none of them, not even Justinian whose regime was as close to caesaropapism as we can find, could dictate church dogma without the clergy's assent.[211] Yet he was the source of all legal authority, and in a *Novel* of the year 536, we find Justinian using the term *nomos empsychos*, though it was applied not to his person but to his *tyche*, which we must construe as a cross-breed between Providence and Fate. God had granted mankind the imperial *tyche* as 'incarnate law', Justinian explained, and thus he, as emperor, was himself not subject to the legislation he promulgated.[212] He does not use the term *nomos empsychos* again.

However, if late Roman kingship borrowed ideology that derived ultimately from Hellenistic monarchy, it was nonetheless sharply different. The imperial office belonged to the traditions of Rome, and the virtues which the bishop of Caesarea extolled in Constantine the Great were the cardinal virtues of any Roman emperor.[213] The theory that the emperor was the choice of the army, the senate and the people was in reality little more than a legal fiction, but it was not moribund, and the coronation ceremony reflected it. Justin was lifted up on a shield by his soldiers, following a custom which was borrowed from the coronation ceremony of the German kings but invested in the Byzantine rite with new overtones. On his head, a soldier placed the trooper's necklace known as a *torques* (in Greek, *maniakis*). The crowd in the Hippodrome, representing the people, acclaimed the emperor, and its acclamations voiced the public will.[214]

But in the fifth century, a subsidiary religious ceremony evolved, which was borrowed from Persia, where the Magian High Priest crowned the king. In 450, Marcian was crowned for the first time in a ceremonial with religious overtones: in the imperial *loge* of the Hippodrome, Anatolius, the patriarch of Constantinople, placed the diadem, which Constantine I had introduced, upon Marcian's head. Seven years later, Leo I, after receiving the diadem as a symbol of imperial power, went to Hagia Sophia for a second coronation. Anastasius, whose orthodoxy was doubtful, was made to take a coronation oath and thereafter such oaths became regular. In 602 the coronation ceremony moved to a church.[215] However, the church did not confer sovereignty on the emperor, nor did the patriarch represent the will of the people. Rather his role symbolized the coalescence of ecclesiastical and temporal power.

Yet, as J. B. Bury once pointed out, anyone who looks at the roll of emperors and notes how they were chosen, will find that only a minority conformed to the theory that the emperor was the people's choice.[216] An emperor on his death generally left a colleague, usually his own son, if he had one, or a son by adoption if he did not. So succession to the throne was punctuated by a series of hereditary dynasties, and when an emperor chose his successor, the army, senate and people were restricted to expressions of joy. When Justin became emperor, Justinian was already his adoptive son,[217] and he took up residence close by the imperial palace in the mansion of Hormisdas, which he remodelled and connected with the palace. At Easter, 527, Justin made the succession clear: he created Justinian co-emperor. The ceremony took place not in the Hippodrome but within the palace in the Triclinium of the Nineteen Couches, while the senate, high officials, the guards and army representatives gathered in the Delphax outside. Justinian received the diadem from the patriarch.[218] When Justin died three months later, Justinian's succession was assured, though not, perhaps, entirely unquestioned.

In the year Justinian became emperor or shortly thereafter, Agapetus, deacon of Hagia Sophia, who may have been one of his tutors, addressed to him an admonitory essay on royal duties that expresses the concepts of Christian kingship which Eusebius had developed. Discourses on statecraft for the edification of princes had been a common vehicle in the past for political ideas, but Agapetus christianized the topos and the influence of his *Mirror* was later to reach even the Tsars of Kievan and Muscovite Russia. It offers counsel under seventy-two headings. 'Like the man at the helm of a ship, the mind of the king ... is always on the watch.' 'The soul of the king, full of many cares, must be wiped clean like a mirror, that it may always shine with divine illumination.' 'In the nature of his body the king is on a level with all other men, but in the authority attached to his dignity he is like God.' 'Impose on yourself the compulsion of observing the laws. ... Thus you will testify to the majesty of the laws.' The emperor should practise philanthropy, but it belongs to a leveller's type: Agapetus counsels the emperor to promote equity by subtracting from the rich, who have too much, and giving to the poor who need help.[219] These are only morsels, but they convey the flavour of this composition, which must pass as a panegyric, though it is unlike most panegyrics offered to emperors. Agapetus was not an original thinker. His essay on imperial duties is conventional enough. The emperor was charged to guide and protect the empire, to respect the law and improve society. His duty was to make the empire better.

This seems to have been a season of speculation about the imperial office, and the qualities of an emperor deemed worthy to hold it.

Besides Agapetus' *Mirror*, we have an anonymous pamphlet of a similar date which revives the political thought of Plato and the Roman Stoics.[220] The emperor should be chosen from the 'best men' (*aristoi*) and his rule should be modelled upon God's. Is this a reflection of views circulating among the senatorial élite? If so, they went underground after the *Nika* Riots of 532. Thereafter there was no public forum for such opinions.

But the pointed suggestion in Agapetus' *Mirror* that the good emperor should take from the rich and give to the poor deserves more than passing attention. It is not a doctrine which would have had a broad appeal to the ruling élite, though in the provincial cities, the decurions were under financial pressure which Justinian[221] did nothing to diminish. They would have welcomed relief. To be sure, there was nothing new to deploring the plight of the poor: it was part of the conventional rhetoric of Christian sermons. 'The peasant works and the landowner harvests', wrote Romanos the Melode in a hymn addressed to monks and ascetics.[222] But there was another source for this sort of counsel, whether the worthy deacon used it or not. It was at this time, during Justin's reign and Justinian's early years, that across the eastern frontier in Sassanid Persia, the Mazdakites were at the height of their influence, and they preached a levelling social doctrine that urged subtraction from the rich and largess to the poor, so as to re-establish the equity of primitive society. The Mazdakites made a convert of King Kavadh as well as his eldest son, and Kavadh tried to induce his Arab allies to accept the Mazdakite doctrine.[223] It would have been surprising if the protobyzantine world escaped Mazdakite missionary zeal, and a garbled passage from the history of John of Nikiu[224] indicates that it did not: a patrician named Erythrius was converted, and introduced a Mazdakite teacher to Justinian, who heard him out before having him executed. Erythrius' wife was to become a victim of the offensive which Justinian launched against the heterodox when he became emperor: presumably she, too, was a convert.[225] The Byzantines confused Mazdak's doctrine with Manichaeism, which Rome regarded with peculiar abhorrence. The law dealt harshly with it: the Manichaeans were heretics *qui ad imam usque scelerum nequitiam pervenerant*[226] ('who had reached the lowest possible depths of crime'). Agapetus cannot have been himself a Mazdakite, but neither can he have been ignorant of their doctrines, and amid the speculation that surrounded the new emperor and empress whose backgrounds were an affront to the old ruling élite, Mazdakite ideas of equity may have raised hopes and fears.

Agapetus' panegyric demonstrates the level of expectations at the start of Justinian's reign. Another unconventional panegyric puts forward the public view nearer to its end. In the late 550s, Procopius of Caesarea was writing his panegyric on Justinian's construction programme, and since the public buildings of emperors served to make statements, Justinian's programme can be taken as a manifestation of his vision of the imperial office. The perception of it as a delegation of divine power remains unchanged. Justinian built for the glory of God and the good of his people, and his inspiration came from God Himself, who went so far as to vouchsafe him the technical skill necessary for raising the great dome of Hagia Sophia! It was God, wrote Procopius, who had given Justinian the mission of watching over the whole Roman Empire and if possible, remaking it.[227] The emperor's own piety was vital, for 'when an emperor is devout, godhead does not cease to attend to the affairs of mankind, but regularly takes part in them, and is fond of the company of men.'[228] Yet this perception of the imperial office posed a dilemma. How could a subject of the emperor explain demonstrations of God's wrath, such as plague, earthquakes, fires and disasters in war, all of which marked Justinian's reign?

The hymnist Romanos provided a pious rationalization. In a psalm which he composed after the *Nika* revolt of 532 to celebrate the rebuilding of Hagia Sophia, he told his congregation that God sent calamities to turn His people from their wickedness.[229] As Brian Croke has pointed out, once that view was accepted, the emperor could take on a new role as the leader of an anxious and penitent populace, with the duty of keeping his subjects from sin. Thus we find Justinian outlawing swearing and blasphemy, with the explanation that they brought earthquakes and plague as retribution.[230]

But there was a contemporary underground hypothesis that was less comfortable. Procopius confided it to his *Secret History*, where Justinian appears as the antithesis of the ideal emperor. He was no true emperor chosen by God, but rather a demon, devoted to evil with all the zeal that a holy man devotes to righteousness! The secret historian was not alone. Evagrius,[231] writing after Justinian's death, passes a comparable judgement, though it is unlikely that he knew the *Secret History*. He had no doubt that Justinian's soul went to Hell. In the world of the sixth century, not only the politics and financial policies of an emperor, but even the natural disasters of his reign could be seen as a manifestation of the emperor's moral character and the pleasure God took in it. This was a habit of thought which colours contemporary assessments of Byzantine emperors.[232] Prosperity marked the reigns of good emperors and manifestations of God's wrath marked evil ones. The connection between Heaven and the imperial office was the golden thread which bound an emperor's subjects in loyalty to him, and it was a thread that could be weakened or even broken. A conceptual drift began in Justinian's reign, and became more pronounced under his successors, whereby the people turned their attention increasingly towards allegiance to the Virgin and saints as their true protectors, who did not share the fallibility of the emperors.

CHRISTIANITY AND ITS DISCONTENTS

The Constantinople of Justinian was very much a Christian city, the seat of a bishop who possessed 'prerogatives of honour after the Bishop of Rome, because Constantinople is New Rome', to quote the third canon of the Second Ecumenical Council of 381. In its churches, services were celebrated daily. At the First Hour there was the opening service, giving thanks for the light of the new day; then about 9 o'clock came the service of the Third Hour commemorating the descent of the Holy Spirit at Pentecost; then at noon there was the service for the Crucifixion and at the Ninth Hour, the service for Christ's death upon the cross. Every Sunday, Holy Communion celebrated the Resurrection. The yearly calendar was punctuated by church festivals, of which the most important were those centring on the Nativity and the Crucifixion. There were as well a host of saints' days commemorating the martyrdoms of the faithful. The cycle of ritual was unceasing, and at the great church festivals, the emperor was a conspicuous participant. The Monday after Easter, he would process through the city, to Constantine's Forum, to the church of the Virgin Diaconissa, then to the domed basilica of St Polyeuktos, on to the Churches of the Holy Apostles, St Christopher and St Euphemia, and finally back to the Great Palace. On Easter Tuesday, he received the people's salutation in the Hippodrome, and then went to Hagia Sophia for communion. To be a pagan in this society was to be an outsider.[233]

Yet paganism in the sixth century was by no means dead. Theodosius II had proclaimed in 423 that 'The regulations of constitutions formerly promulgated shall suppress any pagans that survive, *although We now believe that there are none.*'[234] But he was premature. The *Lives* of the saints present a different picture.

Particularly among the rural population, where the monasteries served as spearheads in the battle for converts, paganism lived on. Data are sparse for Greece, where rural monasteries did not appear until the tenth century, but in the East there is evidence for the survival of pagan cults. In the mid-sixth century, St Abramius found a completely pagan village near Lampsacus on the Hellespont, and at Harran on the eastern edge of Syria, the ancient cult of the Moon Goddess continued into the Islamic period.[235] In Athens, which was crowded with reminders of its classical past, pagans and Christians coexisted, but not, it seems, without tension. In the countryside, archaeological investigation discloses a revival of pagan worship in Late Antiquity at cave sanctuaries and cult places which had been almost abandoned, and it did not die out until the sixth century.[236] Worship at the temple of Asklepios on the south slope of the Acropolis in Athens continued at least until the mid-fifth century, but before the end of the century, the temple was destroyed and a church built in its place. Perhaps a Christian mob was responsible. But the site remained a haven for the sick, for the church was apparently dedicated to St Andrew, patron of healing.[237]

Certainly the legal penalties against pagans were harsh enough. Constantine issued a law against sacrifices, though he did not enforce it, but his son Constantius II confirmed the prohibition.[238] Sacrifices to the gods lay at the heart of paganism, and their prohibition meant a reordering of both the society and the economy along new lines. For it was not merely that the sacrifices had pleased the gods. The meat from them went to the city markets, if it was not eaten during the festivals themselves; deprived of sacrifice, pagan religion could no longer play a role in the redistribution of food in the community, and the church moved into the space which the pagan temples had to vacate. Yet the enforcement of the laws banning sacrifice was clearly a difficult project, for they were iterated again and again. The very Christian Theodosius I forbade pagan ceremonies of any sort: sacrifices, taking the auspices, even entering the temples for prayer.[239] But the pagans were persistent: in 451, the emperor Marcian had to order that temples which had been closed should not be reopened and anyone caught offering sacrifices should suffer loss of their property![240] Two decades later, it was necessary for Leo to issue the ban on sacrifice again.[241] The same emperor banned pagan lawyers, and Anastasius found it imperative to prohibit legacies for the maintenance of pagan rites.[242]

But the laws give an inaccurate impression. Their enforcement was capricious, for it depended on local authorities. The emperors were not anxious to disturb the loyalty of tax-paying citizens, even if they were attached to paganism, and their restrictive laws were inspired not so much by their own prejudices as by ecclesiastical lobbying. What the pagans had to fear was not the imperial officials so much as zealous bishops and gangs of monks. In practice if not in theory, the climate of opinion under the first Christian emperors was still generally tolerant.[243] Zosimus, whose *New History* is a pagan polemic against Christianity, wrote under the emperor Anastasius, and was nonetheless a member of the imperial civil service.[244] But paganism in Late Antiquity was a ragbag of nostalgia and super-stition; what it lacked was a system of belief which could match the intellectual excitement of Christian theology.

In fifth-century Athens, it found a creed. The Neoplatonist Academy there developed a pagan theology and in the early years of the sixth century, the Academy under the leadership of Damaskios set out to become the chief centre of pagan thought.[245] Damaskios gathered there a community of distinguished philosophers, and Athens became, to quote a modern scholar, the 'intellectual factory of late paganism'.[246] The city now had no other claim to fame. Philosophy was the only marketable commodity that Athens produced, a fact which must have helped to blunt the animus of the local Christians. The philosophers were also exemplary citizens, and generous in their donations to civic enterprises, for the teachers were prosperous and the Academy had an endowment.[247] Paganism was no threat to the Christian empire, for power and influence were firmly in Christian hands, but that is not how the situation was perceived. With Justinian, the legislation against paganism betrays a new zealotry.

Justinian's first prohibition dates to 527, while he still shared the throne with his uncle. It was a sweeping measure, applied to all who rejected the Catholic church and the orthodox faith.[248] Then there followed a cluster of statutes, all dating to the early years of his reign. All previous limitations placed upon pagans earlier were validated. Pagans were barred from the palatine service.[249] Only heirs of the orthodox faith might inherit when the parents were heterodox.[250] Not even soldiers were exempt.[251] Baptized Christians who lapsed into paganism, or failed to break completely with it in the first place, were to be put to death,[252] and those persons who had never received baptism were to seek it speedily or lose their property rights. Anyone caught secretly making sacrifice to the gods was to be put to death.[253] Two rulings dating to 529 affected teachers. One denied pagan teachers stipends from the imperial treasury; the other prescribed confiscation of their property and exile if they did not accept baptism forthwith.[254]

How vigorously this last interdict was enforced is uncertain. Not universally, it is clear. Pagan philosophers continued to lecture in the schools of Alexandria until the beginning of the next century. However, this ban seems to have provided the legal grounds for putting an end to the Neoplatonist Academy at Athens. In 529, Justinian ordered the teaching of philosophy and law in Athens to cease, and presumably the endowment of the Academy was confiscated.[255]

There is no regulation in Justinian's law code which specifically mentions the Academy, and our evidence for his interdict comes from a brief reference in the chronicle of John Malalas,[256] who also reports that in the same year, Justinian sent a copy of his new law code, the *Codex Justinianus*, to the law school at Beirut, *and to Athens!*[257] Presumably Athens was sent its copy of the code before the schools were closed, and so it appears that the decision to end instruction in Athens was taken quite suddenly later in the same year. There may have been some incident that triggered it which we cannot identify. Justinian had no grounding in the Greek classics himself, but he did not oppose instruction in them, but rather their teaching by pagans whose ideology was foreign to the Byzantine *Weltanschauung*.[258] So it is significant that the year 529, when teaching in philosophy and law was banned in Athens, was also a year of a general purge. Some pagans in the palatine service lost their lives, though we can name only one: Asclepiodotus who drank poison.[259] There was a general climate of paranoia and fear, and the Academy was caught up in it. It may be that Athens was brought to the emperor's notice first as an unsuitable centre for instruction in law, and then he turned his attention to the city's greater claim to fame, its revitalized Neoplatonic Academy.

After the Heruls sacked Athens in 269, it very nearly lost its reputation as an intellectual centre, but in the fourth century, a revival took place: the future emperor Julian, and the future church fathers, Basil of Caesarea and Gregory of Nazianzus all studied there. Pagans and Christians rubbed shoulders amicably enough. But the climate changed in the last quarter of the fourth century with the foundation of the Neoplatonic school by Plutarch, the last native philosopher of note whom Athens produced. His house, on the south slope of the Acropolis, became the centre of the Academy, and it was still being used by Damaskios, the *diadochus* when the Academy was closed in 529. Its remains were excavated in 1955, and they testify both to the prosperity of the school, and to the fact that pagan sacrifices continued there in spite of the legal sanctions until the building was abandoned.[260]

In the fifth century, the Academy's greatest scholar was Proclus, who had transmuted the philosophy which the school purveyed by combining Platonism with the transcendentalism of the Neoplatonist Iamblichus, and in the process he became as much a theologian as a philosopher. The Academy became a pagan monastery of sorts. Proclus was hard-working and wealthy (the Academy probably owed a large share of its endowment to him), but what he developed was an alternative religious system no more tolerant than contemporary Christianity. Yet that did not diminish its appeal in the intellectual climate of the sixth century. Like the Christians, the late Neo-platonists had sacred books, the dialogues of Plato, and even more important, the series of divine revelations called the *Chaldaean Oracles* which had been presented to the world by a mystic of the second century named Julian, who claimed to be a Chaldaean. Iamblichus adapted these revelations to the uses of his new theology.[261] Prayer, contemplation and hymns of praise to the gods were as important to these late Neoplatonists as they were for a devout Christian. Three times a day Proclus prayed to the sun, asking for purification and enlightenment. Death, he taught, was nothing but the union of the fire of the soul with the divine fire of the stars, and spiritual ecstasy could lead the initiate to union with the Divine.[262]

Damaskios, the head of the Academy at Justinian's accession, was a vigorous scholar, who assembled a group of distinguished philoso-phers at Athens and made the Academy the intellectual base of late paganism. Like all the philosophers in the Academy except Plutarch, the founder, he was an immigrant from the East: he was born in Damascus and was an alumnus of the Alexandrian schools. Relations between the Academy and its Christian neighbours cannot always have been easy. Proclus had had to withdraw from Athens for a year, though we can only guess the reason.[263] But the teachings of the Academy and Christian theology were on a collision course. The ideology that it epitomized was openly non-Christian at a time when to be non-Christian was to be anti-Christian.

At Alexandria, the pagan teachers had learned to keep a lower profile. The atmosphere there had been anything but tolerant in the late fifth century, when the philosopher Horapollo was arrested and interrogated under torture; henceforth he concealed his paganism and eventually he converted. Yet by the time of Justinian, Alexandria had come to terms with the new Christian world. In the same period that saw the closure of the Academy at Athens, John Philoponus at Alexandria was devoting himself to the task of making respectable philosophy out of the Christian doctrine that the Universe is perishable, and not, as Aristotle maintained, indestructible.[264] It may be significant that in the year 529, John Philoponus wrote a treatise attacking Proclus. To appropriate a phrase from Peter Brown,[265] Philoponus was 'the self-appointed hammer of the Platonic Academy at Athens', and as such, he had the backing of the patriarch of Alexandria, who extended his protection. There was nothing about the Alexandrian schools that Christianity needed to fear, and though some philosophers who continued to teach there after Justinian's interdict were still pagan,[266] the prevailing ideology of the schools was not. Not so the ideology of the Neoplatonic Academy in Athens.[267]

Seven of the philosophers from Athens led by Damaskios emigrated to Persia after Khusro I came to the throne in 531. Khusro welcomed them to his court, but he was no philosopher king, and probably the philosophers found that Persia's state religion, Zoroastrianism, was no more tolerant than Christianity. In less than a year they returned to the empire. Their sojourn was hardly more than a lecture tour. But Khusro saw to it that a clause was inserted into the 'Endless Peace' which he signed with Justinian in September, 532 that allowed these refugee philosophers to practise their ancient religion unmolested. It was no doubt the philosophers themselves who suggested this clause to Khusro, and it is the sole example we have of a grant of toleration by Justinian. It may have given him a degree of discomfort, which Khusro in turn probably found amusing, if he was aware of it. Some of these philosophers seem to have settled at Harran (Carrhae) and established there a school which lasted into the Islamic period.[268] In any case, the promise of toleration was kept: Simplicius, after Proclus the most interesting of the Athenian Neoplatonists, produced four commentaries on Aristotle after 529, as well as a commentary on the *Enchiridion* of Epictetus, who was exiled by the emperor Domitian, and Simplicius considered his own experience a parallel, as a few hints in the text indicate.[269]

Some teaching may have continued in Athens, though the archaeological data give little support for that view, and the historical data run thin.[270] With the reign of Justinian we reach the final act of the long, unequal struggle between Christianity and paganism. It is a nice coincidence that the year 529 marked not only the end of the Academy in Athens but also the foundation of St Benedict's monastery at Monte Cassino. More significant, however, is the fact that about this same time, an anonymous Christian author who was a disciple of Proclus or Damaskios produced a literary fiction under the name of Dionysius the Areopagite who was converted by St Paul in Athens in AD 51. It is an astonishing essay, which presents late Neoplatonism in Christian camouflage, and it was to have immense influence in both the eastern and western church.[271] The teachings of the Academy did not die with its closure.

Yet Christianity was divided. Arianism, which denied the consubstantiality of the Father and the Son, had gone down to defeat at the Second Ecumenical Council of 381 held at Constantinople, and henceforth it lived on only as a barbarian religion in the Gothic and Vandal kingdoms. The same council condemned the teaching of the bishop of Laodicea, Apollinaris (ca. 310–ca. 390), a brilliant theologian who had countered Arianism by stressing the divine element in Christ at the expense of his human nature. His 'Christ' was God incarnate, and the Virgin Mary was the Mother of God (*Theotokos*), whose role was to deliver the incarnation of the divine element that was preordained from eternity.[272] The theology of Apollinaris was to have a long afterlife, for he was the precursor of the heresy of Monophysitism, which was to tear apart the empire. But for about half a century after the Council of Constantinople, there was an interlude of theological peace.

The next act began in 428, when the emperor Theodosius II brought the presbyter Nestorius from Antioch to Constantinople and made him patriarch. Nestorius, who came to his post with a reputation as an orator, and swiftly gained another as a tactless moralist, was a product of the school of Antioch founded by two churchmen from the north-east corner of the Mediterranean, Diodore of Tarsus and Theodore of Mopsuestia, and it had an outpost close to the Persian frontier at Edessa, whose bishop Ibas translated Theodore's works into Syriac. The Antiochene school tried to counter Apollinarianism with a definition of Christ as a union of two natures. Thus Christ possessed one 'person', for which the Antiochenes employed the term *prosopon*, but two natures (*physeis*), human and divine, both of them complete in themselves. It was the human Christ who was born of the Virgin Mary and was crucified. Thus the Virgin was not the Mother of God (*Theotokos*) but the

Mother of Christ (*Christotokos*); to call her the 'Mother of God' implied that she had actually given birth to a Divine Being, and hence it was God who had died on the cross. That, Nestorius preached, was blasphemy.

Nestorius' congregation was taken aback. Whatever the Antiochenes might say, the masses in Constantinople were coming increasingly to look upon the 'Mother of God' as their Heavenly Protector, and in Egypt, the cult of the Virgin had taken over the devotion which the Egyptians had once given to Isis and her son Harpocrates. The teachings of Nestorius came as a shock.

Arianism's most resolute opponent had been the archbishop of Alexandria, Athanasius, and Cyril, archbishop of Alexandria since 412, who led the battle against Nestorius, saw himself as Athanasius' follower. Able and unscrupulous, he had the support of a loyal clergy and an army of monks and hospital attendants, both Greek and Coptic. He was absolute ruler of the wealthy see of St Mark, with revenues drawn from tithes and a monopoly of the linen trade. On one level, the contest with Nestorius was a test of strength between Alexandria, which had a tradition for anti-imperial sentiment that went back to the first century, and Constantinople, the upstart see which had been only the suffragan bishopric of Heraclea–Perinthus before Constantine built his new capital. At a another level, it was a theological scrimmage between Alexandria and Antioch, which had generated the doctrine which Nestorius preached.

At the Council of Ephesus in 431, Alexandria won on both levels. The Council was Cyril's triumph. He presided over it, and dominated it completely. Not surprisingly, the Council rejected Nestorianism. Nestorius was banished first to his old monastery in Antioch, then to Petra and finally to Upper Egypt. Nestorian teaching had a great future, but it was to be outside the empire. The successor of Ibas as bishop of Edessa was forced to flee to Persia, where he founded a Nestorian school at Nisibis across the imperial frontier. The empire riposted in 489 by closing the Nestorian 'School of the Persians' at Edessa, which was still a theological satellite of Antioch. Its lecturers found posts at Nisibis. Three years earlier, in 486, the Nestorian bishops in Persia had met at Seleuceia–Ctesiphon and organized a separate Persian church. Nestorianism was to become the Christian creed in Iran and India, and by 631, its missionaries had reached the court of the emperor of China.[273]

But that is another story. Cyril did not have everything his own way. The Council of Ephesus may have rejected Nestorius, but it would not accept Cyril's 'Twelve Anathemas', the twelve propositions which Cyril demanded that Nestorius renounce. The second and twelfth of these were questionable: they spoke of the 'Word' *suffering in the flesh* in a style that smacked of Apollinaris! John, patriarch of Antioch, took a firm line. He excommunicated Cyril and the bishops who supported the 'Twelve Anathemas', and in the end it was Cyril who compromised. The emperor Theodosius II maintained firm control, and a formula was devised which papered over the fissure between the doctrines of Antioch and Alexandria. The formula said that Christ was 'of two natures', using the Greek preposition '*ek*' (out of) for 'of'. Cyril signed.

Yet the issue would not disappear. The fact remained that Holy Scripture spoke of the 'Word' (*logos*) becoming Flesh, and left its meaning obscure. If the divine nature of the *logos* existed before the Incarnation, then after the Incarnation it must have united with Christ's human nature, and what sort of union resulted? Eutyches, a friend of Cyril and archimandrite of the monastery of Job in Constantinople, asserted that the union was complete: Christ's human nature was utterly absorbed by His divine one, so that in Him there was really only one nature. In 448, a local synod chaired by the patriarch of Constantinople, Flavian, condemned Eutyches as a heretic.

But Eutyches had powerful friends, not only Cyril, but also his own godson, the eunuch Chrysaphius who was the power behind the emperor Theodosius II's throne. Cyril's successor at Alexandria, Dioscorus, took up the argument. Dioscorus was a true Monophysite, and though the term 'Monophysite', from the Greek '*monos*' (one) and '*physis*' (nature), did not enter general usage until the seventh century, it is convenient to use it here. At the second Council of Ephesus in 449, the *Latrocinium* or 'Robber Council' as Pope Leo the Great was to term it, the Monophysites came within a smidgen of victory. Theodosius II was amenable. Dioscorus dominated the assembly and the bishops swung their support behind Eutyches' profession of faith. Pope Leo had sent Flavian, patriarch of Constantinople, a letter, the so-called *Tome* of Leo, which supported Antioch's distinction between the Natures of Christ, but the council did not debate it.[274] The Twelve Anathemas of Cyril were declared orthodox. The papal legates uttered protests, but they were ignored. In any case they made their objections in Latin, which was not widely understood among the Greek clergy. The triumph of the see of St Mark appeared complete.

Then everything changed. Theodosius II died from a hunting accident; his sister Pulcheria took over and chose an able soldier, Marcian, as her consort. Eutyches was exiled and Chrysaphius was put to death. In 451, a great assembly of bishops met at Chalcedon and formulated a definition which was to be the touchstone of orthodoxy, and though it recognized the Virgin as *Theotokos*, and stated that Christ was a single, undivided person, nonetheless it was firmly dyophysite. The confession of faith which Marcian and Pulcheria wanted was 'We confess one Jesus, Lord, only Son whom we acknowledge *in two natures*', which conformed with the *Tome* of Leo, the rock on which all future compromise would shatter. The milder formula that defined a Christ *'of two natures'* which Cyril had accepted, and Dioscorus could have also, would not do. The inference was that while divinity and humanity were united in Christ, they did not merge, but each retained its essential property.

Yet the difference was not vast. The majority of churchmen at Chalcedon accepted the 'in two natures' formula only after persuading themselves that it really did not deviate from Cyril's teaching, and Justinian himself was to strain mightily at the Fifth Ecumenical Council of 553 to show that Chalcedon, if interpreted correctly, did agree with Cyril.[275] But the difference by then had grown into a great gulf.

Marcian and Pulcheria got what they wanted at Chalcedon with some arm-twisting. But the Egyptian bishops would not sign. They knew that if they did, they would be lynched when they returned home. Dioscorus himself went into exile, though not for heresy but for strong-arm tactics at the 'Robber Council'.

Chalcedon was a turning point in more ways than one. It decided the order of precedence of the great archbishoprics, which had been called patriarchates since the first Council of Ephesus. Rome had primacy, but Constantinople's ranking above all the other patriarchates was accepted, though not by Rome which refused recognition for six centuries. Antioch and Alexandria were now joined by the patriarchate of Jerusalem, whose suffragan bishop, Juvenal, had supported Dioscorus at the 'Robber Council' and had his diocese elevated to a patriarchal see as a reward. Two years later, at Chalcedon, he shrewdly protected his status by deserting Dioscorus and signing on the winning side. The Palestinian monks were incensed. Juvenal was forced out of Jerusalem and stayed in Constantinople until 453, when he returned with the backing of imperial troops.[276] The monks offered battle at Neapolis, the biblical

Shechem and the centre of Samaritanism, but the imperial troops with some help from Samaritan irregulars worsted them, and their leader Theodosius fled to Egypt with a price on his head.

But the most important result of Chalcedon was an uncompromisingly dyophysite definition of the orthodox faith, which even the aged Nestorius, now an exile in Upper Egypt, could accept, and, as Chalcedon's opponents noted with distaste, it allowed two of Nestorius' old friends, Theodoret of Cyrrhus and Ibas of Edessa, to be received into communion. For Rome, the *Tome* of Leo remained the touchstone of orthodoxy. But Egypt and Syria were lands of monasteries and convents, and the monks represented the non-urban populations, only lightly touched by Greek civilization. Into the struggle between the supporters of Chalcedon and the Monophysites poured the resentments and hurts of indigenous cultures which had long been submerged by Hellenism. It is anachronistic to interpret the Monophysite conflict as a nationalist movement in the modern sense, for the aim of the Monophysites was not separatist: they promoted their doctrine as the correct belief for the whole empire, not for only a part of it. Yet the dispute rapidly became a struggle for empowerment, with the native masses of Egypt and Syria pitted against the Greek-speaking élite. Christianity had given the indigenes a voice, and was the creative force behind Coptic and Syriac literature. Now theological controversy was to give the native masses an identity.

Palestine was a special case. It was Christianity's 'Holy Land' which attracted large amounts of outside capital in the form of gifts and dedications, both public and private.[277] Its monasteries drew pilgrims and monks from all over the empire, whereas a large portion of the native rural population was Jewish or Samaritan. After the first outburst of anger against Juvenal, Palestine edged back into the Chalcedonian camp. In Syria, Monophysitism eventually won, but in the fifth century the outcome was uncertain. But in Egypt, with few exceptions, notably the *Metanoia* at Canopus, the monasteries rejected the hated *Tome* of Leo, and the accursed creed of Chalcedon.

It took a large detachment of imperial troops to install the man chosen by the Council of Chalcedon to replace Dioscorus as patriarch of Alexandria. Proterius had supported Dioscorus but that did him no good when he became Dioscorus' successor. The masses regarded him as a turncoat, and when he advised a prudent policy of flexibility, the emperor turned a deaf ear. Dioscorus died in 454, and the emperor Marcian followed him to the grave not quite two and a half years later, whereupon the Monophysites chose a successor to Dioscorus, Timothy *Aelurus*, 'the Cat', a monk and a moderate Monophysite. Proterius was lynched in his cathedral in 457 as he celebrated the eucharist on Maundy Thursday. The murder was the fault of the Alexandrian mob and need not have disqualified Timothy as patriarch, but he no more than Proterius was able to find a formula which was acceptable to the Monophysites as well as Proterius' supporters. At the end of the year 459, he was exiled in his turn, and replaced by a monk from the *Metanoia* monastery at Canopus, Timothy nicknamed Salofaciolus, a word which combines the nouns for 'teetering' and 'turban': his turban, perhaps, wobbled as he walked. The 'Cat' was to come back: during the putsch which replaced the emperor Zeno by Basiliscus from January, 475 to August 476, Monophysitism enjoyed a brief period of favour at court and Timothy was able to return triumphantly to Alexandria. The other Timothy, of the teetering turban, went back to the *Metanoia*. But Zeno recovered the throne, and the 'Cat' would have gone again into exile except that he anticipated the imperial order by dying at the end of July, 477.

Zeno attempted a compromise with the help of Acacius, patriarch of Constantinople, who recycled a formula supplied originally by the patriarch of Jerusalem. Zeno issued a constitution known as the *Henotikon*,[278] which stated clearly enough that Christ was both God and man, but omitted the offensive words 'in two natures'. It pointed to the Nicene Creed as the common definition of faith, and detoured around Chalcedon. Nestorius and Eutyches were both condemned again. Zeno tried to follow a middle road, and his attempt to find an acceptable formula did satisfy the moderate Monophysites. But the *Henotikon* came to grief on the rock of Roman intransigence. Pope Felix excommunicated Acacius and the 'Acacian Schism' still divided Rome and Constantinople when Justin became emperor.[279]

The emperor Anastasius was Monophysite by conviction, but the populace of the capital was generally orthodox and Anastasius perforce kept his inclinations in check. Even so, a riot in 512 nearly brought him down after the patriarch, with Anastasius' blessing, introduced into the liturgy of Hagia Sophia the Monophysite version of the *Trisagion*. Three years later, he faced a rebellion by Vitalian, the count of the federate troops in Thrace, who marched on the capital with a huge force of soldiers and peasants and inflicted a disastrous defeat on the imperial army that Anastasius mustered against him. Anastasius perforce appointed Vitalian Master of the

Soldiers of Thrace, and promised a new church council. But Rome remained adamant; Pope Hormisdas insisted on the Creed of Chalcedon pure and simple, and the retrospective condemnation of Acacius, and to that Anastasius would not agree. Vitalian marched on Constantinople again, but this time he was defeated in battle and three of his generals were captured and executed. Vitalian himself escaped to Anchialos in his native province of Scythia Minor, ten days' march from the capital, and there he lurked with what remained of his Gothic and Bulgarian army, awaiting an opportunity.

Not two months after Justin succeeded Anastasius, he dispatched a letter to Pope Hormisdas inviting him to send legates to Constantinople, and at the same time, Justinian dispatched a more peremptory letter summoning Hormisdas in person. 'Apart from any delay, we expect your arrival. ... Therefore hasten, most holy lord, lest in your absence should be ordained what ought to be ordained in your presence.'[280] Hormisdas did not come to Constantinople, though his successor John II was later to make the journey, but by that time, his mission was a different one: he was under orders from Theodoric the Ostrogoth to urge Justin to cancel his decrees against the Arians. At the start of Justin's reign, Chalcedon appeared triumphant. Vitalian returned to the capital and was appointed Master of Soldiers *in praesenti*, and in 520, consul. The Monophysite patriarch of Antioch, Severus, who had enjoyed Anastasius' favour, fled into exile in Egypt, narrowly escaping arrest. The papal envoys arrived in the capital, and on Holy Thursday of 519, John, the patriarch of Constantinople, accepted Rome's conditions, though without pleasure. Five of John's predecessors were condemned, as well as the emperors Zeno and Anastasius, and to seal the reconciliation, the papal legates celebrated communion with the patriarch in Hagia Sophia.

The victory was illusory. Within a matter of months Justinian realized that he could not build unity on the *Tome* of Leo, and pondered the wisdom of extending an olive branch to the Mono-physites by sanctioning a doctrine that a group of monks from the province of Scythia Minor put forward, that one of the Trinity had suffered in the flesh. It had been the addition of something very like this to the *Trisagion* which had nearly brought down Anastasius in 512, but the Scythian monks sought to repackage the offensive words so as not to challenge Chalcedon so much as to defend it against the charge of Nestorianism. The 'Sleepless Monks' in the capital vigorously denounced this so-called 'Theopaschite' doctrine as a deviation from Chalcedon, but Vitalian, whose Chalcedonian credentials were impeccable, was a native of Scythia Minor himself and saw to it that his countrymen got a hearing.

Eventually, in 533, Justinian was to decree with Pope John II's approval that the Theopaschite doctrine was orthodox, but that was in the future.[281] In 520, he sent Pope Hormisdas a letter urging him to give the Theopaschite formula fair consideration and counselled patience 'lest, while we wish to win souls, we should lose both the bodies and the souls of many persons'. Justinian was already aware that there was a body of support for a 'middle way', if only he could find it. For the moderate Monophysites who looked to Cyril as their teacher, the phrase 'who was crucified for us' applied to God the Son was vital, for they believed it was the *logos*, the Word, which had to suffer in the flesh so that man might fulfil his divine destiny.[282] In Rome, Hormisdas temporized, though Justinian's formula may have won the support of Theodoric's Master of Offices, Boethius, and perhaps it was his effort to bring about a *rapprochement* between the pope and the emperor that cost him the Ostrogothic king's good-will.[283] But in the end, Hormisdas would not yield. The Easter service of 519 in Constantinople was only the *mise-en-scène* for theological battle theatre of Justinian's reign, in which the middle way somehow disappeared.

THE NEIGHBOURS OF THE EMPIRE

For almost all its life, Byzantium was a beleaguered empire with permeable frontiers. Justinian's reconquests in Africa, Italy and Spain did nothing to alter that fact. In theory, the emperor ruled the *oikoumene*, the civilized world, as God's representative, but the hard reality was that the *oikoumene* was beset by neighbours, some of them heretics, others non-Christian, who were outside imperial control. Imperial diplomacy had a double mission: to secure the frontiers and to spread Christianity, and to these, Justinian added a third: the recovery of the lost provinces. The empire had an arsenal of weapons ranging from manipulation to war to achieve its ends.

On the vulnerable Balkan front, the emperor Zeno had used Bulgars against the Ostrogoths until he removed the Gothic threat by prompting Theodoric to invade Italy and oust Odoacer. The Bulgars remained, and in 493, they launched their first raid, crushing a Roman army and killing its commander, and six years later, they won another victory. In 517, a horde of Bulgars and Antai raided

Macedon and Thessaly as far south as Thermopylae, but Germanus, the emperor Justin's nephew, defeated them decisively enough that they left the Balkans in peace for a decade or so.[284]

The Bulgars were a Ural–Altaic group who had moved westward from Central Asia and had reached the Volga river by the fourth century. At some point in that century, they split to form the Kutrigur state north of the Black Sea, and the Utigur state further to the east. The Byzantine authors called these protobulgars Huns, or if they sought a classical label, they borrowed the name 'Massagetae' from Herodotus. They raided Thrace again in 528, and the next year, they were probably the organizers of a damaging Slavic inroad into Illyricum. In 530, a Byzantine army led by Mundo, a Gepid prince who had only just transferred his services from the Ostrogoths to Justinian, defeated them and captured the Bulgar king.[285] But the threat remained, all the more so because it was under Bulgar leadership that the Slavs first entered the empire.

In Justinian's reign, the Slavs were to take control of the north bank of the Danube from Belgrade to its estuary, but it is a matter of dispute how soon they moved into the area. In 533, they defeated and killed the Master of Soldiers in Thrace, Chilbudius, who was himself a Slav. Justinian replied with a counter-offensive, and in 535, retook Sirmium (*mod.* Sremska Mitrovica) from the Ostrogoths, though he held it for only a year. Yet in a law of 535, he could boast that both banks of the Danube were full of 'our cities', though he named only three north of the river.[286] However, from the archaeological evidence it seems clear that imperial control persisted well past Justinian's accession on a strip of territory north of the Danube. Yet there was one Slavic inroad after another, usually in concert with the Bulgars. In 527, the year of Justinian's accession, there was a massive Bulgar–Slav invasion; in 539 or 540, there was an incursion of Kutrigur Bulgars and thereafter the situation was precarious. Justinian tried to maintain the Danube frontier with a chain of forts so that when the barbarians raided, the local villagers might have places of refuge where they could be safe until an imperial army regained control, or the barbarians went home satisfied with their loot.[287] But this kind of defence could only limit the damage caused by these incursions; it could not put an end to them. Writing in the 550s, Procopius reported,

> The Huns, Sclaveni and Antai, almost every year since Justinian took control of the Roman Empire, have overrun Illyricum

and Thrace in its entirety, comprising the whole expanse of country from the Adriatic to the outskirts of Constantinople, including Greece and the Balkan peninsula.[288]

The Sclaveni and Antai or, as the Germans called them, the 'Wends', were both Slavic: the home base of the Sclaveni stretched from the Danube to the Dniester, and the Antai occupied the territory from Bessarabia to the Donets. By the end of the sixth century, the Slavs were to have settlements all over the Balkans.[289]

In Africa, there was the Vandal kingdom, which occupied somewhat less that half of the old African diocese as it had existed on the eve of the Vandal conquest. The kingdom was a century old when Justinian became emperor, and beginning to show faultlines. In the spring of 429, Gaiseric had led his Vandals across the Strait of Gibraltar and eastward into the diocese, taking advantage of a temporary quarrel between the count of Africa, Boniface, and Galla Placidia, the empress in Ravenna. He quickly overran most of Mauretania and Numidia, though for the time being, the fortified cities of Hippo Regius and Cirta were beyond his reach. But a treaty with Rome in 435 delivered Hippo to him, and four years later, a surprise attack won him Carthage. Another treaty in 442 confirmed him in the heartland of Roman Africa: the emperor recognized him as lord of eastern Numidia, Proconsularis with its capital, Carthage, Byzacium to the south and Tripolitania to the east. The rest of Numidia and Mauretania Sitifensis reverted to Rome, and the emperor Valentinian III made some land grants there to a few of the dispossessed proprietors from Proconsularis and Byzacium, but after Valentinian's murder, we have no report of further Roman activity there.[290]

Carthage was the Vandal capital. It was a city which had prospered greatly in the fourth and early fifth centuries, and the Vandal conquest markedly abridged its public life.[291] Its Catholic churches with their treasures were confiscated and those not destroyed were converted to the Arian rite. The Vandals allowed some Catholic churches to conduct services outside the city walls, but among those that they seized were the shrine marking the site of St Cyprian's martyrdom, and the church where his body lay. Quodvultdeus, the bishop of Carthage, was banished to Italy with most of his priests; Victor of Vita,[292] the chronicler of the Vandal persecutions who never understated reality, reported that God brought their leaky vessels safely to Naples, where they were received with honour. Africa had been Italy's chief supplier of imported wheat, and once it was lost, there remained only Sicily and Sardinia, which the Vandals attacked the year after Carthage's fall. It was Rome's turn in 455: through two weeks of June, Gaiseric sacked the great city far more thoroughly than had the Visigoths forty-five years earlier, and returned to Africa with as much portable wealth as he could take, as well as the empress Eudoxia and the two daughters of Valentinian III, who had been murdered earlier that year. In the Forum of Peace at Rome, he found the spoils taken from the Temple of Herod in Jerusalem which Rome had destroyed in the year 70, and these too he carried off to Carthage.

Gaiseric survived a fruitless campaign against him by the emperor Majorian, and a much more serious expedition mounted by the eastern emperor Leo in 462 which ended in a disaster that still haunted the ruling circles in Constantinople some seventy years later, on the eve of Justinian's own expedition. Leo made peace, but after his death, the Vandal raids against the coast of Greece began again, and Zeno again sued for peace. Thus, before Gaiseric died in 477, he had won Zeno's recognition as king of all Roman Africa, Corsica, Sardinia, the Balearic Islands and Sicily, though the last of these he made over to Odoacer. His aim was to control the sea lanes and as much as anything, it was his maritime dominion that strangled the western Roman Empire.[293]

Of all the barbarian chieftains who led their hordes into the Roman Empire, Gaiseric was the most brilliant warrior. He left the Vandals an aura of invincibility which they soon ceased to deserve. A fragment of the historian Malchus notes that after Gaiseric's death, they grew soft and lost the capacity for swift, unexpected military action which had once been the undoing of the Romans. The distress suffered by the Catholics arose not so much from deliberate persecution as from the effort to maintain a German state as a distinct society dominating a Roman majority. The Vandals were given tax-free allotments,[294] the *Sortes Vandalorum* taken from confiscated landholdings. Roman owners relinquished their villas to new Vandal proprietors, though the management of the estates and the condition of the tenants remained largely unchanged. The Vandal royal family had estates in Byzacium to the south, and it was at one of these, at an unidentified site named Hermiana, that the last king, Gelimer, was staying in 533 when he learned of the Byzantine invasion.

The city of Carthage itself was firmly Arian: Gaiseric in his treaty with Zeno of 476 was willing to grant Catholics freedom of worship there, but he would not allow the appointment of a new Catholic bishop to its vacant see. However, with Gaiseric's successor, Huneric, the situation changed.

Huneric began with an appearance of tolerance. He permitted the consecration of a new Catholic bishop of Carthage. But once it was clear that he had nothing to fear from Constantinople, he initiated a fierce persecution of the Catholics. His successor allowed the persecution to subside, but it was renewed by Thrasamund, who became king in 496, though without Huneric's overt brutality. He closed Catholic churches, prohibited further consecration of bishops and punished disobedience by deporting the Catholic bishops to Sardinia. For more than twenty years, the African Catholics were without bishops or churches.

Nonetheless, Thrasamund remained on good terms with the emperor Anastasius, as well as Theodoric the Ostrogoth, whose sister he married, thereby marking an alliance between the two most powerful Arian kings of the Mediterranean world. The nomad Berbers on the frontiers, or Moors, as the Romans called them, were another matter. The Romans had coped adequately with the native problem. The frontier had always been permeable. The defences on the southern border of the diocese, such as the *fossatum* system that surrounds the base of the Hodna massif, was intended to control passage to and fro, and collect customs dues, not to keep the nomads isolated from the agricultural settlements. Many of the Berber tribes had become semi-Romanized allies before the Vandal conquest, and Christianity, not always of the orthodox variety, had spread widely.[295] These tribes did not automatically transfer their allegiance to the new Arian conquerors.

Before his death, Gaiseric had already lost control of most of Mauretania, and under Huneric, the highlanders of the Aurès massif near the border of modern Algeria made good their independence: the ruined city of Thamugadi (*mod.* Timgad) in the Aurès piedmont is mute evidence of the effects that their raids had on the African cities, for it was largely destroyed at this time.[296] In the mid-530s, a sheikh named Iaudas who could muster 30,000 men controlled the area.[297] In the frontier zone of Tripolitania, the confederacy of Laguatan tribes challenged the Vandals. The Laguatan were nomad worshippers of the Libyan bull-headed god Gurzil, and of Ammon, whose worship had spread along the oasis routes from Siwah, where Alexander the Great had visited his shrine.[298] The Laguatan had migrated westwards along the frontier of Cyrenaica. In Thrasamund's reign a sheikh in Tripolitania named Cabaon almost annihilated an army of Vandal cavalry that attempted to storm his camp, which he defended by ringing it with camels tethered one to another. The Vandal horses refused to face the camels, and the result was the worst disaster that the Berbers inflicted on the Vandals.[299] In the aftermath, the Vandals lost control of the territories of Sabratha, Lepcis Magna and Oea (Tripoli), and the cities themselves were defenceless, for the Vandals had left no walls standing except those of Carthage. Lepcis was depopulated, and so probably were Oea and Sabratha.[300]

About 510, a chief named Guefan built up an emirate in the Grand Dorsale south of Thugga, and when Thrasamund's unwarlike successor, Hilderic, sent an army against it, it was defeated by Guefan's son and heir, Antalas. Antalas was to become a Byzantine ally, though the alliance did not endure. The Byzantines were to inherit the native problem from the Vandals, just as the Vandals had from the Romans, but with the difference that the zone of nomadic control had greatly increased and now penetrated deep within the province. One result is apparent from a recent survey of the Kasserine area of central Tunisia: there the increase in farming settlement in the fifth century came to a standstill and began to decline in the sixth.[301] Another straw in the wind is the sharp increase in food imports in the half century or so before Justinian recovered Africa: for the first quarter of the fifth century, amphoras of east Mediterranean origin account for only one-tenth of all amphoras found in the Carthage excavations, while a century later, they have reached a level of 25 to 30 per cent. The amphoras were food containers, and the import growth indicates that something was going wrong with domestic production.[302] Berber raids on the farming settlements must count as a major reason.

The Vandal weakness was not all enervation, though the Vandals enjoyed to the full the opulence their conquests had won them. Procopius[303] thought them the most voluptuous people he knew, whereas the Berbers were the toughest. But the Vandal problem was a military one: the Vandals fought as horsemen armed with spears and swords, and could not cope with an enemy that fought with javelins and rode camels. Some fifteen years after the Vandal disaster in Tripolitania, a Byzantine army was to face a Berber force which used the same tactics that frustrated the Vandal horsemen, and the Byzantine general, Solomon, countered successfully by ordering his men to dismount and fight on foot. The Vandals paid the penalty for their own inflexibility.[304]

In Italy, Theodoric died in 526 after a reign of thirty-seven years. He had settled his Ostrogoths in the peninsula with remarkably little stress, thanks largely to the competence of his praetorian prefect Liberius, who had once served Odoacer and transferred his services to Theodoric after Odoacer's murder. Liberius was an able Roman collaborator whom we shall meet again. He settled the Goths into the third portions (*tertiae*) of the estates vacated by Odoacer's less numerous followers. The Goths acquired a privileged position and income from the land that was sequestered for their upkeep, as well as a royal grant of some 5 *solidi* each year.[305] But there seem to have been no widespread expropriations from Roman property owners, who could count on royal protection on the official level at least. The Roman senate continued as before, and one consul continued to be appointed in Rome[306] each year from the senatorial order, which retained at least some of its wealth. Theodoric himself was well liked: 'love for him among both Goths and Italians flourished mightily', wrote Procopius.[307]

From Boethius, Theodoric's Master of Offices until his arrest for treason, we have a contemporary judgement that is less flattering, though he had reason for his bias: 'I have countless times', he wrote, 'interposed my authority to protect wretched men from danger when they were hounded by the endless false accusations of the barbarians in their continuous and unpunished lust for wealth.'[308] Those were words written in bitterness in Theodoric's final years, while Boethius was in gaol, but they were based on reality. The Gothic rank and file were a rapacious lot, who believed their conquest had given them the right to plunder Italians and take over their landholdings.[309] They slipped easily into the role that the rich Roman proprietors, the *potentiores*, had played in the past, and like them, plundered smaller and weaker landowners.[310] Theodoric's nephew Theodahad gobbled up most of Tuscany! Procopius' encomium reflects Theodoric's reputation among the Roman élite after the Byzantine reconquest: he bore the title of *rex* like any barbarian king, he wrote, but he had the qualities of a true emperor (*basileus*).[311] The Roman senatorial class was a casualty of the Byzantine reconquest, and in retrospect, Theodoric's reign seemed a Golden Age, far more than it was in reality.

The Ostrogoths themselves were not numerous. Theodoric may have led no more than 40,000 followers into Italy, whereas Gaiseric had twice that number when he crossed from Spain into Africa. Theodoric's power base was narrow, but while he was alive, his authority was respected, and his *saiones*, as his officers were called, maintained law and order.[312] The Arianism of the Goths had a double-edged consequence. On the one hand, it prevented their assimilation into the Italian majority, which would have been fatal to the Ostrogothic monarchy. But on the other hand, it meant that there could be no real *rapprochement* with the Romans, who considered the emperor in Constantinople their rightful ruler.

As long as the Acacian schism endured, and the sees of Rome and Constantinople were not in communion, Theodoric could count on the compliance of the Romans, for they were unwilling to shift their allegiance to an heretical emperor. But once a Chalcedonian took over the imperial throne, the risk of collaboration increased. Yet relations with the new regime in Constantinople began well enough. Justin and Theodoric's son-in-law, Eutharic, became consuls together in 519, and Justin adopted Eutharic according to Germanic custom, thereby assuring his succession after Theodoric died. By implication, Eutharic gave his recognition to the subordinate status of the Ostrogothic kingdom. His liking for the arrangement is questionable, for he was a true-blue Ostrogoth with no love for Catholics, but Theodoric's daughter Amalasuintha was half assimilated: she had been educated as a Roman and admired Roman culture. The Gothic nobles, who had been Theodoric's mainstay, regarded her as a *vendue*. But we can only guess at what might have happened if Eutharic had succeeded Theodoric, for in 522, he died, leaving a 4-year-old son as Theodoric's heir.

Justin was not only orthodox himself, but also put an end to toleration of the Arians within the empire. The news of Justin's anti-Arian legislation roused Theodoric to action and he determined to champion his fellow heretics in the East. He dispatched Pope John II to Constantinople to remonstrate. But the magnificence of the pope's reception there increased the king's paranoia, and when John came back to Ravenna, Theodoric put him in prison where he died. He was promptly hailed as a martyr by the western church. The Catholics expected persecution. It did not happen; yet there were legends, as Sir Charles Oman[313] noted, that at the moment of Theodoric's death, certain holy hermits in Italy saw his soul being carried off to Hell by the Devil himself!

The old king's last years were marked by gloom and suspicion, and not without cause. A year after Eutharic's death, Theodoric's brother-in-law, the Vandal king Thrasamund, died, and his successor Hilderic reversed Thrasamund's anti-Catholic policy. Thrasamund's widow, Amalafrida, protested and Hilderic threw her into prison where she was murdered, and her Gothic entourage was massacred. In the same year Theodoric learned of secret contacts between some Roman senators and Justin. The result was a treason trial where Boethius, the Master of Offices, and Boethius' father-in-law, Symmachus, the head of the senate, were sentenced to death. Boethius' *Consolation of Philosophy*, written in prison, has made him a secular martyr, though he was undoubtedly a Christian, but there is some justice to Thomas Hodgkin's estimate of him, written over a century ago: he was a brilliant man of letters, irreproachable so long as he remained in his library, but unfit for public affairs and incapable of recognizing more than one viewpoint on any question. Yet Procopius reports that after his execution, Theodoric died of remorse. Another source, the so-called Anonymous Valesianus, makes the cause of Theodoric's death dysentery, which was not an uncommon fate for heretics.[314] At any rate, on 30 September, 526, the great Ostrogoth died, leaving his grandson Athalaric to succeed him, with his mother Amalasuintha as regent.

In the East, where 'the land of the Romans' faced 'the land of the Persians',[315] there was a century and a half of equilibrium after the death of Theodosius I in 395. The frontier line followed the river Khabur and the river Nymphios west of the modern Iraq–Syria border. South of the junction of the Khabur and the Euphrates, the latter marked the boundary. But the eastern frontier of the diocese of *Oriens* was a permeable one where the Romans and the Bedouin lived in a permanent state of conflict and symbiosis. The Romans were never able to prevent Bedouin raids, and their *castra* and *castella* served as bases for monitoring Bedouin movements and places of refuge for hermits and travellers when the countryside was unsafe. The 'inner limes', that is, the part of the frontier most removed from settled habitation, was a no-man's land. The situation was reminiscent of the nineteenth-century American frontier, except that here the settled area never could dominate the outback. Climate and geography guaranteed that the nomads would hold their own on these margins of cultivation to which they were superbly adapted.[316]

Within the boundary of the *Oriens* prefecture, but ranging as far as the Euphrates, the Saracen banu-Ghassan had established dominion. Sometime around the end of the third century, they had migrated from south Arabia to the basalt hills of the Hawran, where they became bilingual in Arabic and Aramaic, and two centuries later, they had adopted Monophysite Christianity and come within the Byzantine sphere of influence. Before the sixth century, they had established themselves in north-east Jordan.[317] With Justinian, they acquired new importance: Justinian appointed the sheikh of the banu-Ghassan, al-Harith ben Djabala, patrician and phylarch. He had the 'dignity of a *basileus*' bestowed upon him, according to Procopius who considered him an unlucky warrior if not a traitor, though he later modified his judgement. Justinian used Ghassanids as a buffer against Persia's Saracen allies, the Lakhmids, headed by the formidable al-Mundhir III (ca. 505–554), whose centre was al-Hira not far from Babylon.

The Romans had used local sheikhs to secure the frontier since the fourth century, unreliable though they might be. Side by side with the imperial dukes were Bedouin phylarchs: federate sheikhs who held the nominal rank of *clarissimi* and received regular food subventions in return for restraining *razzias* on Roman territory. Before the Ghassanids, the Romans had had a pact with the Kindites, who at the height of their power had controlled the island of Iotabe (*mod.* Tiran, or alternatively Jazirat Fara'un) at the entrance to the Gulf of Aqaba. A sheikh known to our sources as Amorcesos, who had been a Persian client but was possibly a Kindite nonetheless, won the emperor Leo's recognition as phylarch and ruler of Iotabe, which he held for a quarter-century.[318] On the island was a profitable customs post which straddled an important trade route from south Arabia, and Leo's recognition of Amorcesos, we may believe, was not entirely voluntary.

In 498, Anastasius recovered Iotabe and its customs post, but four years later, he recognized the Kindite sheikh Harith as phylarch and the compact lasted until 528 when Harith quarreled with the duke of Palestine and retreated to the inner *limes* where his son-in-law and nominal vassal, Mundhir the Lakhmid, caught and killed him.[319] Harith's successor was his grandson Qays, for whom Justinian found a flattering sinecure, but the Kindite star was falling, and Justinian needed a more effective counterbalance against the Lakhmids. He revived a strategy which had fallen into disuse since the second century, and created a client kingdom on the frontier. He recognized Harith of the banu-Ghassan first as the successor of the Kindite sheikh, and then, sometime before 531, as supreme phylarch with the status of a king, charged with defending the whole frontier from the Red Sea to the Euphrates river. About the same time, he gave Harith's brother Abu-Karib the phylarchate of Third Palestine in return for the gift of the 'Palm Groves' which lay beyond the imperial boundaries.[320]

The gift was a nominal one; the 'Palm Groves' were of no value anyway, but Justinian got an ally who helped suppress a Samaritan rebellion in 529, and served as an alert guardian of Palestine. Abu-Karib in return secured control of the terminus of the trade route from Mecca, which now lay under Ghassanid control, for Ghassanid dominance stretched as far as the environs of al-Madinah.[321] Along the route passed spices from India, silk from China and slaves on their way to Axumite and Indian markets: after the Samaritan revolt was crushed, 20,000 captive boys and girls travelled along this route to eastern markets.

The Lakhmids had been tented Arabs calling themselves Tanukh who migrated from Yemen to the Tigris–Euphrates valley about the time that Sassanid Persia replaced Parthia as the ruling power there. In due time they established a permanent settlement within the Kindite orbit at Hira. The indigenous population was Christian and some Tanukh became converted, but the royal house did not; only one Lakhmid dynast became Christian and he was the last of the line. Persia found them valuable allies: al-Mundhir ibn Nu'man III, whom the Greeks called 'Alamoundaras', was sole ruler of the Saracens in Persia, whose domain extended to Bahrein and Oman.[322] The north-west edge of his territory impinged on the Ghassanid domain midway along the Palmyra–Damascus road about the region called Strata, where the two clans disputed ownership of a sheep-walk. Mundhir was a formidable enemy, who made his *razzias* at will deep into the eastern provinces of the empire. 'No one at all stood in his way', wrote Procopius.[323]

> For he never made his raids without reconnoitering, and his movements were so unexpected and well-timed for his purposes that as a rule he was already off on his way with all his booty before the generals and the soldiers began to learn what had happened, and muster against him. But if they happened by some chance to catch him, this barbarian turned and fell upon his pursuers before they were prepared or in battle order, routing and crushing them effortlessly. One time he made all the soldiers pursuing him prisoners along with their commanders.

That time was 524, when the emperor Justin had had to retrieve his captive officers with a generous ransom.

In the spring of 529, on the eve of the Samaritan revolt, Mundhir's Bedouin horsemen swept into northern Syria as far as the walls of Antioch, capturing 400 nuns from the church of St Thomas at Emesa and sacrificing them to their goddess 'Uzzai.[324] But the Ghassanids were to prove worthy antagonists: in 544, Harith routed Mundhir, though not before his own son was captured and sacrificed by his Lakhmid rival, and ten years later, Harith killed Mundhir himself in battle.[325]

The long period of stability on the frontier which Byzantium shared with Sassanid Persia ended in 502 with an attack by King Kavadh on Roman Mesopotamia. The reign of Kavadh's father Peroz had been luckless: his empire had suffered from a seven-year drought and famine which had long-lasting effects, and from their base in the Pamir foothills, the Ephthalites launched attacks, capturing Peroz in 469 and finally vanquishing and killing him in 482. The Ephthalites or 'White Huns' (the *Hsien-ta* in Chinese sources) for a century dominated the territory from the south-east of the Caspian Sea to Afghanistan and India, and north as far as the Tarim basin, and they disrupted the caravan trade with China which was an important Persian source of revenue.[326] Peroz's brother and successor ruled over a humbled empire which had to pay the Ephthalites tribute. A revolt of nobles and clergy in 488 brought Kavadh to the throne, who had spent part of his youth as a hostage at the court of the Ephthalite king.

Kavadh's attack on Byzantium was perhaps partly an effort to unite his own empire. He had allied himself with the Mazdakite movement, and was for a period a genuine convert. But at the end of his reign, he found that the Mazdakites were plotting against his choice as heir, who was his third son Khusro, and he engineered a massacre of the Mazdakite leaders.[327] Mazdak had led a religious revolt against Zoroastrian orthodoxy, which was the state religion of Persia, and his theology had elements that were similar to Manichaeism, though our knowledge is scanty. Greek, Syriac and Armenian sources refer to Mazdakite doctrine as Manichaeism, which was the Persian heresy *par excellence*.[328] There was a strong socialist component to Mazdak's gospel: he taught that the Supreme Being had granted men the means of subsistence, which all should share equally. No man had more rights than another to wealth, women or personal property. Land was to be redistributed. The evidence suggests a peasants' revolt, after a series of disasters which weakened the power of the nobility. But there were nobles too who became Mazdakite converts, including Kavadh's eldest son.

We cannot know whether Kavadh gave this doctrine his support out of conviction or because he thought it a useful weapon against

the nobility, but he did encourage it, and a group of nobles and
Zoroastrian clergy reacted by deposing and imprisoning him in 496.
His brother Zhamasp became king in 496. But his rule lasted merely
some three years and was marked by Mazdakite uprisings. Kavadh
escaped to the Ephthalites and with their help regained his throne.[329]
The help came at a price, however, and Kavadh turned to Byzantium.
In the past, the empire had paid a subsidy to garrison the Derbend
and Darial passes in the Caucasus against nomad invaders. Kavadh
demanded a renewal of the subsidy from Anastasius and Anastasius
refused.[330] Whereupon Kavadh attacked.

Byzantium owed a great deal to the stubborn loyalty of the
Mesopotamian cities. Theodosiopolis (*mod.* Erzerum) fell quickly,
but Amida (*mod.* Diyarbakir), behind its walls of black basalt, resisted
desperately. Finally, the defenders of Amida became overconfident.
Some guardians of the walls – a mischievous tradition identified
them as monks – fell asleep, having overindulged in wine, and the
Persians scaled the walls.[331] Next year a Roman army laid siege to
Amida, but abandoned it to march to battle with Kavadh and suffer
defeat. The next year, Kavadh laid siege to Edessa. In the final assault,
the whole population of the city, including women and children,
defended their city and beat Kavadh off.[332] As for wretched Amida,
the Romans returned in 504 and the city suffered another terrible
siege before Persia and Byzantium agreed to a truce, whereby Persia
gave up Amida for 1,000 pounds of gold. The Huns in the Caucasus
were threatening again, and in 506 Kavadh was willing to negotiate
a seven-year treaty. It called for the imperial treasury to pay Persia
500 pounds of gold annually: not an exorbitant amount, though in
subsequent treaties Justinian would reduce the sum.[333]

Thereupon, having secured a peace with Persia on terms more
favourable than the Romans had had for a century, Anastasius
proceeded to bolster his border defences with a new forward base
in Mesopotamia, east of the cities of Constantina and Amida. He,
or rather his generals, chose the village of Dara, on the edge of
the north Mesopotamian plain, some 30 kilometres from Nisibis,
and transformed it into a strong fortress that was renamed after the
emperor. It says something for the importance of the church that
the village had been the property of the see of Amida, which sold
it to Anastasius, and that the construction of the fortress was supervised by the bishop and his clergy.[334] Dara's circuit wall followed the
crests and flanks of three hills which were separated by a narrow
strip of level land from the mountains to the north, and through

the centre of the fortress flowed the Daraçay river, a tributary of the Khabur. Dara's supply of water was secure, even in the dry season.[335]

War with the Ephthalites kept Kavadh occupied, and though the new stronghold at Dara violated a treaty of 442 which stipulated that neither Persian nor Roman should build a new fort in the border region,[336] peace survived Anastasius' death nonetheless. But by 513, Kavadh had curtailed the Ephthalite raids. The Mazdakite movement was suppressed in 528, and a traditional Persian monarchy reemerged in the kingdom.[337] The internal situation was stable, and Kavadh was free to deal with Byzantium.

Armenia had been partitioned between Persia and the Roman Empire by a treaty dating to 387. Rome's share, making up about one-fifth of the kingdom, consisted of two 'treaty states' (*civitates foederatae*), 'Inner Armenia' and 'Other Armenia', the latter a vassal pentarchy ruled by five dynastic families that acknowledged Rome's suzerainty. The privileges they had enjoyed under the Armenian crown remained unchanged. The portion under Persian dominion, the 'Persarmenia' of Byzantine sources, retained a king of the Arsacid house, which traced its lineage back to a Parthian prince who had obtained Armenia in the emperor Nero's reign. But in 428, most of the remaining Armenian princes in Persarmenia transferred their vassalage to the Great King of Persia. The royal house remained one of the great Armenian families, but the monarchy came to an end.[338]

Christianity came early to Armenia. Gregory the Illuminator had converted Trdat the Great in the year 314, which antedated Constantinople's foundation, and from Armenia, missionaries went to Iberia (*mod.* Georgia) and Albania (*mod.* Azerbaijan) in the Caucasus, and under Justinian, it was an Armenian bishop, Kardutsat by name, who led a group of priests to the land of the 'Huns' in the Caucasus (probably the Sabiri) where he baptized and made translations for their use. Justinian lent support. Kardutsat and his successor missionary among the Christianized Huns, Maku, were both Monophysites (the Armenian patriarch had rejected Chalcedon in 491) but Christianity, Chalcedonian or not, widened the Byzantine sphere of influence, and in any case, spreading the Christian gospel was an imperial responsibility.[339]

The northern littoral of the Black Sea was critical for two reasons. First, the northern, so-called 'Scythian' Silk Road from Loyang in China over the southern Urals had its western terminus at Bosporus, ancient Panticapaeum on the Straits of Kerch, and in the sixth century this link was particularly important, for the Ephthalites had disrupted the route that ran south of the Caspian Sea. Second, the empire was uneasily aware that the north shore of the Black Sea bordered on a vast region from which new enemies constantly appeared. Cherson, some 3 kilometres from modern Sebastopol, lay at one end of the Crimean Tauric frontier (*limes Tauricus*) and Bosporus at the other, and it is a measure of the importance which Justinian attached to the area that he not merely restored the walls of both cities, but constructed a line of forts along the coast, and another line further inland along the mountain ridge that separates the Crimean Riviera from the interior. Both cities were in decline; Cherson's exports of wine and salted fish were dwindling to nothing and Bosporus was dominated in the fifth century by the 'Huns', perhaps either Utigur or Onogur Bulgars. In the 520s, however, it offered allegiance to Constantinople. Then, in 528, Grod, king of the local 'Huns', came to Constantinople for baptism, and on his return home, tried to wipe out paganism, to the fury of the native priests. Grod was slain, his pagan brother made king, and then the rebels struck at Bosporus and took it.

Justinian reacted by sending a fleet and a force overland to Bosporus, and the rebels withdrew.[340] But as a result, Justinian tried to make Bosporus a centre of resistance to the 'Huns'. Walls and forts were not his only means. In the Crimean mountains were the remnants of the great Ostrogothic kingdom in south Russia which the Huns had overthrown in 370. Unlike their cousins in Italy, they were orthodox Christians and Justinian cultivated their friendship. They served as dependable custodians of the northern approaches.

East of the Straits of Kerch was Tmutorokan, the ancient Greek colony of Hermonassa, and beyond the Kuban river was Zichia, which was once a Roman client kingdom but had become independent at some point before Justinian's time.[341] Further eastward, Byzantium had two strongholds, both rebuilt by Justinian: Pityus (*mod.* Pitzunda) and Sebastopolis,[342] near modern Suchumi, which clung to the coast of Abasgia. This was the area of ancient Colchis, bisected by the Rioni river (ancient Phasis) and inhabited in the north by the Abasgians and in the south by the Lazes.

Lazica in the fourth century had been a client kingdom of Rome, but somehow after 457, it shifted to the Persian sphere of influence. Its kings went to Ctesiphon for investiture. The Zoroastrian religion had a quasi-official standing, though Christian missions were active: bishops came to the Ecumenical Council of Nicaea in 325 from Trebizond, Lazica's principal seaport. But in 522, in Justin's reign, there was a shift: the Laz king Damnazes died, and Tzath, heir to the throne, came to Constantinople to request baptism. This was a political act, which gave Christianity official status in Lazica. Tzath, who may have been a Christian already, came to Justin less for the baptismal ceremony than to forge a closer tie with Byzantium. Persia's reaction was bitter and it was to result in war. But for the moment Kavadh accepted Justin's reassurances.[343]

To the north, the Abasgians in their dense forests had won a degree of independence from Lazica. Abasgia was a prime source of eunuchs for the empire, and pagan until a mission dispatched by Justinian converted the people, though at the Council of Nicaea a bishop had attended from their port city of Bichvinta. In the Caucasus to the north-east of Lazica lived the Suani, rough mountaineers whose chieftains were at least nominally appointed by the Laz king,[344] and further east were the Iberians, ruled by a royal dynasty that was a branch of the Mihranids, one of the seven Great Houses of Persia. The dynasty lasted until Khusro I of Persia suppressed it, and one of its princes became the great Monophysite churchman, Peter the Iberian. Procopius,[345] speaking for his own time, reported that the Iberians were devout Christians but long-standing subjects of the Persian king.

In the central Caucasus, controlling the Darial pass, were the Alans, a Sarmatian remnant whom the Byzantines coupled with the Abasgians and counted as friends.[346] Beyond them to the north were the Hunnic Sabiri, who guarded the 'Caspian Gates', the Derbend pass skirting the west coast of the Caspian Sea, which was the main route for invaders from the Russian steppes. They furnished mercenaries with equal readiness to both the Byzantines and the Persians. East of Iberia and north-east of Armenia, bounded by the Kur river, the Caspian Sea and the Caucasus range was Albania (*mod.* Azerbaijan), which until about 510 was an independent kingdom with its own language and literature, all of which was lost after Persia suppressed its monarchy.[347]

South of the Black Sea near Trebizond were the Tzani, mountaineers who lived by plunder. Rome paid them an annual subsidy as protection payment, but their habits died hard. They continued their marauding way of life until Justinian sent a force against them commanded by Theodora's brother-in-law Sittas, who reduced them to peace and Christianity for the time being. The Tzani were a new addition to the empire, and Justinian was proud of their conquest, which marked an expansion rather than a restoration of imperial boundaries.[348] But it did not prove lasting; in 557 the Tzani had to be subdued again and subjected to tribute.

These were neighbours on the fringes of the empire. But Byzantine diplomacy reached further. In Gaul there were the Franks, in Spain the Visigoths. In the northern highlands of modern Ethiopia was the kingdom of Axum. It was Christianized in the mid-fourth century, and was a suffragan see of the patriarch of Alexandria. In the region between the Nile and the Red Sea were the Beja tribes known as the Blemmyes, who dwelt in the harsh environment of the eastern desert, with the First Cataract marking the approximate mid-point of their range. Sometime in the third century, they acquired camels which transformed their culture, in much the same way as the horse changed the lives of the Plains Indians of North America. By the end of the century, the Blemmyes were trading desert gold and emeralds, and raiding Roman garrison points south of the First Cataract, until Diocletian, as an economy measure, withdrew from Nubia and stationed the Legio I *Maximiana* at Philae, thereby making the First Cataract (*mod.* Aswan) the effective frontier.[349]

To the south were the three Nubian kingdoms of Nobadia, stretching from the First to the Third Cataract, Makouria, perhaps extending to the Fifth Cataract, and Alodia, whose capital was a short distance upriver from modern Khartoum.[350] All three were converted to Christianity between 543 and 580. But before the conversion, Philae was a centre for the cult of Isis: a holy city that attracted pilgrims who might be Greeks, Romans, Egyptians, Nubians or desert nomads. The priestly oligarchs at Philae ruled over a little 'Vatican City', and they maintained their cult intact until Justinian suppressed it.[351]

The desert fringes to the west of the Nile were insecure. From the fourth to the start of the eighth century they were under constant attack by Blemmyes, Nobadians and a nomad tribe known as the Mazikes, whose nerve centre was in the vicinity of the Dakleh oasis. In 407–408, the Mazikes raided Libya and devastated the monasteries of Scetis; in 578 they made a murderous raid on the Khargeh oasis and shortly afterwards attacked Scetis again and emptied its four lauras.[352] Before the first half of the fifth century was out, the empire had abandoned the area south of the great Khargeh oasis. A military detachment stayed at the Dakleh oasis further west until the early sixth century, but in the end, the best the army could do was to secure the communications between the oases and the Nile Valley.

In south Arabia, Himyar occupied present-day Yemen, which was a trans-shipment station for the trade between the Mediterranean markets and India. Christianity and Judaism both struggled for the allegiance of the Himyarite kings, and at Justin's accession, Christianity with the support of Axum[353] had the upper hand. The king was a Christian and an Axumite vassal. But for the Himyarite ruling élite who were abandoning the ancient paganism, Judaism was an attractive option, not only because Himyar was home for a colony of Jewish merchants, but because it was neither Christianity nor Zororastrianism, the faiths of the two empires that wanted Himyar as a satellite. Both Persia and Constantinople had interests there, for Himyar controlled the trade in myrrh, frankincense and balsam, and it was an entrepôt for a portion of the silk imported into the empire. Historically, the main entrepôt for the silk trade had been Seleuceia–Ctesiphon, and the Persian merchants were anxious to maintain Ctesiphon's dominance. However, the alternative route through Himyar would deny this profitable trade to Constantinople's old enemy and give it instead to her Christian ally, Axum. The potential for trouble was great, and in Justin's reign there was to be a pogrom which resulted in a collection of Christian martyrdoms and assemblage of martyr literature in six languages.[354] But more of that later.

Constantinople kept its finger on the pulses of all these various regions. The Byzantine empire defended itself as much by diplomacy as by armed force, but its concern was not merely self-interest. In Byzantium's view of the world, the empire was coextensive with the *oikoumene* – the civilized world – and if some barbarian nations remained beyond her effective control, that was with the permission of God. It did not alter the divine plan, according to which the emperor was the universal sovereign, ruling as God's vicar on earth, whose duty it was to propagate the faith. And indeed, with some exceptions, such as Persia with its own state religion to propagate and Axum which was far away, Byzantium's neighbours accorded that notion a degree of acceptance.[355]

2

THE NEW DYNASTS
Their early years of power

THE ACCESSION OF THE NEW DYNASTY

Sometime about 470, three young peasants from upper Macedonia abandoned their struggle with poverty at home and left for Constantinople, travelling on foot, with only some toasted bread wrapped up in their cloaks for food. We know their names, and two are recognizably Thracian; Zimarchus, Dityvistus. The third, Justin, was probably of Thracian origin as well. Justin, and perhaps his companions too, were from Bederiana, the name of which has survived in a village called Bader near modern Skopje in Macedonia. When these three reached the capital, they found that the emperor Leo was organizing the *Excubitores* as a new corps of palace guards intended to counterbalance the influence of the German federate troops, and since they were strong, healthy young men, they were promptly enrolled. Zimarchus and Dityvistus thereupon disappeared from history, but their companion was to become the emperor Justin I.[1]

Justin made a good, if undistinguished, soldier, and having improved his own lot, he brought his sister's son, Petrus Sabbatius,[2] along with other relatives, to the capital and saw that they got the education which circumstances had denied himself. In fact, his nephew's name, Justinianus, indicates that Justin formally adopted him as his own son, and the adoption must have taken place by 520, and possibly even earlier, before Justin became emperor. Of Justinian's own antecedents we can say little. His native language was Latin ('*our* ancestral tongue' he calls it in a law of 535),[3] his native province fell under papal jurisdiction, and his religious leanings were firmly Chalcedonian. Some eight years after Justinian became emperor in his own right, he rebuilt the town of Tauresion (*mod.* Čaričin Grad) where he was born, renamed it Justiniana Prima, and made it the metropolitan see of Dardania and the archbishopric of a clutch of provinces filched from the see of Thessaloniki. He intended to make it the seat of the praetorian prefect of Illyricum as well, though we cannot be certain that he did. Procopius, in his panegyric on Justinian's building programme, called it a great, well-populated city. But its ruins at Čaričin Grad today show a city of a mere 7 hectares, with a population reckoned at 3,000 souls.[4] Justinian's beginnings were indeed humble and provincial.

Once Justin was emperor, Justinian became virtually his partner, and the power behind the throne. The old man's reliance upon Justinian requires some explanation, for Justinian was not Justin's only nephew: one other, Germanus, was already winning a military reputation. But Justinian was already Justin's adopted son, and Justin had learned to rely on him. Procopius, who had a mandarin's disdain for the semi-literate, maintained that Justin was stupid and unlettered, and that his nephew's rule really began with his accession in 518,[5] and this may have been a widespread perception: the *History of the Patriarchs of Alexandria*[6] omits Justin's reign entirely! It is true that Justinian thrust himself into public affairs eagerly as soon as his uncle became emperor. Justin had not been on the throne for three months before we find his nephew writing to the pope in impatient prose, summoning him to Constantinople.[7] But Justinian as yet had no power base of his own, and his succession was not a foregone conclusion: in 518 he was only a member of the imperial guard, a *candidatus*. His advance was rapid: by the spring of 519, he held the rank of count (*comes*); next summer he was one of the two Masters of the Soldiers 'in the Presence' stationed in Constantinople, and in 521, he took up the consulship and celebrated his inauguration with games costing 4,000 gold pounds for shows, chariot races and distribution of largesse![8] Justinian was making an imperial statement with a stridency that betrays insecurity.

Amantius the Grand Chamberlain and Vitalian were soon removed. Amantius fell immediately, not ten days after Justin's coronation, 'on no worse charge than that he spoke some reckless remark against the patriarch of the city, John', to quote Procopius, but it appears that he defended Anastasius' anti-Chalcedonian stance, and after his death he became a Monophysite martyr.[9] Vitalian's fall took longer. He had revolted against Anastasius a second time in 516 after the emperor dismissed him as Master of the Soldiers in Thrace, but the imperial navy led by Anastasius' praetorian prefect, Marinus the Syrian, burned his fleet at the mouth of the Golden

Horn, and Vitalian retreated to lurk in his native province of Scythia Minor (*mod.* Dobruja). There he remained until Justin recalled him, and made him a patrician in 518 and consul two years later. Early in 519, a band of Scythian monks, among them a relative of Vitalian, Leontius, arrived in Constantinople to settle a conflict with their bishop and, with greater consequence, to press for their own formula for healing the Monophysite schism. The Theopaschite doctrine that they preached smacked of Monophysitism; yet these Scythian monks got the support of their countryman, Vitalian, whose Chalcedonian credentials were above suspicion. Justinian was wary at first, but then he too lent them support. He was quick to recognize an opening for theological peace, and he could not afford to allow a formidable rival like Vitalian the credit for consummating it.

But the legates whom Pope Hormisdas had sent to Constantinople had come to re-establish the Chalcedonian credo, not to debate it. Rebuffed, the monks headed for Rome, where they spent almost fourteen months promoting their doctrine and annoying the pope. In mid-520, they were expelled from Rome. They were, wrote the pope, 'scatterers of poison under the pretence of religion', but on the Theopaschite doctrine itself, he remained for the moment evasive. About the same time, Vitalian and some of his supporters were summoned to a banquet in the palace and murdered on their way. Procopius[10] blamed Justinian, who feared Vitalian's high profile, though on the Theopaschite formula they were ostensibly allies. The pope, however, was not ready to be flexible. In the spring of 521, he answered another impatient letter which Justinian had written him almost six months earlier, and iterated the *Tome* of Leo, thereby by implication spurning the Theopaschites.[11]

It was about 522, when Justinian was not much less than 40, that he met the woman he was to marry. Theodora was in her early twenties, and she already had a bastard daughter.[12] Most of our information about Theodora's background comes from Procopius' *Secret History*, where he poured out all the venom of an insecure élite that despised the powerful upstart empress. He coupled Theodora with Antonina, the wife of the general Belisarius, as two dominant, conniving women, adept at manipulating husbands who were putty in their hands. Both ladies had been mime actresses in the theatre, and acting was an infamous profession, to which no Christian should belong, though the law allowed them to receive the sacraments on their death-beds; should they, against expectation, survive, they were never to return to the stage.[13] Procopius granted Theodora no talent, but she had a quick wit, she was an artist in obscenity, and her sexual appetite was insatiable.

> Often she would go picnicking with ten young men or more, and dallied with them all, the whole night through. When they wearied of the sport, she would approach their servants, perhaps thirty in number, and fight a duel with each of these; and even thus found no allayment of her craving.[14]

This is men's locker-room humour, and about as trustworthy. Yet we should remember that malicious gossip is the final weapon of disempowered groups in society, and Theodora represented a threat to the status of the ruling élite. But we do have some independent evidence as well.

John of Ephesus was a Syriac historian and Monophysite churchman under Justinian, who in 542 sent him as a missionary to the pagans in Asia Minor. His *Lives of the Eastern Saints* is a vivid glimpse of the afflictions which the Monophysites suffered and the part Theodora played as their imperial protector. John[15] relates how Mare, bishop of Amida in Mesopotamia, sent his deacon and notary Stephen to Constantinople to intercede for the persecuted Monophysites, and God directed 'the virtuous Stephen to Theodora who came from the brothel and was at that time a patrician but eventually became queen.' John wrote without malice. For him and almost everybody else, the theatre embodied immorality, and not without reason he equated it with a brothel. And there can be no doubt that Theodora had been an actress.

As long as Justin's wife Euphemia was alive, Justinian encountered adamant resistance to his marriage. Justin's wife was fond of her adoptive son, but on this she would not budge. She had herself been a slave named Lupicina, and it is a name which must arouse suspicion, for it was an appropriate one for a prostitute. But Justin had bought her, manumitted her and married her, and when she became empress, she assumed the name Euphemia and became an upholder of respectability.[16] But once she was dead, Justin was easily persuaded. He promulgated a new law: imitating the clemency of God, he ordained that a penitent actress might apply for an imperial grant of all marriage privileges. An ex-actress admitted to the patriciate would be henceforth able to marry anyone; all blemishes of the stage and *any other blemishes whatsoever* were wiped out.[17] Thus, complained Procopius in his *Secret History*, all men were made free to marry courtesans.[18] Only penitence was necessary.

Procopius gives us a tabloid journalist's reportage of Theodora's early life, but except for some legends, it is the only story we have, and he was in a position to know. Her father, whose name was Acacius, had kept the bears that the Green faction used for bear-baiting shows in the Hippodrome. He took ill and died, and Theodora's mother was left in poverty with three young daughters. In the bearkeepers' guild, positions generally passed from father to son, and so Theodora's mother remarried with the expectation that her second husband would take over the post of her first one. But the lead pantomime dancer, with whom the decision rested, took a bribe from another candidate and rejected Theodora's stepfather. Destitute, the mother garlanded her daughters and set them as suppliants before the spectators in the Hippodrome, where the Greens rejected their petition, but the Blues, who had recently lost their own bearkeeper, accepted it.

As soon as the sisters reached puberty their mother put them on the stage as mimes. She had little choice, for children of actors were required to keep to the occupation of their parents. Comito, the eldest, became a well-known courtesan, and Theodora followed in her footsteps. Her stripteases were shameless, and she preferred buggery to normal intercourse. Respectable folk meeting her in the market-place shrank from her. But at some point she escaped her duties in the theatre by joining the entourage of a native of Tyre, Hecebolus, whom she followed to Libya when he was appointed governor there. Procopius reports that she served his unnatural appetites. But he abandoned her. Hecebolus had done what the law forbade: he had removed an actress from the stage so that she could no longer serve the pleasures of the public, and legal complications may have been the reason he discarded Theodora. We cannot know. But the experience gave her an insight into the seamier side of the palatine service. Years later, when Justinian issued a constitution prohibiting the purchase of public offices by officials,[19] which was an inducement to corruption, he included the comment that he had discussed this measure with his wife.

Theodora made her way from the Libyan Pentapolis to Alexandria, and thence back to the capital, supporting herself as best she could. Good sources for this portion of Theodora's life seem to have run thin, but Procopius' invention did not fail him and he preferred to believe the worst. But since only a clear commitment to Christianity could free an actress from her obligation to the theatre,[20] it is probable that she was converted in Alexandria, and since this was a stronghold of Monophysitism, the churchmen she encountered there would be Monophysites. Monophysite tradition related that she considered a 'Bishop Timothy' to be her spiritual father, and it may be that this Timothy was Timothy III, patriarch of Alexandria from 517 to 535, who sheltered Severus, the Monophysite patriarch of Antioch, when he was driven from his see when Justinian's uncle became emperor.[21]

Procopius does not report how she met Justinian, if he knew. It was a genuine love affair, and perhaps Justinian had his own experience in mind when, years later, he set forth a legal definition of marriage in one of his laws: 'Mutual affection creates marriage, and it does not need the addition of a dowry.'[22] He made Theodora a patrician, and after the old empress died, he married her. The title 'Augusta' became hers in 527, and for her it was no empty honour.[23]

Just as Justin's family had shared his good fortune, so did Theodora's family and friends share hers. Her sisters Comito and Anastasia made good marriages, and Theodora found a husband for the daughter of a friend from the burlesque theatre, Chrysomallo.[24] The law that smoothed the way for Justinian and Theodora's marriage also opened the ranks of the élite for others, though not many, one suspects. Yet Constantinople had a new royal family sprung from peasants and actresses, that thrust itself into the ruling classes. We may imagine how the old élite regarded these upstarts. The remains of the church of St Polyeuktos, built between 524 and 527 by the aristocratic Anicia Juliana, carry an eloquent message. Her father had been an emperor, albeit a transitory one in the western empire; she was a descendant of the Theodosian House and her son had married a daughter of Anastasius. St Polyeuktos was Constantinople's largest church until Justinian rebuilt Hagia Sophia, and inscribed within it was a poem which compared her achievement with King Solomon's. The analogy was an imperial one, appropriate for emperors.[25] The great church of Anicia Juliana made a statement on behalf of her class.

Justinian and Theodora made it no easier for the old élite. They enforced court etiquette strictly. Earlier emperors had required senators to genuflect in their presence, whereas patricians kissed the emperor's right breast and received a kiss on the head in return. Empresses had received no salute. But the two upstarts Justinian and Theodora required all who approached them to kowtow,[26] and Procopius[27] relates a couple of stories of how Theodora went out of her way to humiliate the old élite. We should take them *cum grano salis*; Procopius did not tell the whole truth where Theodora was concerned. But on one point he was right: under Justinian and Theodora, court ceremony took on increased importance, and Theodora in particular used it to assert her new status.

Theodora's bastard daughter made a good marriage into the family of the emperor Anastasius, and there was a grandson also named Anastasius whom Theodora planned to marry to the daughter and heiress of Belisarius, but the marriage had not yet taken place when the empress died, and Belisarius' wife, Antonina, aborted the plan. Theodora had another grandson as well, named Athanasius, a monk who was a prime mover among the 'Tritheists', a Monophysite splinter group that sprouted in the 550s and won a number of converts, particularly in Edessa and Alexandria. In addition, John of Ephesus mentions a third grandson named John.[28]

Procopius reports that Theodora herself had a son named John as well, conceived while she was still on the stage. She failed to abort, and once the unwanted boy was born, his father saved him from infanticide only by abducting him to Arabia. On his death-bed the father told the boy who his mother was, and he came to Constantinople to introduce himself. The empress entrusted him to reliable attendants, and he was never seen again. Why Theodora should have openly recognized her grandson, and yet have done away with this John for fear of scandal is a conundrum.[29] Procopius has perhaps given us less than the whole truth: 'John' sounds like an impostor who tried to impose upon the empress. In any case, after Theodora met Justinian, she turned away from her previous life. If there had been any rumours of dalliance after her marriage, we can be sure that Procopius would have reported them, and in fact, he does report a tale that she once conceived a passion for a handsome young steward named Areobindus. Areobindus disappeared. Theodora did not subject herself needlessly either to temptation or to spiteful gossip.[30]

She was a convinced Monophysite; on that score, Monophysite sources amply corroborate Procopius. The Monophysite John of Ephesus called her 'the Christ-loving Theodora, who was perhaps appointed queen by God to be a support for the persecuted against the cruelty of the times'.[31] A Syriac tradition pretended that her father was a pious old senator, who would not assent to her marriage with Justinian until he swore never to force her to accept the impious doctrine of Chalcedon.[32] The Chalcedonians recognized her as an enemy; the stout Chalcedonian St Sabas, who led a group of

Palestinian monks to the capital in 531, refused her request that he pray to God that she conceive, for the son she bore to Justinian might bring worse trouble upon the empire than the old Monophysite Anastasius himself![33] Procopius[34] accused Justinian and Theodora of intensifying theological conflict by pretending to take opposing positions, and he was not the only contemporary to speculate that the two acted as complicit partners.[35] It was well-founded speculation only to this extent: the Monophysites, feeling that they had a powerful lobbyist concerned for their welfare at court, remained faithful supporters of the empire, and Constantinople continued to be the focus of their loyalty. The Chalcedonians might have imperial government backing, but the Monophysites had the empress as their patron. The alienation of the Monophysites came later, after Justinian was dead, and the empire was governed by successors who were less aware of the political advantages of having a loyal opposition.

Theodora's sympathy for the Monophysites was understandable. She had been in Alexandria when the first persecutions of the Syrian Monophysites under Justin began, and saw the refugees coming to Egypt. She may even have planted some doubts in her husband's mind, though they did not germinate until after her death. But in the last year of his life, he issued an edict proclaiming as orthodox a radical variation of Monophysitism, which taught that there was in Christ only divine substance, and thus His flesh was incorruptible. Justinian's mind was not closed to his wife's arguments, and it should be remembered that what contemporaries saw as peculiar in Justinian's house was not that his wife's beliefs differed from his but that she openly followed her own policy. Houses had been divided by theology before: the old emperor Anastasius had been Monophysite but two of his nephews, Hypatius and Pompeius, were Chalcedonian. Where Justinian was unconventional was that he respected his wife's opinions and gave them full rein. But he was himself a native of Illyricum, and he inherited a deference to Rome as the trustee of right belief that Theodora could not share.

It was probably Theodora's early life too that formed her compassion for society's unfortunates. The great inscription still to be seen on the entablature of the church of Sts Sergius and Bacchus in Istanbul proclaims it: she is 'the God-crowned Theodora whose mind is adorned with piety, and whose constant toil lies in unsparing efforts to nourish the destitute'.[36] It was probably her own experience, too, that moulded her perception of women's rights. We may recognize her fine hand in Justinian's ordinances prohibiting pimps from requiring sureties or oaths from the prostitutes in their stables to guarantee that they would not abandon the profession.[37] She closed the brothels in Constantinople, and rid the Augustaeum of the whores who plied their trade there. On the Asian side of the Bosporus the imperial pair endowed a convent which provided refuge for these presumably penitent harlots, though some found their new lives so distasteful that they threw themselves over its walls.[38] Evagrius[39] noted the severity with which men charged with rape were punished under Justinian, and thought the motive was avarice, but the instigator may well have been Theodora.

She intervened on behalf of women who were wronged. The Armenian Artabanes, who had suppressed a mutiny in Africa and killed its leader Guntarith, planned to marry the emperor's niece Preiecta and the emperor was willing. But Artabanes already had a wife in Armenia, and when she appeared at court and begged for Theodora's help, Theodora stepped in. Preiecta was given to a great-nephew of the emperor Anastasius, who made a suitable if unloved husband, and Artabanes willy-nilly remained faithful to his Armenian wife until Theodora's death cleared the way for a divorce. The empress, remarked Procopius who related the tale, was by nature inclined to help unfortunate women.

Procopius adds another case where we may suspect her hand. Boraides, the emperor's cousin, died and left left most of his property to his brother, Germanus, and his sons, leaving his own daughter the bare minimum required by law. To Germanus' annoyance, Justinian intervened on the daughter's behalf.[40]

Only one certain portrait of Theodora has come down to us. In San Vitale, in Ravenna, a mosaic of Theodora and her attendants faces Justinian and his court across the chancel. Procopius acknowledged that the bearkeeper's daughters were comely children, and Theodora herself was attractive, though not tall, and her complexion was sallow and her glower intense. That was the opinion of the underground opposition, but in Procopius' last work, a panegyric intended for public consumption on Justinian's building programme, he had fulsome praise for Theodora's beauty.[41] She was to have one great moment when her courage saved the regime. In the *Nika* revolt of 532, when the court panicked and prepared to flee, it was Theodora who kept her nerve and convinced the imperial council not to give up too soon. She was tougher and readier to be severe than Justinian, who was by nature charitable and approachable, and apt to overlook the misdemeanours of his officers.[42]

Her death in 548 resulted in no marked change in Justinian's policies, except that his grip on reality may have grown less firm. Procopius was not wrong when he claimed that Justinian and Theodora worked as a team, but it was not to stir up trouble. Theodora was a Monophysite by conviction, to be sure, and no doubt she was self-willed, but Monophysites were still loyal subjects whom Justinian hoped to unite with the Orthodox under a single creed, and the theological battle lines were not yet as rigid in the eastern empire as they were in the West. Monophysites were by no means on a par with irredeemable heretics like Manichaeans, Montanists, Donatists or even Arians.[43] Justinian was happy enough to have his wife act independently to keep the bridges open between the Monophysites and the imperial court. Modern historians have the benefit of hindsight, which, coupled with a western European perspective, has led to a harsh judgement upon Theodora's forays into theology. But to a large slice of contemporary opinion in the Asian sector of the empire, they appeared constructive.

THE MONOPHYSITE PERSECUTION

The last years of Anastasius marked a high point in the fortunes of Monophysitism. Egypt was lost, though that was not yet apparent. The courier that brought the emperor Zeno the news of Timothy the Cat's death in 477 also brought the news that the Monophysites had elected a successor, Peter Mongus (the Stammerer). This was a challenge to imperial prerogative. Zeno threatened exile, Mongus withdrew to the safety of the Monophysite desert monasteries and his Melkite rival, Timothy of the Teetering Turban, emerged from his monastery and took over. But the populace supported Mongus, and though Timothy did his tactful best, at his death four years later, when Zeno ordered a free election to choose a successor, it was Mongus who won, and Zeno recognized him on the condition that he accepted the *Henotikon*. Mongus' Melkite rival, John Talaia, a monk like Timothy from the *Metanoia* monastery at Canopus, went off to Italy, where he got Pope Felix III's support, but he had to console himself with a bishopric in south Italy in place of the lost see of St Mark. Mongus was politic, steering a careful middle course, all the while harassed by the extreme Monophysites known as the 'Headless Ones' (*akephaloi*), who had broken with him over the *Henotikon* but did not go so far as to elect their own leader (hence their name). However, before he died, Mongus cursed Chalcedon and the *Tome* of Leo, and his successors followed suit.[44]

At Antioch, the patriarchy was in the hands of Severus of Gaza, the 'leader of the *akephaloi*', the 'friend of trouble', who 'resurrected every sort of heresy against orthodox belief and the decrees of the church'. The words come from Cyril of Scythopolis' biography of Severus' great enemy, St Sabas, who in 492 had been chosen archimandrite of all the lauras in the Judaean desert east of Jerusalem.[45] The portrayal exaggerates. Severus in his youth had been destined for a legal career, but before he began to practise as a lawyer, he made a pilgrimage to Jerusalem, and there opted for the monastic life. In 508 he went to Constantinople to plead the cause of the Monophysite monks in Palestine, and the emperor liked what he heard. Anastasius was prepared to throw his weight behind the Monophysites. The patriarch of Constantinople, Macedonius, was exiled, and in Antioch, the patriarch Flavian, a moderate Chalcedonian, was denounced in a synod held at Sidon in 512, which was orchestrated by the bishop of Mabbug, Philoxenos, by origin a Persian. Flavian might have survived the synod, but Monophysite monks in Antioch rioted, and Flavian took fright. To keep the peace, he withdrew from the city at the governor's request. His opponents declared the see vacant and elected Severus. The author of one of our two extant biographies of Severus, John, archimandrite of Beith-Apthonia, states succinctly the Monophysite perception of the matter: the emperor and God approved the choice of Severus.[46]

Upon Justin's accession, Philoxenos was to be arrested, and Severus to escape to Egypt where, by one of the ironies of the tale, he clashed with a fellow exile and erstwhile ally, Julian of Halicarnassus, who developed the Aphthartodocetist doctrine that Christ's flesh was incorruptible from the instant of conception. But for the moment, Severus had Anastasius' ear, and the Monophysites held the initiative. In Constantinople, however, the reaction came quickly. Anastasius was nearly ousted from the throne by a riot of Chalcedonians who caught a whiff of Monophysitism in the Sunday service at Hagia Sophia on 4 November, 512. He appeared in the Hippodrome and offered to step down, but the sight of the old emperor without his crown softened the mood of the crowd, and Anastasius pulled through.

In the East, Palestine remained Chalcedonian, and Severus enountered doughty antagonists in the desert monks: when synodical letters from Severus arrived in Jerusalem along with a detachment of soldiers, St Sabas and his fellow abbots hurried to the city, expelled

Severus' couriers and gathered a great crowd of monks and laymen before the church of St Calvary, where they chanted 'Anathema to Severus and his fellow communicants'! But Severus still had the support of Anastasius, and in 516, he managed to replace Elias, the patriarch of Jerusalem, with a monk named John, who promised to curse Chalcedon. But once John was patriarch, St Sabas and his monks convinced him to renege. When the duke of Palestine threw John into prison, he promised that if he were freed, on Sunday two days thence, he would pronounce the anathema. Sunday came; a great crowd of people gathered in the basilica of St Stephen, among them Hypatius, the nephew of the emperor. John the patriarch, flanked by two of Severus' foes, Sabas and Theodosius, the archimandrite of the cenobitic monasteries in Judaea, mounted the pulpit and cursed all who rejected the creed of Chalcedon. They followed this up with a petition to the emperor, who thought further interference impolitic.[47] The revolt of Vitalian in Thrace was keeping his hands tied. He wanted to find a settlement, but Pope Hormisdas wanted nothing less than surrender, and the attempt at compromise led nowhere. On 11 July, 517, Anastasius wrote his last letter to the pope, with the words: 'We can endure insults and contempt, but we cannot permit ourselves to be commanded.'[48]

Second Syria, with a large Greek population, was also unhappy with Severus. But the province of First Syria, on the limestone massif north and east of Antioch, had shifted its allegiance to Monophysitism. The conversion was the work of the Syriac monks, who sympathized with Cyril's teaching far more than with the dyophysite doctrines of Diodore of Tarsus and Theodore of Mopsuestia which Nestorius preached, and it is worth noting that in First Syria, the monasteries, from their physical appearance, seem to have been integrated into their communities: monastic buildings were not closed units; rather they were open on all sides, with wide verandas and chapels directly accessible to passers-by.[49] Further east, in Mesopotamia, Monophysitism won over the countryside. The Nestorian school at Edessa had been forced across the Persian border to Nisibis in 489, and five years later, it declared its independence from Antioch.[50] Now Severus made the breach final; henceforth 'Nestorian' was a slur hurled at the Chalcedonians, who hurled back the epithet 'Eutychian'. In fact, as a theologian Severus steered a course between Chalcedon and the heresy of Eutyches. The grounds for disagreement were narrow. Severus had no quarrel with the *Henotikon*, but he insisted on the denunciation of the *Tome* of Leo and the creed of Chalcedon that recognized it. Chalcedon was the problem, the symbol of the otherness of the western church.

All changed with the new emperor Justin and the concordat of May, 519 between Rome and Constantinople. Bishops in *Oriens* were directed to accept the doctrine of Chalcedon or forfeit their sees, and orders were issued for the arrest of Severus' supporters. Vitalian, who in the estimation of most people still overshadowed Justinian as the champion of Chalcedon, was appointed Count of the Orient and would have carried out the orders with gusto except that Justinian saw to his assassination. Severus escaped to the safety of Egypt, which the imperial government was circumspect enough to exempt from the persecution. Less lucky, Philoxenos of Mabbug was banished to a hospice in Gangra in Paphlagonia, where he was confined in an airless room above the kitchen, and there he died of asphyxiation. But on the whole, the imperial order was obeyed. Only fifty-five bishops refused and they were deposed.[51]

It was time for Chalcedonian revenge. The monks in the northern Syro-Arab areas had the choice of conforming and signing a certificate to vouch for it, or being turned out into the desert. Most chose the desert. Severus' Chalcedonian successor at Antioch, Paul 'the Jew', was pitiless. He was removed after two years, but the next patriarch of Antioch, Euphrasius, who was moderate only by comparison, continued the persecution until in 526[52] he died in an earthquake when, according to one story, he fell into a pot of boiling wax, while another told that he was buried alive in the ruins of a house. At Edessa, Bishop Paul took refuge in his baptistery, where he was seized and deported to Syria. Forty days later he was permitted to return, but since he still rejected Chalcedon, he was banished again in 522. His successor as bishop used imperial troops against the local monks until a flash flood indicated God's disapproval with sufficient clarity to mobilize Monophysite passions, and the bishop prudently withdrew to Antioch to avoid death by stoning. Finally, in 526, Bishop Paul wrote to the emperor accepting Chalcedon, and was allowed to return to his see.[53]

We can grasp the reality of the persecution from the *Lives of the Eastern Saints* by John of Ephesus.[54] John was born about 507 in a village near the metropolitan city of Amida in Mesopotamia. The sixth century brought Amida a series of disasters: swarms of locusts, famine, pestilence, earthquakes, floods, two eclipses of the sun, and as if that were not enough, a sack by the Persians in January of 503, in which 80,000 Amidans perished, and after it, a double siege by the Romans that reduced the Amidans to cannibalism. Then came the persecution, unleashed by Paul 'the Jew'. The metropolitan seat of Amida was taken over by Abraham bar Kaili, who became the archfiend of Syriac tradition, and in 526, Justin, or more correctly, Justinian, selected as patriarch of Antioch a former Master of the Soldiers in the East, Ephraim.[55] He was a native of Amida but no more compassionate for that reason. Ephraim, who was to be patriarch for eighteen years, knew how to use military power effectively for ecclesiastical ends.

The monastic movement in the East had been an indigenous growth, stressing celibacy and extreme asceticism. The ideal was single-minded dedication to Christian purity. The elder St Symeon the Stylite had set the standard: at Qal'at Sem'an near Beroea (*mod.* Aleppo) he had perched upon a pillar which grew higher by stages until it reached 40 cubits (16 metres?), and there he passed the last thirty years of his life.[56] His imitators sprang up all over the East. Once death removed a saint from his column, new aspirants came forward with their claims on it. John of Ephesus as an infant had been saved by the village stylite saint named Maro, a neophyte in the business, for he had only just mounted the pillar on which his brother Abraham had lived for twenty-eight years. John's parents brought their dying child to the saint, who prescribed lentils. John recovered. Holy men such as these, whether on pillars, in caves or monasteries, served not merely as low-level physicians and medicine men, but also ombudsmen for their communities. Habib, the 'Great and Divine Old Man' whose biography is the first of John's *Lives*, intervened when a poor widow who taught drawing was defrauded of her fee by two of her students, and another time when a rich notable tried to collect his debts twice! Habib's interventions were not easy to ignore!

The first wave of Chalcedonian persecution after Justin's accession drove the monks from the Amidan convents, but after ten years, they were allowed to return and set about rebuilding.[57] Yet they still rejected Chalcedon and Ephraim of Antioch sent troops against them. In mid-winter they were once again forced out. More than twenty years on, the remnants regrouped at Amida, only to be expelled by a third order. Outside Egypt there was no refuge, and the peril must have forced many ascetics to mingle with the general populace, for the persecution was not directed at the laiety, but rather at the Monophysite clergy and the monks. The result was the spread of their doctrines among the common people. Thus the anchorite

Simeon, whose life John[58] relates briefly, left his solitary hut when the persecution struck and went to Amida, where he baptized and gave absolution to the faithful. John also describes in vivid detail the stubborn resistance of one Sergius, a holy man from John's own village in the territory of Amida, the home of the holy man Maro who had saved John's life as a child. Sergius came to Maro on his lonely mountain-top pillar and described to him what was happening. Maro beat his breast and wept. But Sergius was anxious for a more heroic act of defiance, and with both a warning and blessing from Maro, he departed for the metropolitan seat of Amida. He reached it at dawn on Sunday, and went to the church where the whole populace was gathered, for though the Monophysites would not take communion with the Chalcedonians, they still gathered in the same church, and there was as yet no separate congregation with its own hierarchy. During the sermon, Sergius appeared at the church door, clad in a patchwork of sackcloth rags and bearing a cross on his shoulder. He advanced to the chancel, climbed to the third step, seized the preacher by the neck and, abjuring him not to cast pearls before swine, knocked him down. From the top step he hurled curses against Chalcedon.

Then bishop Abraham bar Kaili arose and calmed the congregation, saying that he and his clergy would speak privately in the vestry with this man. After the people dispersed, 'like ravening beasts who find a sheep in the field and all attack it', the Chalcedonians fell upon Sergius, shaved his head and imprisoned him in a monastery in Armenia where all the anchorites were zealous dyophysites. Sergius, who was an agile man, escaped this affliction by leaping from a third-floor window, and set again about the task of building monasteries.

Theodora helped where she could. Mare, the deposed Monophysite metropolitan of Amida and his clergy nearly perished in exile at Petra, and Theodora persuaded Justinian, who was not yet emperor, to get Justin's sanction for them to go to Alexandria. After Mare died, it was Theodora who had his bones returned to Amida. Her influence reached its height in the early 530s. Justinian, who had begun his reign as an harasser of the unbelievers, relaxed the pressure, and in 531, a delegation of Monophysite clergy and monks arrived in Constantinople, where they were welcomed and given quarters in the Palace of Hormisdas adjoining the palace. Theodora visited them every two or three days, and occasionally Justinian came with her. The handsome church of Sts Sergius and Bacchus was built for them as a centre of Monophysite worship in the imperial capital.[59]

Justinian tried to promote dialogue. In the spring of 532, he sponsored a three-day conference of bishops in the Hormisdas Palace, five of them Chalcedonian and five or more Monophysite disciples of Severus. But the *Tome* of Leo remained the sticking point: the Monophysites anathematized it, and though Justinian was willing to be flexible, he would not reject it.[60] In the winter of 534/5, Severus himself came from Egypt to Constantinople at Justinian's invitation. Thither too came Z'ura, a pillar-saint from First Syria who baptized Theodora and, if we can credit John of Ephesus, cured Justinian of an illness that had bloated him beyond recognition.[61] Severus, along with Theodosius, who was chosen Alexandrian patriarch in early 535 and was impeccably anti-Chalcedonian though not rabid enough for the Alexandrian masses, and Anthimus, the newly consecrated patriarch of Constantinople, came to an agreement. Anthimus accepted the moderate Monophysite position of Severus and Theodosius.

That was a stunning success for Severus, and a hollow one. Even in Egypt Severus had divided support. Both he and Theodosius were facing a challenge from the Aphthartodocetists led by Julian, whose extreme Monophysitism was growing popular. In March, 536, came the peripeteia. Pope Agapetus arrived in Constantinople on a mission for the Gothic king Theodahad. He came backed with all the prestige of the Roman see and easily won Justinian back to the creed of Chalcedon. Anthimus was removed and Theodora rescued him from Justinian's wrath by secreting him in her palace, where he remained in hiding until her death.

Pope Agapetus had forced the issue. The Chalcedonian reaction was harsh, and by the end of 536, soldiers were scouring Mesopotamia for Monophysites. Theodosius was bundled off to exile in an uncomfortable fortress in Thrace, and Justinian undertook to find a soundly orthodox patriarch to replace him at Alexandria. His first choice was Paul, abbot of the *Metanoia* monastery in Canopus, and it was lamentable: Paul was implicated in the murder of a church-warden. But he was a fierce defender of Chalcedon. He 'loved to shed blood' wrote John of Nikiu,[62] not without justice, and during his brief tenure, he made Alexandria safe for Chalcedon. The second choice was a Palestinian monk named Zoilus. For the moment, Egypt submitted. But the muddled *History of the Patriarchs of the Coptic Church* correctly dates the split to this point. Henceforth the Melkite patriarchs, whose name derived from the Coptic word for 'king', were foreigners ordained by Constantinople. The Melkites ruled in Alexandria, but the Coptic patriarch, safe in the monastery at Enaton, had the allegiance of Egypt. Yet the passionate quarrels of Alexandria made no great difference in the countryside, where we can find Monophysite priests in the Fayum obeying the orders of the Melkite patriarch, apparently unaware of the theological divide. The peasant masses were poor and ignorant, and they mingled pagan survivals innocently with Christianity. They had little comprehension of what the theological quarrels were all about. For them, Christianity was a protest movement promising liberation, and though their loyalty to the patriarch might be confused, it was absolute.[63]

But the sequel must await a later chapter. In 527, Justin's health was failing. On 1 April, he made his nephew co-emperor,[64] and four months later he died. Justinian was now sole emperor. The empire was Justinian's to remake and restore, and he took up the task eagerly.

THE HIMYARITE AFFAIR

In 524, an embassy headed by a priest, Abraham son of Euphrasius, reached the Lakhmid capital of Hira on a mission of peace. The previous year, the Lakhmid emir Mundhir had made devastating raids on Roman territory. But Mundhir was not at Hira but in one of his camps in the Syrian desert, and thus the envoys continued on for ten days until on 30 January, they reached him at Ramlah, the 'hills of sand'. There they encountered a large gathering, including pagan Arabs, who hurled taunts at the envoys as they entered camp. Their Christ, they said, had been driven out by the Himyarites.

In the embassy was the bishop of Beth Arsham, Simeon, and two letters of his are our best source for the incident.[65] The embassy's mission was successful: it did make peace with Mundhir. But during the conference at Ramlah, an envoy arrived from Yusuf As'ar Yat'an of Himyar with a letter which was read out to the assembly. 'The King whom the Ethiopians [i.e. Axumites] set up in our country died', wrote Yusuf,

> and because the winter season had begun, they were not able to march out into our country and appoint a Christian king as they generally do. Accordingly, I became king over the whole country of the Homerites [i.e. Himyarites], and I resolved to slay all the Christians who confessed Christ unless they became Jews like us.[66]

The letter went on to tell how Yusuf had massacred the Christians in his kingdom and urged Mundhir to do likewise. Simeon's embassy brought the news to Justin, and a refugee who had escaped the massacre brought word of it to the king of Axum, Ella Atzbeha, also known as Kaleb, which was apparently the Christian name which was given to him at baptism, for it appears on his coins. Kaleb had reason for concern; not only was he a Christian himself but the Ethiopian garrison in Zafar, the royal city of the Himyarites, had been annihilated.

Yusuf, the 'wicked Jew' of the surviving accounts, also known as Masruq and, in the Arabic tradition, as Dhu Nuwas, was a Jewish convert, and strongly anti-Christian, though his coup was also a bid for freedom from Axumite dominance. The exact dates are uncertain, but it was about the year 522 that he captured Zafar by promising the Ethiopian garrison safe conduct home if it surrendered, and then slew it after his terms were accepted. Then he killed all the Axumites in the city, destroyed their church and ordered all the Christians in the kingdom to accept Judaism or die.

Next Yusuf moved north against Najran, a Christian centre.[67] The same trick that had won him Zafar won him Najran too. The Christians were given the choice of Judaism or death. The Najran church was burned with the bones of the martyrs and some 2,000 live Christians inside it. The persecution spread to Saba, the old Sabaean capital, to Marib and other cities.

Kaleb and Justin got in touch. Justin's interest was commercial as well as theological: Himyar lay strategically on the route to India. The go-between was Timothy III, the Monophysite patriarch of Alexandria. In the winter of 524–525, a flotilla of Byzantine merchantmen from the Red Sea fleet mustered at the port of Adulis, and as soon as the weather allowed, it carried an Axumite army across to Yemen. Yusuf's coup was broken in two campaigns. Arab legend has it that when Yusuf recognized defeat, he spurred his horse into the sea and disappeared under the waves. Kaleb spent some three years restoring Christianity, and returned home, having set up a vassal king of Himyar. But Kaleb's vassal did not last long. Fugitive slaves from Kaleb's army led the revolt which overthrew him and set up instead one Abraha, by origin the slave of a Greek trader of Adulis. Kaleb dispatched a punitive force, but it deserted, and a second one was crushed. Abraha kept his autonomy, but nonetheless paid Axum tribute.

Abraha has two claims to fame. He moved his residence from Zafar to Sanaa, the present capital of Yemen, and at Justinian's urging, he made a fruitless expedition against Persia. He died in 569/70, the year that the Prophet Mohammed was born, and the Sassanid court moved astutely to secure its interests. Khusro I received the pretender to the Yemenite throne, and sometime between 570 and 575 returned him to Yemen backed by a small force. Within two years, the pretender lost his life to a revolt, and Khusro sent a larger force, which reduced the country and installed a Persian governor. By Khusro's death, Persian ships controlled the Bab al-Mandab, the entrance to the Red Sea.[68]

The *rapprochement* between Constantinople and Axum is an interesting sidelight on the period of Justinian. For an historical moment, it brought Axum within the Byzantine commonwealth, though the incident had more effect upon the traditions of Ethiopia than on those of Byzantium. Later, Justinian, who lacked modern maps and thought Axum was a neighbour of India, tried to establish a trade route via Himyar and Axum which would bring silk into the empire, bypassing Persia, and to stir up trouble between Abraha of Himyar and Persia. The Monophysitism of the Himyarite Christians made no difference. By now, the Nestorians had largely removed themselves from Byzantine dominion, but for Chalcedonians and Monophysites alike, the emperor was still God's vicegerent.[69] Byzantine diplomacy was willing to propagate Christianity of either variety beyond the imperial borders, and thought it in its imperial interest to do so.

RENEWED WAR WITH PERSIA

In the last years of Justin, war broke out again with Persia and the fuse of the powder keg was the Caucasus, where Persia faced a cluster of Christian kingdoms. The Persian king Kavadh's options were limited for the moment. When the new king of Lazica, Tzath, elected baptism in Constantinople and took a Christian wife whom Justin provided, Kavadh retorted by manipulating a Roman federate chief, Zilgibi of the Sabiric Huns, into attacking his former ally. But imperial diplomacy succeeded in turning the move to Byzantium's advantage: Justin sent Kavadh a friendly dispatch to tell him that Zilgibi had taken payment from him to betray the Persians, whereupon Kavadh slew the Hun leader and most of his force. Then Kavadh, with equal cordiality, turned to Justin with a problem of his own. His chosen heir was Khusro, who was not his eldest son, and in order to ensure his succession, he asked Justin to adopt him.

Probably his aim was to forestall any Byzantine move to take advantage of dynastic complications that might follow his death. The proposal attracted both Justin and Justinian, but the quaestor Proclus spoke against it. Proclus was an upright legalist, a prudent conservative and a closet pagan. He argued that adoption under Roman law would give the adopted son a claim on the imperial throne. Whatever modern historians may think about the matter, Proclus evidently believed that the succession was hereditary. He urged the emperor to offer an alternative: adoption following the custom of the Germans.[70] There was a precedent: Justin had already used this protocol to adopt the son-in-law of Theodoric the Ostrogoth, Eutharic. But the young Khusro was no Ostrogoth and considered Justin's offer an insult.

Kavadh retorted with a move against Iberia. He demanded that it abandon Christianity and accept Zoroastrianism. The Iberian king got a pledge of help from Justin, but the Persian invaders were too strong, and the Iberian royal household fled with all the Iberian notables to neighbouring Lazica, and thence to Constantinople. Meanwhile (this was Justin's last year) the Byzantines raided Persarmenia to obtain bodies for the slave trade. The commanders were the empress Theodora's brother-in-law, nicknamed Sittas,[71] and Belisarius, duke of Mesopotamia. The first raid was a success; a second one was defeated by a force led by two scions of the Armenian feudal family of Kamsarakan, who some three years later were to go over to the Byzantines.[72] At the same time, a Roman force incompetently led by one Libelarius advanced across the frontier near Nisibis and then retreated hurriedly for no good reason. Libelarius was removed, and Belisarius was put in command of the troops stationed at Dara. His *assessor*, that is, his legal adviser and secretary, was Procopius of Caesarea.

Thus in Justinian's first year as emperor, two important players make their appearance. Belisarius was to conquer Vandal Africa for Justinian and to lead the attack on Ostrogothic Italy, though there final victory eluded him. Procopius was the leading historian of the age, and thanks to him we are better informed about Belisarius than any other of Justinian's generals. Belisarius had attracted the future emperor's attention while he was himself still Master of the Soldiers and Belisarius was an officer in his bodyguard. Procopius was to follow Belisarius to Africa and to Italy, and eventually his admiration was to change to disillusion and even dislike. Yet Procopius was an effective press agent. It is unlikely that, without him, Belisarius would enjoy the stellar reputation that he does among historians of warfare.

The armies he led were never large, but he knew how to use them effectively, and a military analyst as astute as Liddell Hart has recognized him as the father of the strategy of 'tactical defence' which was to serve the Byzantine Empire well in the future, and might have saved it from the defeat at Manzikert in 1071 had the emperor Romanos followed it.[73] That, perhaps, is an extreme judgement. What is apparent from Procopius' narrative is that a number of Justinian's generals were as effective as Belisarius, and many of them had limited respect for him. Belisarius, good tactician though he was, had great difficulty controlling his subordinates. Jealousy among his staff members played a part. Yet there were probably other reasons as well. Belisarius seems to have been the only general whose wife accompanied him on campaign, and Antonina was no ordinary wife. The *Secret History* of Procopius portrays her as a forceful woman who cuckolded her husband and at the same time kept him completely in her thrall. How much of this rumour was common gossip in Belisarius' army we cannot know, but even half of it would have damaged the respect his soldiers had for him, for an army that laughs at its general is one that is prone to insubordination and desertion.

However, in 527, Belisarius was a rising young officer. Justinian, now sole emperor, ordered him to build a forward post 'in the district of Mindous',[74] facing Nisibis on the Persian side of the boundary, and the Persians demanded that he stop work. Justinian responded with a military strike led by a couple of brothers from Thrace: rash young men who suffered a humiliating defeat. Thereupon Justinian made Belisarius Master of Soldiers in *Oriens*, though he shared power with the Master of Offices, Hermogenes.[75]

In midsummer 530, a large Persian army advanced against Dara. What had aroused the old king Kavadh to war was an embassy from the Samaritans in First Palestine, who promised him their help. Justinian's attempt to force the Samaritans to convert to Christianity had reopened old wounds. The Samaritans, the remnant of the old Northern Kingdom of Israel, were an unloved sect, disliked by both Jews and Christians and detesting them both in return. Their centre was the old religious capital of Shechem, which the Romans had renamed Flavia Neapolis, and their temple on the slopes of Mt Gerizim had been destroyed in 484 after an uprising against the local Christians. In 529 the Samaritans revolted again, captured

Neapolis and restored their temple on Mt Gerizim. Their leader Julian held a chariot race at Neapolis to celebrate his success, and when a Christian charioteer was victorious over all the others, he cut off his head. But the omen told the truth. The news of the Samaritan revolt and Julian's own severed head both reached Justinian at the same time. The revolt was ruthlessly suppressed. Twenty thousand captives were sold as slaves in Persia and India, with the Ghassanids acting as middlemen. The damage to the economy of Palestine was extensive: two years after the uprising, St Sabas led a delegation of Palestinian monks to the capital to petition for remission of taxes in First and Second Palestine,[76] and more than twenty years later, Procopius could complain that great tracts of land in Palestine had gone out of cultivation because their Samaritan tenants had been destroyed.[77]

The Persian offensive of 530 was based on illusory hopes. A battle was fought at Dara three and a half kilometres from the fortress, and for the first time in many years, the Persians suffered a sharp defeat. Further north, Sittas foiled a Persian advance into Armenia led by one of Persia's ablest generals, Mihr-Mihroe,[78] and the year 531 ended with Kavadh hinting to a Byzantine envoy that in return for a fee, he was willing to make peace.

Next spring, Kavadh decided to strike where the Byzantines were weak, not in Mesopotamia but west of the Euphrates. The Saracen warriors of the Lakhmid emir Mundhir along with a force of 15,000 Persians made for the province of First Syria. Belisarius followed swiftly with a strong detachment of Romans and Harith's Ghassanid Arabs, and reached the caravan city of Chalkis ad Belum before the invaders realized their danger. They withdrew, with Belisarius dogging their heels, careful to avoid battle. At the Euphrates, near the city of Callinicum, the armies made contact.

It was Easter and the Byzantines were weakened with fasting. The Persians were on the point of leaving Roman territory and Belisarius wanted to let them go peacefully. But his soldiers wanted a fight. What was prudence for Belisarius was cowardice in their eyes. Under protest, Belisarius offered battle and was defeated, although he avoided a complete rout by dismounting his cavalry and joined the infantry who, with their backs to the river, fought off the Persians. The Persian commander returned to Kavadh, and according to Procopius, he was displeased and considered the raid anything but a success. Procopius' narrative of the battle may be based upon the report he drew up as Belisarius' secretary, and he did his best for

Belisarius' reputation.[79] He relates that the turning point in the battle came when Harith and his Saracens on the right wing fled before the Persian onslaught. But Justinian sent the Master of Offices Hermogenes to investigate, and we get an inkling of his rather different report from the chronicler Malalas, who seems to have used sources that emanated from the court.[80] Hermogenes' conclusions were less complimentary: he disclosed that it was not Belisarius but the two dukes, Sounikas and Simmas, who dismounted and held off the Persians, and that the story of Harith's flight was greatly exaggerated. All in all, Belisarius must have had some explaining to do.[81]

Justinian replaced Belisarius at Dara with the more experienced Mundo, fresh from a victory over the Bulgars in Illyricum, and on the northern frontier Sittas took over. A few months later, Mundo was reassigned to Illyricum, with the result that with the new year of 532, both Belisarius and Mundo were in Constantinople. And that, as it turned out, was fortunate for Justinian and Theodora.

On 13 September, 531, Kavadh died after a stroke, but before his death, he crowned Khusro to ensure his succession. The old king's choice was sound. Khusro *Anosarwan* (531–579), the greatest of the Sassanids, was to consolidate the power of the monarchy by creating a standing army recruited from the lesser nobility and a civil bureaucracy which paralleled Constantinople's.[82] Justinian was to find him a worthy rival. Yet at the same time, Khusro seems to have admired the cultural traditions of Greece, and he was a student of Greek philosophy. But in 531, the future was clouded, and Khusro was ready for peace. So was Justinian. The negotiations between the Romans and the Persians were drawn out, but a year after Kavadh's death, they had an agreement. Each side returned the territory it had won, and Justinian agreed to pay Khusro 11,000 gold pounds and to base the duke of Mesopotamia at Constantina rather than on the Persian frontier at Dara. In the summer of 533, the 'Endless Peace' came into effect. It was supposed to endure forever, and Justinian had paid handsomely for it, but it lasted barely seven years.[83] Whether or not Justinian had already made up his mind to send an expedition against the Vandal kingdom of Africa is not clear, but when the oppportunity offered itself, the 'Endless Peace' had left his hands free.

Khusro was not slow to recognize his supporting role in the Vandal overthrow, and his embassy which congratulated Justinian on his victory asked for a share of the booty. That may have been Khusro's joke, but his domestic reforms did require money, and Justinian realized that the joke was at least half in earnest. He sent Khusro a present.[84]

But before the Vandal expedition got under way, the *Nika* revolt very nearly brought Justinian's regime crashing down.

THE *NIKA* REVOLT

There are many questions which remain unanswered about the *Nika* revolt which took place in January of 532, but the outline of events seems clear. On Sunday, 11 January, there was an encounter in the Hippodrome between the Greens and the emperor. The Greens recited a chant complaining of the wrongs they had suffered at the hands of Kalopodios, the *spatharius*, that is, a eunuch officer of the *cubicularii*. We cannot identify him, though one of our sources identifies Narses as a *spatharius* and *cubicularius* at this time;[85] we shall meet him again as the commander who quashed the resistance of the Ostrogoths in Italy. Kalopodios may have been his immediate predecessor. Such protests in the Hippodrome were not uncommon; what is unusual is that the text of this one has been preserved in two sources, fully in the one[86] (who titles it the *Akta dia Kalopodion ton koubikoularion kai spatharion*) and partially in the other.[87]

The crowd that gathered in the Hippodrome was one that was familiar with the resonances of the church liturgy; the Greens chanted in accentual metre led by a precentor whose name is given as Antlas, and Justinian's spokesman, his *mandator*, standing before the imperial *loge*, replied in metre. 'Long life to you, Justinian Augustus!' the Greens began. 'May victory be yours! I suffer wrongs, O best of princes, and, God knows, they are beyond bearing. I am afraid to name my oppressor, for fear his success will increase and my future will be in peril.'

Mandator:	'Who is he? I do not know him.'
Greens:	'The man who takes advantage of me, O Thrice Royal, is to be found in the shoemakers' quarter.'
Mandator:	'No one does you wrong.'
Greens:	'One man, one man only does me wrong! Mother of God, may we see the end of him!'
Mandator:	'Who is this person? We do not know him.'
Greens:	'You don't need our help to recognize him, Thrice Royal. You know who oppresses me this day.'

119

Mandator:	'If there is anybody, we don't know him.'
Greens:	'Kalopodios the *spatharius* wrongs me, Lord of All.'
Mandator:	'Kalopodios has nothing to do with you.'
Greens:	'Sometime he will have the fate of Judas. God will requite him for wronging me, and swiftly.'
Mandator:	'You are come not to see the Games, but to insult your rulers.'

The dialogue grew more heated. The *mandator*, speaking for the emperor, called the Greens Jews, Samaritans and Manichaeans, and told them to go and be baptized: the equivalent of 'Go to Hell!' The Greens protested that they *were* baptized! 'Would that Sabbatius had never been born, to have a son who is a murderer!' they cried. Sabbatius was Justinian's father. The exchange was becoming more pointed.

A murder had been committed. It was the twenty-sixth in a series of murders. The Greens thought that Justinian was implicated, and Justinian's identification with the Blues was such that they considered the attack was directed against them. The Blues broke in:

Blues:	'You yourselves are the only ones in the whole Hippodrome who commit murders.'
Greens:	'Whenever you commit murder, you get away scot-free!'
Blues:	'You are murderers and rioters. It is you who are the only murderers in the Hippodrome.'

Justinian conspicuously supported the Blues, and the Blues reciprocated. The Greens instanced two recent murders, and the herald accused the Greens of perpetrating both of them. The Greens protested bitterly. 'Farewell, Justice! No one cares about you any more! I shall convert and become a Jew! It is better to be a pagan than a Blue, God knows!' And, with a curse on the bones of the Hippodrome patrons, the Greens walked out.

That evening, after the Greens had left the Blues and the emperor to watch the chariot races by themselves, Eudaimon, the urban prefect who was holding some malefactors from both the Blue and Green parties, ordered the execution of seven of them who had been convicted of murder. It was perhaps an effort to show impartiality. Justinian was still a Blue patron, but since his accession he had sought to enforce law and order with an even hand.[88] But the scaffold broke and two of the convicts, a Blue and a Green, fell to the ground. Thereupon monks from the monastery of St Konon rushed out, saved the two men, whom they found lying on the ground, still alive, and took them to the church of St Lawrence for asylum. Learning this, the urban prefect set a guard at the church, evidently to prevent the convicts from escaping.

On Tuesday, the Ides of January, there were races in the Hippodrome with the emperor present, and both the Blues and Greens begged the emperor to show mercy. No reply. Then, at the twenty-second race, the Blues and Greens together raised the chant, 'Long live the merciful Blues and Greens!' The two parties had joined to become the Constantinople mob, and to prevent the military from infiltrating, they took as their watchword 'Nika' (Conquer!). Nika was the cry with which the parties cheered on their chariot teams, and it gave the revolt its name.

Some of the rioters were hoodlums, but street violence had been decreasing since Justin's crackdown in 523,[89] and this outburst in the fifth year of Justinian's reign cannot be dismissed as a case of mindless crowd fury. Like mobs at other times in other places, this mob seems to have had a sense that its goal was legitimate.[90] The rioters included women as well as men, even though women did not attend the races, and that in itself indicates that the Nika revolt was more than a brawl of Hippodrome fans that got out of control. Somehow Justinian's refusal to show mercy to the two men who had escaped the gallows snapped the bond of fealty between him and his subjects. This was an uprising that gave voice to a broad spectrum of discontent, and its ultimate aim was to replace Justinian with a legitimate emperor.

On Tuesday evening, the mob demonstrated outside the Praetorium, the urban prefect's headquarters, and getting no response, they killed the guards, released the prisoners incarcerated there and set the building ablaze. That evening, Justinian must have seen parts of the city alight virtually on the doorstep of the palace. The mob set fire to the Brazen House, and the flames spread to Hagia Sophia. On Wednesday, Justinian tried to calm the crowd by giving another series of games, but the rioters ignited the Hippodrome seating, and the blaze spread to the Baths of Zeuxippus.

The outcry was now aimed at Justinian's three unpopular ministers, Eudaimon the urban prefect, Tribonian, the Quaestor of the Sacred Palace, and John of Cappadocia, the praetorian prefect of the East. Justinian replaced them forthwith. The replacements, Phocas, the new praetorian prefect, Basilides, the new quaestor, and the new urban prefect, Tryphon[91], whose brother had held the office four times, were men who enjoyed the respect of the senators, and their appointments show where Justinian recognized a nexus of opposition.[92] But the aim of the rioters now was to replace Justinian himself, and the alternatives with the best claims to legitimacy were the nephews of Anastasius. The most likely of these were Pompeius and even better, Hypatius, an army officer of considerable experience and indifferent ability. Both these men were in the Great Palace with Justinian.

By Saturday, 17 January, all Justinian's efforts had failed. The clergy had tried in vain to intervene, and the guards were unreliable. Street fighting spread along the central part of the city from Hagia Sophia to Constantine's Forum. Fortunately Justinian had Belisarius, who had returned from the Persian front with a corps of battle-hardened soldiers, and Mundo, who had a cadre of Heruls, and loyal troops had come in from Thrace. On Saturday evening, Justinian decided to order Hypatius, Pompeius and other senators to leave the palace and guard their own homes, and they left reluctantly. On Sunday, before sunrise, he appeared in the Hippodrome with the Holy Gospels and tried to rally the people to his side with a bit of theatre. He repented publicly of rejecting their petition on Tuesday, and pledged a general amnesty if peace returned. Some voices raised the acclamation, 'Justinian Augustus, *tu vincas*', but there were more who silenced the emperor with the cry, 'You are a breaker of oaths, you ass!', and he beat a retreat. By now the mob knew that Hypatius was at his home. It had its legitimate emperor.

Hypatius was taken against his will to the Forum of Constantine, and on the steps of Constantine's Column, he was crowned with a gold collar and dressed in the white robe that emperors traditionally wore prior to coronation. From there, he was taken to the *kathisma* in the Hippodrome for the coronation ceremony. Frightened at first, Hypatius gained heart: word came that Justinian had fled. In fact, Justinian almost lost his nerve. According to Procopius of Caesarea, who may have been inside the palace himself during the riot, the emperor and his court were arguing whether to stay or flee, when Theodora spoke out, and made a brave speech, which ended with the maxim that 'royalty is a good winding-sheet.' Theodora can hardly have uttered the exact words which Procopius reports, but it is not at all unlikely that it was this tough little graduate of the streets who recognized what had to be done to save the regime, and did not hesitate to do it. Theodora did not frighten easily, and if a massacre was needed, she had no misgivings. Justinian and his ministers decided to strike as ruthlessly as they knew how.

Belisarius made his way past the charred ruins of the Brazen House to the Hippodrome, while Mundo entered it through the passage called the *Nekra*, the gate by which the corpses of crashed charioteers were removed. Together they fell upon the supporters of Hypatius, who were crowded into the Hippodrome. Two of Justinian's nephews dragged Hypatius from his throne and took him and Pompeius to the emperor. They protested their innocence, and Justinian might have yielded, except for Theodora. The two men were put to death and their bodies cast into the sea. Their property was confiscated, and eighteen senators were exiled and their property seized.[93] More than 30,000 people had been slaughtered in the Hippodrome.[94]

The sources which we have for the revolt agree on the main lines, but differ on omissions and viewpoints. Only two record the *Akta dia Kalopodion* on Sunday, 11 January, but these seem to be independent reports. There is nothing in the *Akta* itself which ties it to the subsequent events of the week, but it gives us a glimpse of popular sentiment. The Greens uttered an orchestrated complaint in the Hippodrome and Justinian treated them roughly, commanding them to be silent, and calling them 'Jews, Samaritans and Manichaeans'. 'Jew' and 'Samaritan' were customary slurs applied to heretics, but we should not take the vocabulary of Justinian's *mandator* too literally. The Greens insisted on their orthodoxy. But it appears that in the street violence, the Greens had been getting the worst of it. Greens had been killed, and they blamed Justinian, whereupon the Blues intervened to claim that the Greens alone had murderers in their number. There may have been a grain of truth to their charge: the perception of Procopius in his *Secret History* was that the Blues were comparatively moderate, and it should be noted that, on the final Sunday of the revolt, 200 or 250 of the 'Young Greens' turned up wearing full armour, which is testimony to their militancy.[95] The Greens were in a dangerous mood when they left the Hippodrome.

That evening, the urban prefect attempted to mete out even-handed punishment to both Blue and Green felons in his custody. In the past, Justinian had kept the mob divided by favouritism for the Blues. The executions of 11 January marked a change of policy, and the Blues realized it. Before the Tuesday demonstration in the Hippodrome, the Blue and Green leaders must have worked out a joint plan of action, however tentative.

Count Marcellinus, whose report of the revolt is almost contemporary, laid the blame for the revolt on the nephews of Anastasius, who conspired with a group of nobles.[96] He may reflect Justinian's own immediate reaction. Procopius, who may have been inside the Great Palace himself, and if he was not, had access to Belisarius who was there, emphasizes the reluctance of Hypatius, but by the time he wrote, Justinian had restored the property of Hypatius and his brother Pompeius to their heirs. Only Procopius gives Theodora her great scene: with the splendid fearlessness of a Clytaemnestra, Theodora puts the case for staying and fighting. She concludes by quoting the old proverb that kingship makes a good burial shroud. But the proverb conceals a sting. Theodora misquotes. The maxim was a piece of advice once given to Dionysius I of Syracuse, a tyrant with a bad reputation, when he was faced with revolt, and if Theodora had quoted it correctly, she would have said, 'Tyranny is a good winding sheet.'[97] The Byzantine world knew the difference between a tyrant and a true king, and the old élite to which Procopius belonged must have chuckled at Theodora's mistake and at the same time thought that if she had quoted correctly, she would have been accurate in double measure.

We must deny Theodora her great scene. But we may be sure that during the revolt, Theodora did not lose her nerve, and was prepared to do anything necessary to save the regime, whether it smacked of tyranny or not. It is fair to note that the anonymous *Easter Chronicle* of the early seventh century assigns Justinian a more vigorous personal role in the attack on the mob in the Hippodrome on the last day, and a more critical part to Narses, who infiltrated the Blues and bribed some of them to support Justinian. Procopius is alone in portraying Belisarius as the hero of the last day. The *Easter Chronicle* has Hypatius try to send a message to Justinian urging him to fall upon the mob assembled in the Hippodrome, but he got the reply that Justinian had already fled. One source alone attributes the executions of Hypatius and his brother to Theodora's severity.[98] But it is a credible morsel of evidence.

The revolt was a major disaster but it cleared the decks. The mob was cowed. Senatorial opposition, forced underground, was reduced to futile griping, of which Procopius' *Secret History* is a literary example. There were widespread confiscations of senatorial property after the revolt. The old propertied élite had shown their degree of alienation, but Justinian was now free to push on with his plans with or without their support.[99] The *Nika* revolt left the levers of power firmly in his hands. But he did not misuse them. By the next year, the healing process was under way. Hypatius and Pompeius were rehabilitated posthumously, and rebels whose property had suffered confiscation had it restored, though perhaps not completely.[100] The rebuilding of Constantinople went ahead swiftly. Only forty-five days after the Hippodrome massacre, Justinian began the construction of a new Hagia Sophia to replace the church that was burned. It was to be his statement of imperial sovereignty, and he pushed its completion impatiently. But why did the revolt break out when it did?

There was no single cause, but rather a collection of them which came to a head in the week of 11 January. Justinian's law code had come into force in 529, and Tribonian, the moving force behind its creation, was at work on the *Digest*.[101] History may judge that Justinian's codifications were the lasting success of his reign, but they must have unsettled the legal fraternity and added to the anxiety of the age. John the Cappadocian's fiscal reforms were no better. The old establishment was worried. The empress Theodora in particular displayed calculated disrespect for the senatorial class, and senators looked back with nostalgia to the reign of Anastasius, the thrifty old emperor who had managed to steer a careful course between Monophysites and Chalcedonians. Anastasius' nephews seem to have been men of limited ability and ambition, but they were a natural focus for discontent.

The Greens, the most militant of the parties in the Hippodrome, were aggrieved because they were outsiders who felt that the emperor treated them unfairly and cared nothing for their wrongs, while the Blues were startled into an alliance with them by the sharp realization that the days when they were the imperial favourites were past, though they were, it seems, still open to negotiations with Narses when he came, offering bribes. In the background, there were rising expectations among the masses which raced ahead of reality. Overall, the empire still enjoyed the prosperity it had known under Anastasius, but in Constantinople itself the indigent population was growing, fed by an influx of economic refugees from the country-side, some of them victims of John the Cappadocian's ruthless officials.[102] Change was in the air. To some, it brought anxiety, to others unrealistic hopes. All these factors came together in the week of 11–18 January.

3

THE RESTORATION OF THE EMPIRE
The wars of Justinian

THE RECOVERY OF AFRICA

On 1 April, 536, three months after Sicily had fallen to the victorious army of Belisarius, Justinian issued a law on the administration of the province of Cappadocia. Its provisions do not concern us, but its codicil does, for there Justinian refers both to the cost of his wars, and his hopes:

> God has granted us to make peace with the Persians, to make the Vandals, Alans and Moors our subjects, and gain possession of all Africa and Sicily besides, and we have good hopes that He will consent to our establishing our empire over the rest of those whom the Romans of old ruled from the boundaries of one ocean to the other and then lost by their negligence.[1]

To us, with the advantage of hindsight, there is a whiff of irony to Justinian's prose. But in 536, the push to renew the Roman Empire was still going well, and success seemed to justify the cost of it all.

The Vandals in North Africa had provided an opportunity. In Byzacena, too close for comfort to their estates within the *Sortes Vandalicae*, they had lost a battle to the Moors. The Vandal king, Hilderic, the grandson of the emperor Valentinian III, was no warrior but Justinian had reason to like him. He had ended the maltreatment of the Catholics, sought a *rapprochement* with the emperor and had consequently alienated the Ostrogothic kingdom in Italy. In mid-June, 530, he was deposed in a *coup d'état* led by a great-grandson of Gaiseric, Gelimer, who was considered an able soldier and whose Arian sympathies were not in doubt. Justinian promptly remonstrated, but Gelimer turned a deaf ear. He told Justinian, as one king to another, not to meddle. Justinian was understandably irritated, and there was an influential lobby of merchants, African churchmen and dispossessed landowners in Constantinople to play upon his sense of grievance. Hilderic had aroused expectations, and now he was fallen, they pressed Justinian to avenge him.

But the consistory was dismayed. The Persian War had just come to a conclusion, the 'Endless Peace' was costly, and the treasury empty, and most of all, the councillors remembered the disastrous expedition that the emperor Leo had dispatched against Gaiseric. But only the praetorian prefect John the Cappadocian dared speak against the venture, according to Procopius, who was no friend of John's, but here calls him the 'most daring and clever of all his contemporaries'. John felt no romantic yearning to recover the western provinces. He might have won over Justinian, except that Christian faith intervened. One account has it that a bishop from the eastern provinces appeared, and reported a dream which promised success if the emperor would preserve the Christians of Africa, and another story[2] relates that it was the African martyr Laetus, slain in a Vandal *auto-da-fé* in 484, who came to Justinian in a dream to urge him on. The African lobby had its way.

The field army that was readied for the expedition numbered about 18,000 men, 10,000 of them infantry, who needed 500 transport ships with 30,000 crewmen, most of them Egyptians or Ionian Greeks. To convoy them, there was a flotilla of 92 fast warships (*dromones*) with 2,000 fighting men as rowers. The generalissimo was Belisarius, whose wife Antonina accompanied him, and his immediate subordinates were Dorotheus, commander of the troops from Armenia, and Belisarius' *domesticus* Solomon, a eunuch castrated by accident rather than intention. Procopius, our chief source for the expedition, went along as a member of Belisarius' staff.

Just before departure, the Byzantines had two strokes of luck. A Roman Libyan named Pudentius led a revolt in Tripolitania, and in Sardinia, a Gothic retainer named Godas, whom Gelimer had placed in charge of the island, rebelled and sought Justinian's aid. Gelimer had to let Pudentius be, but he was anxious to reclaim Sardinia, and dispatched his brother Tata with 5,000 men and 120 ships – probably the whole of his effective fleet, for as it turned out, he offered no resistance at sea to Belisarius. The Vandals seem to have been completely unaware of the threat in store for them.

About the time of the summer solstice of 533, the Byzantine fleet anchored off Julian's harbour on the Sea of Marmara within sight of the Sacred Palace, received the patriarch's blessing and set sail. The voyage to Africa was to take more than two months. The rift between the Vandals and the Ostrogothic kingdom served the imperial interests well: Amalasuintha provided a market in Sicily for Belisarius' army. It was in Sicily too where Belisarius discovered that the Vandals did not expect an invasion. Their ignorance is extraordinary, for news travelled well enough over the trade routes, and the fact that no forewarning had reached them demonstrates how separate the world of the Arian Vandals was: they had little contact with traders from the eastern empire, and regarded them with suspicion.[3] Procopius describes how he went to Syracuse to glean what intelligence he could, and there he met a childhood friend from Caesarea whose merchantmen journeyed regularly to Carthage, and a slave agent of his who had come from Carthage only three days before had reported that the Vandals anticipated no danger: their best troops had sailed with Gelimer's brother to suppress the revolt in Sardinia! Procopius relates how he led the agent down to his boat at the waterfront, and hijacked him off to the roadstead where the fleet lay at Porto Lombardo, and there the slave repeated his story to Belisarius. It was welcome news. It helped dispel the gloom occasioned by the death of Dorotheus, which had only just happened.

At the end of August, the army disembarked along the east coast of Tunisia, at Caput Vada (*mod.* Ras Kaboudia), some 200 kilometres south of Carthage.[4] It built a stockaded camp, and chanced upon a stroke of luck: as the soldiers dug the moat, they struck a spring of fresh water sufficient for both men and pack animals. It was a good omen. From Caput Vada, the army proceeded warily towards Carthage. Belisarius allowed no pillaging; his war was pointedly directed against the Vandal occupiers of Roman Africa, not against the Roman inhabitants.

The fleet had sailed with the patriarch's blessing and the promise voiced by the unnamed bishop who had provided the compelling argument for the Byzantine invasion. But thus far it was no anti-Arian crusade.[5] Belisarius' mission was to free Africa from a tyrant who had dethroned and imprisoned its rightful king, Hilderic. Justinian had provided Belisarius with an open letter to that effect, which Belisarius in turn gave to an overseer of the public post who had defected, with orders to broadcast it. As the army advanced, Belisarius was careful to maintain discipline and allow no looting that might antagonize the civilian population. And he took no chances. John the Armenian led a vanguard of 300 of Belisarius' *bucellarii* some 4 kilometres or more in front of the main army, and on the left there was a company of 600 Bulgars, all mounted archers. On the right was the sea, where the fleet kept pace with the army.

Gelimer was caught unawares. He was staying at a royal estate in Byzacium when he learned of the Byzantine landing. But he reacted swiftly. He sent word to his brother Ammata in Carthage to kill Hilderic and his followers, who were imprisoned there, and to order his men to action. His strategy was sound enough. He planned to trap Belisarius in a natural defile at the tenth Roman milestone from Carthage. Ammata was to attack from the front, and himself from the rear, while another brother, Gibamund, would circle around and attack from the left. The action at the Tenth Milestone (Ad Decimum) was a battle of mounted troops, for Belisarius' infantry remained in camp, and that was where the Vandal strength lay.

But the plan went awry. The Vandal scouts made contact with the Byzantine army while it was still about 45 kilometres from Carthage and for four days the two armies continued a wary advance to the locale of Ad Decimum, which is now covered by the northern suburbs of modern Tunis. The battle took place on 13 September, which was the eve of the feast of St Cyprian, but instead of the concerted effort Gelimer had planned, it was a series of isolated engagements. Ammata left Carthage too soon without his whole force, and he was defeated and killed by John the Armenian. Gibamund's force fled and Gelimer himself, unmanned by grief at the discovery of his brother Ammata's body on the battlefield, threw away his one chance for victory.

The road was open to Carthage. The city walls had been rebuilt in 425, in the last years of Roman dominion, but the Vandals had neglected them and the city could not stand siege. The populace welcomed the victors. Belisarius was careful to keep his army under firm discipline: he allowed no violence that might have alienated popular opinion. The Byzantine fleet sailed around Cap Bon and most of the ships preferred the Bay of Utica as an anchorage instead of the small harbour of Carthage known as the Mandracium. The victory had given the navy a safe haven just as the sailing season came to an end. The victory also decided the Berber sheikhs who had been waiting to see which side would win; now they sent envoys to offer allegiance to Justinian and ask for imperial investiture in return.

On 15 September, Belisarius entered Carthage, took possession of Gelimer's palace in the emperor's name and sat upon Gelimer's throne. Gelimer had ordered a banquet prepared to celebrate the triumph he anticipated and now Belisarius and his officers feasted on it. Meanwhile, at St Cyprian's basilica, the Arians fled, and for the first time in two generations, the Catholics celebrated the festival of the martyr Cyprian there, only one day late.[6]

In the meantime, the Vandal expeditionary force which had suppressed the revolt in Sardinia returned, and Tata rejoined his brother. Gelimer moved on Carthage, but although Belisarius had not yet had time to complete repairs on the walls, and the city might have fallen easily enough to an enemy equipped with a siege train, the Vandals were horsemen, and the best Gelimer could do was to blockade the city by land and cut its great aqueduct. He also tried to contact the Arian troops in Belisarius' army and win them over. The Arian clergy had for the most part fled Carthage along with the Vandals, but thus far, the anti-Arian character of the Byzantine expedition had been very low-key. It seems that Justinian thought initially that the Arian clergy could be integrated peacefully into the Catholic hierarchy, and changed his mind later only under pressure from the African bishops seconded by the pope. At this point, Gelimer's attempt to tamper with the loyalty of the Arian troops came to nothing, but Belisarius took it seriously.

Some three months after the victory at the Tenth Milestone, which gave the Byzantines the city of Carthage, the decisive engagement took place that ended the Vandal kingdom. The Vandals had encamped with their wives, children and treasure about 30 kilometres from Carthage, at a place called Tricamarum which was protected by a small stream. The actual site is unknown, but probably it commanded the main road to Numidia. The Vandals apparently neglected to fortify their camp; their earlier defeat had not taught them prudence. The Byzantine vanguard under John the Armenian with all but 500 of the cavalry made contact with the enemy first, and camped close by, waiting for Belisarius to come up with the infantry and the rest of the horse. But the next day near noon, the Vandals drew up a battle line behind the stream, and repelled two feints against their centre led by John the Armenian, but without moving from their defensive position. But the third charge resulted in a fierce struggle along the whole front. All the Byzantine cavalry moved in and joined battle (Belisarius had joined the vanguard with his horse just as the action began, leaving the slower infantry to catch up). The Vandal centre sagged, Gelimer's brother, Tata, fell fighting and the rout began. At this point, the two companies of Bulgar mounted bowmen in Belisarius' army, whose loyalty was precarious and who were ready to swing over to the victor once they perceived who he would be, joined in the pursuit, and the Vandals fled to their camp.

Now, towards evening, the Byzantine infantry came up, and Belisarius advanced against the Vandal camp. Gelimer's nerve broke. He mounted his horse and fled, and as soon as his departure was known, the Vandals fled after him, leaving a great wealth of booty behind them. The Byzantine troops abandoned all order and turned their attention to plunder, for they were all penniless men, and here were the riches of Vandal Africa before them for the taking. Had the Vandals rallied and counterattacked, they must certainly have won the day. But Gelimer was galloping along the road to Numidia.

The end came quickly. John the Armenian pursued Gelimer hotly for five days, but then he was killed accidentally by one of his own men who aimed an arrow at a bird while he was drunk, and struck down his own commander instead. Gelimer found refuge among the Moors who lived on Mt Papua near the western edge of Numidia, probably in the Kroumirie range. Meanwhile, Belisarius advanced as far as Hippo Regius, where Gelimer had deposited his own treasure for safekeeping, and dispatched a force to take Sardinia and Corsica.

Winter was at hand, and Belisarius returned to Carthage, handing over the siege of Mt Papua to a Herul officer named Pharas. Three months passed: terrible months for Gelimer who, like most of the Vandals, had come to love luxury, and now had to endure the austere life of the Moors. Pharas invited him to surrender but Gelimer declined: he asked only that Pharas send him a loaf of bread, a lyre and a sponge. The messenger who brought Pharas Gelimer's strange request explained: the loaf Gelimer wanted because he had not seen one since the siege of Mt Papua began, the sponge he wanted to wash his eyes, which had become swollen, and the lyre was to accompany the ode which he had composed on his misfortune. Pharas wept for the king and sent him what he wanted, but he did not slacken the siege a whit.

When spring came, Gelimer at last accepted Belisarius' assurances that he need have no fear for his own safety, and surrendered.

Belisarius was staying in a suburb of Carthage when Gelimer was brought to him, and according to Procopius, the Vandal king laughed uncontrollably. Some thought him mad, but his friends said that his mind was sound; he was laughing merely at the caprice of fortune which had granted him royal birth and great wealth, and then brought him low. Four generations after Gaiseric, the Vandal kingdom had been brought down with astonishing ease.

Justinian must have waited anxiously for news of the victory that he hoped for. By 21 November 533, however, he knew of the capture of Carthage, for on that day he issued the decree which introduced his *Institutes*, and its third sentence reads:

> The barbarian peoples who have passed under our yoke have come to learn of our warlike labours, and witness to them are both Africa and countless other provinces, which by our victories won by Divine Grace, have been restored to Roman rule within our empire.

and in the preamble the titles of Justinian proclaim himself victor not merely over the Alamanni, Goths, Franks, Germans, Antai and Alans, but over the Vandals and the Africans as well. He had grasped the chance to invade Vandal Africa, and his move was vindicated.

Yet the emperor must also have felt a degree of apprehension, for he received a secret message from some officers that Belisarius was plotting to set himself up as an independent king in Africa. He moved with circumspection. He sent back another commander, Solomon, who had reported back to Constantinople after the capture of Carthage, and he let Belisarius know that he might accompany Gelimer and the other Vandal captives to Constantinople, or, if he preferred, he might send them on and remain in Africa himself. But Belisarius had learned about the denunciation. He was anxious to return to the capital, and even though the Moors in Byzacena and Numidia broke out in revolt before he left, he handed over his command to Solomon and set sail.

In Constantinople, the victory was celebrated with a triumph which recalled the traditions of imperial Rome, in particular the triumph of the emperor Vespasian's son, Titus, over the Jews. The comparison was fitting: the procession of Titus through Rome to the Temple of Jupiter on the Capitol put on public display the treasures taken in AD 70 from the Temple of Herod in Jerusalem, and the Vandal triumph in Constantinople exhibited the same treasure, which Belisarius had found in Carthage. The parade started at Belisarius' house, but Belisarius processed on foot, not in a chariot, and the culmination of the triumph took place in the Hippodrome: having reached its entrance near the starting gates for the chariot races, the parade made its way down the arena to the imperial box, where Gelimer was stripped of his purple, and both he and Belisarius prostrated themselves before Justinian and Theodora. This was the climax of the triumph and it contrasted sharply with the ancient triumphs which it recalled: where the triumphant general in pagan Rome had laid down his command before Jupiter Optimus Maximus, in the Christian empire, he humbled himself before the emperor and his empress. Gelimer himself snatched a modicum of dignity from defeat: when he reached the Hippodrome and saw the crowds and the imperial pair in their box, he repeated over and over the verse from *Ecclesiastes*, 'Vanity of vanities, all is vanity.'[7] His enforced stay on Mt Papua had given him time to adapt the story of his downfall to poetry, and in his defeat, he assumed the persona of a hero from Germanic saga, and accepted his fate with words that suited the occasion.[8]

But Justinian did Gelimer no harm. He was granted an estate in Galatia and allowed to live there with his family. Some 2,000 able-bodied Vandal prisoners were conscripted into five battalions called the *Vandali Justiniani* and sent to the Persian front. The treasures from the Temple, including the Menorah, the seven-branched candlestick, were returned to Jerusalem on the advice of a leading member of the Jewish community in Constantinople, and there they remained lodged in various Christian churches until the Persian sack of 618. As for Belisarius, he was honoured with the consulship for the next year, 535, and his inaugural celebration on New Year's Day was a reprise of his triumph. Justinian had another conquest in mind for him.

These must have been months of high hopes and anticipations. Justinian had moved to organize his new conquest even before word reached him of Gelimer's surrender. By a rescript dated to April, 534, he created an African prefecture with an accompanying bureaucracy.[9] The capital was to be Carthage and the first prefect was the patrician Archelaos, who was already in Africa as paymaster of the army. But by New Year's Day, Solomon had returned as praetorian prefect and commander of the army, and thereafter the military and civil jurisdictions in Africa were never separated.[10] It was a symptom of the future.

Justinian's rescripts of April, 534 show that he intended to re-occupy all of Roman Africa as it had existed before the Vandal conquest, but much of the area was still controlled by the Berbers. Most of them had come to terms after the fall of Carthage, and some had given hostages. But their wise women had predicted that the Berber conquerer would be a beardless Roman general, which foreshadowed the coming of Solomon who was a eunuch. Belisarius' staff had full beards, and the Berbers concluded that their conquest was not yet fated. The Libyan landowners had reason for apprehension too, for under the Vandals the tax-collection system had fallen apart, and with the new regime, the imperial tax assessors arrived to restore it. Solomon faced a crisis. The Berbers were plundering Byzacium freely and a detachment of cavalry had already been wiped out.

Solomon advanced into Byzacium, made contact with the Berber camp on the south-east fringe of the Tunisian Dorsal and there fought a pitched battle which was a complete victory. But no sooner had he returned to Carthage for the winter than word came that the Berbers were again plundering Byzacium. Next spring, Solomon brought them to battle on the lower peak of an unidentified mountain called Bourgaon, defeated them again, and captured so many women and children that a Berber slave boy could be purchased for the price of a sheep. Except for the sheikh of the Frexes, Antalas, and his clan, who were still loyal allies, the Berbers left Byzacium and retreated south to the Aurès massif on the Sahara rim, a forbidding range to one approaching it from the north,[11] where bare mountain peaks alternated with cultivable valleys. There the sheikh Iaudas had his base from which he raided the plains south of Constantine. In the summer of 535, a small Byzantine garrison gave him a trouncing as he returned from a *razzia*, and he retreated into the Jebel Aurès where Solomon tried to run him down. But he accomplished little in 535. He distrusted his guides, and prudently withdrew to winter in Carthage, and prepare for a campaign next spring.

However, the plan went awry. On Easter Day (March 23), 536, a mutiny broke out in the army.

Solomon's troops were a multicultural group that included at least 1,000 Arians. Justinian's initial impulse had been tolerant: his rescripts of 534 had allowed the Arian priests to retain their posts, but by the next year, the urging of the Catholic bishops had hardened his attitude. Church property still in Arian hands was to be returned forthwith. Non-Catholics, soldiers not excepted, were denied the right to religious services, and barred from public office. Quite naturally, when the Vandal priests complained, the Arian troops lent a sympathetic ear. In addition, some soldiers had married Vandal heiresses, and were anxious to retain their wives' estates. Justinian's regulation that allowed the descendants of landowners evicted by the Vandals to reclaim their lands affected them directly. Then too, there was the problem that was becoming increasingly prevalent: army pay was in arrears.

But what sparked the mutiny was the denial of the sacraments to the Arians at Easter.[12] Solomon, all unsuspecting, would have been murdered at the Easter service if his assassins had not lost their nerve, but five days later the army gathered in the hippodrome, chose as leader Theodore of Cappadocia, one of Solomon's officers whom they believed was at odds with Solomon, and then turned to looting and rioting. But Theodore was not disloyal, and with his connivance, Solomon escaped to Sicily to join Belisarius, who had just conquered the island.

The rebels, meanwhile, withdrew from Carthage and chose a more committed leader, Stotzas, who moved to reoccupy Carthage, and the city was on the point of surrender when Belisarius appeared, with 100 of his *bucellarii*.

Of the city garrison, only 2,000 were reliable, but with these Belisarius moved to the attack. At Membrasa on the road to Numidia, he brought the mutineers to battle with the *sirocco* blowing in their faces, and sent them off down the road in flight. But Belisarius' own army in Sicily was mutinous, and he could not stay. Meanwhile, the troops in Numidia made common cause with the rebels and killed their officers.

In the crisis, Justinian turned to his cousin Germanus, no favourite of Theodora's, but at this juncture, Justinian needed a commander of prestige and ability. Germanus arrived to find that only a third of the army, the portion garrisoning Carthage and other African cities, remained loyal.[13] Stotzas outnumbered his forces by more than two to one. So Germanus' first move was to win back as many mutineers as he could, with pay and promises, and he succeeded well enough that Stotzas decided to attempt a battle in the hope that Germanus' men would refuse to fight their old comrades-in-arms. But Germanus' troops did not waver, and Stotzas retreated again to Numidia, pursued by Germanus. He brought his quarry to battle at a site called Cellas Vatari (*mod.* Fedj es-Siouda?). It was a furious struggle, but it ended with the rout of the mutineers. The Berbers, who up to this point had watched the action as neutral onlookers, joined in pursuing the mutineers and pillaging their camp.

Germanus returned to Carthage to face another plot led by one of the bodyguards of Theodore of Cappadocia. But Germanus was warned in time. The conspirators were killed or captured in the hippodrome where they had gathered, and the leader of the mutiny was crucified close by the walls of Carthage. For nearly two years Africa remained calm.

THE INVASION OF ITALY

Once Theodoric was dead, the frailties of the Ostrogothic regime soon became apparent. Theodoric's successor, his grandson Athalaric, was still a child, and his mother Amalasuintha ruled as regent. She was an accomplished woman, fluent in Greek, Latin and Gothic, and well grounded in the humanities,[14] but she sparked no great enthusiasm among the Goths: not only was she a woman but she was also too pro-Roman. She reversed the anti-Roman policies of Theodoric's last years and conciliated the senate: thus when the senators and the Roman people swore loyalty to young Athalaric, he in return promised the Romans good government. The properties expropriated from Boethius and Symmachus were returned to their families. Quite possibly Amalasuintha envisaged the cultural fusion of Romans and Goths, and among a few Goths, the fusion was already beginning to take place. Amalasuintha was already half-assimilated. She had had a Roman education herself and that was what she wanted for her son.

Athalaric's education was delegated to three civilized Gothic gentlemen who were versed in the humanities. But Theodoric's retainers had their own traditions, and they included drinking and fighting more than classical learning. There was a tradition that Theodoric himself could not write his name, though that may have been a myth designed to gratify the Goths, for he spent his formative years from the age of 7 to 18 at the imperial court in Constantinople and it is hard to understand how he could have avoided all learning.[15] The Goths insisted that their young king have a genuinely Gothic upbringing. He was given Gothic youths as friends, and learned how to become a drunken lecher.

Dissatisfaction with Amalasuintha increased. Discovering a plot against her, she found tasks for three of the ringleaders at separate locations on the northern frontier, but the conspiracy remained alive nonetheless. So she contacted Justinian and requested sanctuary with him if she should need it. Justinian readily agreed. Thus reassured, she laid her plans carefully, dispatching to Dyrrhachium a ship with loyal retainers and her possessions, including a large sum of gold, while at the same time commissioning the assassination of the three conspirators. The assassinations took place as planned; Amalasuintha summoned back the ship and stayed in Ravenna.

But she was increasingly isolated. Athalaric's Gothic education had destroyed his health, and in October 534, he died. Amalasuintha turned to the last male scion of the Amal house, the son of Theodoric's sister Amalafrida who had died in a Vandal prison. Theodahad was a Tuscan landholder with a reputation for philosophy, particularly Platonism, and one that was more deserved as a grasping proprietor who seized property illegally both from his neighbours and from the royal estates. Amalasuintha had already brought him to book, and earned his hatred by making him repay his illegal gains. But there was no other ally available. Amalasuintha proposed an *entente*: she would rule, but Theodahad would be king in name. Theodahad swore to cooperate, and Amalasuintha addressed a letter reporting the partnership to the Roman senate. 'Rejoice, now, fathers of the Senate', she wrote,

> and make your prayers for us to the heavenly grace, since I have appointed as my fellow prince a man who will both execute the good deeds that spring from my justice and display what belongs to his own devotion.[16]

She could hardly have been more mistaken. Before her envoys could report her action to Justinian, Theodahad had thrown her into prison, and dispatched his own delegation to Constantinople to reassure the emperor.

Meanwhile Justinian, still unaware of Athalaric's death, had sent his own envoy, Peter, ostensibly to negotiate about Lilybaeum (*mod.* Marsala) in Sicily, which the Goths refused to surrender,[17] but also to carry on some private bargaining with Theodahad and Amalasuintha. Peter met Amalasuintha's envoys at Thessaloniki and learned of Theodahad's accession, and shortly afterwards, while he was waiting at Valona on the shore of the Adriatic for the weather to allow him to cross to Italy, he met Theodahad's embassy and learned that Amalasuintha was in prison and her life in danger. He reported to Justinian, who gave him a letter full of support for Amalasuintha, which he was instructed to make public. But before Peter reached Ravenna, Amalasuintha was dead, strangled in her island prison on Lake Bolsena. Theodahad claimed that the murder was done without his approval, but the honour he paid her assassins argued for his complicity.

The Roman senatorial class watched with ambivalence. Its members had collaborated with the Goths and in return had maintained their status and much of their wealth, but now there was an orthodox emperor in Constantinople and in Ravenna, a corrupt, vicious king. The performance of Theodahad's embassy is a case in point. It was composed of senators, headed by Liberius and Opilio, the former of whom had served both Odoacer and Theodoric. On reaching Constantinople, all denounced Theodahad except Opilio, whose family connections with the Ostrogothic court were too great.[18] Liberius switched sides with impeccable timing, maintaining all the while his reputation for integrity. He moved into Justinian's service, where he continued his long public career: in 550, we find him, aged 85, leading a military force to Sicily and Spain!

However, there was intrigue behind the scenes. Our best source, Procopius, reports for publication that Peter arrived too late to do anything more than denounce Amalasuintha's murder, but the *Secret History* adds that Theodora feared Amalasuintha: if she were in Constantinople, her beauty and culture might give her an influence at court that outweighed Theodora's own, and so she bribed Peter to arrange her death. The source is malevolent, but we cannot dismiss the story completely. There are two odd letters in Cassiodorus' *Variae*, his carefully expurgated collection of state papers. One of them, from Theodahad's wife, Gudeliva, is addressed to Theodora. It contains a curious reference to 'an affair . . . which should make me still dearer to your justice'. The other, from Theodahad himself addressed to Theodora, refers to his ordering 'what I trust will agree with your intention' in the case of 'that person'.[19] The dates of both are the spring of 535, not long after the murder, and two years before the publication of the *Variae*. Peter, who was allegedly Theodora's agent, received the title of 'patrician' not much later and thereafter enjoyed Theodora's favour.[20] The verdict of a Scots judge on Theodora's guilt would be 'not proven' rather than 'innocent'.

For that matter, Justinian's indignation was contrived to some degree. He now had grounds for invading Italy. His policy was opportunist, but his success in Africa had given him confidence. Theodahad appealed for peace. So, under duress, did the Roman senate. So did Pope Agapetus, who was dispatched to Constantinople at his own expense, where he seized the opportunity to correct any diffidence Justinian had about the truth of the Chalcedonian doctrine. But on the question of Italy, Justinian's mind was made up.[21]

The attack was two-pronged. Mundo, Master of Soldiers in Illyricum, moved against Dalmatia, defeated the Goths and captured Salona, near modern Split. Belisarius landed at Catania in Sicily with a small army less than half the size of the expeditionary force he had led against the Vandal kingdom. His subordinate commanders were Bessas, a Goth from Thrace, no longer young, Constantine, a Thracian, and Peranius, a prince of the royal family of Iberia which had fled to Rome. His orders were to take Sicily if it could be done with no great effort, but if he met stubborn resistance, he should sail for Carthage.

However, Justinian was confident. Overconfident, as it turned out. The Vandal conquest had been easy, and the Ostrogothic regime was tottering. At first, the campaign went well. Only at Panormus (*mod.* Palermo) did the Gothic garrison put up any resistance. Belisarius, who held the consulship for 535, made his entry into Syracuse on 31 December, and there, on the last day of the year, he laid down the office.

The loss of Sicily left Theodahad in a state of consternation. He struck an agreement with Justinian's wily negotiator, Peter. Peter was to propose that Theodahad cede the independence of Ostrogothic Italy and rule as a subordinate. But if that did not do, Peter was authorized to offer surrender, in return for an estate which would yield a satisfactory revenue: 86,400 *solidi per annum*: a not ungenerous sum, since a poor man might feed himself on 2 *solidi* a year. Justinian rejected the first offer and accepted the second. Belisarius in Sicily was told to prepare to take control of Italy, and Peter was sent back to Ravenna to look after the details of carrying out the agreement.

But Theodahad's confidence had revived. A Gothic army had gone to Dalmatia, where it caught Mundo's son Maurice scouting with a small force and killed him. Mundo, overwhelmed with grief, had attacked the Goths and routed them, but was killed himself in the pursuit. Gothic reinforcements arrived and occupied Salona, but their leaders were cautious, and Mundo's successor, Constantinian, Count of the Stable, retrieved the situation easily enough. The Gothic army retired to Ravenna. But for the moment, Theodahad thought it safe to blink at his agreement and detain Justinian's envoys. Belisarius received orders to invade Italy.

Just after Easter, however, Solomon arrived from Carthage with news of the mutiny in Africa, and Belisarius took time out for his swift campaign against the rebels. But on his return, he crossed the

Strait of Messina. The Gothic corps guarding the crossing was commanded by Theodahad's son-in-law, who deserted to Belisarius and was made a patrician as a reward. Belisarius' advance encountered no resistance until he reached Naples. The Neapolitans felt no joy at Belisarius' arrival: the Jews in the city, who knew Justinian's reputation for intolerance, were devoted Gothic loyalists, and as for the Catholic citizens, whatever their private feelings may have been, it was important to be on the winning side.

Naples fell after a siege of twenty days. Winter was approaching and Belisarius was about to abandon the siege and make for Rome, when an Isaurian soldier discovered that the Naples aqueduct, if widened at one spot, would give passage into the city. At nightfall on the last day of the siege, a picked group of some 400 men crept through the aqueduct, killed the guards in two towers on the north rampart and then signalled the rest of the army to storm the wall. The city fell in a welter of plunder and slaughter in which the Bulgars particularly distinguished themselves, and it did not cease until Belisarius himself intervened.

Theodahad, who was in Rome, might have saved Naples, but he ignored the appeals of the Neapolitans and did nothing. The Goths suspected him of treason. They met in assembly at a locale half-way between Rome and Naples, and chose another king, raising him on a shield amidst drawn swords, according to German custom. Their choice, Witigis, was an unassuming man, not of the royal Amal house but a soldier who had fought with some distinction under Theodoric.[22] Theodahad fled for Ravenna, but Witigis sent in pursuit a Goth with a private grudge against him, and Theodahad was over-taken and butchered like a sacrificial victim.

Then Witigis entered Rome, and held a council. There were two immediate dangers, Belisarius in Naples and the Franks in the north, whom Justinian had incited to attack. The bulk of the Ostrogothic army was in Provence and Venetia. Witigis' next move must have seemed not unwise at the time. Belisarius' little army was less formidable than the Franks at the moment, and Witigis had to regroup. He left a force of 4,000 troops in Rome and left for Ravenna, having first extracted oaths of loyalty from Pope Silverius, the senate and the people. The pope owed his election to Theodahad's pressure, and the Goths counted on his fidelity.

In Ravenna, Witigis married Amalasuintha's daughter, Matasuintha, much against her will, and undertook to buy off the Franks. Theodahad had already offered them the lands in Gaul which the Ostrogoths claimed, and 2,000 gold pounds in return for their help, and Witigis concurred. The three Frankish kings were happy to take the territory and the money, but they were as embarrassed as the Merovingian Franks ever were by the fact that they had already agreed to help Justinian. So to avoid breaking their pact with the empire, they promised to provide the Goths with auxiliaries from tributary tribes. In the meantime, Belisarius advanced on Rome. The pope, his loyalty oath notwithstanding, urged the Romans to avoid a siege and invite the Byzantine army into the city. So on 9 December, 536, Belisarius entered by the Porta Asinaria near the cathedral church of Rome, St John Lateran, and at the same time, the Gothic garrison withdrew by the Porta Flaminia. Leuderis, the Gothic commander, remained behind, and Belisarius sent him along with the keys of the city to Justinian.

Then Belisarius prepared to stand siege. The Romans had never imagined such a consequence of their welcome for Belisarius. The walls of Rome had a circuit of 18.8 kilometres: too long for Belisarius' little force of 5,000 to man adequately. Probably Belisarius never expected a siege as long and difficult as it was, while in Constantinople, Justinian still dreamed of an easy conquest. But the siege was to last a year and nine days. Witigis had with him 150,000 men, most of them mailed horsemen, or at least that is what is reported by Procopius,[23] who saw his army. He exaggerates: no doubt the Goths greatly outnumbered the Byzantines, but not by thirty to one.

Belisarius himself almost fell into Gothic hands before the siege began. The Gothic army reached the Ponte Salario over the Anio where Belisarius had built an outpost to slow the Gothic advance. But the garrison panicked and slipped away during the night. Next day Belisarius, having heard nothing of the garrison's flight, rode out with 1,000 horse to the bridge and encountered the Goths. Deserters recognized his mount and urged the Goths to aim at him. But Belisarius and his contingent escaped with heavy losses, and got back to the Porta Salaria where the guards refused to admit them. Word had reached Rome that Belisarius was dead, and the guards could not believe that this horseman covered with sweat and dirt was he. Belisarius then turned and charged his pursuers, who pulled back in fright, and with this exploit he succeeded in persuading the guards to open the gate. It was a near thing.

The Goths built seven camps around the city, one on the west of the Tiber in the Vatican area, and the rest to the east of the river.

Rome was too large for them to envelop completely, and as it turned out, the blockade was somewhat negligent. The Romans soon began to suffer discomfort. The aqueducts were cut, and the great baths ceased to function. The aqueducts had supplied water power for Rome's flour mills, but Belisarius improvised a substitute: he moored two boats with mills on them two feet apart in the middle of the Tiber, and suspended a water wheel between them where the force of the current turned it. The Romans followed his example, and these floating mills provided all the flour needed.

The siege dragged on. The Romans were unused to the sufferings they had to endure, and Witigis, learning of their discontent, sent envoys to offer Belisarius safe conduct if he would evacuate the city. Belisarius' reply was a stern refusal. Then Witigis launched a massive assault, which was driven back. The chief casualties on the Byzantine side were the statues which had adorned the Mausoleum of Hadrian, which stood just beyond the Aurelian Gate. The defenders threw them down on the heads of the enemy, who attacked protected by large shields. The Goths almost succeeded in setting their scaling ladders against the wall, but in the end, they failed and retreated with heavy losses.[24]

The next day, Belisarius ordered the women, children and those slaves not needed to man the walls to leave the city. The Goths did not dare to leave the safety of their camps to prevent the departure, for Belisarius followed a strategy of keeping them on the defensive with constant sallies, and the Berber units were particularly effective. The able-bodied Romans were conscripted into the companies guarding the wall, and paid a wage which gave them the where-withal to buy food. Witigis in his turn ordered the death of the Roman senators whom he kept as hostages at Ravenna, and seized Portus, the harbour built by the emperor Trajan just north of the Tiber mouth, and connected to Rome by a good road and a towpath so that barges could be pulled upstream by ox teams. The older harbour at Ostia was unsatisfactory, and dangerous once Portus had a strong Gothic garrison. Supply ships for Rome had to put in at Anzio, a day's journey distant.

Some three weeks later, a force of 1,600 cavalry, mostly Bulgars and Slavs, reached Rome, and Belisarius decided to risk a pitched battle outside the walls. Procopius, who was still Belisarius' *assessor* and admirer, wrote that his hero was pushed into it by the clamour of his soldiers, but he was probably willing enough. There was a chance of success, and it was worth taking: supplies were getting low and though the reinforcements were welcome, their small number was disappointing. Belisarius committed both his cavalry and infantry, which included the Roman militia, many of them without full armour, fighting under the command of two of Belisarius' *bucellarii*. It was a hard battle, but in the end, the Goths drove the Byzantine forces back to the city walls. Belisarius did not dare try again. He resumed his former tactics: constant sallies by mounted troops, and whenever he used foot soldiers, they attacked in company with the cavalry.

About the spring equinox, money arrived from the emperor to pay the soldiers, and about the same time, famine and disease began to take their toll. The Gothic blockade grew tighter. They fortified a place a few kilometres south of Rome where two aqueducts crisscrossed, and stationed some 7,000 men there to prevent supplies entering the city from Campania. The Romans could subsist for a while on greens that were grown within the walls, or grain which some soldiers gathered on night raids and sold – there was even a black market for sausages made from dead mules – but soon there was nothing left in the fields near Rome, and the greens had to be shared with the horses, which needed fodder. The Romans begged for another battle, and promised that every able-bodied Roman would fight alongside Belisarius' troops. Belisarius refused. But he announced that the emperor had a great army and fleet on its way, and he expected it in a few days.

The 'great army and fleet' was the product of rumour, but Belisarius was desperate enough that he ordered Procopius to slip out of the city and go to Naples to discover if the rumour was true, and in any case to gather whatever soldiers and grain he could and ship them to Ostia. He sent out patrols to cut off Gothic foraging parties, seizing what strongholds they could in Latium to serve as bases for their sallies, and he dispatched his wife Antonina to Terracina with 1,000 horsemen: Antonina was to continue to Naples, and the cavalry was to use Terracina as a base for raids on the Gothic supply trains. The result was that the Goths, too, began to feel the pressure of famine and disease.

In Naples, Antonina found that Procopius had mustered 500 troops and had a convoy of grain transports loaded and ready. But the reinforcements did not arrive until November: 3,000 Isaurians, 800 Thracian horsemen led by John, the nephew of Vitalian, and 1,000 regular cavalry. From Naples, the Isaurians continued by sea to Ostia, and the rest headed overland for Rome at the head of a supply train. To prevent interception by the Goths, Belisarius made a surprise attack in force on the Gothic camp nearest the Flaminian Gate, so that the Goths were occupied north of the city while the supply train entered on the south side of the city. 'And immediately the barbarians gave up the war as hopeless', wrote Procopius,[25] 'and considered how they might retreat from Rome.' The Goths sought peace, offering Sicily and part of Italy – Campania and Naples – and yearly tribute, but Belisarius would not negotiate. However, he accepted an armistice, so that Witigis' envoys could go to Justinian himself.

Meanwhile, the convoy from Naples reached Ostia with its grain cargoes and 3,000 Isaurian troops, and the Goths did not interfere with the trans-shipment to Rome. Then the arrangements were completed for a truce of three months: hostages were exchanged and the safety of Witigis' envoys to Justinian guaranteed. Rome now had food, and the Goths were on short rations, so much so that Witigis removed his garrisons from Portus, Città Vecchia and Albani, all of which the Byzantines promptly occupied, truce or not. John, the nephew of Vitalian, whom Belisarius found a difficult colleague, was sent to winter in Picenum, which was empty of Gothic warriors, for they were all at Rome. John's orders were to remain quiet for the moment, but if word came that the Goths had broken the truce, he should raid Picenum, plunder the estates of the Goths, and enslave their women and children, but do the Romans no harm.

The Goths soon broke the truce. First they were discovered trying to penetrate the city by the empty aqueduct called the Aqua Virgo which entered Rome from the north. A guard spotted what he thought was the glint of a wolf's eyes through a chink in the masonry, and when word of this came to Belisarius, he ordered the aqueduct explored, and found evidence of lamps and torches which the Gothic sappers had used. Then there was an open attack on the Porta Pinciana, which was repelled, and finally an attempt to bribe two Romans to drug the guards on the low north-west section of the circuit wall on the Tiber bank, where attack was not expected. One of the Romans betrayed the plot. Belisarius judged the truce broken and unleashed John in Picenum.

John swept aside a Gothic army and killed its commander, Ulitheus, Witigis' uncle. He bypassed Osimo and Urbino, which were hill towns strongly held by the Goths, but at Rimini, the Romans opened the gates. Rimini was only a day's march from Ravenna, and John thought that when word of the threat to Ravenna reached Witigis, he would raise the siege of Rome and hurry to save his capital. But he had ignored Belisarius' strict orders to leave no stronghold in Gothic hands in his rear. John was a bold, independent commander, in no way overawed by Belisarius' reputation, and trouble was brewing. It did not help, perhaps, that when Witigis' reluctant wife in Ravenna, Matasuintha, learned that John was only a day's journey distant, she was delighted and contacted him with an offer of marriage and betrayal of the city.

As John hoped, the Goths did retreat from Rome, suffering heavy losses as they crossed the Milvian Bridge under assault from Belisarius' troops. It was mid-March, 538, and the terrible first siege of Rome was at an end.

Through it all, Roman sentiment remained with the Byzantines.[26] Roman militia manned the walls and fought alongside the Byzantine troops in one pitched battle, and if they had had their way, they would have fought a second. However, the treatment which Belisarius and Antonina had meted out to Pope Silverius must have given them pause. It had been Silverius who had urged them to open their gates to Belisarius and his army in the first place. But not long after the siege began, Procopius' *History* notes briefly that Silverius came under suspicion of collaborating with the Goths, and Belisarius removed him, exiled him to Greece and appointed a successor, Vigilius.[27] The *Secret History*[28] adds the information that Silverius was a victim of Theodora's intrigue, with Antonina acting as her agent, and promises to tell all in a later narrative. The promise is not kept.

Vigilius was a deacon who had accompanied Pope Agapetus to Constantinople, where the pope refused to communicate with Theodora's henchman, the patriarch Anthimus, had him deposed and then died before he could return home. Anthimus went into hiding in Theodora's apartments, where he remained until Theodora died. Vigilius was an ambitious Roman aristocrat: the papal throne had been almost within his grasp once before when Boniface II died in 532,[29] and now he intimated to Theodora that he was willing to help her in return for her favour. But when he got back to Rome, he found that Silverius had already been chosen pope. Yet the empress did not find that an insurmountable obstacle. Silverius, who refused to recognize Anthimus as adamantly as his predecessor, found himself accused of treason. A letter was produced which showed that he was plotting to betray Rome to the Goths. Belisarius summoned him to the Pincian palace, and indicated that he could save himself from the perilous position he was in if he followed Theodora's wishes.

But Silverius would not yield. To lessen suspicion, however, he did move from the Lateran palace near one of the city gates to St Sabina on the Aventine some distance from the walls. Belisarius summoned him again. This time he was arraigned before Antonina with Belisarius sitting at her feet, and when he proved as inflexible as ever, he was deposed. Vigilius was duly elected, and ordained bishop of Rome on 29 March, 537.[30]

The unfortunate Silverius was banished to Patara, a city on the south coast of modern Turkey. There the local bishop took up cudgels on his behalf and journeyed to Constantinople to tell Justinian that while the world had many kings, it had only one pope. Justinian was sufficiently moved to order that Silverius be returned to Rome and his treasonable correspondence scrutinized. But when Silverius reached Rome, Belisarius handed him over to his successor, and Vigilius took no chances. He deported Silverius to the little island of Palmaria in the Tyrrhenian Sea some 40 kilometres from the Italian coast, and there Silverius starved to death before the year was out.[31]

The Gothic army that retreated from Rome moved slowly north-wards towards Rimini, foraging along the way, and pausing to leave garrisons in places like Orvieto, Chiusi, Todi, Urbino and Osimo. Belisarius sent 1,000 horse under Ildiger and Martin directly to Rimini, with orders that the defence of Rimini should be handed over to a company of infantry drawn from soldiers who had just arrived at Ancona. John's squadron of 2,000 horse would then serve as a mobile force that could harass the Goths if they laid siege to Rimini. Martin and Ildiger moved north swiftly, forcing the Gothic fortress at Petra Pertusa (*mod.* Passo di Furlo) and reaching Rimini, only to find John quite unwilling to obey orders. So Martin and Ildiger departed to report to Belisarius, taking with them the company of Belisarius' *bucellarii* that had been serving under John. By April, Rimini was under siege.

Belisarius acted with due deliberation. During the winter of 537–538, while the truce was in force, the metropolitan bishop of Milan had come to Rome leading a little embassy of notables, and told Belisarius that a handful of troops could take the province of Liguria and its metropolis without difficulty. Once spring arrived and the siege of Rome was abandoned, Belisarius sent Mundilas, one of his bodyguards, with 1,000 Isaurians and Thracians by sea to Genoa, and they quickly took over all Liguria except Pavia. But Milan was soon beleaguered by a large Gothic force led by Witigis' nephew, Uraias, and it was joined by 10,000 Burgundians sent by the Merovingian king of Austrasia, Theodebert. Mundilas had only 300 troops, for the rest of them were distributed among the other towns of Liguria, and so it was the Milanese themselves who bore the brunt of the defence. Meanwhile, in June, 538, Belisarius marched from Rome, took Chiusi and Todi, and was about to attack Orvieto when a new army led by the eunuch Narses and Justin, the Master of Soldiers in Illyricum, reached Ancona.

Narses' star had been rising since the *Nika* riots, when he had shown himself both loyal and effective, and he had proved himself again in Alexandria where Theodora sent him in 535 to confront the fanatical mobs who wanted to unseat the patriarch Theodosius.[32] He was now *praepositus sacri cubiculi,* on a par with the Masters of the Soldiers. He was also a friend of John, the nephew of Vitalian, and dissent with Belisarius arose as soon as the two met to confer at Fermo. Rimini, where John was under siege, could not hold out much longer, but Belisarius argued, with the support of most of the generals, that it was too risky to advance on Rimini with Gothic strongholds still in their rear. After all, as everyone knew, it was John's insubordination which had brought him into his predicament. But Narses pointed out accurately enough that John's insubordination was a separate issue; the real question was whether Rimini, with a large force of cavalry with a first-rate, if disobedient, officer in command, should be allowed to fall into Gothic hands.

Then, while the question was still being argued, a message arrived from John, brought by a soldier who had managed to elude the blockade of Rimini. John stated simply that he could hold out only seven days longer. Belisarius was genuinely worried about a Gothic ambush, or so Procopius[33] would have us believe, but his plans for the relief of Rimini were masterly. He made a three-pronged attack: Ildiger led a force by sea to Rimini, Martin led another along the coast road and Belisarius with Narses took the rest of the army by an inland, mountainous road. It was a well-coordinated assault, and successful: the Goths fled to Ravenna. John emerged, pale and emaciated, from Rimini, and when Belisarius told him that he owed thanks to Ildiger, who commanded the first force to reach the Gothic camp, John replied drily that it was Narses to whom he owed thanks.

The rupture between Narses and Belisarius now became dangerous. Narses declined to accept orders. Belisarius called a staff conference and urged the generals to make a concerted effort to take Osimo with part of the army, and with the other part to raise the siege of Milan. Narses argued that it would be better for his forces to operate separately in the Emilia. Belisarius produced a letter from the emperor, which made it clear that Belisarius was commander-in-chief, and urged all to follow him 'in the interests of our state'. Narses, who was a veteran of bureaucratic warfare, perceived a loop-hole in those last words: Belisarius' plan, he argued, was not in the interests of the state. Thereupon Belisarius sent a force to take Orvieto while he laid siege to the hill town of Urbino, while Narses, considering Urbino impregnable, withdrew his troops, thus cutting the besieging force in two, to the great satisfaction of the Gothic garrison. But they exulted too soon: Urbino was dependent on one spring for its water, and it went dry, leaving the garrison no choice but to surrender. Narses, who had retired to Rimini, learned of Urbino's fall with great chagrin. Belisarius then joined the siege of Orvieto and starved out the defenders.

Famine now stalked central Italy. Sowing and harvesting had become impossible, and in Picenum some 50,000 farmers died. Some turned to cannibalism: in the territory of Rimini, two women who kept a little inn ate seventeen of their lodgers. The eighteenth, who caught them just in time before he was consigned to the cooking pot, extracted their story from them and then killed them. There were more plausible reports of starving people dying as they tried to eat grass. But there was worse to come. In 539, Milan fell, and the Goths, bitter at the disloyalty of the Milanese, slaughtered the adult males, gave the women as slaves to the Burgundians and destroyed the city. It was a disaster which might not have happened if the general staff had worked together, and though Justinian assigned fault to no one, he recalled Narses.

Early in 539, the Goths made a move which portended danger for the empire. They appealed to Persia. They had first tried to secure help from the Lombards beyond the Danube, but the Lombard king was a friend and ally of the emperor. Then they bribed two priests from Liguria to deliver a letter to Khusro, urging him to open a 'second front'. Khusro was a willing listener, and the Gothic message may have brought home to him how overstretched the empire was. But when Justinian discovered that Persia was planning an attack in *Oriens*, the 'Endless Peace' notwithstanding, he recognized the danger, and determined to seek a negotiated peace in Italy. With the keen vision of hindsight, we can see that he was right. But Belisarius wanted Gothic surrender, unconditional or not, and he had his way.

Belisarius laid siege to Osimo and Fiesole and planned to advance against Ravenna after they fell. The two strongholds resisted stubbornly: the Goths in Osimo gave up only after Fiesole fell, and Belisarius paraded the captured leaders of the Fiesole garrison before the walls of Osimo. Finally, overcome by famine and convinced that no help was coming from Ravenna, the Goths surrendered Osimo, and Belisarius moved on Ravenna.

There the Goths were on the horns of a dilemma. The Franks offered help, but they had already proved themselves treacherous allies. While Witigis' nephew, Uraias, had been moving with an army to relieve Fiesole, a huge Frankish army under Theodebert moved into the Po valley, and crossed the Po at Pavia, assisted by the Goths, who imagined that the Franks were coming to help them. Once the Franks held the bridge, they slaughtered the women and children in Pavia, then advanced against Uraias at Tortona, and put his army to flight. The Byzantine commanders at Tortona, Martin and John, seeing the Goths in flight and thinking that Belisarius had arrived unexpectedly, came out to greet him. They encountered a great army of Franks, which routed them. But fortunately what arms failed to achieve, dysentery did. The water of the Po and the oxen which the Franks slaughtered for food made them ill, and they retired across the Alps, having lost about a third of their men to disease.

So with good reason, Witigis and his council hesitated to trust the Franks again. But Ravenna faced hunger. The Po had fallen to an abnormally low level, and was temporarily unnavigable. Arson had destroyed the public granaries in Ravenna; Procopius[34] reports that Belisarius bribed a Roman in Ravenna to set fire to them, but there was also a rumour that Witigis' unhappy wife, Matasuintha, was responsible. Witigis' nephew, Uraias, raised 4,000 men from the Gothic strongholds in the Cottian Alps, but many deserted, for John, the nephew of Vitalian, and Martin managed to capture their families. Uraias could only retire to Pavia and wait. Thus the Goths were ready to negotiate.

What Justinian offered the Goths was Italy north of the Po river, and half the royal treasure. It was a reasonable offer which would have freed imperial resources to meet the anticipated attack of the Persian king, who next year was to destroy Antioch.[35] It would also have preserved Witigis as king of the Ostrogoths, and Witigis had proved himself the sort of leader who would be no great danger to the empire. His kingdom would have been a buffer between Italy south of the Po and the barbarian incursions from the north.

Justinian's offer was shrewd, and it might have saved Italy much anguish. But as it turned out, the Goths found an abler leader, and the war dragged on for fourteen more bitter years. The Italian campaign was to demonstrate the truth of the dictum of Georges Clemenceau, the leader of France in World War I: 'War is too important to be left to generals.'

In this case, the general in question was Belisarius, who wanted an unqualified victory. He refused to put his name to the peace accord, and the Goths, their suspicions aroused, refused to accept a treaty without Belisarius' signature and oath. Belisarius' officers roundly condemned his disobedience, whereupon Belisarius had them all put their opinions in writing so that none of them could try to change the record later. He did this knowing that the Goths were becoming desperate, and sensing a rift between Belisarius and the emperor, the Gothic notables, with Witigis' fearful cooperation, offered Belisarius himself the throne. What they apparently had in mind was the revival of the western imperial office which had lapsed in 476 when Romulus Augustulus was hustled off into retirement, and in some part of his psyche, Belisarius probably found the suggestion more attractive than his *assessor* Procopius was prepared to admit in his *History*.[36] He pretended to accept, though he postponed swearing an oath. He entered Ravenna, sent home those Gothic troops in the city who lived south of the Po, thereby ensuring that the imperials were not outnumbered, and prepared himself to return to Constantinople at the summons of the emperor. It began to dawn upon the Goths that Belisarius had tricked them.

They were soon left in no doubt. Belisarius returned to Constantinople with Witigis, a small company of Gothic prisoners and the royal treasure. Justinian welcomed him with mixed feelings. He was impressed by the Ostrogothic treasure and put it on display for the private viewing of the senate. But the year that Ravenna fell was a season of disaster. In 540, a Persian army sacked the Queen City of the East, Antioch. It was about this time, too, that a horde of Kutrigur Bulgars launched a two-pronged strike into the Balkans: one spearhead pillaged Greece as far south as the Isthmus of Corinth, while the other swept down the Strymon river valley, took the walled city of Cassandra in the Chalcidike and menaced Thessaloniki. Then the horde moved eastwards, forcing the Long Walls and approaching the Theodosian Wall of Constantinople themselves before they withdrew, loaded down with captives, and leaving an unnerved city behind.[37] The optimistic decade of the 530s was petering out, and it may already have occurred to Justinian that a negotiated peace in Italy, of the sort that Belisarius had aborted, might have brought the empire savings more valuable than Theodoric's treasure. John the Cappadocian, who had no sympathy for the western adventure, made no secret of his dislike for Belisarius.[38] He judged the victory in Italy in terms of profit and loss to the treasury, and he was not pleased at the finding.

Belisarius was not granted another triumph like the one after the conquest of Africa. Instead, he was dispatched to deal with the crisis on the eastern front.

In Italy, those Goths who had not surrendered, realizing they had been deceived, determined to fight on. Uraias, Witigis' nephew, declined the crown but suggested the Gothic commander at Verona, Ildibad, whose uncle was king of the Visigoths in Spain. Ildibad's reign was short, though long enough to open a Gothic mint at Ticinum which produced gold coins to pay the Frankish auxiliaries.[39] Uraias' wife, who was beautiful and wealthy, snubbed Ildibad's queen one day at the public baths, and Uraias' murder soon followed. Gothic resentment was bitter, though the assassin of Uraias was not a Goth but a Gepid officer of the royal guard. At this point, certain Rugians who had followed Odoacer into Italy and survived, unassimilated, in northern Italy proclaimed one of their own, Eraric, as king, and the Goths tolerated him for five months. Eraric had a secret scheme to hand over northern Italy to Justinian in return for a generous subsidy and the title of patrician, but before he could accomplish his betrayal, a cabal of Gothic nobles killed him and made Ildibad's nephew, Totila or Baduila, king.[40] Totila was commander at Treviso, and had been so near despair that he was about to surrender the town. He was proclaimed king on the very day that he had agreed to open the gates to the Byzantines. The Goths had at last found a worthy leader, and Italy would pay heavily for Belisarius' duplicity.

NEW BATTLE FRONTS:
REVOLT IN AFRICA, FRESH WAR IN ITALY AND THE PERSIAN OFFENSIVE

Justinian's anticipation of an easy victory over the Ostrogoths had proved to be an error. As the war dragged on in Italy, trouble brewed on other fronts. Africa, the Balkans, the Caucasus region and the Persian frontier all needed attention, and it is to them we must turn next.

First, Africa. In the early summer of 539, the eunuch Solomon returned to Africa as praetorian prefect and Master of the Soldiers. The army in Africa had been bled white, first by Stotzas' mutiny, and second by pressure to get reinforcements to Belisarius when he was besieged in Rome.[41] But in 539, Justinian anticipated a peace settlement in Italy, and decided the time was ripe for a new offensive against the Berbers. He also decided, perhaps at Theodora's urging, that Germanus was not the man to lead it. Hence Solomon was reappointed to Africa, and he came with fresh troops.

Once there, he weeded out any seditious elements still in the African army, and got rid of the remaining Vandals and the Vandal women. Subversives were sent to Constantinople or dispatched to Belisarius in Italy. Prosperity increased and tax revenues along with it, some of which went to rebuild the walls of the African cities, which the Vandals had destroyed. The imperial programme of restoration and reconstruction got under way,[42] and by the summer of 539, Solomon was ready to carry out the offensive against the Berbers which he had intended three years earlier.

The first spearhead, led by Guntarith, a *bucellarius* of Solomon, was defeated at the River Nahr bou Roughal and besieged in its camp, which the Berbers tried to inundate by redirecting the irrigation ditches that were fed by the river, and thus turning the plain around the camp into a swamp. Solomon, not quite 13 kilometres away, came up quickly, and forced the Berbers to withdraw to the foot of the Aurès massif, where he inflicted a sharp defeat on them. Some Berbers then withdrew to Mauretania while others retreated south of the Aurès, but Iaudas himself pulled back to a mountain fortress called Zerboule. Before attacking it, Solomon laid waste the grain lands around Thamugadi to deny the Berbers food. Then he beleaguered Zerboule, which Iaudas' garrison abandoned after three days, and from there he moved against a second stronghold named Toumar, an arid place where he had to ration his troops to one cup of water per day. Toumar fell when an adjutant in Solomon's own detachment started the assault on his own. His comrades joined him, and stormed the fortress.[43]

There was one last Berber stronghold to fall: the rock of Geminus, where Iaudas had placed his treasure and his harem, leaving only one old Moor to guard them, for he thought the place impregnable. One of Solomon's soldiers scaled the rock and cut off the old Moor's head. So ended the Aurès campaign. Iaudas, defeated and wounded, took refuge in Mauretania.[44]

Mauretania Prima or *Stitifensis,* so called after its metropolis Setif, was annexed and Solomon began the construction of a string of forts to protect imperial territory. No doubt most of the funds came from African taxes, though Iaudas' treasure made a contribution. The situation was stable, and Africa appears to have been prosperous. When trouble started again, the cause was the incompetence of one of Theodora's favourites, Sergius, Solomon's nephew, who was appointed duke of Tripolitania with headquarters at Lepcis Magna. In the year of his appointment, the pandemic of bubonic plague reached Africa, but it affected the cities most, and left the nomad Berbers largely unscathed. The plague tipped the balance of power, but it was Sergius who provided the spark for the next burst of Berber insurrection. In 544, he massacred seventy-nine Laguatan subchiefs who had come to Lepcis to receive their customary gifts and honours: he had invited them to a banquet under safe conduct sworn on the Holy Scriptures, but when the Laguatan chiefs aired complaints of how the troops rifled their lands, he would not listen, and the quarrel turned violent. One chief who escaped aroused the Laguatan, who were camped outside the newly built walls of Lepcis.[45] In the skirmish that followed, Sergius was successful, but the day ended with his withdrawal behind the city walls, taking with him a good number of Berber women and children to sell as slaves. The Laguatan rose in rebellion and they were joined by Antalas in Byzacium, whom Solomon had alienated. The insurrection that followed was to take four years to suppress.

In Italy, once Belisarius was recalled, no one was appointed in his place. Constantinian, the Count of the Stables whom we last met as Mundo's successor in Dalmatia, was dispatched to Ravenna with orders to pacify Italy in cooperation with the other generals there, but there was no clear chain of command. The civil administration, however, was vigorous and maladroit. The *discussor* (*logothetes* in Greek) Alexander, nicknamed 'Scissors' because of his skill at clipping coins, arrived in Ravenna to put the finances in order. He proceeded pitilessly. He abolished the retinue of the Roman imperial court, which had survived the Ostrogoths. He introduced John the Cappadocian's money-saving measures, and pursued tax arrears dating back to Theodoric's reign. His parsimony alienated the soldiers, who in turn plundered civilians. As well as collecting wealth for the imperial treasury, he reputedly collected a good deal for himself, and we can believe the rumour. Qualms about conflict of interest were alien to the culture of the civil *militia.*

When the news reached Justinian that the Goths had chosen Totila as their king, he prodded his generals into action. They mustered some 12,000 men at Ravenna, and marched on Verona, which they might have taken except that a dispute over the division of the loot they expected to get delayed the assault. Falling back south of the Po, they met Totila again at Faenza at the head of 5,000 Goths and suffered another defeat. Then Totila sent a force to lay siege to Florence, where the Byzantine commandant Justin was utterly unprepared: he had no provisions and he sent a desperate appeal to Ravenna. An army under three commanders, two of them well known to us: Bessas and John, Vitalian's nephew, set out to relieve Florence, but the commanders could not agree, and in the Mugello valley a day's journey from Florence, they snatched defeat from the jaws of victory. Thereafter the Byzantine army took refuge behind the walls of the Italian towns and left the countryside to Totila, who moved south, bypassing Rome, laid siege to Naples, and occupied Campania and much of the rest of southern Italy.

The wives and daughters of Roman senators whom he captured he allowed to go free, but the senators had reason to hate him, for he confiscated the revenues from their estates. He did not harm the tenant-farmers, who were, for practical purposes, serfs: their condition improved with Totila's revolution. He freed slaves and enrolled them in his army. His strategy was to create a social and economic upheaval which shattered the underpinnings of the Roman senatorial class, and it never quite recovered. Its immediate effect was to make it harder than usual for the imperial treasury to meet the payroll of the army.

On the eastern front, there was a sense of disquiet. A four-day mutiny had broken out in the great fortress of Dara in 537, but it was quashed by loyal troops at the urging of the bishop seconded by a local notable.[46] Had it been wartime, the mutiny would have been a serious matter, but Khusro of Persia was bound by the 'Endless Peace'.

Yet Khusro grew apprehensive and a little envious as news of Justinian's conquests reached him, and he looked for a valid reason to break the treaty. The continuing rivalry between the Saracen Ghassanids and Lakhmids provided one. Mundhir III and Harith disputed the possession of a sheep-walk along the old Palmyra–Damascus road called the *Strata Diocletiana*, which still went by the name 'Strata'. The Ghassanids, who defended this sector of the frontier as imperial allies, had a solid claim to this old Roman road.

But Mundhir, with his suzerain's encouragement, nursed the dispute into open hostilities.[47] Another came from Italy: the envoys from Witigis arrived, two Italian priests, one posing as a bishop and the other as his attendant, and they warned him that what had befallen the Vandals and Ostrogoths was in store for Persia. This message coincided with another that came from Armenia, where Sittas, the husband of Theodora's sister, Comito, had just lost his life, and discontent had come to a head.

Justinian's zeal for reform had extended to Armenia. The five princely families of Other Armenia across the Euphrates were shoved aside. In 528, a Master of Soldiers took up residence in Erzerum (Theodosiopolis), and assumed command of the imperial forces in Armenia. Justinian overrode the immunity from imperial garrisons which the princely families of Other Armenia had enjoyed and their right to maintain private armed forces. A few years later, he reorganized the Armenian territories into four provinces,[48] and attacked the basis of Armenian feudalism by abolishing agnatic inheritance and applying Roman law to Armenian marriage customs, which he condemned roundly for their barbarity. His *Novels* dealing with Armenia betray a zeal for reform. To quote one fiat, 'We have taught [Armenia] to make use of Roman systems and laid down that there should be no laws among them except those honoured by the Romans.'[49]

Sittas had been on furlough in Constantinople since the 'Endless Peace' ended the war with Persia, but when trouble broke out in Armenia, Justinian dispatched him to deal with it, and expected immediate results. Sittas, who understood the Armenian problem, was pushed reluctantly into military action. After Sittas' death, his successor was another veteran of the eastern front, Bouzes, but he was not a man the Armenians trusted. One Armenian, a member of the Arsacid royal house who had once been Bouzes' friend, did come with a small party for a parley, and paid for it with his life. After that, an Armenian deputation led by the Arsacids came to Khusro and urged him to take up the war. Justinian, they claimed, had already broken the 'Endless Peace'. Khusro heard them out with pleasure.

In the spring of 540, Khusro opened war, advancing up the west margin of the Euphrates, avoiding the fort of Circesium at the junction of the River Khabur and continuing to the city of Sura, which defended itself vigorously for a day until the garrison commander, an Armenian named Arsaces, was killed. Then the bishop of the city

tried to negotiate, but the Persians forced the city gate while negotiations were still in progress, plundered and burned the city, and
killed or enslaved the populace. He then demanded ransom for the
survivors from the bishop of Sergiopolis, the nearest large city to the
south, and when the bishop claimed to have no money, Khusro
accepted a promissory note.

Bouzes was with a force at Hierapolis (*mod.* Mabbug), and in the
absence of Belisarius, he was in command of the eastern defence.
But he stayed out of Khusro's path. Justinian sent his cousin
Germanus with 300 of his *bucellarii* to Antioch. But the Antiochenes
refused to follow his advice to strengthen the circuit wall, and when
it became clear that no reinforcements were coming, Germanus gave
up hope of saving the city. The Antiochene notables held a council
and decided that the best course was to try to buy off the Persians.
So they sent the bishop of Beroea (*mod.* Aleppo), Megas, who
happened to be in Antioch, to beg for mercy and offer Khusro
money to leave them unscathed.

Money was Khusro's object. This offensive was a *razzia* on a grand
scale. But Khusro was in a recalcitrant mood. Taking Megas with
him, he advanced on Hierapolis, where he collected 2,000 pounds
of silver in return for breaking off his assault. Then he yielded –
ostensibly – to Megas' entreaties and agreed to leave imperial territory
in return for 1,000 pounds of gold. Seventy-two thousand *solidi*,
and a poor man might feed himself for almost half a year on one
solidus!

Megas hurried back to Antioch and Khusro followed at a slower
pace. Half-way there, he came to Beroea, which failed to produce
sufficient ransom money. Khusro took the city and set it ablaze. At
Antioch, meanwhile, two emissaries had arrived from Constantinople
on their way to Khusro, and stiffened resistance, though the patriarch
Euphraemius fled the city for Cilicia, and Germanus soon followed
him.[50] Megas returned to the Persian camp empty-handed, to find
his own Beroea on fire, and his flock putting up a hopeless resistance
on the acropolis. Megas begged with tears for their lives, and Khusro
yielded. The Byzantine garrison for the most part deserted to Khusro:
their wages were in arrears.

In June of 540, Khusro's army was before the walls of Antioch.
The Antiochenes, cheered by the arrival of 6,000 troops led by the
dukes of Palmyra and Damascus, were in no mood to pay ransom,
and taunted Khusro from the walls. When he pressed home the
assault, citizens and soldiers fought side by side, and after the soldiers

fled, it was the young men of the Blue and Green parties from the Antioch hippodrome who fought on, even though most of them had no armour and only stones as weapons. Khusro turned his best troops against them, and they were forced back. Then there was only slaughter. Antioch was sacked and burned, and as many as 30,000 survivors were transported to Ctesiphon to populate a new Antioch which Khusro built for them, officially named '*Veh-Antiokh-Khusro*', but commonly called '*Rumaghan*': 'City of the Romans'.[51]

Justinian's two emissaries approached Khusro again, and worked out an agreement whereby the king would receive 5,000 pounds of gold immediately, and a yearly payment of 500 pounds for the defence of the Caucasus passes. Then Khusro went to Seleuceia, the port of Antioch, where he bathed in the Mediterranean, a variation of the boast of the ancient conquerors who came from Mesopotamia, beginning with Sargon of Akkad, that they washed their weapons in the Great Sea. Then, after a visit to Daphne where a few buildings were set ablaze, chiefly the church of the archangel Michael, he advanced south to Apamea, having promised Justinian's envoys to plunder no more than 1,000 pounds of gold.

When news of the sack of Antioch reached Apamea, the people begged their bishop Thomas to bring out the city's most precious relic, a fragment of the True Cross, and Thomas agreed to display the relic on designated days, so that the villagers might come into the city to share its saving power. The historian Evagrius was taken as a child to see it and witnessed the miracle: as the bishop, holding up the relic in his arms went round the church, a flame rose from it, harmless but brilliant.[52] Once Khusro arrived, he took all the treasure he could find, though he left Apamea its precious relic. Then he held a chariot race in the hippodrome of the city, and insisted that the Green charioteer should win, for he knew that Justinian was a Blue *aficionado*. To keep Khusro in good humour, Bishop Thomas, who usually did not attend chariot races, attended this one.

Khusro now turned back to Mesopotamia by a more southerly route, collecting 200 pounds of gold from Chalcis, and then advancing due west to cross the Euphrates by a pontoon bridge and threaten Edessa. Edessa could easily withstand a siege, but it paid 200 pounds of gold to save its territory from pillage. Here Khusro learned that Justinian accepted the treaty that he had negotiated after Antioch's fall, but nonetheless, on his route home, he attacked Dara. The great fortress withstood him, and disgusted, Khusro accepted

1,000 pounds of silver as a consolation prize and departed for Ctesiphon. Justinian judged the treaty broken.

Khusro had administered Roman prestige a telling blow and one result was that an embassy from Lazica arrived at Ctesiphon to renew the Laz vassalage, which King Tzath had broken off in 522. The Byzantine Master of Soldiers in Lazica, John Tzibus, was an able but unscrupulous administrator, who prompted the emperor to build the strong fortress of Petra on the Black Sea coast, and John made it the port of entry for all imports into Lazica. From the Byzantine viewpoint, an import–export monopoly was a fair way of making the Lazes meet the cost of their own defence, particularly of maintaining an imperial garrison in the country. But the Lazes did not see it that way, and they handed themselves over to Khusro. Khusro had misgivings about the difficult terrain of Lazica but the Lazes relieved them. They would guide a Persian army through the forests and prepare a road. Khusro was easily persuaded, and he gathered an army, pretending that his object was to meet the Hun threat in Iberia.

In the spring of 541, Khusro advanced into Lazica where the Laz king Gubazes made his formal submission. John Tzibus concentrated his troops at Petra, which put up a good fight until John himself was killed by an arrow in the neck. The Persians then brought down one of the two great towers which dominated the ramparts, and Petra came to terms. Khusro appropriated John's treasure, but did no further harm; the Roman survivors joined his army. His own losses were great, not only from combat, the harsh environment and scarce rations, but from disease as well, and his subjects were in a discontented mood.[53] As for the Lazes, they discovered they had only changed masters and soon found their new ones less to their liking than the old.

Meanwhile Belisarius arrived on the eastern front to conduct a circumspect campaign. He had his usual problems with insubordinate officers and perhaps, behind the scenes, there was a distrustful emperor. Unaware of events in Lazica, Belisarius moved into Persian territory and camped some 9 kilometres from Nisibis, hoping to tempt the Persian commander of the Nisibis garrison to come out and fight. Two of Belisarius' subordinates, however, Peter, who had seen duty in Lazica as an exploitative Master of the Soldiers, and the duke of Mesopotamia, John Troglita, whom we shall encounter again in Africa, went their own way and camped five kilometres closer to the fortress, where a Persian sally caught them by surprise.

However, Belisarius came up quickly to retrieve what might have been a disaster. The Persians retreated quickly before the onslaught of the Gothic horsemen whom Belisarius had brought with him from Italy.

Leaving Nisibis, which was impregnable, Belisarius advanced a day's journey further east and laid siege to the fortress of Sisauranon. He sent his Ghassanid ally Harith ahead to plunder Persian territory, and – perhaps because he did not trust Harith – he sent with him 1,200 troops taken mostly from his *bucellarii*. Sisauranon was unready for a siege and fell easily. But Harith failed to return. Finding rich booty and no resistance, Harith saw to it that his scouts reported a Persian army nearby, and he advised the commanders of the *bucellarii* to avoid this non-existent army and retire to the safety of Roman Mesopotamia. No news reached Belisarius, and his troops began to sicken in the suffocating heat of the Mesopotamian summer. The dukes of Damascus and Palmyra, who had withdrawn their troops from Phoenice Libanensis, were apprehensive: their province was exposed to the raids of Mundhir, Khusro's Saracen ally. So the Romans retreated, with a train of carts bearing the sick leading the column.

An imperial summons brought Belisarius back to Constantinople for the winter.

It had been a cautious, almost timid campaign, marked by the commander's inability to control his subordinates. The one major success of the year 541 was in Roman Armenia, where the Master of Soldiers Valerian wiped out a Hun army dispatched by Khusro.[54] The *Secret History* of Procopius provides an explanation, and there is probably some truth to it, though we should never forget Edward Gibbon's warning to beware the 'malevolent whisper of the *Anecdota*'.[55] Antonina, Belisarius' wife, who usually accompanied her husband on campaign, had stayed behind in Constantinople where she helped the empress bring about the fall of John the Cappadocian. Antonina was a lusty lady of a certain age, and she had an amour with a young Thracian, Theodosius, whom Belisarius had adopted on the eve of the Vandal campaign. Antonina's natural son, Photius, saw to it that the details of his mother's adultery were reported to Belisarius. Belisarius, sick with jealousy, left Sisauranon to meet his wife when he got the news that she had set out for the East. The imperial summons to Constantinople came from Theodora, who was anxious for Antonina's welfare. But had Belisarius advanced, wrote the secret historian with wild exaggeration, he might have captured Ctesiphon and freed the captive Antiochenes![56]

In the spring of the next year, Khusro crossed the Euphrates, aiming at Palestine. Sergiopolis withstood him, but its unfortunate bishop, who could not pay the promissory note he had given to ransom the survivors of Sura two years before, was carried off a prisoner. Justinian sent back Belisarius by imperial post to take command. Belisarius made his camp at Dura-Europos, and there he received Khusro's envoy with an elaborate charade which so impressed him that Khusro retired across the Euphrates, pausing, however, to take the Roman customs post of Callinicum, where the wall was being rebuilt and the city was unready for a siege. Yet Belisarius was blamed for the loss of Callinicum, nonetheless.[57]

The next year, the theatre of war changed to Armenia. Belisarius and Bouzes had been recalled, Belisarius to return to Italy and Bouzes to be thrown into an oubliette in the palace dungeon. But bubonic plague had broken out in Constantinople and took a heavy toll of its population.

542: THE PLAGUE YEAR

In the spring of 542, bubonic plague reached Constantinople.[58] It may have originated in Axum, as Evagrius claims, but it is likely that it travelled up the Nile from the Central African plague reservoir in Kenya, Uganda and Zaire. At any rate, it appeared in Egypt in 541, and spread along the trade routes, always moving from the coast to the interior. No place was to be free of it. It appeared in Italy in 543, and reached the diocese of *Oriens* in the same year;[59] from there it migrated to Persia, infecting the Persian army and Khusro himself, who beat a retreat east of the Tigris to the highlands of Luristan, which were still free of the pest.[60] It reached France by 543, where Gregory of Tours[61] relates how St Gall saved his flock in Clermont-Ferrand, and by 544, it had spread to Ireland.[62] Moreover, like the Black Death in Europe eight centuries later, it was recurrent; Agathias, writing of a second outbreak in the capital in 558, relates that since the plague's first visitation in the fifteenth year of Justinian's reign, it never completely abated, but simply moved from one place to another. Demography is the science of informed guesswork; yet it is probable that the plague coupled with other disasters reduced the population of the Mediterranean world by the year 600 to no more than 60 per cent of its count a century earlier.[63]

Our best diagnostic of the disease comes from Procopius, who used Thucydides' report of the Athenian plague of 431 BC as his literary model. The first symptoms were fever and lassitude, neither of which seemed life-threatening. But soon, if not on the same day, then shortly thereafter, buboes appeared in the groin or armpits, or sometimes beside the ears or on the thighs. Then the disease progressed rapidly. The victim might fall into a lethargic state or else become delirious, and eating was difficult. Some suffered from none of these symptoms but died painfully when their buboes gangrened, though there were cases where the bubo grew to great size, ruptured and suppurated, after which the patient recovered. A number of victims broke out with black blisters like lentils over their bodies, and these died swiftly.[64] Others died vomiting blood. Pregnant women who contracted the disease generally died through miscarriage or in childbirth, though Agathias reports that overall, young males suffered the heaviest toll. The contagion differed in a significant way from the plague which fell upon Periclean Athens: Thucydides noted that those who cared for the sick contracted the disease. In Constantinople, they did not.[65]

Evagrius adds a personal touch. He himself was a schoolboy when the plague first broke out, and was infected; since then, its various recurrences had cost him several children, his wife, many of his kin and slaves. He mentions inflamed eyes and faces, followed by a sore throat and death; others suffered from diarrhoea, and for still others, a high fever followed the appearance of buboes. Death was swift: in two or three days – five at the most, Agathias reports. Animals – dogs, mice and even snakes – were affected. Those who recovered often continued to have muscular tremors and 'it was known', wrote Zachariah of Mytilene, 'that it was a scourge from Satan, who was ordered by God to destroy men.'[66]

The poor were the first to suffer, but the pestilence moved quickly into the homes of the well-to-do. Houses became sepulchres, and John of Ephesus relates that ships at sea lost all their crew to plague and were left derelict. Men saw terrible visions. Some reported sightings of a spectral boat of bronze with headless oarsmen, and many told of seeing apparitions before they were smitten by the disease. In Syria and Palestine, the plague reached the farmlands of the interior between the planting and the reaping, and the crops ripened with no one to harvest them.[67] Close by Antioch, seated upon his pillar on Mons Admirabilis, the stylite saint Symeon the Younger prayed to Christ in tears, and got the reply, 'The sins of this people are manifold, and why do you bother yourself about their diseases? For you love them no more than I.' But to save the saint grief, the

Lord granted Symeon the power to heal those who invoked Him in Symeon's name, and many who were smitten called on St Symeon and were cured. Others who fell ill would light a lamp in their houses and sprinkle over it a pinch of incense, praying 'Christ, God of Your servant of Mons Admirabilis, have pity on me', and they obtained pity.[68]

This was the first great pandemic of bubonic plague to affect Europe: less famous than the Black Death of the fourteenth century, but quite as deadly. Plague is a disease of wild rodents that are hosts to fleas which carry the bacilli to new victims. Humans enter the chain of infection from a flea bite. The rodent which carried the Black Death was the black rat, and it may also have been the carrier in the sixth century. But we cannot be certain when it invaded Europe, and it need not have been the only carrier; the dogs that died on the streets of Constantinople must have hosted colonies of infected fleas. But the rat is the chief suspect, and since rats found urban areas most congenial, it was the cities that suffered most: the nomad Berbers in Africa and the Arabs on the desert fringes in *Oriens* were not greatly affected. In the cities and towns of Syria the plague became endemic, whereas it seems not to have penetrated the Hedjaz at all.[69]

Plague occurs in two forms. One is the bubonic or bubo-septicaemic type which results when a flea bite injects the bacilli into a human victim, and its tell-tale symptom is the bubo: a gangliform reaction of the lymph nodes closest to the site of the flea bite. Since the legs are an easy target for fleas, it is no wonder that more often than not it is the lymph nodes of the groin that become swollen. Septicaemia occurs when the infection enters the bloodstream, and death can be swift, even before buboes are detected. Agathias reports victims dying as if by an attack of apoplexy. The other type of plague is pulmonary, which develops after the disease becomes septicaemic, and the bacilli invade the lungs and cause plague pneumonia. Pulmonary plague is directly communicable to another person, and is very contagious: a victim speaking normally can spread saliva droplets laden with germs a distance of some 2 metres. On the other hand, simple bubonic plague itself is not directly contagious unless the patient harbours fleas, or perhaps lice, which may also serve as carriers.[70] Procopius' observation that those who cared for the ill or handled the dead did not necessarily contract the disease is a clue that this was bubonic, not pulmonary plague, which we may also infer from the lack of another symptom of the pulmonary type: shallow breathing and tightness in the chest.[71] Bubonic plague without modern treatment results in death in from 40 to 70 per cent of cases; pulmonary plague, if untreated, leaves no survivors.

Justinian, who contracted the plague himself and recovered, turned to Theodore, one of the legal secretaries (*referendarii*) who served as his channels of communication,[72] and mandated him to get rid of the bodies. He placed the palace guard at his disposal. Tombs already in existence were full, and so Theodore had great pits dug across the Golden Horn in Sycae (*mod.* Galata) that could hold 70,000 corpses each. Then he hired men to collect the dead. When the pits overflowed, corpses were heaped inside the towers on the walls of Sycae, where they putrefied with a stench that pervaded the whole city. Streets were deserted and trades abandoned; bread became scarce, and some of the sick died of starvation. John of Ephesus tells of a house that men avoided because of its foul odour, and when it was entered, some twenty rotting corpses were found.

John[73] provides us with vivid descriptions of havoc: of how men collapsed in public places, with bellies bloated and mouths gaping, how ships at sea floated aimlessly with all their crew dead and how monsters appeared in the waters off the Palestine coast. Yet the modern reader must be struck by the soberness of the accounts, and the degree of acceptance by the general populace. We hear of no processions of flagellants, or choreomania or persecutions of Jews. The apparition of a bronze boat rowed by headless boatmen, which John of Ephesus reported, pales beside the overwrought visions which accompanied the Black Death in the fourteenth century. The attitude of the church paralleled the church's interpretation of the later plague: it was caused by the wrath of God, or it was a scourge of Satan, commanded by God to destroy men.[74] But by itself, the visitation of 542 need not have been devastating. The demographic pattern probably resembled the sequel to the Black Death: after the plague, marriages increased sharply, and the unions were prolific. But the disaster of 542 was not unique. The reign of Justinian is a recital of earthquakes, floods, invasions and after 542, repetitions of plague, which established permanent cycles of infection. Constantinople had a severe earthquake in mid-August, 542, while the plague still raged.[75] Nine years later the whole of *Oriens* was shaken by a terrible earthquake which was felt even in Alexandria. Beirut was destroyed and its famous law school moved to Sidon. Neither Beirut nor the law school recovered its splendour. A tsunami destroyed Cos. Agathias[76] describes a visit there after the disaster: the whole city was a heap of rubble. As if that were not enough, in 551 sickness (anthrax?) attacked cattle in Syria, and fields were left unploughed for want of oxen.[77] The bitter *Secret History*[78] of Procopius lists the natural catastrophes that afflicted the empire since the time that Justinian first took charge of it in 518, as his uncle's *éminence grise*: floods, earthquakes – and then half the survivors died of plague. God, hating the works of this demon emperor, turned His face away!

The taxation base shrank dramatically. Taxes on arable land whose holders died of plague were made the responsibility of the neighbouring landholders. The regulation (*epibole*) whereby taxes on parcels of land that went out of cultivation were assigned to neighbouring proprietors had been standard practice long before the plague, but if we may judge by the complaints of Procopius,[79] who regarded it as an innovation, it became far more burdensome, and in 545, Justinian[80] tried to make it more tolerable by ruling that tax arrears on derelict property should not be charged to neighbouring landowners. Evidently they were receiving bills for arrears, and that may have been the point of Procopius' complaint.

Fiscal pressure on the cities increased. To economize, they curtailed civic salaries for teachers and physicians and slashed the budgets for public entertainments. Recruits for the army became harder to find, and the plague must be one of the major reasons for the shrinkage of the army in Justinian's last years. Fortunately for the empire, Persia was also weakened by the plague, but in Italy, the Goths resumed the war, and fresh trouble broke out in Africa. In Constantinople, we know of some eighty monasteries before the plague, but after it, we lose track of most of them.[81] It seems likely that some of the surplus population which fed the monasteries and nunneries disappeared. But at the same time, pietism increased, and the church probably skimmed off a greater share of the private resources that might have supported civic projects in happier times. In the crises that followed the plague, the empire moved into closer alliance with the church.

But it is an ill wind that blows no one any good. The Black Death in fourteenth-century Europe produced a lower people-to-land ratio, and wages rose. In England, money wages rose typically by one-third or more in the three decades after the Black Death and thereafter continued to drift upwards, and though there were other factors, such as higher grain prices, in the plague's immediate aftermath, which dampened real wages, it is still clear that the population decrease benefited the lower economic classes.[82] The trend after the

Justinianic plague was similar: we have the evidence of a law of 544[83] vetoing pay increases for artisans, labourers, sailors and the like which marks an effort to control wage inflation. Building activity in the empire continued, which indicates that the level of prosperity persisted, but it was not unchanged. In Syria, there was a marked shift from civic construction to the building of churches and monasteries by the middle of the century,[84] and one reason for this must be that public sector wealth was hit harder than its private counterpart. The public sector which paid for civic construction relied upon tax revenues, whereas the church could tap private donors whose purse strings were loosened by the fear of death.

Yet for all that, it is clear that Justinian's design of renewing the empire had fallen victim to a series of 'Acts of God', to borrow a phrase which has an ironic overtone in a Byzantine context. The empire was overextended.

CONSOLIDATING THE CONQUESTS:
THE SEARCH FOR PEACE

The campaigning season that passed between Belisarius' recall from the eastern front in 542 and his dispatch to Italy in the spring of 544 was a fearful one for him. There was a moment when it seemed that Justinian might not survive the plague, and it was alleged that Belisarius and Bouzes had declared openly that they would never tolerate a second Justinian as emperor. The empress Theodora acted ruthlessly. Bouzes spent a brief term in prison, and Belisarius was deprived of his command and bodyguard, and feared for his life. His wife's friendship with Theodora saved him, but he returned to Italy under a cloud.[85]

The Master of Soldiers in the East was now Martin. Khusro had retired from the frontier for fear of the plague, and Justinian thought the time ripe for a major offensive against Persarmenia. Martin was hampered almost as much as Belisarius by the curse of Justinianic commanders – an inability to impose authority on subordinates – but it is worth noting that the army of some 30,000 troops that was to launch the offensive was one of the largest that we find in the sixth century. Clearly in Justinian's eyes, the eastern frontier was all-important, plague or not. Yet the offensive was a fiasco. At a small village named Anglon, a Persian force of only 4,000 men routed the Byzantines, but it was too weak to take advantage of its victory.

The following year, Khusro launched an assault on the city of

Edessa, while another army laid siege to Theodosiopolis on the Khabur river. The Edessenes were divided in theology, but against the Persians they stood united, and when Khusro made his final effort to storm the walls, even the women and children helped in the defence. Frustrated, Khusro abandoned the siege. It must have been about this time, too, that news reached him of another setback: the duke of Mesopotamia, John Troglita, had made an effective night attack on the Persian army besieging Theodosiopolis, and followed it up with a sharp defeat of the Persian force attacking Dara, and the capture of the Persian general, Mihr-Mihroe.[86] In 545, Khusro was willing to listen to Justinian's envoys who waited upon him at Ctesiphon. He agreed to a five-year truce on the eastern frontier, but not in Lazica. There Khusro had no intention of losing his advantage. The Persians were to receive 400 pounds of gold per year, and as another condition of the peace, he received the attentions of the Greek doctor Tribunus, for Khusro considered his health precarious and was on a special diet. The Persian court prized Greek medicine, and Greek doctors sometimes served a double role as diplomats. At the end of a year, Tribunus begged Khusro for the release of some prisoners whose names he supplied, and Khusro released not only them, but 3,000 others as well.[87]

The truce was uneasy. The Lakhmids and Ghassanids continued to skirmish: in 546 or thereabouts, the Ghassanid sheikh Harith lost a son to Mundhir, but in June, 554, he inflicted a defeat on Mundhir and killed him. In 547, a Persian plot to capture the Dara fortress failed. But the chief theatre of war was Lazica.

The Persians had soon alienated the Lazes. They were convinced Christians and the Persians convinced Zoroastrians, who, with some reason, regarded Laz Christianity as evidence of imperial sympathies. Moreover, the empire was Lazica's natural trading partner and took Laz slaves, furs and hides in return for salt, wine and grain. Khusro decided to solve the Laz problem by ethnic cleansing: he planned to transplant the Lazes elsewhere and resettle Lazica with more dependable subjects.

The first step was to get rid of the Laz king Gubazes, but he was warned in time. He had willingly become a Persian vassal in 541, but now he begged for Justinian's pardon and aid. Justinian sent a young Master of Soldiers named Dagisthaeus with 8,000 men who joined Gubazes and the Lazes in laying siege to Petra.

The siege had gone on for four months and the defenders were near exhaustion when the Persians managed to reinforce Petra. Mihr-

Mihroe, his prestige undimmed by his capture by John Troglita at Dara, led a large army across the Laz–Iberian frontier through a pass which Dagisthaeus had foolishly left undermanned, and brought 3,000 fresh troops and supplies to Petra, where the garrison had been reduced to no more than 150 able-bodied fighting men. But Mihr-Mihroe lacked supplies enough for his army, which numbered some 30,000 troops, and so he positioned an encampment of 5,000 soldiers near the Laz frontier to maintain the supply route, and retired himself with the bulk of his army to Persarmenia. Next spring, Gubazes and Dagisthaeus surprised the camp, wiped out most of the garrison and seized a great cache of supplies.

Summer came, and Dagisthaeus and Gubazes won another victory, destroying an army of Persians and Alans which had advanced to the river Hippus (*mod.* Tzkhenisdskali), a southern tributary of the Phasis, but at the same time, another Persian force managed to resupply the garrison at Petra. Justinian had had enough of Dagisthaeus, and replaced him as Master of Soldiers in Armenia with Bessas, newly returned under a cloud from the Italian theatre. Bessas acted vigorously at first. Elderly and overweight though he was, he led an assault on Petra himself, took it and dismantled it. But the success burned out his energy, and without making an effort to block the passes on the Iberian frontier, he left for Armenia to see to the collection of taxes. Mihr-Mihroe, who had been on his way to relieve Petra, learned of its fall, and with his army of cavalry and eight elephants turned to attack the fortress of Archaeopolis, where the Romans had a garrison of 3,000 men. His attack failed, and when he died in 555, full of years and so crippled that he had to be carried in a litter, Archaeopolis was still untaken. But the Persians had a stronghold at Onoguris in the same region, and were in control of the countryside, and though King Gubazes himself remained loyal, many Lazes were disaffected, alienated by the treatment the Roman soldiers had meted out to them.[88]

The five-year truce had expired in 550, and while Bessas was attacking Petra, Khusro's envoy, his chamberlain Izedh Gushnasp, was negotiating in Constantinople. Khusro wanted a settlement: he had just quashed a rebellion by his eldest son, who was a Christian. A year and a half of negotiations resulted in a renewed peace on nearly the same terms as before. In Lazica, the war went on, unaffected by the armistice. But the Laz king Gubazes complained bitterly to Justinian about the Roman commanders, naming in particular the two Masters of the Soldiers, Bessas and Martin, as well as

Rusticus,[89] who was not a general but a finance officer with the army. Justinian's patience with old Bessas ran out: he took away his command, banished him to Abasgia and confiscated his property. But Justinian left Rusticus in place and, with some misgiving, put Martin in overall command, and these two plotted Gubazes' death. Rusticus' brother John went to denounce Gubazes before Justinian as a traitor, and got a signed order to bring him to Constantinople for trial; if he resisted, 'he should suffer a tyrant's fate and die miserably'. His assassin need fear no retribution.[90] Armed with the letter, John returned to Lazica, and picking a quarrel with Gubazes before the walls of Onoguris, he struck him the first blow with his dagger and one of Rusticus' bodyguard finished him off.

The Lazes buried their king, and withdrew from further cooperation with the Romans. Martin and Rusticus pressed home an attack on Onoguris, on the premise that a victory there would absolve them, if the truth about Gubazes' murder came out. Instead, they suffered a sharp defeat.

The Lazes, however, decided that a Christian emperor was a lesser evil than a Zoroastrian monarch. They protested Gubazes' innocence to Justinian and asked him to give them Gubazes' younger brother Tzath as king. Justinian agreed readily to Tzath, and sent to Lazica the elderly senator Athanasius,[91] with a commission to investigate Gubazes' murder. Rusticus and John were arrested, and held until a proper trial could be staged. Martin continued as Master of Soldiers with Justin, the son of Justinian's cousin Germanus as second in command, and the year 556 went well for the imperial forces. Mihr-Mihroe's successor[92] suffered such a defeat on the banks of the Phasis river that Khusro recalled him and flayed him alive.

After the imperial victory, Athanasius held his trial with pomp and ceremony intended to impress the Lazes and repair Roman prestige. Rusticus and John were beheaded. Martin's case was forwarded to the emperor, who recalled him and reduced him to the ranks, but inflicted no further punishment. Justin took over as commander-in-chief in Lazica and Armenia.[93]

By now, both sides were ready for peace and in 557, Khusro dispatched his envoy Zich (he was, in fact, his chamberlain Izedh Gushnasp, whose family name was Zich), who negotiated a truce on the basis of the status quo. Constantinople was clearly the winner, and the resources which Justinian mustered for this war refute the charge sometimes levied against him that he neglected his eastern frontiers for adventures in Italy and Africa. It was Italy rather than the East that was starved of troops in the 540s. Justinian was determined to deny the Persians access to the Black Sea, where they might disrupt the trade routes which converged on the Crimean area[94] and instigate hostile forays into the Balkans. His efforts were on the whole successful.

In Africa, Solomon, praetorian prefect and Master of Soldiers, was killed in 544 in a skirmish in central Tunisia at Cillium (*mod.* Kasserine).[95] The enemy was the Laguatan tribes of Tripolitania, who were joined by the sheikh of the Frexes, Antalas, the erstwhile ally whom Solomon had alienated by killing his brother and cancelling the pension with which the emperor had honoured him. Two of Solomon's nephews had been appointed to Africa, the older, Cyrus, as duke of Cyrenaica, and the younger, Sergius, as duke of Tripolitania. The appointments were intended as a compliment to Solomon, though Sergius also had Theodora's backing, and it was he who succeeded Solomon as prefect of Africa. Procopius[96] describes Sergius as a mixture of arrogance and fatuity with an appetite for the wives and the property of other men, and though he was not the only cause of the revived uprising of the Berbers, he was the worst possible choice for a demanding post. To add to the danger, the Visigoths in Spain chose this moment to cross the Strait of Gibraltar and take the Byzantine fort at Septem (*mod.* Tangier).[97] The Visigoths were wiped out by a surprise attack one Sunday, but insurrection in Africa rapidly spun out of control. Stotzas reappeared with a force of deserters and Vandals and joined Antalas, and together they took Hadrumentum by a ruse. The sequel was full of irony: a priest of Hadrumentum named Paul escaped to Carthage and tried with no success to persuade Sergius to send an army to retake his city. But Sergius did agree to give him eighty men, and with these and any others he could muster, he hurried back to Hadrumentum and spread the rumour that Germanus, the emperor's cousin, was on his way with a large army. Germanus' reputation struck fear into the hearts of Stotzas and his Berber allies, and they rapidly evacuated the city. But they soon discovered the truth, and their *razzias* became all the worse.

The complaints from Africa finally moved Justinian, but he did not recall Sergius. Instead he sent out a new praetorian prefect, Athanasius, whose career, as we have seen, was later to take him to Lazica to investigate the murder of the Laz king, and a new, but totally inexperienced military commander, Areobindus, whose party included a company of Armenian troops led by two brothers of the

Arsacid royal line, Artabanes and John. Sergius departed to campaign in Numidia and we do not hear of him again until later in the year, when Areobindus tried to coordinate a campaign against Antalas and Stotzas who were at Sicca Veneria, a three-day journey from Carthage. John, son of Sisiniolus, one of the few able officers left in Africa, carried out his orders, but Sergius ignored his, and John, outnumbered and unsupported, was defeated and killed at Thacia (*mod.* Bordj Messaoudi). But before he died, he had given Stotzas a mortal wound.

Now at last Justinian recalled Sergius, and made Areobindus overall commander, but the disaffection had already spread through all ranks, and Areobindus was not the man to deal with it. He faced a mutiny led by the duke of Numidia, Guntarith, and panicked, fleeing to a fortified monastery in Carthage. The mutineers put the loyalists to death, and Areobindus' sanctuary failed to save his life, though the prefect Athanasius was spared. The sheikh of the Frexes, Antalas, who had assisted Guntarith's coup, was rewarded with Areobindus' head but nothing else, whereupon he withdrew and rethought his position. The Armenian Artabanes professed loyalty to Guntarith, but he and Athanasius planned to grasp the first chance to destroy the usurper.[98] The opportunity came at a banquet which Athanasius held in the prefectural palace on the eve of an offensive to conquer Byzacium. Wine flowed. Guntarith's bodyguards took their portions outside the building to eat, and once they left the hall, Artabanes and his Armenian accomplices struck. Guntarith, his friends and all the Vandals at the banquet were killed.

The ringleaders were rounded up and sent to Constantinople, and Artabanes took over as commander of the army in Africa. But before the end of 546, Justinian granted his request for permission to return to Constantinople. He had a personal motive: he wanted to wed Areobindus' widow, Preiecta, who was the emperor's niece, and he no doubt thought it a very suitable union for an Arsacid prince! The passion was mutual. Artabanes already had a wife whom he had repudiated for the usual reasons, and he saw no reason why she should block his requited love. But the empress rose to the defence of the deserted wife, and married Preiecta instead to the son of Anastasius' nephew Pompeius. Artabanes was left with an unloved wife and his resentment. The story was to end in sedition.

Artabanes' successor was John Troglita, transferred from the eastern front where he was duke of Mesopotamia. The situation was grave. The Byzantine forces had withdrawn to Carthage and the

coastal cities of Byzacium, and the Romans in Africa were subject
to constant Berber *razzias* and the danger of enslavement. John had
more than a year of hard fighting before he ran the Berber alliance
to earth at the 'Fields of Cato', where he cut off their supplies. The
Berbers launched a desperate assault on a Sunday. The Berber leader
Carcasan, emir of the Laguatan, died at John's hand. Seventeen
Berber sheikhs were among the dead, and Antalas submitted.
Diplomacy as well as force played a role in the victory, it is clear,
for we find Solomon's old foe Iaudas on the side of the Byzantines
against Antalas and Carcasan.[99] Evidently he had recovered his
domain in the Aurès massif and come to terms with the empire.

At any rate, peace returned, and though our evidence is mostly
negative, it seems that prosperity returned as well. Procopius,[100] who
devotes only a few lines to John Troglita, opines gloomily that Africa
was left depopulated by war and insurrection. But we should accept
his judgement with a grain of salt. In stark contrast to Italy, there
was an exceptional amount of public building in Byzantine Africa,
some of it carried out by local effort. The Catholics were soon
discomfited, for while the conquest turned the tables on the Arians,
the Catholic churchmen soon found themselves faced with an
emperor whose views they considered unorthodox. Yet the unhap-
piness of the church did not affect the economy. From 548 to 562,
Africa was at peace and though there was sporadic fighting from
562 to the end of the century, the general picture we have is of a
half-century of economic well-being.[101]

On the scale of Justinian's military priorities, Italy occupied third
place. The emperor could muster some 30,000 troops on the
Armenian frontier in 543, in spite of the plague, but when Belisarius
arrived back in Italy in the dying weeks of 544, he had with him
only 4,000 recruits whom he had scraped together with the help of
the Master of Soldiers of Illyricum, Vitalius. Belisarius was to
describe them as a small, pitiful and inexperienced crew.[102] Most of
his own *bucellarii*, on whom he could depend, were left behind in
the East. In Italy, he faced a grave situation. Naples had capitulated,
and Totila made a point of treating the captives with consideration.
Totila had concluded that if the Ostrogoths were to hold Italy, they
must win over the Italians. The misconduct of imperial officials, to
say nothing of the army, was not calculated to make friends, and
Totila intended to capitalize on Italian discontent. He wrote to the
Roman senate reminding it of the kindness of Theodoric and
Amalasuintha, and contrasted their behaviour with the rapacity of

the Byzantines. The letter was entrusted to captives who were sent to Rome, but the commander of the Roman garrison, John, nephew of Vitalian, intercepted it. But Totila tried again: he sent a number of open letters which collaborators in Rome posted at night in public places. It was suspected that the collaborators were Arian priests (it is interesting to note that some still existed in the city) and all these were expelled.

There was little Belisarius could do. His troops were too few, morale was low and desertions were at an unprecedented height.[103] He himself was now a middle-aged commander out of favour at court, with a military reputation that was growing threadbare. At Tivoli, the company of Isaurians who made up the garrison betrayed the city, and the Goths massacred the inhabitants including the bishop. We do not know the reason for the atrocity, which ran counter to Totila's scheme to win over the Italians. At Bologna, Vitalius was deserted by his Illyrian troops when they received the news that a Bulgar raid was laying waste Illyricum. Their pay was in arrears, and under the circumstances they felt greater allegiance to their homeland than to the imperial mission in Italy.[104] A year after Belisarius' arrival at Ravenna, Totila laid siege to Rome itself.

The commander of the Roman garrison was Bessas, replacing John, the nephew of Vitalian, whom Belisarius had sent back to Constantinople to ask for money and reinforcements. The letter which John carried to the emperor was a desperate plea: the imperial army in Italy was small, frightened and disaffected, and decimated by desertions. However, John, who was no supporter of Belisarius, was an unhurried emissary; he took the time at court to marry the daughter of Justinian's cousin, Germanus, to the annoyance of the empress, who would have been happy to see all Germanus' children remain celibate! But in any case, Justinian had few troops to spare for Italy. He dispatched the eunuch Narses to recruit troops among the Heruls settled in the Balkans around Belgrade, and this had an unexpected bonus: Narses encountered a horde of Slavs who had crossed the Danube to plunder Thrace, and mauled them badly. This was the first Balkan invasion of the Slavs acting independently without the Bulgars, and it was a sign of danger ahead.[105] John, newly married, was sent by the emperor to Italy with a mixed force of regulars and federates and a colleague, the Armenian officer Isaac Kamsarakan.

Belisarius was waiting for John at Durazzo. The situation was desperate, but the two men could not agree on strategy. Belisarius wanted to sail immediately for the port of Rome and use it as a base to raise the siege, whereas John wanted to cross to Calabria and advance with due deliberation up the peninsula. In the end, they agreed to disagree: Isaac and Belisarius, accompanied as usual by his wife, sailed for Portus, while John recovered southern Italy. But a small force of 300 Gothic cavalry which Totila sent to Capua was enough to deter him from advancing further north. His caution seems excessive. Antonina may have been the reason: John's marriage had displeased the empress, and her crony Antonina was quite capable of carrying out any skulduggery that Theodora proposed to express her anger. Behind the walls of Portus, Belisarius waited for John in vain, while Rome starved.

Finally Belisarius made an attempt to get supplies to the besieged city. The Goths had closed the Tiber to foodships by means of a boom that stretched between two towers manned with guards on either riverside. Belisarius planned to destroy one of the towers with a fireship, break the boom and then push up the Tiber with 200 light warships loaded with supplies. The ships were fitted with little pillboxes to shelter soldiers acting as marines. Meanwhile, a sortie by the garrison in Rome would distract the enemy.

There was no sortie. Bessas, the commander of the garrison, was in no rush to have the siege lifted, for he was selling the last remnants of his supplies at inflated prices to those few Romans who still had money with which to buy. Or so it was reported. What Bessas had to gain is hard to understand, for though greed was an endemic vice among imperial officers, Bessas' profits were likely to fall into Gothic hands if the siege were not lifted, and in fact that is what happened, though Bessas himself escaped to hold a last command in Lazica.[106] Worse, Isaac Kamsarakan, who was left behind in Portus with Antonina, under strict orders to stay there, disobeyed and attacked a Gothic camp in the Isola Sacra. The Goths were surprised; their commander Roderick was wounded, and they retreated, but as Isaac and his troops turned to plunder, the Goths rallied and counter-attacked. Isaac's force suffered heavily, he himself was captured and when Roderick died of his wounds two days later, Totila put him to death.

Meanwhile Belisarius' assault on the boom was proceeding according to plan, when word reached him that Portus had been taken. He reacted with panic. Abandoning the attack, he galloped back to Portus to find that both his military base and his wife were safe. He might still have retrieved the situation if he had returned immediately to the offensive, but he lost his nerve. Mortified, he fell ill, developed a fever and nearly died.

Rome fell on the night of 17 December, 546, betrayed by four Isaurians in the imperial army, who opened the Porta Asinaria by prearrangement. Bessas and his fellow officer Conon had picked up rumours of sedition, but had not taken them seriously. Now they fled with most of the soldiers and some senators; the rest of the population, reduced by now to about 500 souls, fled into the churches, and when morning came, Pelagius, a deacon of St Peter's and future pope (the present pope Vigilius was making a compulsory journey to Constantinople), persuaded Totila to put an end to the slaughter.

But Totila did not want to dissipate his manpower by leaving a garrison in the city, and considered razing it to the ground so that it need never be besieged again. What deterred him was, it seems, an appeal from Belisarius at Portus: Rome, he contended, was a monument to a civilized past and by sparing it, Totila, if he won the war, would have spared his own city, and if he lost, he would at least have gained the victor's gratitude. Totila thought it over. His aim was still to restore the Gothic kingdom as it had been under Theodoric, and on the heels of his victory, he sent a deputation consisting of the deacon Pelagius and a Roman barrister to Constantinople to propose peace on those terms. Justinian's reply, when it came, was to refer the matter to Belisarius. But meanwhile, Totila decided to spare Rome, and informing Belisarius of his decision, he evacuated the city and removed the bulk of his army to a camp west of Rome.

Totila was campaigning in south Italy against John, the nephew of Vitalian, who fell back and entrenched himself in Otranto and Taranto, and he was already moving north to make a thrust somewhere – perhaps against Ravenna – when news reached him that Belisarius had reoccupied Rome. In April of 547, Belisarius had shoved aside the Gothic force that was dogging him, taken Rome and was now restoring its walls. The move was unexpected, and to Totila's way of thinking, it was treacherous. When Totila launched an assault on the city before the gates could be restored, and failed, he had to face the bitter reproaches of his Goths, who felt that he should never have left Rome standing when he had the chance to level it. This was Totila's first check, and it was a turning point, though it went unrecognized at the time. The war continued with each side winning local successes, with the Goths on the whole having the upper hand, but when Belisarius left Italy, Rome was still under imperial control.

In June of 548, Belisarius sent his wife Antonina to Constantinople to use her influence with the empress to secure more troops. But Theodora succumbed to cancer on 28 June, and Antonina, discovering the news on her arrival, concluded that the climate at court was unfriendly, and that Italy would be starved for troops as long as her husband was in command. She asked for his recall, and in early 549, Belisarius left Italy for the last time. The judgement of J. B. Bury on him is unduly harsh, but not so far from the truth that it cannot be quoted:

> He [Belisarius] might vanquish a general of mediocre ability like Witigis, but it was a different story when he had to do with a foe of considerable talent and unflagging energy like Totila. Belisarius might have much to say in extenuation of his failure, but the broad fact was that he had failed.[107]

But we should not reach a verdict purely in terms of absolute success or failure. Justinian wanted to hold on in Italy until he had achieved some stability on other more important fronts, and when that happened, then he could shift military manpower there. Belisarius had had his share of glory, and Justinian cannot have been unaware that the quagmire in Italy was the result of a policy which Belisarius had forced upon him by sabotaging the negotiated peace which would have left the land north of the Po river in Gothic hands. It was not unfair that he should slog up and down Italy, and the 'broad fact' was that his campaign was not by any means an utter failure. He had avoided a débâcle.

At any rate, Belisarius was given all the marks of imperial favour when he returned to Constantinople. He held the title of Master of Soldiers of the East and was put in charge of a guards corps, and perhaps it was at this time that Justinian erected a gilded statue in his honour.[108] But he was to wait a long time before he returned to active service.

This was the historical moment when the greatest theological controversy of Justinian's reign, the 'Three Chapters' dispute, was in full cry, and it was a period of transition and unease. Theodora's death was one of a series of events significant to contemporaries if not to historians: Slavic incursions into the Balkans, an abnormal Nile flood which caused famine in lower Egypt, earthquakes, one of which levelled Beirut. A great killer whale which had plagued shipping at the entrance to the Black Sea for fifty years ran aground near the mouth of the Sangarios river, and was hacked to death by the locals.[109] The power structure at court shifted: Theodora's death removed a powerful opponent of the emperor's cousin, Germanus, whose star began to rise. While Belisarius was still on his way back from Italy, two Armenians hatched a plot and tried to involve Germanus and his son Justin. The Armenians were two members of the Arsacid royal house, Artabanes, bitter at Theodora's veto of his marriage to Preiecta, and Arsaces, who bore a grudge against Justinian. Justin revealed the plot to his father who told Marcellus, the Count of the Excubitors. Marcellus, an austere man who had no use for gossip, required proof, and even when he had it, he postponed action. When at last he informed the emperor, Justinian's suspicion of his cousin was intense until Marcellus took the blame on himself. But against the conspirators Justinian acted mildly: Artabanes lost his post of *magister militum praesentalis* and he and the others were kept under guard in the palace.

In the west, a Gothic fleet ravaged the Dalmatian coast in the spring of 549, and in the summer, Totila began the third siege of Rome. The garrison, commanded by one of Belisarius' bodyguard, Diogenes, fought well, but on 16 January, some Isaurian soldiers opened the Ostian Gate, and only a handful of imperial soldiers managed to escape with Diogenes to Città Vecchia. Once again Totila tried to come to terms with Justinian, but Justinian refused his envoys an audience, and Totila decided to carry the war to Sicily. The Italian lobby at Constantinople pressed for action, and it contained influential aristocrats from Rome whom Totila's capture of the city at the end of 546 had sent scurrying for refuge. But Justinian was unhurried. He sent a force to Sicily under the aged Liberius, who in his long career had served Odoacer, Theodoric, Amalasuintha, Theodahad and now Justinian. Then, changing his mind, Justinian rehabilitated Artabanes and dispatched him to relieve Liberius, whom he recalled to the capital. Evidently he decided that a seasoned soldier was needed in Sicily; nonetheless, hardly had Liberius reached Constantinople when he was commissioned to lead an expedition to Spain.

However, by 550, after much hesitation, Justinian decided on a plan which must have roused the hopes of the Roman refugees in the capital. He put his cousin Germanus in charge of the war against Totila, and Germanus, whose wife was long since dead, married Matasuintha, the grand-daughter of Theodoric and a genuine princess of Amal blood.

The strategy, which Germanus and the emperor must have worked out together, is clear. Germanus was an able general whose ambitions Theodora had thwarted while she was alive. If he outlived Justinian, he was the obvious heir: a given which prompted the emperor to as much wariness as pleasure. Matasuintha's son by Germanus would mingle the royal blood of the Ostrogoths with that of the imperial house. Germanus, with Justinian's acquiescence, was embarking upon a policy that would assimilate the Ostrogoths within an imperial commonwealth, and it marks a shift in Justinian's thinking. How well the plan might have worked we can only guess, for the Arianism of the Goths was a formidable obstacle to any such hopes. But among the Italian refugees in Constantinople, the marriage of Germanus and Matasuintha must have roused hope and great expectations. It was a possible solution to the agony of Italy.

But it was not to be. In the autumn of 550, while Germanus was in Sardica (*mod.* Sophia) and ready to leave for Italy in a couple of days, he fell sick and died. A son by Matasuintha, named after his father, was born posthumously. Jordanes, who was putting the finishing touches on his *Getica*, which was a compendium of Cassiodorus' lost Gothic history, transferred his hopes to this infant. 'In him the family of the Anicii is joined with the Amal lineage', he wrote.[110] But for the moment, Justinian was left to find another general and another strategy, and in April, 551, the eunuch Narses departed from Constantinople for Italy with resources enough for a major offensive. He arrived in Italy with no less than 30,000 men, and money enough to pay the soldiers the arrears to their wages.

Unlike Belisarius, Narses had an easy relationship with the officers under his command, and he was an able tactician as well. Not having transports enough to ferry his army to Italy by sea, he marched around the head of the Adriatic, clinging to the coast so as to avoid the Franks in Venetia and a brigade of Goths under Teias whom Totila had stationed at Verona to block his march. On 6 June he reached Ravenna, where he joined forces with Justin and the patrician Valerian, and nine days later, continued his march south, through the Apennines to a site not far from Sentinum in Umbria, where in 296 BC one of the heroes of republican Rome, Decius Mus, had sacrificed his life to win a crucial battle of the Third Samnite War. The name of the site was *Busta Gallorum*, 'Tomb of the Gauls'.

The battle fought there was a decisive defeat for the Goths, who were outnumbered and outgeneralled. What marked Narses' strategy was his effective use of infantry. Whereas Totila placed his foot-soldiers in the rear so that, if the cavalry was routed, it might fall back to the safety of the infantry line, Narses placed his archers on the wings, where they enfiladed the Gothic horsemen before they reached the Byzantine lines. The struggle was sharp and furious; Procopius[111] gives both sides equal marks for valour. But towards evening the Goths turned and fled, panicking in turn their own infantry line, and the whole army dissolved into a general rout. Totila, accompanied by five Goths, fled through the night, pursued by an equal number of imperial troops who were unaware that their quarry was the Gothic king. Before the night was up, the pursuers came close enough for a Gepid trooper to give Totila a mortal wound, and though the Goths rode on and the pursuers gave up the chase, Totila had reached the end of the road. Another version of Totila's death had it that he was wounded by an arrow during the battle, and it was his departure from the field which sparked the rout. The Byzantines learned of his death only when a Gothic woman pointed out his grave.

The Goths who escaped the rout mustered at Pavia and chose Teias as king. Totila had left enough treasure at Pavia to allow Teias to mint gold and silver coins bearing the likeness of the emperor Anastasius, and he made an unsuccessful attempt to make an alliance with the young Merovingian king of the Franks, Theudobald, even though the Goths had already discovered that the Frankish interests in Italy were entirely selfish. But Theudobald was still a boy, and unwell. Narses, meanwhile, reorganized his forces. His first act after his victory at *Busta Gallorum* was to dispense with the Lombard federates in his army. They were a lawless lot and he was wise to send them home under escort. After Justinian's death, they would become the next in the line of Italy's invaders. Then Narses moved south to capture Rome, taking Perugia and Narni on the way. Once again, the keys to Rome were sent to Justinian.

Meanwhile Teias became anxious for the fortress at Cumae on the western shore some 14 kilometres from Naples, where Totila had deposited the bulk of his wealth. Narses had put the fortress under siege. Teias moved south, slipping past the imperial army in Tuscany, and took up a position close by Mt Vesuvius on the left bank of the river Sarno. There Narses and Teias faced each other for two months, until a Gothic traitor delivered the ships which supplied the Goths into Byzantine hands. The Goths sought refuge on Monte Lattari nearby, but since supplies were even scarcer there, they were forced to fight. It was an infantry battle, man to man, with no room for manoeuvre. Teias fought in the front rank until his shield was full of spears, when he would call for a new one. Finally, when the day was one-third over and twelve spears stuck in Teias' shield, he was struck down as he took a fresh one, and for a moment exposed his chest. But the Goths fought on until nightfall, and next morning renewed battle and refused to acknowledge defeat until the day was nearly over. Then they came to terms, agreeing to leave Italy.

The young Frankish king Theudobald had turned a deaf ear to Teias' plea for help, but two of his subjects were prepared to act on their own. Two brothers belonging to the Alamanni, Leutharis and Buccelin, put together a great army of Franks and Alamanni, invaded Italy in 553 and won a success at Parma, where they ambushed a company of Heruls in imperial service. Narses had spent the winter investing Cumae, but with spring, he left a small force to continue the blockade and moved to central Italy, mopping up Città Vecchia, Florence, Volterra, Pisa and Luna, and, after a siege of three months, Lucca.[112] Then Narses went to Ravenna, where, in due time, Aligern, Teias' brother and the commander of the Gothic garrison at Cumae, arrived to surrender the keys of the fortress. If a choice had to be made between the empire and the Franks, he elected the empire.

Narses chose to spend the winter in Rome and, for the moment, Leutharis and Buccelin had their way. Bypassing Rome, Buccelin advanced down the west coast to the toe of Italy, while his brother advanced down into the heel. Leutharis got back to Venetia safely, though he lost much of his booty when Artabanes, commanding the garrison at Pesaro, inflicted a defeat on him. But once back home, he and a good part of his army fell victim to plague.

Buccelin, meanwhile, was returning northwards through Campania. For want of other food, his troops had filled their stomachs with ripe grapes plucked from the vineyards, and their bowels were loose. At the Volturno river, he met Narses, and the resulting battle was proof of Narses' tactical skill. The Franks in wedge-shaped formation plunged into the Byzantine line, only to find the centre unoccupied. Sindual's cranky Herul contingent, which should have been there, was late coming, but when it did arrive, as Narses calculated, the Franks were surrounded and only a remnant escaped to find refuge at Compsa (*mod.* Conza). Narses had made a tactical advantage out of the tardiness of the Heruls.

The siege of Compsa lasted through the winter. Supplies had run low by spring, and the commander, Ragnaris, sought to negotiate. But after Narses had broken off the parley, Ragnaris, on his way back to the fort, turned and directed an arrow at Narses. He missed, but one of Narses' bodyguard shot back, and Ragnaris was mortally wounded. With his death, the Franks lost heart and surrendered, and Narses sent them off to Constantinople.

In year of the battle of *Busta Gallorum* Justinian dispatched an army to Spain.[113] The Visigothic kingdom had ruled central Spain for several generations, but in the south it was the local aristocracy together with the episcopate which had effective control. It was probably an attempt to change this state of affairs which led to an uprising in Cordoba, whose citizens defeated the attempt of the Visigothic king Agila (549–555) to suppress them. Agila lost his son, his royal treasure and much of his army, and a noble named Athanagild chose this moment to rebel. But Agila was stronger than Athanagild reckoned, and in 551–552 he sent an urgent appeal to Justinian for help. The emperor cannot have welcomed Athanagild's timing, but the opportunity which the appeal presented was one he could not afford to overlook. The Spanish Visigoths were a threat to the restored empire: about 546, they had crossed the Strait of Gibraltar to take Septem, and though the Byzantines had dislodged them, who could tell when they might try again?

The Byzantine campaign in Spain is described by no Byzantine writer, though Jordanes, who finished his *Getica* just as the expedition departed, records Athanagild's rebellion, and adds a muddled note, 'So Liberius the Patrician is on his way with an army to oppose him.'[114] Liberius' force reached Spain by midsummer, 552, and after three years of campaigning, Athanagild got what he wanted with Byzantine help. Agila's comrades killed him and made Athanagild king. Then Athanagild, who had no further use for the Byzantines, discovered that they were not easy to remove. The Byzantine presence remained in Spain until ca. 624.

The boundaries of the Byzantine province of *Spania* are uncertain. It took in the Balearic Islands, south Baetica and part of *Carthaginiensis*, including the city of Cartagena, and Cordoba may have been part of it, though that is uncertain. Its governor was the Master of Soldiers of Spain, who ranked on a par with the Masters of Italy and Africa, and his headquarters was either Cartagena or Malaga. *Spania* was not a large presence in Spain. But the speed with which Justinian seized upon an internal division in another barbarian kingdom as a chance to expand the empire shows that, plague, natural catastrophes and financial stringency notwithstanding, the ageing emperor still clung to his dream of 'renewal'.

The province of Spain marked the furthest limit of the *renovatio imperii*.

In Italy, Narses continued to pacify and consolidate. In 554, responding to a petition of Pope Vigilius, Justinian issued a 'divine pragmatic sanction' designed to restore the social fabric as it had existed under Amalasuintha and Theodahad. It was an effort to turn back the clock: an unsuccessful effort, but well meant just the same. All Totila's donations were to be nullified; all privileges granted by Amalasuintha, Athalaric or Theodahad to the senate and Roman people were to be inviolable. Confiscated property was to be restored; slaves were to be returned to their owners, *coloni* to their estates, and nuns who had wed under Totila's 'tyranny' were to be sent back to their convents. For senators of the higher grades – *gloriosi* – travel between Rome and Constantinople was to be freely allowed, which was a signal for the colony of Italian refugees in Constantinople to go home.[115]

The Franks were in no position to interfere. A swingeing defeat at the hands of the Saxons eliminated them for the moment as a danger. A Gothic insurrection in Aquileia about 561 was successful enough to take Verona and Brescia, but Narses dealt with it firmly, and in November, 562, the keys of the two cities arrived in Constantinople.[116] Sindual and his Herul mercenaries tried their luck at mutiny in 565, and failed. Sindual was hanged and the Heruls pass from history. Italy was firmly under imperial control.

As the decade of the 550s came to a close, Justinian must have regarded his effort to renew the empire as a success. If he did, we cannot blame him. The *renovatio imperii* had been more costly than he could have imagined at the start of his reign. For the Italian senatorial class it was calamitous. But the unification had been accomplished, and the new order imposed.

The accomplishment lasted only until the third year after Justinian's death, when the Lombards invaded and two-thirds of Italy rapidly passed out of Byzantine control. In Africa, however, the conquest lasted longer. The exarchate of Africa under the emperor Maurice (582–602) had roughly the same boundaries as did the prefecture under Justinian. In 647 the caliph Othman commissioned the Arab governor of Egypt, Abdallah ibn Saad, to attack Africa, but the conquest was a drawn-out enterprise and Carthage did not fall until 695. Byzantine Africa seems to have been quietly prosperous. It exported wheat and olive oil to Constantinople, and camels, dates, and probably oil as well to Merovingian France; and the potters of the Carthage area recovered a good deal of their former market for the fine African Red Slip table ware which had dominated the eastern and western Mediterranean before the Vandal conquest.[117] Even judged by the harsh standards of historical hindsight, Justinian's *renovatio imperii* there was a temperate success.

4

THE HOME FRONT
Domestic problems

THEOLOGICAL IMBROGLIO

The Monophysites no longer were united, if they ever were. In Egypt, Severus of Antioch represented 'standard Monophysitism', but his former ally, Julian of Halicarnassus, who came to Egypt with him after both fled from their sees in 518, soon parted company. Severus taught that Christ's body before the Resurrection was corruptible, and that Adam had been created mortal and corruptible, whereas Julian's doctrine had it that both were created incorruptible, though Adam after the Fall became a mortal man. Julian died soon after 527, but his teaching won a large following, and Severus, to his immense chagrin, found himself the leader of a minority in Alexandria. Julian's disciples, known variously as Aphthartodocetists, Julianists or Gaianists, captured the souls of the masses.

The see of St Mark became vacant in 535, and the empress Theodora contrived the election of a Severan supporter, Theodosius. But in the midst of his acclamation, a mob of Julianist monks surged into the church, ejected him and set their own candidate, Gaianus, on the episcopal throne. When Theodora heard the news, she approached Justinian, who gave her a free hand to act.[1] Narses was sent to Alexandria to investigate, with a detachment of soldiers at his back. The ordination of Theodosius was vindicated, and Gaianus was deported to Sardinia after an episcopate of only 104 days. Theodosius held on to his see with the support of imperial troops for almost seventeen anarchic months, during which Narses had to wage street warfare against the Gaianists, at one point even setting part of the city ablaze. But it was long enough for Theodosius to ordain a succession of bishops and ensure that the doctrine of Severus remained 'standard Monophysitism'. Then he left for Constantinople and never returned.

The emperor had already, on 15 March, 533, published an edict which set out his confession of faith. It was a subtle statement with a Chalcedonian flavour, though it left the *Tome* of Leo unmentioned. In the winter of 534/5, he invited Severus to Constantinople, and Severus came, although he had little optimism about the outcome. But when he arrived, with Theodora as intermediary he opened the eyes of the patriarch Anthimus to the unrighteousness of the Chalcedonian creed. Pope John II was not unreasonable; on 25 March, 534, he accepted the Theopaschite formula with its subtle but unmistakable whiff of Monophysitism. But next year, in May, 535, there was a new pope, Agapetus I, who came to Constantinople early in 536 on a mission for King Theodahad.[2] Agapetus achieved nothing for the Ostrogothic king, but he was a more effective champion of Chalcedon. Pope and emperor were both native speakers of Latin, as a Syriac chronicler noted with a feeling of alienation.[3] Agapetus engineered the deposition of Anthimus, and before he died on 22 April, he consecrated a new patriarch of Constantinople, Menas, a native of Alexandria, and the director of Constantinople's chief hospital, the Hospice of Sampson. An imperial edict came down in August, banning Severus, Anthimus and their followers from the capital. Severus departed for Egypt to enjoy the hospitality of a wealthy patron at Xois in the Delta, where he died two years later. Anthimus found shelter next door to the Great Palace, in the house of Hormisdas, under Theodora's protection.

He was soon joined there by Theodosius. Theodosius, having reached Constantinople, remained as stubborn a Monophysite as ever. He would not sanction Agapetus' notion of orthodoxy, which was guarded after Agapetus' death by the Roman deacon Pelagius, the first of a line of papal nuncios in Constantinople. Thereupon Justinian deposed Theodosius, and dispatched his successor to Alexandria, already ordained by the patriarch at Constantinople.[4] Theodosius and some 300 Monophysite clergy were shut up in the fortress of Derkos in Thrace between the Long Wall and the capital, until the empress delivered them. Theodosius was to live on until 566, at first under Theodora's protection in the Palace of Hormisdas, and then, after she died, Justinian, respecting her death-bed wish, continued her protection. Theodosius was to become the unchallenged leader of the Monophysite church, and, like his Chalcedonian rival, he was recognized as 'Ecumenical Patriarch' by his followers, if not by the emperor.[5] Monophysitism and orthodoxy were to develop along separate ecclesiastical paths, with the first drawing its strength from the countryside with its monasteries, and orthodoxy occupying the cities with their episcopal seats. But only in retrospect does the schism seem insuperable. Contemporaries had not yet abandoned the concept of One Holy Church.

Upon his return to Egypt, Severus allowed John of Tella, whom he had already ordained as a presbyter, to consecrate priests across the Persian frontier, but his intention was not, it seems, to set up a rival anti-Chalcedonian hierarchy. The enemy in Persia were the Nestorians, not the Chalcedonians. But John interpreted his commission broadly and consecrated priests on *both* sides of the frontier, taking his catechumens from the monasteries where Greek was a foreign language. He tried to ensure that all his priests were literate and would ordain no monk who could not at least sign his name, but he was prepared to be flexible if the aspiring monk was willing to learn this modest skill.[6] After barely more than a year, John was arrested in Persia, brought to Antioch and put to death by the Antiochene patriarch Ephraim. The priests he had ordained were hunted down. But as John of Ephesus wrote in his *Life* of John, God raised up another John to carry on.[7]

The turning point soon arrived. In 541, while the Ghassanid emir Harith was in Constantinople on other business, he approached Theodora to ask for 'orthodox' (by which he meant Monophysite) bishops for his tribe. Harith's loyalty at this juncture was important to maintain, for imperial prestige was low in the East after the Persian sack of Antioch.[8] With Theodora's blessing, Theodosius consecrated two monks, Jacob Baradaeus as metropolitan of Edessa and Theodore as metropolitan of Bostra, capital of the Roman province of Arabia. Both were nomadic bishops. Theodore, who was himself an Arab, did not reside in Bostra, but moved from camp to camp, usually in the train of the Ghassanids as they roved through the provinces of Arabia and Palestine. Nor did Jacob live in Edessa, where he was liable to arrest, but he ranged across the whole region of the East, and extended his activity even as far as to Egypt. By his death in 578, he had consecrated 27 metropolitan bishops and some 100,000 clergy.

Theodosius himself moved more slowly. Steadfastly loyal, he was essentially a moderate churchman who never ruled out reconciliation. Only in 557 did he ordain a Monophysite patriarch of Antioch, one Sergius of Tella, who did not dare go to his see but remained in Constantinople with Theodosius, with whom he soon quarrelled. But Jacob Baradaeus was ready to disregard the law. Justinian tried hard at first to have him arrested, but he was a master of disguise (hence his nickname, Baradaeus: 'man in rags') and his flock never betrayed him. He was never caught, and eventually the emperor conceded toleration in practice, if not in theory. The new Monophysite clergymen came for the most part from the monasteries, their language was Syriac and their differences with the Chalcedonian hierarchy were cultural as well as theological. It is not difficult to recognize a populist movement in Baradaeus' launch of an alternative communion, and its political effect was separatist.[9]

Meanwhile the search for an acceptable formula went on. As the empress Theodora saw it, the stumbling block was the intransigence of the popes, and she failed to comprehend that behind that intransigence was the full force of popular opinion in the western empire. The Monophysites had the better theologians, but Rome was not prepared to yield to theological subtlety. When Agapetus died, Theodora's choice as his successor was the deacon Vigilius, who had come to Constantinople with Agapetus and showed a promising degree of flexibility. But before Vigilius got back to Rome, the election was held and Silverius, with Ostrogoth backing, carried off the prize. Silverius' father, Pope Hormisdas, had taken a hard line during the Acacian Schism, and Theodora could not expect much from the son. But she was not to be put off. With the help of Belisarius and Antonina, Silverius was hustled off the throne of St Peter and Vigilius was elected his successor.[10]

But the rift between Monophysite and Chalcedonian could not be mended by manipulating churchmen, as the next act in the drama showed. In 544, Justinian issued an edict condemning the teachings of two friends of Nestorius, Theodoret of Cyrrhus and Ibas of Edessa, and along with them, Theodore of Mopsuestia (ca. 350–ca. 428), who along with Diodore of Tarsus had fathered the Antiochene theology which had shaped Nestorius' thought.

Only a smidgen separated the Chalcedonian doctrine of the Trinity from Nestorianism, and in Monophysite eyes, the Chalcedonians *were*, in fact, Nestorians. Hence it was a logical gambit to emphasize the difference by demonizing Nestorianism. The Council of Chalcedon had brought Theodoret and Ibas into communion, and Theodore was respected in Chalcedonian circles but detested by the Origenists whose teachings had taken hold in the Palestine monasteries after Mar Saba's death. By condemning the 'Three Chapters', as the gospel of this trinity of theologians was labelled, Justinian hoped to remove an obstacle to reconciliation.[11]

Origen (ca. 185–ca. 254) had imported Neoplatonist speculation into Christian thought. Did a person's soul exist before birth? And if so, was the preexistent soul of Christ one of many such pure intellectual entities that assumed flesh, though it was the only one to escape the cosmic Fall because of its union with the Divine Word: the *Logos*? The Origenist answer was that Father, Son, Holy Spirit, Angels, Powers and man in the dignity of his soul had once been part of a unique monistic structure encompassing all intellectual entities, and this structure was broken by the Fall of Adam. Thus man's soul was an intellectual being incarcerated in the body, and it sought return to the pure, divine substance whence it came.[12] Origen only speculated, but in the fourth century, the monk Evagrius Ponticus (ca. 345–399) developed his thought into a new doctrine about the nature of the *Logos* which won converts in the monasteries of Palestine, particularly in the New Laura near Jerusalem.

Before his death, Mar Saba, archimandrite of the Judaean lauras, had appealed to Justinian against the abbot of the New Laura, Nonnus, but Justinian made no response.[13] On the contrary, less than four years after the saint's death, two Palestinian monks, Theodore Askidas from the New Laura and Domition from the Origenist monastery of Martyrios, caught Justinian's attention when they came to Constantinople in 536 to take part in a synod. Conflict broke out within the Great Laura itself in 539. The Origenists were banished, and moved to the New Laura, and from there a pious army of ascetics, armed with picks, crowbars and holy rage, set forth to assault the Great Laura. But they were scattered on the way by a violent storm sent, according to Cyril of Scythopolis, St Sabas' biographer, by the 'God of St Sabas'.[14]

Thus far, Origenism was a Palestinian problem. It was the pope's nuncio in Constantinople, Pelagius, who made an issue of it. Probably he hoped to downgrade the influence of Theodore Askidas, who had displaced him as Justinian's theological familiar. Origenism was duly condemned by imperial edict. Justinian produced a long treatise against Origen in 543, which all five patriarchs signed. Theodore survived easily, however, though he developed a marked distaste for Pelagius in the process. So it was with the realization that Pelagius would be annoyed that Theodore suggested to the emperor that the censure of the 'Three Chapters' would be an acceptable correction to the Council of Chalcedon and would dampen the appeal of Monophysitism. His zeal was not decreased by the knowledge that the anti-Origenists in the Great Laura of Mar Saba were admirers of Theodore of Mopsuestia and would be distressed at his inclusion in the condemnation, and in fact, one side-effect of the 'Three Chapters' controversy was to strengthen Origenism in Palestine.[15]

Early in 544, Justinian issued his 'Three Chapters' edict, and the reaction was hardly what he had hoped. For the Severan Monophysites it was irrelevant, and for the Julianists, there was never any hope anyway. The West saw it as an attack on Chalcedon and was hostile. Africa was particularly intractable. Still, from the pope, Justinian anticipated a happier result. But Vigilius refused to subscribe.

Eventually Justinian had his way. The Fifth Ecumenical Council of 553 wrung a partial concession out of Vigilius, and on 23 February, 554, he capitulated and condemned the 'Three Chapters' explicitly. But the intervening years were occupied with bullying and theological manoeuvres. In late November, 545, Vigilius was arrested in Rome in the midst of mass at St Cecilia in Trastevere, and taken to Constantinople, thus missing Totila's terrible siege of the city. The pope travelled slowly, with a long sojourn through the winter of 545–546 in Sicily, where the African bishops made clear to him their bitter opposition to the 'Three Chapters' edict.[16] In January, 547, Vigilius and the emperor had an emotional reunion in Constantinople. But on the edict the pope was not prepared to yield without a fight. He knew too well the antagonism of the western clergy to it. Waiting for him in Constantinople when he arrived was a small band of African and Italian bishops hostile to the edict, chief among them Facundus from Hermiane in Africa, a tough-minded theologian with a good command of Greek who advocated stern measures in defence of Chalcedon. The pope excommunicated the patriarch of Constantinople, Menas, and the bishops who supported the edict, and possibly the empress Theodora into the bargain.

Coercion replaced argument, and Vigilius' position softened. In June, 547, Vigilius made up with Menas and wrote a secret letter to Justinian and Theodora indicating that he personally condemned the 'Three Chapters' but feared that an anathema would harm the rights of Rome. In April of the next year, however, he issued a *Iudicatum* which did anathematize the 'Three Chapters'. At the same time, he upheld the creed of Chalcedon. The *Iudicatum* should have satisfied the West, or so Vigilius hoped.

But then the terrible empress died and Vigilius recovered his courage. It was already clear that the *Iudicatum* was a failure. In

Constantinople Facundus published a denunciation so vehement that he thought it prudent to go into hiding, where he nonetheless continued to follow events closely. In Africa a General Council of bishops in 550 rejected the condemnation of the 'Three Chapters', broke off communion with the pope and sent a protest to Justinian. Vigilius fought back with anathemas. But in Illyricum and Dalmatia there were protests too: the Illyrian bishops deposed their metropolitan, Benenatus of Justiniana Prima, who had accepted the condemnation, and even from Merovingian France there came a concerned letter from the bishop of Arles. Justinian could not afford western alienation at this juncture, for the Byzantine conquest of Italy was still in the balance. He allowed Vigilius to abrogate his *Iudicatum* in return for a secret promise that he would work for the condemnation of the 'Three Chapters'.

In July, 551, exasperated by the pope's failure to keep his promise, Justinian issued a second edict against the 'Three Chapters'. Two years of rigorous negotiation followed. The pope's resistance was founded less on personal conviction than fear of his Latin bishops in the West. A new delegation arrived from Africa, chief among them Reparatus of Carthage, who was deaf to the subtle arguments of the Greek bishops. So his removal was duly arranged: he was charged with complicity in Guntharith's *putsch* in Africa in 546, and bundled off into exile where he died. His fate sufficiently impressed one colleague, Firmus, primate of Numidia, that he was willing to sign anything. But the remaining two Africans stood firm, and followed the pope when he slipped out of Constantinople just before Christmas, 551, and crossed the Bosporus to Chalcedon where he took refuge in the church of St Euphemia. Meanwhile the emperor's agents set to work in Africa, and their operations were effective in spite of a denunciation which Facundus launched from his hiding-place. Reparatus was replaced as bishop of Carthage by a more flexible prelate who used a potent combination of persuasion and force to win over the African clergy.

In August, 552, the patriarch of Constantinople, Menas, died. A replacement was found with breathtaking speed: Eutychius, an abbot, who had been sent to the capital as the nuncio of the bishop of Amaseia, who was ill. He was consecrated while his predecessor's body still lay in Hagia Sophia,[17] and Vigilius absented himself from the consecration. Nor did he appear at the Fifth Ecumenical Council when at last it opened in Hagia Sophia in May, 553. But he issued a *Constitutum* wherein he condemned texts attributed to Theodore and Theodoret, thereby leaving a loophole. Possibly these texts were not authentic? But Justinian refused to accept the *Constitutum* and the Council condemned Vigilius. The emperor applied force. Pelagius, the papal nuncio who had represented the pope at the Council, was incarcerated in a succession of monasteries, and used his leisure to pen a treatise in defence of the 'Three Chapters'. But Vigilius yielded eventually: in February, 554, he published a second *Constitutum*, anathematizing the 'Three Chapters', and abrogating anything he had written in their defence. He was already a sick man, suffering from a kidney stone, and he died on the way back to Rome. He had never been by nature an inflexible prelate, and in his heart, he probably had more sympathy for Justinian's theological position than he could admit publicly, but he knew that the western churchmen expected him to put up a good fight, and he had done his best to meet their expectations.[18] But it was not enough. His body, which was brought to Rome, was interred, not in St Peter's basilica like all other sixth-century popes, but in the church of St Sylvester.

The Fifth Ecumenical Council was not a shining example of ecclesiastical statesmanship,[19] and it made no difference to the Monophysite problem. What emerged were three orthodoxies, if we define orthodoxy as a creed which its disciples accept as correct. There was the western orthodoxy of Rome, the Monophysite orthodoxy represented by a new hierarchy of priests taken for the most part from the eastern monasteries, and between them, the orthodoxy of Constantinople, legislated by Justinian and confirmed at an ecumenical council notable for the absence of western bishops. Rather than uniting Christendom, the Fifth Council defined the Byzantine church of the future.[20]

The battle must have seemed worth fighting to the emperor. Not to us, to be sure, who have the clear vision of hindsight. But to contemporaries, the 'Three Chapters' debate showed Justinian at his most authoritarian, not merely arguing theological subtleties better than most theologians, but using the muscle of imperial power to win his points. If Justinian deserves to be called a 'caesaropapist', it is the 'Three Chapters' controversy on which his claim rests. On the Balkan front, Slavic invaders threatened Constantinople, and there was open criticism of the negligence that Justinian showed in his conduct of the Italian campaign.[21] Yet his resolve remained firm. One is forced to admire his confidence and sense of purpose. The battle for religious unity in the empire was already lost, but Justinian was far from admitting defeat. He soldiered on, doing what he considered his imperial duty.

Justinian was now in a position to choose Vigilius' successor as pope, and his choice fell on Pelagius. But there was a condition: Pelagius was to accept the condemnation of the 'Three Chapters'. Since Pelagius had just written a defence of them, his *volte face* is, perhaps, surprising. But Pelagius was an able church politician and not without ambition. He accepted. He returned to a hostile population in Italy, but Narses and his troops maintained firm control. On Easter Sunday, 556, he was ordained bishop of Rome by two bishops and a presbyter, for the usual complement of three bishops willing to act could not be found. Escorted by troops, he processed to St Peter's basilica where he mounted the pulpit and before the congregation declared his adherence to the doctrine of Chalcedon and his support for the 'Three Chapters' which the Fifth Council had condemned.[22] Rome remained suspicious. But little by little, Pelagius succeeded in imposing his authority on Italy south of the Po river; north of it, however, Milan remained estranged until the Lombard invasion, and it was more than 140 years before the see of Aquileia resumed communion.

Outside Italy, in Gaul and Spain, Pelagius' standing was low. The church in Gaul maintained communion both with Rome and with the schismatic sees north of the Po. The papacy had been dealt a defeat and it did not entirely recover its prestige until the eighth century. In Africa, Justinian used strong-arm tactics when persuasion failed. Recalcitrant bishops went into exile, and it is to one of the most fanatical of these, Victor, bishop of Tunnena in Africa Proconsularis, that we owe much of our information about the African persecution. Exile and imprisonment did not lessen his zeal. In 564, he and five other African prelates were cited before the emperor and patriarch, and since all six refused to yield, they were confined to various monasteries in Constantinople. There Victor wrote a world chronicle from Creation to 567, which as ecclesiastical history is thin, prejudiced and inaccurate, but preserves valuable titbits on secular matters.

But by then, the most obstinate defenders of the 'Three Chapters' were dead, and the passion was spent. Africa was thriving and peaceful. When Justin II succeeded in 565, his first edict was one sending the exiles back to their sees with the provision that they should maintain established religious practice and eschew any novelties.[23] Justinian's successors treated Africa kindly, and the church prospered.

The rift with the papacy began to close before the death of Pelagius, and under his successor, John III, Africa returned to the fold.[24]

Among the Monophysites, the dispute mattered very little. The development of a separate Monophysite hierarchy continued slowly, but irreversibly. Theodosius was the undisputed leader, addressed as 'Ecumenical Patriarch' by his suffragans, including Jacob Baradaeus, and he kept a firm hand on the theological dissensions within his church. To the Aphthartodocetists there was added a new splinter group in the 550s, the 'Tritheists', who argued, like good Aristotelians, that within each person of the Trinity, there were to be found both generalized individuality (*hypostasis*), corresponding to the general characteristics that allow us recognize, let us say, a horse as a horse, and individual nature (*physis*), which marks one horse off from another. This doctrine won over the leading Aristotelian philosopher of the age in Alexandria, John Philoponus, and it made another convert with some prestige: the empress Theodora's grandson, Athanasius, who eventually founded his own little splinter sect. Theodosius pursued the Tritheists with diplomacy, argument and finally excommunication.

The Monophysite centres were the great monasteries in north-east Syria and Egypt, where the bishops found shelter and working space. The Monophysite patriarchs of Antioch and Alexandria in the last part of the sixth century made their diocesan seats in rural monasteries, the former at the monastery of Gubba Barraya between Beroea and Hierapolis and the latter at Enaton, at the ninth milestone west of Alexandria. This was partly because the authorities banned their entry into their primatial cities,[25] but partly, too, out of choice. The Monophysite bishops made a virtue out of necessity.[26] The rural villages were theirs, even if the cities were not, and they were thus better positioned than the Chalcedonians in the contest for the hearts of the people. We must see the success of the Monophysites in the context of the sixth-century decline of the cities, for which they must bear a small share of the responsibility, for their movement diminished the importance of the city as a centre of religious life.

THE ADMINISTRATION OF THE EMPIRE

The emperor's apparatchiks

One of the side-effects of Justinian's concentration on theology was that he had less time to spend on the administrative details of the empire. He grew older, and so did the men about him. Justinian was about 70 years old at the time of the Fifth Ecumenical Council. In the years that followed, he continued to speculate with consuming passion on the nature of the Trinity, but there was no great fire left in his belly when it came to repairing affairs of state.

Yet the earlier part of his reign was full of reforming zeal. To quote his own words, he spent night and day reflecting on measures which were pleasing to God and useful to his subjects,[27] and on this point, or at least the first half of it, his contemporaries agreed: he had an endless capacity for work, and he took time neither to eat nor sleep![28] He had an upstart's passion for attaching his name to reforms: it was his reason for making them, grumbled his secret critic, Procopius.[29] He taxed heavily and spent prodigiously. Evagrius,[30] who wasted no love on him, thought him avid for money, but a generous builder of churches, orphanages, homes for the aged and hospitals for the sick. Justinian took the imperial philanthropic mission seriously.

He laid his plans as heir apparent, and came to the throne in 527 with a clear idea not only of what he wanted to do, but where to find able men to help him. They served him well, and in return received the emperor's support. One was the quaestor Tribonian, whom Justinian dismissed in a futile attempt to appease the mob in the *Nika* revolt of 532. We shall meet him again as chairman of the second law commission which drew up the Justinianic Code. But his career is worth a preliminary glance.

A product, probably, of the Beirut law school, he began his career in the office of the praetorian prefect of the East. Procopius[31] considered him a man of natural ability and good education, but avaricious, and willing to sell justice. When Justinian set up the first commission that drew up his first law code, the *Codex Vetus*, Tribonian was a member, and he must rapidly have proved his worth, for he was named chairman of the committee which produced the *Digest*. By the autumn of 529, he was quaestor. This was a year of McCarthyist fervour directed against pagans, and Tribonian's predecessor as quaestor had been caught by it.[32] He held the office until the *Nika* revolt, when as a sop to the mob he was replaced by the patrician Basilides, a former prefect of Illyricum and Master of Offices, who should have brought the regime some needed senatorial support. But Tribonian's work on the laws continued with no apparent interruption. By late 533, he was Master of Offices, and in 535, he was quaestor again. Information runs thin, but Tribonian seems to have continued as quaestor until 542, the year of the plague, which may have claimed him as a victim. A son and a number of grandchildren survived him. Justinian confiscated a share of his property nonetheless, but the confiscation was more a death duty than a mark of disfavour. It was the emperor's percentage of Tribonian's ill-gotten gains. He may have been a closet pagan: at least the tenth-century *Souda* reports the charge, but it is hard to credit, given the anti-pagan atmosphere of the times.

The same accusation was made by his enemies against John the Cappadocian, but he seems outwardly to have conformed. John, like Tribonian, was sacrificed in the *Nika* Revolt in January of 532, but by 18 October he was praetorian prefect again. John Lydus, who hated him, reports that he wormed his way into the emperor's favour, who was unaware of the Cappadocian's villainy. Lydus has lurid tales to relate. An acquaintance of his, Antiochus by name, was strung up when an informer claimed that he possessed some gold, and he died of the ill-treatment. John's native city of Philadelphia fell prey to one of the Cappadocian's agents who robbed it so thoroughly that it could not recover. One Philadelphian who owned a fine jewel was stripped, flogged and shut up in a mule shed. A discharged soldier named Proclus slew himself when he was unable to produce 20 gold pieces, and the Cappadocian's creatures hurled his corpse into the market place and plundered his property.[33]

Procopius,[34] with a broader perspective, thought John the Cappadocian an evil character who misused his power, but he acknowledged his ability. John was an uncultured man, and his Christianity was questionable: he did attend church, for it would not do to parade paganism under the emperor's nose, but gossip had it that he passed the night in the sanctuary muttering heathen incantations to himself. But he never fawned upon the emperor. Justinian and Theodora supported the Blues in the Hippodrome. John was a Green. When Justinian proposed the expedition against the Vandal kingdom and his courtiers feared to oppose him, John not only spoke out against the proposal, but even won over the emperor until a bishop revealed a dream foretelling victory to the emperor. He had no respect for Theodora and her meddling, and she in return developed a pure, undiluted hatred for him, which eventually brought him down. But until she did, Justinian's confidence in him remained unshaken.

He was an efficiency expert, and the imperial bureaucrats loathed him. It is significant that in the *Nika* revolt, John's predecessor as prefect, who was dismissed to make way for John's appointment, apparently supported the move to replace Justinian.[35] John reformed and retrenched wherever he could. He put limits on the fees that bureaucrats could charge for services.[36] He made entry into the imperial service more difficult, and that, combined with the cutbacks in *sportulae*, reduced the number of entrants, which, in turn, decreased the size of the prefectural bureaucracy. There was thus no time available for the paperwork dear to a bureaucrat's heart. John had no patience with rhetorical elegance in the civil service. His was a style diametrically opposed to that of the praetorian prefect of the Ostrogothic court, Cassiodorus, whose collection of letters, known as the *Variae*, is a monument to bureaucratic preciousness. Opposition was swept aside. Under the emperor Anastasius, the service had survived a reformer of the same ilk, Marinus the Syrian,[37] who had removed tax collection from the jurisdiction of the city councils and set up *vindices* (protectors) in the cities to do the job, and he deserves some of the credit for the full treasury which Anastasius left behind on his death. But John was an even tougher animal.

Greek replaced Latin as the official language of government business in the eastern prefecture. It was the language the people knew: what did it matter if Latin was hallowed by tradition? The imperial post was curtailed.[38] Previous emperors had tried to do likewise, but with John, the law was enforced.[39] The result was unanticipated distress. The imperial post had maintained stables for post horses, which provided a market for the grain harvested by the local farmers. When John closed the stables, the farmers could only leave their grain to rot, for overland transportation to distant markets was prohibitively expensive.

Another of John's economy measures which boomeranged was his effort to scrimp on the chandlery of the fleet which Belisarius led against Vandal Africa. The ship's biscuit which he provided spoiled, for he used the hypocaust of a public bath to bake the dough. Some 500 soldiers who ate the biscuit sickened and died.[40] His exactions[41] drove villagers off their land, and having nothing else to do, they migrated to Constantinople where they became the idle mob that burned the city in the *Nika* riots. John Lydus is the source of this charge, and he gives a vivid picture of one of the Cappadocian's creatures, the obese John Maxilloplumacius, vicar of the diocese of Asia, who released a swarm of 'wild beasts and Cappadocians', otherwise known as tax collectors, upon John's home province of

Lydia. The charge had a measure of truth, but the fiscal and judicial oppression which drove the provincials to the capital antedated the Cappadocian, and the chief source of it, as the emperor himself recognized, was the fact that provincial officials purchased their offices and sought to make a profit out of their purchase.[42] The system encouraged corruption.

By the spring of 535, it was clear that Ostrogothic Italy was not going to fall like a ripe plum into Justinian's clutches, and whether there is a connection or not, it is then that we have the start of a series of reforms intended to increase the efficiency of the provincial administration while at the same time reducing its size. In 536 John suppressed most of the dioceses, thus removing a layer of bureaucracy between the prefect and the provincial governors, who now combined military as well as civil functions in their jurisdictions. The reform was less than an unqualified success, but John's streamlining of officialdom was what the emperor wanted. In 538, John was consul, only the second ordinary consul whom Justinian appointed in the first decade of his reign (the other was Belisarius). By 540, his power was at its height. He knew how fiercely the empress Theodora hated him, and how delighted those groups injured by his reforms would be if he stumbled. He surrounded himself with a huge bodyguard to forestall assassination. But in the winter of 540–541, he toured the East where the masses applauded him, if the officials did not, and while he was away, Belisarius' wife, Antonina, insinuated herself into the confidence of his daughter Euphemia, his only child. Antonina talked openly with Euphemia, vilifying the emperor for his treatment of Belisarius. Euphemia was a naive and willing listener. She promised to sway her father to conspire with Antonina and usurp the throne.

Euphemia may have been naive, but John was not, and it is incredible that he would make an ally of Belisarius, for whom he nurtured a hearty dislike. But Belisarius *was* discontented,[43] and John knew it. Perhaps what attracted him to this conspiracy was the chance to implicate Belisarius in treason. John agreed to a midnight meeting with Antonina outside the city at Rufinianae, a suburb that was Belisarius' property. The empress saw to it that two officers whom Justinian trusted, Narses the eunuch and Marcellus the Count of the Excubitors, were at the trysting place, hidden but within earshot, and she also informed Justinian of her stratagem. John for his part took precautions: some of his bodyguard accompanied him. Rumour had it that Justinian warned John in advance not to meet Antonina, and that may have been true. Justinian would have been in character if he had given his minister a chance to save himself.

John and Antonina talked, Narses and Marcellus overheard him agree to Antonina's treasonable proposals, and out they rushed to arrest him. John's bodyguards intervened; Marcellus was wounded and John got away. But he lost his nerve for the moment and instead of going directly to the emperor and telling his story, he sought asylum in a church, thus leaving the initiative with Theodora.

He was banished to a church at Artace, a suburb of Cyzicus on the Asian side of the Sea of Marmara, where he was ordained a deacon. But he refused to carry out any clerical duties, so as not to wreck his chances of returning to office. Justinian had not yet abandoned him. He confiscated his property but returned a large part of it, and John could still afford a comfortable life. But an unpopular bishop of Cyzicus named Eusebius was murdered by a local youth gang, and John fell under suspicion, for he was a well-known enemy of the victim. It was John's misfortune that it was a commission of senators that was sent to investigate, and he could expect no mercy from them. The élite whose interests John had slighted now got their revenge. He was not convicted, but he was punished anyway. He was flogged, stripped of his property and exiled to Antinoe in Egypt. To add insult to injury, his palace in Constantinople was given to Belisarius.

Even in Egypt Theodora feared him. Four years into his exile there, she found two members of the Green party at Cyzicus who had belonged to the gang that killed Eusebius, and she tried with threats and promises to pressure them into giving evidence against John. With one she succeeded. The other would not yield even under torture. Yet Justinian waited until Theodora was dead before he recalled John to Constantinople. But his career was over, and he dropped out of sight.[44] He was a genius of sorts: a reformer who carried on where Anastasius' minister Marinus the Syrian had left off.[45] But his experience shows how difficult it was to make reforms, even for one as regardless of sensibilities as John the Cappadocian. The empress Theodora and the senatorial class lost no love upon each other, but against John they were united. His enemies brought him down, and Justinian, loyal though he was to his aides, had in the end to give him up.

Phocas,[46] who replaced John as praetorian prefect in the *Nika* riots, was aristocratic, distinguished and cultured. He was also, it seems, a secret pagan who survived one witch-hunt in 529, but just as the 'Three Chapters' dispute began to grow warm, in 545–546, there was another outbreak of anti-pagan McCarthyism, orchestrated by John of Ephesus, who at the time headed a Syrian monastery in a suburb of the capital. Phocas committed suicide, and Justinian directed that he be buried like a donkey, without funeral rites.[47] He was the antithesis of the Cappadocian: no threat to the palatine apparatchiks and consequently well liked by them, and his appointment to the praetorian prefecture was mere window-dressing. He lasted less than a year. But in 542/3 he served on the senatorial commission which investigated the murder of Eusebius, bishop of Cyzicus, and no doubt relished the fate of his old rival, John the Cappadocian.

John's successors in the prefecture had briefer terms. Theodotus, who took over in 541, was a bureaucrat who lasted about two years, and though Procopius sneered that he was too honest for the imperial pair, he did in fact return to the office after 546 and died in it.[48] However, between his two periods of tenure, Peter Barsymes took over, and Procopius[49] has nothing good to report about him. He was Theodora's protégé, a Syrian and a banker, and he moved to the prefecture from the office of the Sacred Largesses. Finance was his speciality. By now, all palatine officers must have known that the need for revenue was beginning to dominate the political agenda, and advancement in the service went to those who could best satisfy it. Barsymes scrimped where he could. He allowed the army payroll to fall into arrears. He issued a light-weight gold *solidus* to husband the gold reserves,[50] and it was perhaps he, too, who issued a *solidus* of adulterated gold in Egypt,[51] which was to provoke a currency crisis there in the late 550s. But what led to his dismissal in 546 was an unlucky speculation with Constantinople's grain supply: he sold off surplus stocks in 544 at good prices, and the next year, a poor harvest in Egypt forced him to make compulsory purchases in Thrace, Bithynia and Phrygia, which probably went hungry to feed the capital. But he returned as prefect of the East in 555 and continued in office some seven years, and possibly longer. In 562, as he was completing his second term, the Blues set fire to his house, which was a measure of his unpopularity,[52] but he built a splendid palace to replace it. His enemies spread rumours about his orthodoxy, as they did with John the Cappadocian: in Peter's case, the charge was Manichaeism, which was as dangerous to a palatine official's career as a charge of paganism. But no hostile coalition brought him down, and he retired wealthy.

Tribonian's replacement during the *Nika* riots, Basilides, was, like Phocas, a career civil servant, a good solid man, who respected the traditions of the past and counterbalanced progressives like Tribonian and John the Cappadocian. When he ended his career, he was Master of Offices.[53] But polish, mastery of the humane arts and reverence for the usages of the past were not the prime qualifications for office under Justinian's regime. The Libyan Iunillus, who succeeded Tribonian as quaestor, spoke bad Greek, but he was a man of standing in Africa, the author of an introduction to the Bible. He enlarged Byzantine Africa's representation in the service, and as an outsider, he had no great attachment to the traditions of the service. Nor, one imagines, did Alexander 'Scissors', the roving auditor[54] from one of the financial sections of the praetorian prefecture, whom we have already encountered in Italy where he was assigned in 540. He collected taxes mercilessly and cut army costs, thereby estranging both the troops and the Italians. He enriched himself, but he enriched the imperial treasury, too. With no thought for tradition, he swept away the officialdom of the western imperial court, thus diminishing the status of the Italian senatorial class and hastening the demise of the senate. Like other imperial bureaucrats, he moved easily from the *militia* of the civil service to the army, but we lose track of him after he suffered a defeat at Totila's hands in 541.

Two other officials made the transition more successfully, Narses and Liberius, and they illustrate another feature of this regime: incompetence or disfavour at court might necessitate retirement but old age did not. In Justinian's later years his regime became almost a gerontocracy. There was a noticeable lack of new blood. Petrus Marcellinus Felix Liberius, to give him his full name, began his career under Odoacer in Italy, and transferred his services to the Ostrogothic monarchy after Odoacer died. But Theodahad was more than he could stomach. He made a second transfer of his services to Justinian. We meet him next as Augustal prefect of Egypt. The prefecture was a minefield: Liberius' predecessor Rhodon had followed orders to support Paul of Tinnis, the Melkite patriarch of Alexandria, and in the execution of his duty, tortured a deacon to death. Liberius was appointed to investigate, and the unfortunate Rhodon was put to death, in spite of his defence that he had acted as Justinian directed. Then the emperor muddled on, ordering an Egyptian named John Laxarion to assume Liberius' post while at the same time instructing Liberius not to relinquish it. In the struggle that resulted, John lost his life, and Liberius was recalled to stand trial before the senate. He was acquitted, but Justinian may have collected a fine nonetheless.[55]

Yet in 549, when Liberius was an old man past 80, Justinian considered him seriously as commander-in-chief in Italy, and a year later, he did dispatch him to meet the Gothic invasion of Sicily, but on second thought, sent a replacement. Yet in 552, Justinian selected him to go to Spain to support the pretender Athanagild. Liberius was too elderly to be ambitious, and Justinian may have been running short of talent. Liberius died aged 89. By then, he had returned to his native Italy, and he was buried at Rimini.

Narses was a eunuch born in Persarmenia beyond the imperial borders, and presumably was a slave brought to Constantinople while still a boy. He had little formal education, but he got the practical training that a rearing in the palace imparted, and made his way up through the ranks by sheer ability.[56] The *Nika* riots gave him his chance; Theodora in particular seems to have noticed him. She sent him to Alexandria to support Theodosius against his Julianist rival Gaianus. By 538, he held the rank of *illustris*, the highest senatorial title, and he not only had the empress as an ally but he was the emperor's confidant. He rapidly emerged as Belisarius' rival. At *Busta Gallorum* in 552 he defeated Totila and smashed Ostrogothic power, but it was not skilful tactics alone that won him victory. He knew that the sinews of war were troops and supplies. He insisted that Justinian give him enough men and money to carry out his task, and got what he demanded: something that Belisarius could never do. At *Busta Gallorum* he outnumbered the Goths.

Narses was still in Italy when Justinian died. He ruled with a firm hand. The Pragmatic Sanction of 554 attempted to restore civil administration in Italy under a praetorian prefect, but Narses did nothing to ensure the success of the effort. In Rome itself, civil government fell into the hands of the pope and the church, and in Italy outside Rome, it was a heterogeneous group of military men, many of them easterners, who took charge of the administration. Narses himself spent much of his time in Rome, where he had an easy relationship with Pope Pelagius and John III after him, though Narses himself probably leaned towards Monophysitism. His residence in Rome was the old imperial palace on the Palatine Hill, overlooking the ruins of the Roman past, but he showed no apparent interest in them.

Justinian's building programme barely touched Italy.[57] In the area of Rome, Narses rebuilt a bridge over the Anio and not much else.

The country was poor. The Pragmatic Sanction tried to restore the social and economic fabric, but the senatorial class failed to recover. The only great office left for the Italian senators after the reforms of Alexander 'Scissors' was the urban prefecture. It was this office that was held in 573 by the future Pope Gregory the Great, who was only a boy of about twelve when Narses crushed the Goths at *Busta Gallorum*. Gregory was born into a wealthy senatorial family, and attended school in Rome, for the Pragmatic Sanction restored the stipends of professors, and himself became a senator. But the senate was a mere shadow which barely survived the end of the century.[58] When Gregory laid down the prefecture and abandoned the secular life for the church, he was moving from the old focus of power to the new.

As for Narses, Justin II recalled him in 568. He seems to have gone as far as Naples, changed his mind and returned to Rome. A few months after his recall, the Lombards invaded Italy, which perhaps determined him not to abandon Rome. There were stories that the empress Sophia was hostile, and that Narses called in the Lombards out of spite, but that is unlikely. He died, immensely wealthy, in the palace in Rome in his ninety-fifth year, and his sarcophagus was shipped to Constantinople.[59]

Justinian's officials who avoided disgrace grew old and rich in his service. The Master of Offices from 539 to the end of Justinian's reign was Peter the Patrician, who won his spurs in the negotiations with Theodahad before the invasion of Italy. He was learned, and long-winded, and the author of three works which survive only in fragments. He was by repute light-fingered, but he was an adroit old diplomat, who negotiated the peace treaty of 561 with Persia, and it was a reasonable settlement, though Justinian's successor was to repudiate it. He continued in office until his death, and after a brief hiatus, Justin II appointed his son to succeed him.[60]

Justinian's generals, too, grew old in the service. Bessas, who tried to enrich himself during Totila's siege of Rome, campaigned in Lazica in his late seventies, until Justinian turned against him and sent him into exile.[61] John, the nephew of Vitalian, was probably still serving under Narses in Italy as late as 560.[62] Belisarius was old, frail and immensely rich when he was summoned from retirement to defend Constantinople in 559. Justinian's cousin Germanus was a brilliant general, but his claim to be old Justin's heir was as good as Justinian's, and if Justinian was trusting, the empress Theodora was not. The two Justins, one of them Germanus' son and the other the future

Justin II, who was the son of Justinian's sister and the husband of Theodora's niece, represent a new generation, and Germanus' son inherited his father's ability. But the cadre of able men who had supported Justinian at the start of his reign was not replaced. The emperor's talent for recruiting faded as he grew older.

Procopius voiced open criticism: Justinian was too lackadaisical and ready to overlook the blunders of his subordinates. His unvoiced complaint which he confided to his *Secret History*, was that Justinian and Theodora were not comfortable in the company of good men.[63] But corruption was a way of life in the bureaucracy, and Justinian was by nature lenient. One modern scholar[64] has compared him to Stalin, but he lacked Stalin's ruthlessness. He maintained faith in his officers, and in return they kept the administrative and military momentum under way. Justinian's administration, in its last years, showed all the defects of an ageing regime, but one way or another, it kept the dark clouds at bay until after his death.

The codification of the laws

'The laws bear the same relation to practical matters as medicines have for diseases.' So Justinian, in the preface to a constitution of 541.[65] The quotation reveals his mindset, unchanged since he became emperor; indeed the project of codifying the law had no doubt germinated in his mind while he waited to succeed his uncle. He was the great physician, and the laws were to be his prescriptions for rehabilitating the empire.

Certainly improvement was needed. The empire had inherited two great masses of jurisprudence. One was the 'Old Law' (*ius vetus*), which consisted of laws and decrees of the senate (*senatus consulta*) that were not yet obsolete, though they dated to the early empire or even the republic, and the writings of jurists from the same period, particularly of those who had the right to make authoritative pronouncements (*ius respondendi*). This was a vast area of literature, sometimes contradictory and not completely available to most lawyers. Theodosius II and Valentinian III had made a modest reform by giving special weight to the opinions of five eminent jurists of the past, Papinian, Gaius, Ulpian, Modestinus and Paulus, but the problem remained. The other mass of jurisprudence was the 'New Law' (*ius novum*), consisting of imperial constitutions later than the second century. These had been brought together into two collections in the fourth century, named after the jurists who produced them,

202

the Gregorian and Hermogenian Codes, and to supplement them, Theodosius II had issued a code which gathered ordinances from the time when Constantine the Great made himself master of the western empire until 438. But valid constitutions outside the Theodosian Code had to be obtained separately.

Justinian attacked the problem with speed and confidence. Hardly seven months after Justin died, he summoned a ten-man commission chaired by John the Cappadocian to update the Gregorian and Hermogenian Codes, as well as the Theodosian Code which, by Justinian's reign, was a century old.[66] The commission was to add later constitutions and weed out obsolete laws and contradictions. The new code was to be limited to what was practical, and its aim was to curtail the ingenuity of lawyers who produced obscure constitutions in court to win a point even when it did not conform to general law.[67] The commission moved quickly, and the new Code came into effect in April of the next year.

Twenty months later, Justinian set up another commission to undertake the great work of collecting jurists' law, that is to say, private as opposed to imperial writings on Roman law. The chairman was Tribonian, who had been a member of the first commission, where he had proved his worth. In October, 529 or thereabouts, he had taken over the portfolio of senior law minister, *quaestor sacri palatii*, when the incumbent was accused of paganism and removed. As such, his duty was to draft imperial constitutions. Probably Tribonian was a product of the school at Beirut, the 'Harvard Law School' of the late empire, with a faculty famous for its historical orientation, intellectual distinction and its Latinity, though since the fifth century lectures had been given in Greek.[68] He was given full power to choose his collaborators, and his choice fell upon another government official, Constantinus, the *magister libellorum* whose function it was to prepare cases for the consistorium which served as the imperial supreme court; Dorotheus, the dean of the Beirut law school, and a colleague from the same school, Anatolius, whose father had served on the first commission; and from the Constantinople law school he chose two professors, Theophilus and Cratinus. These six, all holding the rank of *illustres*, were assisted by eleven barristers from the court of the praetorian prefect of the East. Their role is not clear. Perhaps it was they who noted obsolete rules and advised on procedure.

The work was enormous. The commissioners scanned 1,528 books written by Roman lawyers from the first to fourth centuries, excerpted them and organized them into fifty books divided into 432 chapters or 'titles'. The *Nika* riots came and went; they cost Tribonian his quaestorship but they did not disrupt the work of the commission which Tribonian continued to chair. His energy and acumen were enormous. He organized the commission into three sub-committees, each of which researched separate parcels of legal literature and in the final editing, the excerpts which each sub-committee had selected were arranged under individual 'titles' in the order in which they were read, with no attempt to amalgamate them. To some of the 'titles' were added selections from juristic texts that did not fall within the mandate of any of the sub-committees. These appear to have turned up while the compilation was going on, and in the final stages they were appended to appropriate titles.[69]

The excerpting was meticulous: the texts – 9,123 of them – were changed very little, and by and large, we can read them confident that they are what the jurists of the third century actually wrote.[70] The whole work was finished in three years and published on 16 December, 533, and it received the name *Digest* (in Greek, *Pandects*), following the example of the great casuistical works of the high classical revival. It superseded the 'Old Law' which in future was not to be cited in court.

At the same time, a new official law primer had been completed and published,[71] and came into force at the same time as the *Digest*. The textbook in the eastern law schools had been the *Institutes* of Gaius dating to the second century, and the new Code and Digest made it obsolescent. The new *Institutes* were written by Dorotheus and Theophilus, under Tribonian's supervision. It was, in fact, more than a school textbook, for Justinian gave it, like the *Digest*, the validity of an imperial statute.

As the commissioners worked on the Code, they encountered many arguments and opinions that were outmoded or unjust, some of which could be simply abolished, but there were some questions which required imperial constitutions to reform them appropriately. The emperor was a zealous improver, and in his first three years, there was a copious yield of new laws. In late 530 or early 531, these were assembled and published as a collection known as the *Fifty Decisions*, which is now lost. It contained only those decisions made before work on the *Digest* began, for Tribonian's commission quickly realized that a new edition of the Code of 529 would be necessary. That was the next project. Tribonian, together with Dorotheus and three lawyers, set to work at it, and had it ready for publication on 16 November, 534. The new Code, known as the *Codex Iustinianus repetitae praelectionis* ('Justinian's Code of Resumed Reading') came into force before the end of the year. It assembled in twelve books constitutions from the emperor Hadrian (117–138) up to the year of publication. The old Code, the *Codex Vetus* of 529, was superseded and has not survived.[72]

The whole great work, *Codex, Digest and Institutes*, the *Corpus Iuris Civilis* to give it the name which it has had since the sixteenth century, was intended as a unified body of law, unmarred by contradiction and confusion. Justinian forbade any commentaries on the *Digest*, and probably the rule applied to the whole *Corpus*. Only literal translations into Greek were allowed. Delinquents who breached these rules were to be treated as forgers. Justinian was determined that jurists should not muddy the clear instruction of the laws. But in the ancient world, it was one thing to make rules and quite another to enforce them. The *Digest* was to give rise in later ages to more literature than any other book except the Bible.

In the constitution[73] which prefaced the Code, Justinian indicated that he planned to produce a collection of his subsequent laws under the title *Novellae Constitutiones*, for he continued legislating, though his zeal declined in his later years. He never carried out the plan. However, unofficial collections were made, and we have three of these. The oldest is an abridged Latin version of 124 constitutions compiled by a law professor at Constantinople named Julian shortly after 555, for it contains no Novels dating later than that year. It was probably made for use in Italy. The fullest is the collection of 168 constitutions, which includes some measures of Justin II and his successor Tiberius, and hence cannot be earlier than Tiberius' reign, which ended in 582. It records each Novel in its original language, which is usually Greek.[74] The third is a collection of 134 Novels known as the *Authenticum*, which records the Greek originals in a literal translation into Latin. The *Authenticum*'s latest entry dates to 556, which allows the suspicion that it was made for use in Italy when the empire was trying to restore the status quo ante, that is, society as it existed before the Gothic War.

Justinian's reforming passion also touched legal training. The law schools at Alexandria and Caesarea were suppressed with scornful comment about their bungling teachers and emasculated science,[75] and for the future, legal education was concentrated in the schools of Constantinople and Beirut, though the latter never recovered from the earthquake of the mid-century. A five-year course was mandated, which was no great change, for most law students before Justinian seem to have taken five years. Freshmen took lectures on the *Institutes* and the first part of the *Digest*; the second and third years were also devoted to parts of the *Digest*. The fourth year was devoted to private study, but still centred around the fourth and fifth parts of the *Digest*, and the fifth year was spent on private study of the Code. For some reason that escapes us, freshmen had been named 'two-pounders' (*dupondii*) before Justinian's reform. Justinian considered the sobriquet ridiculous and decreed that henceforth they should be called after himself: 'Justinian's freshmen' (*Iustiniani novi*).[76] The emperor, as Procopius pointed out, had a passion for attaching his name to his reforms.

Two objectives met in the *Corpus* and their coupling was uneasy. On the one hand, the *Code* and the *Digest* were intended for use in the courts of the empire, and in the law schools. Their purpose was practical. They were intended to erase the uncertainties of the law, and by so doing, put an end to long-winded litigation. 'The laws have been delivered from a confused state of overburdened chaos', wrote John the Lydian, 'and the litigious regret their former burning of the midnight oil over contentious points, since for the future no chance is left of disputing them because of the clarity of the laws.'[77] On the other hand, the *Corpus* was a monument to the history and theory of Roman law. It is coloured by the same awareness of the great imperial traditions of the past that provided the rhetoric for Justinian's renewal of the Roman Empire. In the *Digest* in particular, reverence for the past very nearly overcame the needs of the present: it 'shows with peculiar clearness the Janus-like character of Byzantine civilization. The past, even when explicitly abolished ... shines through everywhere.'[78] We must, however, draw a distinction: Justinian's jurists invoked classical legal concepts, but they did not attempt to reinstate classical Roman law.[79] They were innovators in classical dress, using the rhetoric of the great tradition.

The *Corpus* was magnificent and impracticable; the mere fact that it came into force only two weeks after it was promulgated shows that the imperial authorities knew that it would have little effect in the far reaches of the empire, and perhaps they did not greatly care, for outside the capital the civil courts were not greatly used. In Egypt, there is no good evidence that they functioned at all after 500, and in the other provinces, local law and institutions continued to flourish even when they contradicted imperial legislation.[80] The *Code* and *Digest* were written in a language which most people in the eastern empire did not understand, and we need not be surprised to find provincials preferring arbitration and mediation to the civil courts, often using bishops or local holy men as arbiters. For the rural inhabitants of the empire, who were the vast majority, what Synesius of Cyrene wrote about life in the country a century earlier remained true: 'No doubt men know well that there is always an Emperor living, for we are reminded of this every year by those who collect the taxes; but who he is, is not very clear.'[81] Justinian's *Corpus* did not make a great deal of difference to most of his subjects. By the next century, it had fallen into neglect.

But let us not depreciate the achievement. It was the rediscovery of the *Digest* in eleventh-century Italy that led to the rise of the university of Bologna, which claims a foundation date of 1088, and Bologna's alumni sparked a revival of Roman law, which in turn resulted in a literate class of laymen trained in legal science. It is arguable that the European Renaissance began with the production of the *Vulgate Digest* by Irnerius for use as a textbook for his students at Bologna.[82] Whatever the immediate consequence of the *Corpus Iuris Civilis* may have been, it is the great lasting achievement of Justinian's reign.

The flavour of the laws: a look at the *Novels*

'For we are lovers of freedom. . .' Justinian on himself. The law where this remark appears deals with the status of a child born of a free mother and a father who was a tenant tied to an estate (*adscripticius*). Justinian ruled that the child should be free, and not inherit his father's status.[83] One of the golden threads we may pick out of Justinian's laws is a bias against slavery and serfdom. Another is a determination to vindicate the status of women, and their rights in marriage. A third was a determination to do away with corruption and promote efficient administration. And not only civil administration. Justinian's concern for efficiency and good government extended even to the church.

The laws governing slavery were simplified. Obsolete distinctions were removed. Freedmen guilty of a felony or infamous behaviour during their servitude had been classed as *dediticii* (captives) and denied citizenship, and slaves whose manumission was not completely legitimate for some reason had been bracketed as 'Junian Latins' without the right to make a will, inherit or act as guardians.[84] Justinian ruled that the freedom given to slaves should be unqualified.

Freedmen should, he asserted, conduct themselves as if they were freeborn citizens.[85] The rights of former masters as patrons were safeguarded, to be sure. If a patron complained about his freedman to a governor, the governor should pay heed; if a freedman abused any of his patron's family, he should be punished, and if he attacked any of them physically, he should be condemned to the mines.[86] But at the same time, a patron's demands on his freedman had to be reasonable; he must leave him enough time to earn his own living.[87]

Laws dating back to the emperor Augustus restricting the number of slaves one master might manumit and prohibiting the freeing of slaves under the age of 30 were dropped. Minors who had reached an age when they might legally dispose of their other property by their wills were given the right to manumit by will as well: slaves were not to be treated as a special case.[88] Well-born persons might not be condemned to slavery as a punishment, and a master who abandoned a sick slave could not reclaim him if he recovered.[89] A slave who was ordained to the clergy should be free, if his master was aware of the ordination and made no objection; if his master was unaware, then he had only one year in which to reclaim his property.[90] From Thessaloniki there came a report that infants abandoned in churches were being reclaimed as slaves by their parents after the church had reared them. Justinian ruled that such children should be free and their parents punished.[91]

Nothing very revolutionary. Throughout the history of imperial Rome, emperors had legislated to protect slaves. What is remarkable about Justinian's ruling that a sick slave abandoned by his master should be deemed free is that he had to make it, for the law was already on the statute books and dated back to the emperor Claudius in the first century.[92] It had not been observed. The rights of slaves were precarious. It would be anachronistic to expect Justinian to challenge the system, but he was a man who believed that manumission was a commendable act, and there is enough in his *Novels* to justify his own opinion of himself as one eager to grant freedom.[93]

There was not much liberalism, however, in Justinian's measures affecting the *adscripticii*, the tenant farmers who were bound to their lessors under conditions little different from slavery. A class of free tenant farmers still existed in law, but in the sixth century few of them can have remained: in fact, Justinian recognized only two categories of peasants: the *adscripticii coloni* and the free farmers who worked land that they themselves owned.[94] Justinian allowed the tie to be broken only if the *adscripticius* became a bishop,[95] for agricultural labour was scarce and economic considerations occupied the driver's seat. Justinian's ruling that a child born of a free woman and an adscript tenant should be free illustrates the problem. Justinian was merely applying the Roman law of slavery which ruled that the child of a 'free womb' was free, and he was ensuring that an adscript had no fewer rights than a slave. Yet the statute aroused a storm of protest from the landowners, for it seems that a large number of adscripts did, in fact, have free mothers, and if they escaped from their status through this loophole, the labour shortage would become worse. The objections from Illyricum were particularly vigorous, for there the successive forays of Bulgars and Slavs must have decimated the rural population. Their estates, the landowners alleged, were being deserted by adscript tenants who claimed that their mothers were free women, and Justinian had to move quickly to reduce the impact of the law.[96] Yet he was too much of a believer in the sanctity of marriage to stomach a practice that was reported from Mesopotamia and Osroene: there landowners separated married *coloni* from different estates and took away their children. Justinian would not hear of it.[97]

'It is Our wish that everyone lead chaste lives, so far as is possible': Justinian on himself again. The law where these words appear outlawed panders and procurers who exploited girls for prostitution.[98] Protecting woman and vindicating their rights was clearly one of his concerns. Justin's constitution,[99] which smoothed the way for Justinian's marriage to Theodora, set the tone. A slave who was freed had the status of a freeborn citizen: why then should not a contrite actress who repented of the life she had chosen because of the 'feebleness of her sex' (*imbecillitate sexus*) be treated differently? Procopius[100] grumbled that this law opened the door for any number of marriages between senators and courtesans, and probably the example of Justinian and Theodora did diminish social barriers. At any rate, whatever we may think of Procopius' male chauvinist protest, it is clear that Justinian was no exponent of female inferiority. 'In the service of God', he ruled, 'there is no male or female, nor freeman nor slave.'[101] Probably, however, on this matter the historian was at least as much in tune with contemporary society as the emperor.

Dowries and antenuptial donations were a natural concern. The latter was a counter-dowry of the husband to his wife which had developed in Late Antiquity. Justinian ruled that its value should equal that of the dowry, and the same rules governing inalienability should apply.[102] Moreover, before a husband could encumber an antenuptial donation with debt, his wife had to give her consent *twice*.[103] The need for double consent, Justinian explained, was because a woman might be deceived by her husband's blandishments, and after reflection, repent of giving her approval. So Justinian gave legal protection to a woman's right to change her mind. But perhaps remembering his own marriage, the emperor reminded his subjects that mutual affection created wedlock, and a dowry was unnecessary.[104]

No woman was to be put in prison; if she could not give bail, she should bind herself by an oath, and if detention was necessary, then she should go to a nunnery. But she should never be put in gaol, where the male guards might violate her.[105] Divorce was not to the emperor's liking: he prohibited the old custom of divorce by mutual consent (his successor Justin II restored it as soon as he was dead[106]), but he recognized a list of just causes, including a husband's involvement in a plot against the emperor.[107] Women had no less right to own property than men: when Justinian decreed that lands in Africa which the Vandals had confiscated should be returned to the former owners,[108] he ruled that the owner's gender should make no difference, and one of his sharpest laws is addressed to the proconsul of Armenia about Armenian customs of inheritance. Armenian women were purchased by their husbands, he wrote indignantly, and might not becomes heirs, as if females were not, like males, created by God! Henceforth, he ruled, the rights of Armenian women to inherit were not to differ from those of men.[109]

'You must, therefore, take over your office untarnished and without graft and above all you must keep your hands clean in the eyes of God, and of Us, and of the law. You must take for yourself no emolument great or small, nor carry on any underhand traffic to the detriment of Our subjects': These are the principles which Justinian addressed to Tribonian during the *annus mirabilis* of 535, which is crowded with reforms.[110] Of course, the collection of taxes was paramount. 'First, you ought vigilantly to be zealous in the collection of fiscal revenues'; 'You shall see to it that the payment of imperial taxes takes place properly even within the churches, for it is advantageous and very necessary for the soldiers, the private citizens and for the whole state that we should have a record of taxes.'[111] The *defensores* of the churches and their business managers were to help. The budget had to balance somehow, for Late Antiquity had none of the financial instruments that allow modern nations to run up huge national debts.

The decurions in the cities got no relief from their obligations. Their numbers had grown small, Justinian admitted, and under Anastasius, officials known as *vindices* (protectors) had taken over their obligation to collect municipal taxes. 'Destructive hirelings' Justinian called them.[112] The *vindices* had been a flawed solution. Justinian's own answer was conservative: he wanted to restore the curial class. He realized that the status was so unattractive that some decurions preferred to remain childless rather than leave an estate to their heirs encumbered with curial obligations, but his remedy was simply to plug the loopholes. A decurion without issue was to be forced to leave three-quarters of his estate to his municipal council.[113] But a decurion could make anyone he pleased his heirs, including illegitimate offspring, or even a child born of a slave mother, so long as the municipal council did not lose its claims on his estate.[114] Appointment to the palatine service brought immunity from curial burdens, but Justinian restricted this privilege to designated upper ranks of the service, and ruled that children born before an officer reached an immune rank should not inherit immunity.[115] Seepage into the clergy was curtailed as well. A decurion who had been a monk for fifteen years might be ordained, but a portion of his property had to go to the municipal council and the imperial treasury. But let an ordained decurion marry, or take a concubine, and he was to be returned forthwith to his former status, even if he belonged to an order which permitted marriage![116]

There is nothing new here. Emperors before Justinian had tried to legislate municipal councils back into life, and Justinian had no more success than they. Perhaps even less, for the complexion of the cities was changing, and their decline gathered speed as the end of the century approached. But the spirit of the legislation is worth noting. It is innovation disguised as conservatism. It exudes the same spirit that animated Justinian's urge to revive a past that never existed.[117] Justinian's aim was to build upon an idealized historical tradition which he did not hesitate to alter to suit his purposes. We find a similar attitude pervading his provincial reforms. There is a series of them that start with historical prefaces which may come from the pen of Tribonian, but they express Justinian's perceptions, as well as his shallow grasp of history.[118] Pisidia and Lycaonia are to have praetors with civil and military jurisdiction,[119] and the ancient title of the office masks the fact that the amalgamation of civil and military power turned its back upon a tradition that went back to Diocletian. Reduction of administrative expense was the purpose of the reform, and it created a new set of problems which Justinian did not foresee.[120] Yet its alleged justification was that it was a return to the hallowed usages of the distant past. Likewise, legislation curbing the expenses of the games which a consul sponsored when he entered office begins with an historical reflection on the consulship.[121] A fine traditional title might mask an innovative office: witness the law of 535 which replaced the Prefects of the Night Watch with Praetors of the Plebs.[122] The public image which Justinian wanted to present was of a legislator working within a tradition inherited from the great past.

Nonetheless, Justinian's reforms reveal a legislator as bold as Diocletian, though less systematic. One reform carried out by John the Cappadocian was to suppress most of the dioceses and their vicars who had been the link between the provincial governors and the praetorian prefect. The reform worked less happily than the emperor hoped: the diocese of Pontica, which was abolished and its vicar made the 'Justinianic Count of Galatia Prima', was restored after thirteen years: it seems that the Pontic provinces were overrun with brigands and governors were unwilling to pursue them beyond the boundaries of their own provinces. The plague had thinned the ranks of the taxpayers, and the peasants responded to the rapacity of the tax collectors with turbulence. The vicar who was put in charge of the revived diocese was to be first and foremost a police officer, responsible for order. About the same time, Justinian tried to bring peace and quiet to the five provinces of the old diocese of Asia. He appointed a duke with the title 'preventer of violence' (*biokolytes*).[123] The cure was as evil as the disease, and in 553, in response to an appeal from the provincials who alleged that the 'preventer of violence' and his staff members were making their lives unbearable, Justinian removed both Phrygias and Pisidia from his jurisdiction. Lycaonia and Lydia were left in his merciless hands, but if he or any of his staff tried to enter the other three provinces, the bishops were charged to expel them.[124]

In three instances we find two smaller provinces in Asia Minor combined to form one larger province. One of them was the two Cappadocias which were made into one. Justinian had a special interest in Cappadocia for there were large imperial domains there, supervised – not too well – by the 'Count of the Patrimony'. The new single province was entrusted to a 'proconsul' who not only controlled civil administration and military forces, but supervised the agents of the 'patrimony' both in Cappadocia and the other provinces of the Pontic diocese.

The diocese of Thrace was next door to Constantinople, it was a good recruiting ground for the army and it was exhausted by barbarian invasions. Two vicars were in charge, one ruling the Long Wall district and the other Thrace itself. Justinian first joined the jurisdictions under a Justinianic Praetor, and a few years later, in 536, he subtracted Lower Moesia and Scythia from the Thracian diocese and added them to Caria, the Cyclades and Cyprus to form a new jurisdiction under a Justinianic Quaestor of the Army. The reform looks like a jigsaw puzzle. The motive was probably fiscal: rather than cancel the taxes of 'disaster areas' on the Danube frontier which had been hurt by border raids, Justinian united them with richer, more secure provinces which could make up the shortfall.[125]

The Augustal Prefect of Egypt retained his status as vicar of the diocese until Justinian reorganized it in 539, after the anarchic years of 536 and 537 when the Julianists a.k.a. Aphthartodocetists had fought the imperial troops in the streets of Alexandria.[126] The Augustal Prefect was renamed 'Augustal Duke' and given civil and military authority over Alexandria and the provinces of First and Second Egypt, both of which retained civil governors. The 'Augustal Duke' had the *aisia embole* – the 'happy requisition' of grain for the capital – designated as one of his chief responsibilities and it was set at 8 million units, which presumably are *artabae*.[127] The Duke of the Thebaid in Upper Egypt was also titled 'Augustal' and given civil and military authority over the two Thebaid provinces with their governors. That leaves Augustamnica I and II, Arcadia and Pentapolis, and the part of *Edict* XIII dealing with these is lost. But Justinian's reforms must have touched them, too.[128]

'Parkinson's Law' had affected both the civil service and the church. By a constitution of 535, the number of imperial clerks and messengers known as *referendarii* were to be reduced by attrition from fourteen to eight, and any civil servant who tried to increase the number in the future should pay a fine of 10 gold pounds and lose his office.[129] Bishops were to rein in their ordinations: churches were spending more on the stipends of their clergy than they received as revenue from the two main sources of their income: endowments and voluntary offerings.[130] Hagia Sophia was a particular concern: Justinian ruled that when a priest in a dependent church died, no replacement should be ordained until a check revealed that the number of the clergy was within prescribed limits.[131] Churches, oratories and monasteries were not to spring up like mushrooms: their founders should provide sufficient endowments, and if a would-be founder could not do so, Justinian suggested that he use his available funds to restore a church in Constantinople or the provinces that had fallen into disrepair.[132] Church property was not to be sold: Justinian had received reports of sales, particularly in Egypt, where monasteries that fell into financial difficulties were sold, exchanged or even given away.[133] But less than three weeks after he issued this ban, he made an exception for the Church of the Holy Resurrection in Jerusalem, which was a special case because of the pilgrim trade.[134]

Clergy who failed to carry out their duties were to lose their stipends, which were to be transferred to new appointees.[135] Churchmen might not act as lawyers in a civil court nor could a bishop be subpoenaed, though he might give testimony privately to an agent of the court.[136] Yet bishops were made almost an adjunct of the civil government: their courts had jurisdiction when a monk or ascetic was sued,[137] and only when a bishop could not make a decision because of the nature of the case was it to go to the civil governor.[138] Indeed anyone who suffered injustice at the hands of a civil governor might have recourse to the bishop.[139] The ruling recognized a shift of power which had been in process since the fourth century: the real authority in the cities was now in the hands of the bishops. Under Justinian they became a second tier of government with the power of surveillance over the civil *militia*. In some cities, they were the only effective civic authority.

The contrast between the emperor of the *Corpus* and the perception of Procopius' *Secret History* is stark and vivid. The Justinian of the *Secret History* was an innovator and a hypocrite. He banned the purchase of public office,[140] but, claimed the underground critic,[141] the law was barely a year old when he broke it himself and sold offices to the highest bidders. On the one hand, the secret historian complains that soldiers billeted in private houses always took over the best rooms; on the other, Justinian rules that soldiers were to take whatever quarters were vacant, leaving the principal rooms of the house to the owners, and they were to accept the supplies which a city could provide from local sources and not demand victuals that had to be imported.[142] On the sanctions against paganism and homosexuality, the Code and the *Secret History* agree, but for the latter, they existed only to further the villainous schemes of Justinian and his appalling empress.[143]

Yet it is well to remember that laws are passed to prevent wrong-doing *that does exist*. No legislator bothers to outlaw delicts that never occur. Thus the *Novels* of Justinian can be taken as evidence for the abuses that were to be found in the empire. Civil and ecclesiastical offices could be bought and sold like merchandise, and officials were corrupt. Cities suffered cruelly when army contingents passed through their territories, requisitioning supplies and living quarters. Lay aside the venom and the exaggeration of the *Secret History* and the picture it presents is not entirely inaccurate. The Justinian of the *Novels* is a confident reformer, prepared to legislate on any subject. Personal morality, provincial administration, theology: all lay within his purview. Past tradition received due reverence, but never hindered reform. But he was not infallible and he knew it. The final verdict on Justinian's regime must put as much weight on the *Secret History* as upon the laws. But it is the *Novels* which give us better grounds for passing judgement on his aspirations and his character.[144]

SOCIAL AND ECONOMIC DEVELOPMENTS

The imperial building programme

All Roman emperors built to make statements, and not only emperors. Public buildings, and, with Christianity's coming, churches and monasteries, were the medium by which wealthy men and women advertised their euergetism. Justinian followed in a well-worn path. What is different is that a panegyric has survived which describes his buildings, and it was written by the greatest historian of his age, Procopius, whose *Secret History* is an invective directed at Justinian's regime.

Procopius' *Buildings* is an odd panegyric, but nonetheless that is what it is, and the reader must remember that while literary skill is a requirement for a successful practitioner of the *genre*, sincerity and devotion to accuracy are not. Procopius kept to the rhetorical rules for imperial encomiums rather than historical truth, and gave Justinian all the credit for being the supreme planner, master builder and architect of his empire, even when his role was only to repair what was already built. Yet Procopius displays a knowledge that could probably have come from only one source: the imperial archives. We need not assume that they were completely accurate, but if Procopius had access to them, then he wrote with the emperor's permission, or even with his urging. The date of the composition is uncertain, but the easiest solution is probably the right one: Procopius wrote his first book before 558 as a separate encomium on Justinian's buildings in Constantinople, and later added five more books to cover the construction programme throughout the empire.[145] He passed over Italy, but Justinian had little to boast of there. Thus the panegyric as we have it belongs to the emperor's last, troubled years when he began to believe that the statements which his buildings made were not clear enough by themselves, and needed a publicist to articulate them in the literary prose which the élite appreciated. For the panegyric was not aimed at the masses, but rather at the small élite that had never accepted Justinian or his empress, and whose approval he was still anxious to obtain.

There are three themes to the panegyric: churches, defensive fortifications and water supply, including flood control.[146] Constantine I's conversion had sparked an orgy of church building. There was no correlation between the number of churches that mushroomed in the cities and villages and the requirements for worship. Justinian ruled that private foundations must have adequate endowments; apparently many did not.[147] But at the same time, church building was an expression of Christian patronage and it was a necessary activity of a good emperor,[148] all the more so for Justinian, because he was a *parvenu*, and on the *Mese*, between the Forum Tauri and the church of the Holy Apostles, stood the great church of St Polyeuktos, which Anicia Juliana, of impeccable pedigree, had completed just before Justinian's accession.[149] A riposte was necessary.

Justinian must have planned his own great church before the *Nika* revolt cleared the site of Hagia Sophia. Construction started on 23 February, 532, only forty-five days after the revolt was crushed, and even today, with the aid of computer imaging, forty-five days would not be long enough to solve the engineering problems which the great dome of Hagia Sophia presented. That means that the planning for the church must have begun before the revolt, perhaps as early as Justinian's accession, and it may even have been intended for some other location in the city before an inscrutable Providence cleared a site opposite the imperial palace.[150] One factor Hagia Sophia's architects could not know: under much of the building, extending in places to within a metre of the floor, lay a bed of Devonian rock which was weak enough to be compressed by the weight of the piers which held up the great dome. But in 532, Justinian was an impatient man. He was not willing to allow time for the mortar between the bricks to cure properly. The masonry was required to withstand the lateral thrusts of the dome before it was ready.[151] But Hagia Sophia was Justinian's reply to Anicia Juliana's church of St Polyeuktos,[152] and he wanted his church not only to be architecturally more adventuresome and bigger (it was half as large again): he wanted it finished quickly. His new church was dedicated on 26 December, 537. For a thousand years it was to be the largest church in the world, until the Cathedral of Seville surpassed it.

The architects were Anthemius of Tralles and Isidore of Miletus. It was a daring design: a ground plan that was nearly square, two narthexes, a nave with a small east apse, and side aisles; and over the middle part of the nave hung the great dome. Isidore was a mathematician who produced a new edition of Archimedes and wrote a commentary on Hero of Alexandria's treatise *On Vaulting* of the first century BC. Anthemius was an inventor and experimenter who worked from models. A theoretician and an engineer. They pushed the technology that was available to its limit, and the wonder is not that the dome fell, but that it was built in the first place.

The weight of the dome soon began to tip the piers and buttresses backwards, but the building survived an earthquake in 553 and another in 557, but on 7 May, 558, part of the dome fell. Justinian entrusted the restoration to Isidore the Younger, nephew of one of the original architects. He consolidated the piers and arches, and raised a new dome, making it 6 metres higher than the old one in order to reduce its lateral thrust. Much of his dome still remains: the western arch of the four supporting it came down in 986 (or 989) and was rebuilt by an Armenian architect named Trdat, and the eastern arch fell in the fourteenth century and was rebuilt with contributions raised in Russia.[153] But Hagia Sophia in modern Istanbul is still Justinian's church, evoking past aspirations and still making its imperial statement, however tattered it may be in our century.

Hagia Eirene, originally built by Constantius II as the patriarch's cathedral, was enclosed in a single court with Hagia Sophia, with which it shared clergy. It was destroyed by the same fire that consumed Hagia Sophia in 532. Justinian rebuilt it, but it burned down again in 564, and only the lower part of the walls of the present church belong to his rebuilding.[154] Between the two churches was the Hospice of Sampson, a hospital and orphanage to whose director Justinian entrusted supervision of the capital's other hospices in 537.[155] One director, Menas, had moved from the post to the patriarchate the year before. The hospice burned again in 563 and was restored, and was still in operation when the sack of Constantinople in the Fourth Crusade of 1204 ended its life.

Only two of Justinian's churches in Constantinople have survived, Hagia Sophia and Sts Sergius and Bacchus, both built in the sanguine 530s, but one other must be mentioned, the church of the Holy Apostles, which Justinian rebuilt. It was begun in 536, before Hagia Sophia was complete, but the Vandal treasure had arrived in Constantinople and provided the resources for it.[156] Beside it was the mausoleum for the emperors, but for himself and Theodora, Justinian built a separate shrine, a *heroon* just north of the church where each was to have a sarcophagus. The mosque of Mehmed II Fatih now stands on the site, but Justinian built a similar church dedicated to St John the Evangelist on the barren hill of Ayasuluk above Ephesus,[157] and the church of San Marco in Venice replicates its plan.

When Procopius' encomium on Justinian's building programme moves beyond the capital, the emphasis switches to defence works and water supply. But not entirely. He gives a full description of the *Nea*, or the 'New Church of the Theotokos' dedicated to the Virgin, which Justinian built in Jerusalem, on a hill where the site was too narrow, and on the south and east the construction had to be carried on a vaulted substructure 'artificially added to the hill by the emperor's power'.[158] Here Procopius was accurate: in 1970, excavations in the Jewish Quarter of the Old City revealed part of the foundations of a great basilica with two rows of interior columns, a large apse at the east end of the nave and at the end of each side aisle, a *pastophorion* or chamber for the use of the clergy, with a small apse on the back wall. In the substructure south of the basilica the excavators discovered a great vaulted cistern, and on the top wall of one of the vaults, there was an inscription in bold relief on the plaster, with letters picked out in red paint, which proclaimed that this was the 'work which our most pious emperor Flavius Justinianus undertook in his beneficence, with the vigilance and devotion of the most holy Constantine, priest and *hegoumenos*, in the thirteenth year of the indiction'. The *hegoumenos* Constantine is attested elsewhere: he was abbot of the *Nea* in the late sixth and early seventh centuries,[159] and the cistern, if the inscription refers to Justinian's second indiction (549–550), dates to 562, near the end of the great emperor's reign.

The *Nea* itself was inaugurated in November of the plague year, 542, and destroyed by an earthquake in the late eighth century.

There were in the territory of Jerusalem eleven monasteries and churches, and one hospice, all of which Justinian restored, and five monasteries were given wells to supply them with water.[160] Procopius reports nothing of Bethlehem, where a late tradition has it that Justinian reconstructed the church of the Nativity which Constantine I had built, but both Procopius' silence and the archaeological evidence justify scepticism.[161] But in Third Palestine, at Mt Sinai, he did build a famous church to the Mother of God and a fortress.

In fact, the monastery of St Catherine at Mt Sinai was a fortified monastery, and was presumably part of the frontier defence system. But for a fortress it was poorly sited and designed. Justinian's primary interest was not to defend the frontier so much as to safeguard the monks who had appealed for protection against the Bedouin, or at least that is what a tenth-century patriarch of Alexandria, Eutychius, reports.[162] St Catherine's marked the traditional location of the Burning Bush, and rising above it was Gebel Musa, reputed to be the Mt Sinai where Moses received the decalogue. On three beams of the monastery church there are inscriptions, which a worshipper could at one time have seen from the floor: one for Theodora, who was already dead when it was made, one for Justinian and the last for the builder of the church.[163]

In Africa, Justinian restored 150 cities. That, at least, is the testimony of Evagrius.[164] He exaggerates, but a recent authority suggests that the number may not be altogether unrealistic if it refers to the sum of the *municipia* which paid tax. At any rate, cities were numerous in Byzantine Africa, to judge from the number of bishoprics there: we know the names of forty-five cities dated securely to Justinian's reign and a probable twenty-four for which the evidence is of a later date, and the minutes of the last council of the African church held under the Byzantine regime bears the signatures of sixty-nine bishops from Africa Proconsularis alone.[165] The city walls which Justinian's officers rebuilt show signs of hasty construction and economy: where possible, the builders reused masonry and incorporated earlier structures, and the dimensions of the walls reveal a shrunken urban life: for instance, the circuit at Theveste (*mod. Tebessa*), built in 535, encloses only a quarter of the space that its Roman predecessor did.[166]

We find similar shrunken dimensions at the Libyan cities of Sabratha and Lepcis Magna, which were rebuilt by Justinian with new walls, public buildings and churches: the splendid floor mosaic of the basilica at Sabratha has survived. At Thamugadi at the foot of the Aurès massif, spoil from the ruined buildings went to build a huge citadel with barracks inside. Procopius, describing Justinian's building programme in Africa, puts his emphasis on defence construction: he mentions only five churches, but thirty-five forts. The security of the empire mattered. And it is clear that the strategy for frontier defence had undergone a change.

A story in John of Ephesus' *Lives* takes it for granted. The Huns attacked on the eastern frontier, and the blessed Habib and his monks, leaving their monastery, sought refuge in a fort. There they stayed until Habib thought the danger was past, and he sent out the holy man Z'ura to inspect the monastery for damage. He encountered a band of Huns one of whom would have slain him, except that Z'ura resorted to a not uncommon miracle of the holy man: he froze the belligerent Hun in position until the band had gone on its way.[167] But it is not the miracle so much as the defence strategy against the Hun attack which we should note. The monks retired to a fort which served as a refuge while the raiders made the countryside unsafe. No military garrison is mentioned,[168] and the abbot seems to have been in charge. When the raiders departed, the monks returned to their monastery and repaired the damage.

Though he may have been unaware of it, Habib was only following the strategy of St Severinus in Noricum Ripense in the later fifth century. There from ca. 400 on, we find forts built on protected slopes, often with a church in the midst of them, where the provincials could find shelter. The saint's counsel was to fly to one of these refuge centres when the barbarians came to plunder the countryside, and to 'put all your possessions within the safety of your walls, so that the enemy on his terrible march may find nothing that men need to support life'. The frontiers were pregnable, and the cities could not be protected; it was to these refuge settlements that urban life moved and in the sixth century, after the old cities had collapsed, they emerged as towns in their own right.[169]

In Africa, these *Fliehburgen*, to borrow a useful German term, were not placed on the southern border of the prefecture, but in the midst of populated areas, where Berber raiders could find the richest plunder: slaves, valuables and farm produce. They gave the country-men of the district a refuge centre, and if they were large enough, they housed garrisons of *limitanei* who could counterattack the raiders, or if they were themselves inadequate for the job, they could summon *comitatenses* units. If the situation became truly serious, the

Master of the Soldiers himself would have to intervene, but until he could, these forts protected the provincials and curtailed the freedom of the invaders to pillage.

But Sassanid Persia in the East was a more dangerous enemy than the Berbers, and Syria and Palestine were more important than Africa ever was. Here Justinian's fortifications were concentrated in the north where they protected the road to Antioch and the passes through the Amanus and Taurus mountain ranges. For central and southern Syria, the imperial defence strategy relied heavily on the loyal Ghassanids, whose centre was at Djabiya on the Golan Heights but who wandered over the desert marches from the Negev in the south, and north to Sergiopolis (*mod.* Rusafa), some 25 kilometres from the Euphrates, where the Ghassanid sheikh held an assize every year during the festival of St Sergius.[170] Over this area, Justinian let the imperial defences run down. But his policy on the north-eastern frontier was sharply different. There Justinian began his programme of reconstructing frontier defences in 527, when he dispatched Belisarius to attempt to build an advance post on the very edge of Persian territory,[171] and his effort continued until the peace with Persia of 562, only shortly before his death. The private sector also helped: many forts were built by local magnates or bishops, and villages built their own ramparts using whatever skills they had at hand.[172] But constructions for which the imperial treasury did not pay went unrecorded in the archives which Procopius used to write his *Buildings*.

The great fortress of Dara thrust against the Persian frontier, a mere 30 kilometres from the city of Nisibis. The rhetoric of the *Buildings* that presented Justinian as the protector of his people, righting the inadequacies of his predecessors, is particularly apparent in its glowing report of his work at Dara, which goes so far that Procopius disaffirms what he himself wrote earlier in his *History of the Wars!*[173] The truth seems to be that Justinian maintained and improved a strong fortress built by the emperor Anastasius. The river Cordes (*mod.* Daraçay) traversed the city, and Justinian's engineers improved the canalization of its water, but the *Buildings* overstates Justinian's role as the builder of Dara. Another frontier city, Martyropolis, capital of Fourth Armenia, where the late fourth-century bishop Marutha had gathered the relics of many martyrs, was strengthened with a ditch and a second wall which surrounded the first.[174] Sergiopolis on the northern fringe of the Ghassanid domain had been protected by a wall proof against only Bedouin raids; Justinian replaced it with one that could withstand the Persian army. Zenobia (*mod.* Zalebiye) on the left bank of the Euphrates lay abandoned inside a dilapidated wall, but Justinian restored it as a garrison post, and Theodosiopolis (*mod.* Erzerum) on the Khabur river, which Theodosius I had built as a garrison post and Anastasius expanded into a city, had its circuit repaired. A century and a half ago, extensive remains of the walls of Theodosiopolis still existed, but it would be hard now to distinguish what belongs to Theodosius I or Anastasius from Justinian's work.[175]

Even from this brief sketch, it is clear that Justinian gave particular attention to the protection of his north-east frontiers, as had the emperor Anastasius before him. In the Balkans as well, which opened into the hinterland of Constantinople itself, Justinian continued what Anastasius and Justin had begun. For that matter, the imperial defence strategy was one that was inherited from the emperors Constantius II and Theodosius I. Its two features were a broad band of small garrison posts and *Fliehburgen*, and beyond them, a screen of barbarian allies whose allegiance was won by imperial diplomacy and money. The Hun invasions of the mid-fifth century had destroyed the Roman fortresses on the Lower Danube, and if they did not quite wipe the frontier clean of urban life, it was a very near thing. The countryside was pillaged at will, and the population fled or took refuge in *Fliehburgen*.

But in the reign of Anastasius, we find new military constructions, first along the Black Sea coast, where commerce was reviving. At Tomis (*mod.* Constantza) the fortifications were rebuilt, financed not by the imperial treasury but by local citizens. Further north on the coast at Histria, the fortifications were reconstructed about the same time, and, to judge from the remains of their town houses, the city had a few well-to-do residents. Anastasius, too, rebuilt the forts on the Danube frontier of Scythia (*mod.* Dobruja),[176] and excavations at Nikup in northern Bulgaria, which was Trajan's foundation of Nicopolis, show that the site was reoccupied in his reign. By about 543, Justinian had pushed the reconstruction west to the Serbian border. In Moesia along the Iron Gate region of the Danube, archaeologists have found over a distance of 180 kilometres seven forts that were restored, another seven new constructions and five camps for auxiliaries, two of which were river ports.[177]

It was also Justinian's contribution to add greater depth to the defence. Procopius aroused Edward Gibbon's[178] scepticism by listing over 600 sites in the Balkans where Justinian had defences built or improved: Gibbon surmised that most of them were no more than solitary towers surrounded by moats, and in fact, if one were to look at Cyrenaica rather than the Balkans, one would find Gibbon's surmise well founded: there, on almost every hilltop stood a watchtower with a ditch around it, well sited to transmit coded signals to alert each other of nomad raids.[179] But the picture that Procopius conveys is not inaccurate. *Fliehburgen* of various sizes sprang up in the interior of Illyricum, some new, some refurbished strongholds, many, no doubt, built on private initiative. Procopius confines himself to Justinian's activity, but even so, he reports that cities such as Serdica (*mod.* Sofia) and Naissus (*mod.* Nish) had their walls restored; fortresses (*polichnia*) were built and at Čaričin Grad in Serbia, 45 kilometres due south of Naissus, Justinian constructed *Justiniana Prima* as the new capital of Illyricum. It was the only completely new city founded in Illyricum in the sixth century.[180]

All this activity took place under the increasing hostile pressure on the Danube frontier, which must have constantly disrupted the construction programme. The relative stability of the 530s was followed by the grim 540s. In 539 or 540 the protobulgar Kutrigurs made a two-pronged invasion. One spearhead reached the environs of Constantinople. Again, in 544, they raided Illyricum. In 545 or 546, the Slavs pillaged Thrace, and in 548, they were back, looting Illyricum and pressing as far south as Dyrrachium on the Adriatic coast. In 550, there were two Slav raids; the later of the two aimed at Thessaloniki but failed to take it. The next year once again, in the autumn, the Slavs entered Illyricum to plunder and maraud. There followed a short breathing-space until the autumn of 558, when the khan of the Kutrigurs, Zabergan, arrived at the Danube, found it frozen and crossed over. The following year, one spearhead of the Kutrigur horde came within a whisker of taking Constantinople, and a second reached, but failed to pass, Thermopylae.

By then, the defence strategy which Anastasius had begun and Justinian continued was showing its inadequacies. The forts protecting the Dobruja region were destroyed about mid-century. The latest coin found at Histria on the Black Sea belongs to 543–544.[181] The Danube frontier defence required greater resources than the post-plague empire could muster. But most of the forts were not abandoned until late in the century or at the beginning of the next. Justinian's defences continued to protect the Balkan provinces more or less until after his death. For that, he deserves the kudos which Procopius bestowed upon him. His successors did not give up on the Danube frontier by any means: we find, for instance, the Dobruja forts reoccupied, but there is little sign of extensive defence construction in the Danubian provinces after Justinian, and a strategy which had guarded the Balkan frontier reasonably well for a century and a half came to an end.

Thermopylae was the key to the defence of southern Greece, and Procopius produced a grandiose report of Justinian's defence works at that famous pass: fortresses, water reservoirs, walls and a garrison 2,000 strong. In the *Secret History*, he is less flattering. Yet recent carbon-14 dating has shown that most of the monumental work at Thermopylae which has been credited to Justinian on Procopius' authority was built a century or so earlier.[182] Justinian's contribution was to maintain the Thermopylae defences and replace the militia that guarded them with regular troops.[183] If Thermopylae failed to stop invaders, there was the Isthmus of Corinth, south of which the cities were unwalled, and the *Buildings* asserts that Justinian rebuilt the old trans-Isthmus wall, which had fallen into disrepair.[184] The rebuilding of the *Hexamilion* wall across the Isthmus belongs to the years after 550, and an otherwise unknown official named Victorinus left an inscription to commemorate the project: 'Light of light, true God of true God, guard the emperor Justinian and his faithful servant Victorinus along with those who dwell in Greece according to God.'[185] Earthquake damage made reconstruction necessary, it appears, and it may have been the great earthquake of 551 that was responsible. At least Victorinus omits mention of Theodora in his dedication, which dates the rebuilding to some year later than her death in 548.

In Italy, nothing worth mention. At Ravenna, the Arian churches built under Ostrogothic rule were rededicated to the Catholic faith, and the church of San Vitale was founded, with its famous mosaics of Justinian and Theodora and their retinue. But though San Vitale may have had imperial blessing, it was not built with imperial funds. The 26,000 *solidi* that it cost were supplied by a Ravenna banker of eastern origin, Julius Argentarius, who also contributed to the cost of San Apollinare in Classe.[186] The powerful circuit walls at Terracina on the Appian Way between Rome and Naples, which were once attributed to Belisarius, have now been redated to a century earlier, and the line of defensive towers and *castra* along the fringes of the Alps that used to be assigned to Narses were for the most part erected in the early fifth century.[187] The demands of war prompted Belisarius to repair the walls of Rome, and in the last year of Justinian's regime, Narses restored the Ponte Salaria outside the city.[188] It all amounts to very little. By the time the Ostrogothic War was over, Italy had ceased to be high on the emperor's list of priorities.

It matters very little whether Justinian worked out a new defence strategy or merely refined one which had been developed more than a century earlier. The important point is how well it achieved its aim. The boundaries of Justinian's empire were still intact at his death, increasing pressure notwithstanding. The vital areas were the eastern frontier and the Balkans, and it could hardly be otherwise: these were the sources of the empire's revenues and her army recruits. Justinian was not a spendthrift builder, though when one adds his churches to his defence works, the drain on his treasury must have been immense. The *Buildings* of Procopius, which represents an emperor repairing the neglect of his predecessors with unlimited resources and divine inspiration, presents an imperial ideal, which conforms to the ideology of the imperial office. The rules of rhetoric required some slighting of Anastasius' achievement, but the encomium remains a valuable document, and any assessment of Justinian as builder must do more than merely score points against it.

Cities and villages: change and decline

Cities as the classical world had known them were undergoing change, and by 600, the amenities of urban life which still existed a century earlier had disappeared in most of them. City councils ceased to function. They died with a whimper, and there is no date we can pinpoint for their demise. In Egypt, there is some evidence that they continued well into Justinian's reign, and in Italy we find survivals into the seventh century.[189] The reason was not poverty, though there was great regional variation: the beleaguered cities of Illyricum were anything but affluent, but in the east, the city notables and the church between them could dispose of an impressive amount of wealth. But the social and economic drift was moving against the classical city and the civilized life it embodied, and by the end of the century, it was fading out in many parts of the empire.

City dwellers watched with apparent unconcern as their theatres and amphitheatres decayed for lack of maintenance.[190] In Syria, we know of no new theatre construction before Justinian since the emperor Philip the Arab three centuries earlier built one to embellish his birthplace.[191] At Gerasa (*mod.* Jerash) and Thessaloniki, the hippodromes were apparently despoiled for building material before they passed completely out of use![192] Public baths survived, and Justinian himself thought them an important amenity of urban life: he built, or rebuilt, them not only at Antioch, but at Justiniana Prima, Nicaea and Helenopolis in Bithynia, where he built a new bath and repaired another, and at Nicomedia he renewed a great bath establishment, which was an unexpected boon, for the size of the bath made it something of an anachronism.[193] For the public baths had grown smaller. They ceased to be the social centres that they used to be in the classical period. At Gerasa, the two great baths of the Roman period were deserted sometime in Late Antiquity and by Justinian's day, the city was served by a relatively modest establishment which the bishop built in the mid-fifth century near the cathedral.[194]

Justinian set his face against these developments.

Antioch is a case in point. The second quarter of the sixth century brought it a series of hammer blows. In 525 there was a disastrous fire, and next year, on 29 May, a terrible earthquake with great loss of life. The aftershocks lasted eighteen months. Both Justinian and Theodora took part in the reconstruction: Justinian built churches to the Virgin, and to Sts Cosmas and Damian, and a hospice, baths and cisterns; Theodora constructed a basilica and a church to the archangel Michael. But another, more terrible quake on 29 November, 528 destroyed Antioch again. There was another reconstruction effort: the patriarchal church must have been almost complete when the Persians sacked Antioch in 540, leaving only one church standing and removing a portion of the population to Ctesiphon. Two years later, the plague arrived. Thereafter the blows seem to have been less intense: the terrible earthquake of 551 which destroyed Beirut must have affected Antioch, and there were other quakes or tremors in 554, 557 and 560/1, but the destruction they caused paled by comparison.

A lesser emperor might have given up on Antioch. The Persian sack in 540 had left the city in ashes and, as Procopius describes its rebirth, Justinian cleared away the debris and laid out a new city, complete with stoas, market places, baths – and theatres! 'So it came about that Antioch is more magnificent now than it was before.'[195] In fact it was not, but Procopius at least expressed the emperor's aspirations, and excavations at Antioch before World War II have shown that Justinian did rebuild the city's splendid main street and the porticoes that bordered it with the same dimensions as before.

Only the roadway was made narrower to allow room for a side-walk.[196] The sack of Antioch had been a blow to the prestige of the empire, and its reconstruction was a bid to restore confidence. It was also a statement of faith in the classical city.

Likewise Justiniana Prima in Illyricum. Justinian made its metropolitan an archbishop, thus ranking him with the metropolitans of Ravenna and Carthage. Its city plan borrowed traits from Constantinople: in the centre was a round plaza and in the middle of it a statue of Justinian. Radiating out from it like a four-spoked wheel were the main streets lined with porticoes. Its churches, wrote Procopius,[197] were not easy to number. Justiniana Prima was to be the new capital of Illyricum, though it is doubtful if the praetorian prefect ever left Thessaloniki. Yet there is a note of defiance to the diminutive grandeur of Justiniana Prima. The waves of invasion notwithstanding, it was to be a worthy marker of Justinian's birth-place.

It seems that not only the ruling élite in Constantinople but Justinian himself were still wedded to the idea of the city as the bearer of civilization. Procopius acknowledged the fact in a significant passage: at Caputvada in Africa, where Belisarius made his landing in the Vandal kingdom, Justinian built a city, complete with an *agora*, so that the rustics could sample the refinement of urban life![198] But the hammer blows of plague, warfare and what insurance companies define as 'Acts of God' were transforming the cities, and they were not the only forces at work. Christianity also left its mark. Churches became the urban focal points, and the classical city pattern that centred on an *agora* gave way to neighbourhoods centred on churches. Public space no longer had its former importance. Private houses invaded avenues; in Athens, where Justinian's reign was a time of ebbing prosperity, we find them invading the *agora*. Wooden partitions divided porticoes into market stalls, which sometimes served as dwellings as well as places of business, and private buildings spilled over on to the public thoroughfares. In Justinian's rebuilt Antioch, small, poorly constructed buildings soon encumbered the new main street, while in Carthage, we find similar encroachments upon streets as early as the Vandal period.[199] Cities came increasingly to look like villages. Before occupation faded out at Justinian's new city of Justiniana Prima in the late sixth and seventh centuries, it became a *Fliehburg*, a walled place of refuge for the local rural population. Its porticoes were taken over as living quarters, empty spaces filled up with huts and even churches became dwelling places.[200] We may perhaps recognize similar forces at work in the capital of Epirus, Nicopolis near modern Preveza, where from the end of the fifth century the population actually increased.[201] Was this the result of an influx of farmers, seeking protection from Bulgar and Slav raids, or of increased local trade or, paradoxically, of both?

One marker of the change is the shift in burial customs. Church porches, narthexes and precincts became favourite places for interment. The cemetery churches of Late Antiquity were built outside the walls as a general rule, though there is an entry belonging to 381 in the Theodosian Code[202] which pointedly bans funeral urns and sarcophaguses inside the city, and further, prohibits burial at martyrs' shrines. We may infer that some Christians were already challenging the time-honoured custom that the dead should be interred beyond the city limits. But in the late sixth century at Corinth, a cemetery church was built on Temple Hill, near the centre of the protobyzantine settlement.[203] By the next century, the ban on burial within the city walls no longer held. In the last years of the Byzantine occupation of Tripolitania before the Arab conquest, we find Christian graves in the forum of Sabratha, a city which Justinian had rebuilt.[204] The ancient concept which separated the cemeteries for the dead from the urban space for the living had ceased to exist.[205]

Every city had a bishop, chosen by the clergy and the important landowners in collaboration with the metropolitan, and he served as leader of the civil government as well as of the church. We can see bishops at work in 540, when the Persians broke the 'Endless Peace' and overran Syria. It was the bishops of the cities in the path of the invasion who trudged back and forth to Khusro, negotiating ransom and pleading for mercy. The gallant bishop of Beroea, Megas, negotiated on behalf of Antioch as well as his own city, and the bishop of Apamaea on the Orontes, Thomas, bargained with Khusro on his city's behalf.[206] But *ad hoc* councils still functioned, though in most places, the old *curiae* or *boulai* of the classical cities had dwindled away. Before the sack of Antioch, a council of Antiochenes met.[207] We do not know its composition but we can guess. The unheroic patriarch Euphraemius was present; so was Germanus, representing his cousin, the emperor, and so, we may imagine, were various Antiochene notables. We glimpse such a council again during the plague year at Myra in Lycia, when the *Life* of St Nicholas of Zion reports that the notables met in council with the governor of the province and metropolitan to complain of the saint. They alleged that he was causing shortages of wine, flour, grain and wood in the city because he advised the peasants to avoid the market at Myra in order to avoid infection. As a result, two clerics of the metropolitan church were sent to arrest the saint. We do not know the result.[208]

Justinian's laws intended to revive the curial class in the provincial cities had little effect, and, for all we know, may have made matters worse as the *curiales* tried to shift their burdens on to the small freehold farmers who in turn deserted the smaller cities for larger ones, notably Constantinople.[209] Yet the notables who met in council with the bishop occupied the same slot in the social hierarchy as had the decurions who staffed the *curiae* a century earlier. We find them described as *protoi* or *proteuontes* (leading men), or *possessores* (in Greek, *ktetores*), that is, landowners, or sometimes *protectores*. They were the establishment of the protobyzantine city, and like the *curiales* in earlier centuries, they were, in some cities at least, expected to collect state taxes and supply horses at the imperial post-relay stations.[210] But they held no civic offices; they were merely local persons of influence whom it was prudent to consult. Among them, more and more (one suspects) there were to be found imperial officials resident in the provincial cities. But the real power was in the hands of the bishops. The union between church and state on the level of city government was complete.[211] Symptomatic of the new reality was Justinian's measure of 545 which directed that a city's standards of weights and measures, which had hitherto been kept in the *prytaneion* or town hall, should henceforth be kept in the bishop's cathedral.[212]

The decline of the cities was not uniform across the empire, nor was there any single reason for it. We should avoid generalizations. Cities that attracted imperial patronage, such as provincial capitals, fared better than others. The fortunes of war hurt the cities of the Balkans and Greece, but left Anatolia unscathed. The recurrent outbreaks of plague were part of the cause, for they hit the cities and villages harder than the countryside. In Africa and in *Oriens*, the nomads were little affected. In Syria, the plague caused the balance between the nomad herders and the settled agriculturists to shift in favour of the former.[213] The cities of *Oriens*, which were to show little resistance to the Arab invaders of the seventh century, had already become partly Arab.

The constant succession of earthquakes that afflicted the eastern Mediterranean in Justinian's reign met an increasing lack of resilience. Cities that were laid low failed to recover on their former scale.

Berytus (*mod.* Beirut) never quite recovered from the quake that flattened it in 551, and at Anemurium (*mod.* Eski Anamur) on the coast of Rough Cilicia opposite Cyprus, only makeshift rebuilding followed a natural disaster in the mid-570s.[214] The community that occupied the site at the end of the sixth century was a shadow of what it was a century earlier. Population decline must often have been the reason, though Christian theology must bear some blame for the decline of resilience: a people who ascribes earthquakes and plague to God's anger accepts them with resignation.[215] Yet there are two causes which deserve special examination.

One was a shift of attitude. The effect of the Christian church and monasticism was to cloud the social differences of the classical city. Peter Brown sums up the change: 'The compartmentations, the hierarchies, the sharp distinctions on which the life of the city continued to be based, had been blurred and softened by the impressive communal rituals in the Christian basilicas.'[216] The élites of the classical cities were proud to call themselves 'lovers of their home towns'. For the Christian notable, the preferable epithet was 'lover of the poor'. To an extent we can hardly grasp in a secular age, religion, including the finer points of theology, took hold of the minds and passions of the populace. Priorities changed. Churches, hospices and monasteries skimmed off the wealth which had once paid for the great public monuments of the classical city. Not only that: the monasteries alienated large tracts of land from city territories which no longer contributed to urban revenues.

The second cause was a shift in the balance of power between city and countryside. The village (*chorion*), not the city, was the social unit where most people lived, and though it generally lacked the monumental architecture of the city, it had churches, priests, and even 'country bishops' who seem to have been declining in number in Justinian's day, but were still to be found. They might also have monasteries nearby, and sometimes holy men who attracted pilgrims seeking advice or aid against the oppression of the landowners. Large villages might have markets for local produce, and walls to defend themselves against marauders. We find cities in Africa that were smaller than villages in Syria. But the language of their streets was frequently not Greek or Latin, and in great areas of the empire, their religion was not orthodox. What had distinguished the classical and protobyzantine city was its domination of its territory.[217] But in the sixth century, the city's economic dominance was fading, and its social and religious dominance was insecure.

The city was the seat of the bishop, possessing both civil and ecclesiastical authority. But his power was not unchallenged. The monasteries and holy men of the countryside were outside the church hierarchy, and their relationship with the bishops was edgy. Bishops had to be politicians as well as priests, while monks, ascetics and holy men occupied a happier situation, wielding influence without responsibility, and a prudent metropolitan had to move deftly at times to keep them in line: St Nicholas of Zion in sixth-century Lycia was precipitately appointed bishop of a remote see at one point in a move that was clearly intended to check his authority.[218] Monophysitism offered a further challenge, for its strongholds were the monasteries, and in the East it drove a wedge between the upper ranks of the church hierarchy and the villages. The monasteries themselves could be little cities: when the Persians invaded Egypt in the seventh century they found a community of wealthy monasteries at the Monophysite stronghold of Enaton outside Alexandria. Coptic tradition numbered them at 600, filled with insolent monks.[219]

One symbol of the classical and protobyzantine city's dominance of its territory had been its aqueducts. They stretched out for miles into the hinterland, sucking in the available water with insouciant selfishness for their baths and fountains. They were statements of urban authority as well as engineering achievements. Any reader of Procopius' *Buildings* will be impressed by Justinian's attention to the water supply of the cities. The unvoiced reason was concern for the status of the city. As with many other aspects of his reign, Justinian, the catalyst of change, attempted at the same time to hold it back.

Yet, at the same time, the villages seem to have escaped many of the ills which altered the shape of the cities. They resisted not only the cities whose territories they filched, but imperial authority as well: we find Justinian in 535 addressing a problem in Pisidia where large, well-populated villages were defying the tax collectors.[220] It was a sign of the times. A new type of urbanism was emerging, one that cared little for the ordered space and the amenities of the classical city. Urban settlements responded to the changing pressures that beset them by developing new forms. The pressures varied from region to region and so did the changes. But all over the empire, Justinian's reign was a time of waning for the social, economic and demographic milieu which had allowed the classical city to flourish.

COMMERCE

Most trade was local trade. That is easily forgotten in the investigation of imports of silk from China, pepper from India and amber, furs and slaves from the Baltic region. It was the movement of goods over a 20-kilometre radius from the market centre or thereabouts that was most important. The city was a magnet for the market gardeners outside the urban area, who would set off before dawn with their donkeys laden down with goods, and by sun-up would fill the bazaars and suqs. The dependence of the cities on this traffic between their markets and the farms in their territories is illustrated by an incident in the *Life* of St Nicholas of Zion: in the plague year of 542, the saint advised farmers around Myra not to come to the city market with their produce for fear of contracting the disease, and Myra was soon in danger of starvation.[221]

The large cities always had buyers with good purchasing power, and traders with non-perishable goods came from far away. The Pachomian monks at Pbow near modern Chenoboskion in Egypt regularly brought their baskets and mats for sale at Alexandria, the greatest commercial and industrial city of the empire. But the small villages in the countryside also needed markets to exchange their goods. But they lacked the commercial attractions of the large cities, and hence their commerce centred on regular market-days, festivals and fairs.[222]

We are familiar with farmers' markets, for they existed in most of our country towns until modern shopping centres shoved them to the margins of mercantile life. It is the festivals (*panegyreis*) which have no good modern counterpart. The best occasion was the holy day of a god, when there was much merriment, sometimes athletic contests, poets or orators performing, and a solemn procession to the temple followed by the sacrifical meal. And commerce. Pedlars came, pitched their tents and sold their wares, which might be cloth, metal work, livestock or slaves. The festival that combined religion and commerce was an important mode of exchange in the pagan world.

Christianity made no immediate difference to the *panegyreis*. In the fourth century, the villages in the hinterland of Antioch still sold their surplus and bought what they needed in *panegyreis* which had changed little from the pagan past. Some fairs drew international trade: at Batnae, a short distance east of the Euphrates in Osroene, an annual festival in early September attracted merchants with goods from India and China to sell,[223] and another fair at Aegae in Cilicia attracted shippers from Ostrogothic Italy and Vandal Africa.[224] At Sergiopolis (*mod.* Resafa), some 25 kilometres from the river Euphrates, the festival of St Sergius on 15 November drew merchants as well as pilgrims. There the Ghassanid sheiks built an audience hall for themselves which has left extensive remains.[225] The festival must have been an opportunity for commerce between the nomads and the agricultural communities.

The church was wary of these fairs at first, for they tempted good Christian men to waste their money, or chase painted ladies, for among the items for sale was sex. Constantine I was outraged when his mother-in-law told him that at the Oak of Mamre near Hebron, hallowed as the site where Abraham had welcomed three angels, a fair took place every summer and attracted pagans, Christians and Jews who traded and feasted together. He reproved the bishops of Palestine for allowing it, and ordered the statues burned and a church built on the spot, which henceforth was to be devoted to divine service.[226] But the fairs were necessary vehicles of exchange. By degrees the Christian cycle of martyr celebrations evolved into *panegyreis* with social and economic functions similar to their pagan antecedents.

The larger fairs and markets attracted merchants in the import and export trade. At Gaza, for instance, they bought dates and wine and imported commodities which could not be produced locally, such as timber: the local synagogue was donated by two Jewish timber merchants who evidently prospered.[227] From the pottery found at Carthage, it seems that olive oil from Palestine and Syria, where the limestone massif north of Antioch specialized in its production, found markets in Vandal Africa, and the fine table ware manufactured in the vicinity of Carthage which we know as 'African Red Slip' was exported to all the major Mediterranean markets. It need not surprise us that when the imperial fleet anchored off Syracuse in Sicily on its way against the Vandal kingdom, Procopius found a trader there whom he knew from his youth at Caesarea, and his vessels evidently travelled regularly to Carthage.[228] One of his agents had just returned from Africa, and his timing was fortunate, for when Gelimer learned of the Byzantine landing, he incarcerated the eastern merchants whom he found in Carthage.

John of Ephesus' *Lives* relates the biographies of two traders from Amida, Elijah and Theodore, brothers who from boyhood had travelled with the caravans to Persia. They were honest dealers who played no tricks and sold at a fixed price. Their performance pleased their employers, who raised their salaries from 5 or 6 denarii a year to 10, and then they offered 30 denarii, in return for which they wanted exclusive use of their services, for they had large warehouses and served an extensive area. But the brothers preferred to go into business for themselves, and eventually became wealthy.[229]

There were probably few traders as honest as Theodore and Elijah, and perhaps not many as successful, but otherwise their lives followed the usual career pattern of a merchant.[230] For twenty years they travelled, following the markets, until they were able to open their own merchant house at Melitene in Cappadocia, and had agents of their own. They prospered under Anastasius, but when Justin began to persecute the Monophysites, they responded by selling their property and giving it to the poor and the refugee monks. But it seems clear that in its heyday, theirs was a prosperous merchant house.

Spices, silk and cotton were imported along trade routes which were centuries old, and the tariffs on these luxury items were an important source of revenue. The silk trade had always been closely supervised, and silk textiles were produced for court use within the imperial palace itself.[231] But silk manufacture was not an imperial monopoly until Justinian, or rather his praetorian prefect, Peter Barsymes, made it one, and how the deed was accomplished is described in an indignant but confused passage in the *Secret History*. Raw silk was bought from the Persians by *kommerkarioi*, who were traders acting in an official capacity,[232] and resold to independent raw-silk merchants (*metaxopratai*), who either employed the spinners, weavers and dyers themselves or jobbed out the work. Justinian fixed the purchase price for raw silk so low that the Persian merchants would not sell. His immediate aim was to deprive Persia of revenue which went to support the Persian army, but the result was that the silk-textile workers concentrated in Beirut and Tyre were ruined and had the choice of seeking work in the imperial silk mills or emigrating to Persia, which many did. The imperial mills were apparently unaffected by the shortage of raw silk. Either they had ample stocks on hand, or they bought at the market price.

Once Justinian had his monopoly, the price of silk fabrics soared. But bypassing Persia was hard to manage. Justinian tried to find an alternative silk route with Axumite help, and it is easy to see why. Pepper came from India via Himyar and cinnamon was traded by

the Chinese for cloves in Indonesia, then carried by outrigger boats
to Madagascar, thence up the east coast of Africa to Somalia and
from there to the imperial ports of entry. Justinian probably imagined
that silk could travel along a similar route, and encouraged King
Ella Atzheba of Axum to bypass the Persian middlemen and divert
the silk trade to Himyar. But the Persian traders were closer to India,
and when the Indian merchant-ships put into the harbours where
trading fairs took place, the Persians bought up their cargoes before
the competition could arrive from Himyar.[233]

But about 553, another solution emerged. Two Nestorian monks
appeared before Justinian to tell him that silk came from a land
named Serinda, and it was produced by worms, whose eggs could
easily be carried over a distance. At Justinian's urging, they smuggled
some eggs out of China, thus founding the Byzantine silk-growing
industry which was later to become a source of imperial prestige.[234]
The story strains the limits of credulity. To feed the silk-worms, one
needs the leaves of the white mulberry tree, to say nothing of skilled
workers to process the cocoons into yarn. However, the technology
may already have been known: the island of Cos had once been
famous for its 'silk' fabrics which were woven from thread obtained
from a cocoon, and the insect which produced this pupa may have
been some sort of native relative of the Chinese silk-worm. Some
technology transfer may have been possible, and some may have
come from Sassanid Persia, for Persia had acquired smuggled worms
in 410 and already had a silk industry.[235] In any case, the techniques
were mastered, and domestic production of silk began. By the seventh
century, sericulture was established in Asia Minor, and Byzantine silk
was to become a prestige export that was carefully controlled.

State monopolies did not belong to Roman tradition,[236] and the
emperor Zeno outlawed them in 483, as had Leo before him. But
the *Secret History* claims that Justinian ignored Zeno's interdict and
granted private monopolies right and left, but these cannot have
been monopolies in the usual sense of the term.[237] What Justinian
did was to allow the tradesmen's guilds to purchase the right to fix
the prices for their own commodities, first in Constantinople and
then in other large cities. But there was one imperial monopoly that
Justinian did establish: the imperial ordnance factories took over the
manufacture of all arms, and private arms makers were drafted into
them. The arms were stored in the imperial armouries or local
armouries established in designated cities.[238] Illicit export of arms
was stopped as far as possible.

The export of gold and silver was guarded with equal jealousy. The *Secret History* reports that a native of Edessa had the misfortune to be given to Persia as a hostage, and when his grandmother offered 2,000 pounds of silver as ransom, the emperor refused, for he would not let so much Roman wealth pass into foreign hands.[239] Silver, however, was not minted for commercial purposes in the sixth century. It was the gold *solidus*, introduced by Constantine and minted at seventy-two to the Roman pound, that was respected in foreign markets. All nations, wrote the Alexandrian trader, Cosmas Indicopleustes, used the *solidus*, or *nomisma*, to give it its common name in the East, and it was universally admired from one end of the world to the other. Minting was an imperial monopoly, and in Justinian's reign, twice as many mints were in operation as in that of Justin I. Bronze coinage was for domestic usage, and served as the currency used by the poor, but gold paid the stipends of the soldiers and the civil service, subsidized the building programme, and served as the principal weapon of Byzantine diplomacy and trade. The drain on the treasury must have been immense, and new sources to replenish the reserve were not abundant. Gold and silver mines in the Balkans and Anatolia continued to be worked, and there were gold-bearing mountain streams in Armenia which were a bone of contention between the empire and Persia. Outside the empire, there was gold in Nubia, and in the Caucasus and Ural mountain ranges, which helps explain Justinian's interest in both areas. Yet access to these sources became more difficult in spite of Justinian's best efforts. The *Secret History*[240] concludes with a story of how hangers-on at court would ask each other where all the Roman money had gone: some said that the barbarians had it all, others that the emperor hoarded it in secret chambers. There was ground for their complaints. The empire's supply of gold was diminishing.

It was probably for this reason that Peter Barsymes began to issue a light-weight *solidus* shortly before the empress Theodora's death. The find-spots of these coins *within* the empire seem to rule out the hypothesis that they were intended for the northern European trade rather than internal use.[241] They must have been employed to pay off debts tariffed in gold where the state had captive creditors, for in free commerce, Gresham's Law would have quickly driven them from circulation. So the best guess is that Barsymes introduced them as a means of remunerating the civil militia and perhaps the soldiers while at the same time, reducing the drain on the treasury.[242]

The *Secret History*[243] gives some grounds for this hypothesis: light-weight gold coinage was among the sins that it imputes to Barsymes, and Procopius himself would be sensitive to salary cuts, for he himself belonged to the civil service, whereas northern European trade lay beyond his horizon. But Justinian was not above tinkering with the bronze coinage too, in an effort to increase the purchasing power of gold. That, at least, seems to explain a report in John Malalas' *Chronicle* that the poor in Antioch, who used bronze, rioted in 553 over the debasement of the coinage.[244] Apparently government decree had made the *follis*, the common bronze coin, cheaper in relation to gold. The result would have been devaluation at the expense of the poor. But faced with rioting in the streets, the government retreated.

In the second half of the sixth century, the economic outlook darkened. The signs, however, are not equally clear everywhere. The reconquests in the West hurt the economies of Africa and Italy. In Africa, there was stagnation: African wheat was exported as part of taxation once Africa became an imperial province, and her exports of African Red Slip pottery, which had revived in the final period of the Vandal regime, began to tail off in Justinian's last years, though production continued into the late seventh century.[245] But this decline may be due to the increased competition which African Red Slip pottery encountered in the eastern Mediterranean from similar earthenware exported from Cyprus, Egypt and particularly Phocaea in Asia Minor, which shipped table ware even to Carthage itself.[246] When Procopius[247] reports that Africa was ruined, we must distrust him. The reconquest may have dampened the economy, but we get a general impression of economic well-being lasting past Justinian's death.

Yet Africa was well-off compared with Italy, where the distress caused by years of war was compounded by tax collectors and corrupt officials dispatched from Constantinople. When Procopius states that Italy was reduced to a desperate state, he was not far off the mark.[248] There was no relief from taxes, for the treasury's need was too great. When Tiberius II became emperor in 578, the compulsory donative known as the *aurum oblaticum* which Rome contributed was exacted at the same high rate as in the past. Three thousand gold pounds was the city's assessment, its ruined state notwithstanding.[249] The reconquest meant that a large share of the West's capital surplus was siphoned off to Constantinople.

Italy got little in return. At Ravenna, the headquarters of the *strategos autokrator*, the reconquest was followed by an influx of Byzantine officials and soldiers, and yet the economic ties of the city with the eastern Mediterranean grew markedly anaemic compared with what they were under the Ostrogothic regime. The ironies of history have made the church of San Vitale in Ravenna the place where the ghosts of the great emperor and his empress emerge most clearly from the shadows of the past, for the mosaics in the chancel which represent them are as vivid today as when they were first installed. But most of the Ravenna churches consecrated in Justinian's reign were begun under the Ostrogoths, and the costs were borne by local benefactors or bishops. Imperial benevolence, however, did benefit the see of Ravenna in other ways, for Justinian soon recognized that he could use it to clip the power of Rome, and in 546, he appointed as its bishop an outsider, a native of Pola in Istria named Maximian, who moved in imperial circles in Constantinople, and perhaps had Theodora's favour. Pope Vigilius was ordered to consecrate him, and like the metropolitans of Carthage and Justiniana Prima, he was raised to the rank of archbishop by imperial edict. He appears in the San Vitale mosaics wearing the *pallium*, which was probably a gift from the pope. But the papacy regarded this wealthy, upstart see with apprehension.[250]

In the Balkans and in Greece proper, the signs of decline are everywhere, once the relatively peaceful decade of the 530s was past. The one exception was Thessaloniki, the headquarters of the Illyrian praetorian prefecture, which remained a commercial centre. In 545, faced with a crop failure in Egypt, Peter Barsymes requisitioned wheat from Thrace as well as Bithynia and Phrygia,[251] and this has been taken to show that the farms of Thrace could still produce a surplus. It is, however, more likely that Barsymes considered it more vital for the regime that the Constantinople masses be fed than the Thracian peasants. Three novels of Justinian illustrate the plight of the small landholders in Thrace and Illyricum who fell into debt to lenders who made loans in money or kind: for the former Justinian limited interest to slightly over 5 per cent and for the latter, 12.5 per cent.[252]

The picture is much better in the East, where the huge estates which ground down the peasants in the western portion of the empire were less widespread. The olive production on the limestone massif that lies between the coastal plain of northern Syria and Aleppo continued, unaffected by the Persian sack of Antioch in 540. The village communities enjoyed growth and prosperity from the fourth century until the plague interrupted it. Even then, there is no evidence of marked population decline. These villages were surveyed before World War II and yielded evidence for a thriving rural economy based solely on olive oil production.[253] Further work has modified the picture: excavations in the 1970s at Déhès, an ordinary village in the Gebel Barisa, has shown that the villagers also raised livestock and in the off season quarried building stone. From the mid-sixth century on, there are signs of economic slowdown, but no depopulation until the start of the ninth century, and it was not until a century later that Déhès was deserted.[254]

Moreover, the prosperity of these hill villages was not unique: parallels can be found elsewhere in eastern Syria and the Negev.[255] In the villages of the Gebel Barisa region, there was no lack of money in circulation well into the seventh century. The economic life of the villages appears to have been more active than that of the cities in the same period. In Palestine, the construction of new synagogues and churches points to general prosperity, and Justinian's building programme brought in public capital on a scale not seen since the death of Theodosius II's consort, the empress Eudocia, who had been a munificent patron. The Samaritan revolt of 529 did great damage; Justinian had to remit taxes for two years and Procopius reports that long afterwards, many farms once tilled by Samaritans remained abandoned.[256] But we are left with the impression of a thriving economy in Palestine which declined only after Justinian's death.

Part of the reason for this prosperity was the pilgrim trade, which might lend prosperity to a settlement whose only resource was a martyr's shrine nearby. But in southern Syria too, in the basalt hills of the Hawran, villages continued to thrive into the seventh century. Trade with the nomad peoples of the desert and southern Arabia may be part of the reason.[257] From Nessana, a caravan station in the Beersheba region of Third Palestine there is supporting evidence for this hypothesis, for it became, for practical purposes, an Arab settlement, and bred and raised camels, which earlier was a purely nomad activity.[258] The late blooming of Nessana was based on the nomad trade. But elsewhere the likely cause of prosperity is the development of autonomous rural economies centred on independent villages, which traded their surpluses for what they could not produce themselves. Some were more successful than others, and the overall picture is not uniform. But the growth of these rural economies went hand in hand with the decline of the cities, and that is another story.

THE 'OUTSIDERS': JEWS, SAMARITANS, PAGANS, HERETICS

'He [Justinian], finding that belief in God in former times had wandered into error and was forced to go in many directions, wiped out the paths that led to error and succeeded in placing it upon the strong foundation of one faith.' So Procopius,[259] neatly expressing the *Zeitgeist* of the age. But every state with an official ideology has minorities which do not fit. They are the outsiders. In Justinian's empire, they were the Jews, the Samaritans, the pagans and heretics.

The Jews were relatively privileged. Late Antiquity inherited a series of laws dating back to the first century BC, which recognized Judaism as a lawful religion.[260] Thus when Diocletian launched the last great persecution against the Christians and ordered that all Roman citizens offer sacrifice to the pagan gods, Jews were exempt.[261] No similar exemption was given the Samaritans, who found the command equally repugnant. There was also an exemption from the general ban on circumcision: Jewish children might be circumcised, Gentile children, with some exceptions for the Egyptians, might not. The interdict may in part have been intended to discourage conversions, for Judaism was a religion which attracted proselytes from the Gentile world. However, conversions continued nonetheless, and in the early centuries of our era, Judaism was a worthy rival of Christianity: a fact of which the church remained uneasily aware.

However, the prohibition of circumcision, which dates to the emperor Hadrian, may have been one of the reasons why we find groups of people attached to synagogues known as 'God-fearers' (*theosebeis*). A 'God-fearer' was a Gentile who was attracted enough by the Jewish way of life that he imitated it to some degree. He might abandon his ancestral gods, though not all did so. He might even take the final step and convert, which involved a ritual bath and circumcision, but until he chose to do so, he remained a welcome member of the synagogue.[262] 'God-fearers' were allies and friends of the Jewish communities, and in a society where to be friendless was to be vulnerable, they provided valuable support.

There was a change of rhetoric with Constantine, but not much else. Constantine fulminated, but he had no stomach for persecution, and except for a brief assault on the Donatists in Africa, he left the outsiders alone. There is a dichotomy between the rodomontade which Constantine employs in his letters to Christian bishops on the subject of Jews, and his legislation. The former is hostile and vehement, but the latter conforms reasonably well with the usages of the past. Rabbis, like Christian clergy, were exempted from compulsory public services;[263] municipal councils were encouraged to nominate Jews;[264] the rights of Jewish rabbinical courts were protected.[265]

The legal standing of Judaism in the fourth century changed very little: its status as a lawful religion was reiterated, and insults against Jews and their patriarch were forbidden.[266] Their Sabbath was respected by law: no Jew need perform a liturgy on that day, and their privilege of being excused from summonses to the law courts on the Sabbath, which dated back to Augustus, was confirmed.[267] Rabbis and synagogue elders of the curial class had the same exemption from liturgies that Christian clergy had,[268] and Christian and Jewish decurions alike tried to use the loophole to escape their curial obligations.[269] No soldiers were to be billeted in synagogues,[270] a privilege apparently not extended to Christian monasteries, for the Pachomian mother house at Pbow in Egypt hosted an army detachment! We find a series of laws forbidding attacks on synagogues, which serve as evidence that such attacks were not uncommon, for laws do not prohibit fictitious delicts.[271] Synagogues, once they were seized and consecrated as churches, could not be deconsecrated, but the Jews were to receive adequate compensation and a new site for a synagogue equivalent to what they had lost.[272] In January, 438, Theodosius II issued the last imperial constitution on the subject of Jews until we reach Justinian. It banned Jews from office in the imperial service, and forbade the construction of new synagogues.[273] Neither interdict seems to have been taken too seriously, even in Constantinople itself.[274] In 442, while Theodosius II was absent in Asia, the urban prefect authorized a new synagogue in the quarter of the bronzesmiths (*Khalkoprateia*) opposite Hagia Sophia's west gate. The pious emperor returned to find his law disregarded, and ordered the synagogue converted into a church.[275]

At the same time, the law took care to protect the interests of Christians from Jews. Marriage between a Christian and Jew was treated as adultery.[276] No Jew should assail another Jew who had converted to Christianity;[277] Christians, on the other hand, who converted to Judaism would have their property confiscated.[278] Jews might not disinherit children or grandchildren who converted to Christianity;[279] and Christian slaves owned by Jews might not be converted to Judaism and circumcised.[280] In particular the law targeted purchase of Christian slaves by Jews. Constantius II banned it, and the ban was repeated, but the law was prepared to be reasonable if a Jewish master already owned Christian slaves whom he had acquired by other means.[281] This ban on the purchase of Christian slaves encountered determined resistance, since it must have hurt Jewish merchants who were active in the slave trade between the western and eastern Mediterranean, for slaves from the West were a commodity which helped to pay for the trade deficit which western Europe had with the East.[282] The ban also hurt Jewish farmers who used a few slaves on the family farm, and tradesmen who used slave labour in their shops. Using their co-religionists as slave labour was no solution, for Jewish law prevented Jews from owning Jewish slaves.[283] Thus, caught between Roman and Jewish law, Jews were left to buy slaves legally only from non-Christian areas outside the imperial boundaries.

Theodosius II's constitution of 438 may have given some comfort, for it defined the concern of the Christians more narrowly. Theodosius prohibited Jews, on pain of death, from converting any Christians, slave or free, against their will or by illegal persuasion. It was not the purchase or the ownership of Christian slaves that was singled out for interdiction, but rather their conversion. Probably, if a Jewish owner allowed his Christian slaves free exercise of their religion, the imperial authorities looked the other way.

Yet there was a great gap between issuing an edict and enforcing it. New synagogues were constructed, no matter what the law stated. In the fourth and fifth centuries, there was a building boom of synagogues in Galilee and on the Golan Heights that continued into Justinian's reign, and in the diaspora, Jewish communities enjoyed status and respect.[284] The fourth century was the period when the Jewish patriarch (or *Nasi* as he is known in rabbinical sources) with his seat at Tiberias in Palestine, achieved premier rank in the imperial system: the last *Nasi*, Gamaliel VI (d. 425) was an honorary praetorian prefect, and his courts seem to have been used by Christians as well as Jews. His rights and privileges were confirmed by a law of 404.[285] Eleven years later, however, in 415, Theodosius II issued a stiff edict stripping him of his honorary prefecture (but not his other honours) for exceeding his powers.[286] The charges against him seem to have been authorizing new synagogues, circumcision of non-Jews and owning Christian slaves.

Gamaliel had no surviving son, and there was no obvious heir within the dynasty of Hillel. Perhaps the imperial government made no great effort to find one. At any rate, after a decent delay of four years, it abolished the patriarchate, and annexed the crown tax (*aurum coronarium*) which the patriarch had levied on the synagogues.[287] However, the rabbinical school at Tiberias maintained its reputation and its chief rabbi, called by the Greeks the archipherecite (*archipherekytes*), continued to exercise many of the *Nasi*'s powers. The office again became hereditary in the sixth century. About 520 there arrived in Palestine Mar Zutra, son of the leader of the Jewish community in Babylon, who had rebelled against King Kavadh of Persia and was killed when the rebellion was crushed. The rabbis at Tiberias received Mar Zutra cordially, and he was soon chosen archipherecite of the sanhedrin there. His dynasty lasted seven generations, and the Tiberias school remained the nerve centre of Judaism until after the Arab conquest, when it was transferred to Jerusalem.[288]

The real danger which the Jews faced was not from the laws, but from a rising tide of intolerance. In popular perception, Jews were lumped together with pagans and heretics; in fact, heretics were commonly vilified as 'Jews'. From the *Lives* of the saints, we get occasional glimpses of how Jewish communities fared in the diaspora. At Amida, in Mesopotamia, the Jewish community made a regular donation as a protection fee of sorts to the church. That assured them of allies in the defence of their interests. The judicial system of Late Antiquity depended heavily on self-help, and vulnerable parties were disadvantaged if they lacked powerful friends.[289] When the holy man Sergius and his disciples from the village of Ar'a Rabtha in the territory of Amida, the capital of Mesopotamia, burned the local synagogue and built a church on its ashes, the Jews laid a charge against him, apparently in the bishop's court, and it was heard sympathetically. The Jews got another site for a synagogue, as the law prescribed, and they also struck back at Sergius by burning the huts where he lived with his followers. No civil officials seem to have been involved. On the village level, there may have been none. The bishop and his clergy had the only effective authority in the villages, and even they had only limited control over the monks and hermits, whose charisma often outmatched their own. At Amida, the Jews and Sergius continued to fight out their battle, and Sergius had the better of it until Justin I's persecution of the Monophysites directed his energies against new and tougher enemies.[290]

This was no isolated incident. Jewish communities fared well enough where they were able to defend their interests, but poorly if they had only the meagre palatine *militia* to vindicate their rights.

At Sardis, the Jewish community acquired the south hall of the city's largest bath–gymnasium complex near the end of the third century, and transformed it into a splendid synagogue which continued in use for worship and teaching (there was a school attached to it) until Sardis was destroyed in 616.[291] The community was clearly influential and affluent enough to keep any Christian zealots at bay. On the other hand, at Apamea on the Orontes, a large Christian basilica off the main street took over the site of a late fourth-century synagogue shortly after it was built,[292] and at Stobi in Macedonia, a basilica was erected in the fifth century over a synagogue which was in regular use until it was expropriated.[293] We can only guess at the reasons, but perhaps what we witness at Stobi and Apamea is evidence for the activities of local counterparts of the holy man Sergius. The life of a Jewish community in a late Roman city was uneasy.

The Jewish pogrom against the Himyarite Christians in Justin's reign added to Christian martyr literature, and must have strengthened the popular perception of Jews as enemies of Christendom.[294] In any case, with Justinian, the 89-year hiatus during which we have no new laws on Jewish matters came to an end. In the brief interval in 527 when Justinian shared the throne with his uncle, he passed a sweeping measure against all heterodoxy, Jews included.[295] He did not single them out; rather he associated them with pagans, Samaritans and heretics as a problem which needed his attention. Justinian never explicitly rescinded the status of Judaism as a 'lawful religion', but the tone of his legislation indicates that he did not recognize it. Laws against heretics and pagans were extended to cover Jews, and whether they were enforced or not, they contributed to a sense of unease in the Jewish communities across the empire.

An incident in the first year of Belisarius' campaign in Italy illustrates the point. In mid-535, Justinian had issued a constitution on ecclesiastical matters in Africa, admittedly a response to pressure from the grim African bishops, who had just met in council at Carthage, and hence harsher than it might otherwise have been. Its chief targets were Arians, Donatists and pagans, but Jews were included: they were again forbidden to possess Christian slaves and their synagogues were to be made into churches.[296] These anti-Jewish measures were not enforced, but there was one consequence. The following year, when Belisarius laid siege to Naples, the Neapolitan Jews supported the Goths, and the section of the circuit-wall facing the sea, which the Jews defended, was the last to fall.[297] The Jews had taken Justinian's measure and recognized an enemy.

The rest of Justinian's anti-Jewish measures were pin-pricks. Jews, along with Samaritans and heretics, were barred from purchasing real estate from a church: indeed a Catholic owner of any property where a church was situated might not sell, bequeath or lease it to a Jew, or even entrust it to Jewish management.[298] Another novel ruled that Jews who were decurions were not to be excused their curial duties; apparently Jews, along with Montanists, Samaritans and others, claimed that since they were legally outlawed, they should be excused these duties, and John the Cappadocian had seen some merit in their argument. Justinian affirmed that he hated heretics, but nonetheless he would not release them from their curial duties, though they were to have none of the honours attached to them.[299] He also legislated that the Scriptures might be read in synagogues either in Greek or the local language of the congregation, but he prohibited the use of the Mishnah,[300] for he reasoned that Jews who understood the Holy Scriptures, unfiltered by rabbinical interpretation, would perceive that they foretold Christianity and willingly convert. Another charge, this one from the malevolent *Secret History*, has it that Justinian compelled Jews to postpone the Passover Feast if it fell before Easter, and that many Jews paid heavy fines for disregarding this interdict.[301] However, no law in the *Corpus* confirms this charge, and a recent explanation connecting the allegation with a problem calculating the date of Easter for the year 552 may be right.[302] If so, the interdict was an isolated incident which Procopius, ever eager to malign Justinian, has seized upon. Yet these two incidents show that Justinian's caesaropapism encompassed Judaism as much as Christianity. He waded into Jewish theology with as much confidence as he did into Christian dogma.

Justinian may not have enforced the laws against Jews much more rigorously than his predecessors.[303] He was not unreasonable: to give one instance,[304] he was indulgent to the Jews of Tyre when they broke his laws governing marriage. He did not prevent the building of synagogues: recently the remains of a large synagogue with a basilical plan have been discovered at Nabratein in Galilee, which the Jewish community there completed the year before Justinian's death, unworried by his legislation,[305] and the evidence of archaeology shows that there was, if anything, a synagogue-building boom in Palestine in the sixth century.[306]

Nonetheless, Justinian's reign marks a watershed in Jewish–Gentile relations. The sticking point was not so much that Jews were barred from public offices such as that of *defensor civitatis*, which Avi-Yonah has cited as an example of intolerance.[307] The example is ill-chosen, for the office had become so unattractive that it would be hard to say who suffered the greater discrimination: the Jews who were barred from the office, or the Christians who were barred from refusing it.[308] Nor need Justinian's recognition of the judicial powers of the bishops[309] have caused trouble, for Constantine I had also recognized them, and Jewish well-being seems not to have suffered thereby. Anti-Semitic rhetoric aside, as long as many of the bishops and rabbis shared the Greek *paideia* that marked educated men, the gulf between Judaism and Christianity was not insuperable. Their leaders were still bound together by a degree of mutual understanding.

But the age of Justinian was a period of unsettling change, during which the norms of society shifted in ways hostile to the 'outsiders'. More and more in the sixth century, the bishops and clergy came from the monasteries: virtually all the Monophysites did, and an increasing number of Chalcedonians. They brought with them the intolerance of their institutions, and they set the tone for the intellectual currents of Justinian's empire. Isolated, the Jews turned increasingly to their own learned culture: it is significant that this was also the time when Hebrew was replacing Greek in the synagogue services.[310] The *modus vivendi* between Jewish communities and the Greek-speaking ruling élite, which had lasted into the fifth century, was breaking down.

The alienation of the Jewish communities was eventually to grow into open antagonism. When the Samaritans rose in revolt in 556, some Jews joined them. And when, in 614, the Persians attacked Jerusalem, the Jewish community sided with them, and after the city fell, the Jews actively assisted in the massacre of the Christians and purchased captive monks as slaves.[311]

Justinian was not unaware of the danger of an alienated, resentful minority. He made no attempt to force Jewish conversions, with one exception. On the frontier of the Libyan Pentapolis was the outpost of Boreum, situated on the inhospitable promontory of Ras Bu Grada by the Gulf of Sidra. Barley was the only cereal crop that could be grown, as well as a few herbs for sheep, and its only attraction was that it was a tax-free zone.[312] Yet Boreum occupied a strategic site on the edge of the Pentapolis. Justinian surrounded the town with a wall, and within a 5-kilometre radius there lie the ruins of at least twelve watchtowers with a larger one 10 kilometres distant, most of them Justinianic, and evidence of how seriously the government took the Berber threat. Nearby was an ancient colony of Jews with a synagogue[313] that local tradition attributed to King Solomon. The Byzantines turned it into a church and converted the Jews, by what methods we do not know. The reason was probably more military than religious. An alienated minority was a latent threat to a frontier stronghold like Boreum, and Judaism was a potential rival for Berber allegiance. To the Byzantine mind, Christianity, loyalty to the empire and even civilization itself went hand in hand.

The Samaritans were outsiders in the eyes of both Christians and Jews. They were numerous in Palestine, where they probably made up the majority of the rural population. Claiming descent from the tribes of Ephraim and Manasseh, they had their centre at the old city of Shechem, which was rebuilt by Vespasian in 72 as Flavia Neapolis (*mod.* Nablus), and nearby, on Mt Gerizim, they had built their temple by permission of Alexander the Great. It was the destruction of this temple by the Jewish Hasmonean state under John Hyrcanus in 128 BC that gave rise to much of the Samaritan antagonism towards the Jews, which was heartily reciprocated.

Relations with the Romans were not smooth either, but in general, the Samaritans prospered. Their temple was rebuilt in the second century after the failure of the Jewish Bar Kokhba revolt (132–135), which the Samaritans helped to quell, and lands vacated by Jewish rebels were settled by Samaritan farmers. But Christian monasticism introduced an intrusive element. How much the monastic settlements in rural Judaea contributed to the bitterness between Christian and Samaritan is hard to measure, but until the mid-fifth century the Samaritans were generally loyal, even providing recruits for the Roman army, and their disaffection began when the anti-Samaritan laws, which had been disregarded until then, started to be enforced.[314] For that, we can no doubt thank the monks, and when their influence was combined with the natural antagonism between the cities, where Christianity was dominant, and the countryside, which was to a large degree Samaritan, the situation was explosive.

The Samaritans rebelled in 484, capturing Caesarea, slaughtering the Christians and burning the church of St Procopius.[315] The emperor Zeno retaliated by turning their temple on Mt Gerizim into a church dedicated to the Virgin, and banning Samaritans from the public service. Another uprising under Anastasius was repressed, though not before the offending church was set alight. When Justinian became emperor, the Samaritan 'problem' was quiescent. At Caesarea in Palestine, attests Procopius, who was a native and had first-hand knowledge, many Samaritans feigned conversion to

Christianity, but others turned to 'Manichaeism', that is, the Mazdakite doctrines, which had not yet been stamped out in Persia.[316]

In 529, they rebelled again. The incident which sparked the insurrection was a Samaritan attack on Christians and Jews in Scythopolis. John Malalas[317] describes how it started. It was a custom in Palestine on Sunday for Christian children to leave their churches after the reading of the Holy Gospel, play near the Samaritans synagogues and throw stones at their houses. The Samaritans usually kept to themselves on these days. But one Sunday in 529 their patience snapped, and when the children started throwing stones at their synagogues, they came out armed with swords and killed many of their tormentors. The time was ripe for revolt: Persia's Lakhmid allies were raiding First Syria and the Samaritans hoped for Persian help. The uprising was no small matter, and it was ruthlessly suppressed. Justinian responded harshly: Samaritan synagogues were to be destroyed and Samaritans were denied the right to leave legacies to anyone other than orthodox Christians.[318] Enforcement was enjoined upon both the civil authorities and the bishops.

Procopius put the number of Samaritan dead at 100,000, and if we include among the casualties those sold into slavery, it may not be greatly exaggerated. The result was a shortage of farmers, and Christian landowners in the cities suffered, for though their land lay fallow, they remained responsible for the taxes. Sergius, the metropolitan bishop of Caesarea, appealed to Justinian on behalf of the Samaritans, and in 551, Justinian responded by repealing his law that took away their right to make wills, though in cases where a Samaritan had both Samaritan and Christian heirs, the Christians should be sole heritors.[319] But in the midsummer of 556,[320] the Samaritans rose again, not in Neapolis, which had been strongly fortified after the earlier revolt, but in Caesarea. This time they had Jewish allies. They massacred the Christians, looted churches and slew the proconsul Stephanus in his *praetorium* when he tried to interfere. We do not know what sparked the insurrection: perhaps a brawl in the local hippodrome?[321] Justinian dispatched Amantius, the Master of Soldiers in the East, to Caesarea and he suppressed the revolt without pity.

However, in 572, after the old emperor was dead, Justin II, noting that efforts to convert the Samaritans had had poor results and some of the baptized had returned to their 'evil doctrine', renewed Justinian's ban on Samaritan wills and the holding of public office.[322]

The Samaritans rose for the last time in revolt. The emperor dispatched a soldier named Theophilus to restore order, and he carried out orders with an iron fist. The Samaritans continued to exist (a few do up to the present day) but the Samaritan 'problem' was effectively extinguished.

Pagans could expect no quarter. Justinian's first law against the heterodox, promulgated in 527,[323] was followed by his sweeping edict of 529[324] which prescribed various penalties for pagans and once again forbade sacrifice on pain of death. 'In that year, there was a great persecution of Hellenes', wrote Malalas. 'Many had their property confiscated.'[325] The law was effective, almost embarrassingly so. In Jerusalem, the patriarch Peter sent a query to the Grand Old Man of the monastery at Thavatha in the territory of Gaza. What should he do about the number of pagans seeking baptism after Easter, 529, as a result of Justinian's edict? The Grand Old Man, who was an Egyptian monk named Varsanuphius, replied from his cell that they should be baptized on Ascension Day on the Mount of Olives, so that they would still have a week of feasting before Pentecost. Another query sent to the Grand Old Man begins with a significant introduction, 'Since the *dux* has lately become a Christian by zeal of the Christ-loving emperor . . .'[326]

In 545–546 there was another outbreak of anti-pagan zeal in Constantinople which swept up a throng of teachers, lawyers and doctors, and even touched the élite: the patrician Phocas, whose pagan sympathies had already been investigated once in the purge of 529, poisoned himself rather than face a second inquisition. In 562, when Justinian was old and more pietistic than ever, pagan theurgists were paraded through the city and their books burned, along with pictures and statues of their gods.[327] But it was in the provinces where paganism remained a stubborn growth. John of Ephesus, Monophysite though he was, was sent in 542 on a rural mission to the provinces of Caria, Asia, Lydia and Phrygia, with instructions to convert unbelievers, and he claimed to have won over 70,000 souls, who turned away from the errors of their ancestors. Temples were demolished, idols, altars and sacred trees destroyed, and 96 churches were built, 55 of them paid for by the imperial purse.[328] At Sardis, the capital of Lydia, there has been found an inscription dating after 539 which refers to pagans interned there. It may be connected with John's campaign to stamp out paganism, for he used strong-arm tactics as well as persuasion. We hear no more of paganism in the area.[329]

At Philae on the southern border of Egypt, the Christian bishops and the pagan priests of Isis continued to coexist until 537, when Justinian dispatched Narses Kamsarakan, duke of the Thebaid,[330] to suppress the pagan cult. The priests were arrested, and the cult statues with their precious metals and jewels were sent to Constantinople, where they no doubt added some welcome gains to the imperial treasury. The Isis temple was handed over to the bishop of Philae, Theodore, to become the church of St Stephen, and it was he who had the cross carved that may still be seen on the entrance to the *naos*, with the inscription, 'The cross has conquered! It ever conquers!' thus proclaiming victory and at the same time forestalling any pagan spirits that might try to creep back into their old sanctuary.[331] What the Blemmyes thought when they found their treaty rights to worship Isis at Philae disregarded is not recorded, but in 566–567, we find them at war with the empire.

The closing of the temple was the prologue for vigorous missionary activity among the Nobadae. Theodosius, the patriarch of Alexandria exiled in Constantinople, became alarmed that the Nobadae would accept the Chalcedonian faith and become attached to the patriarchate of Constantinople rather than his own. Julian, a priest in his entourage, volunteered to go as his missionary and preach Monophysitism to them. As John of Ephesus relates the story, Julian approached Theodora, who promised help and informed her husband of what she intended to do. But Justinian preferred to have Chalcedonians preach to the Nobadae, and he not only urged Theodore of Philae and other Chalcedonian bishops in the Thebaid to convert them, but he sent envoys with gold and baptismal robes to Silko, the Nobad king.

The empress was not to be foiled. She sent a dispatch to the duke of the Thebaid instructing him to make sure that Julian reached the Nobadae before Justinian's envoys. The duke decided that he would rather face Justinian's wrath than Theodora's, and with his help, Julian's party reached Silko first with their gifts and baptismal robes and explained to him the advantages of joining the Monophysite camp. When the emperor's envoys arrived, they found Silko well inoculated against Chalcedonian doctrines.[332] But the climate of Nubia was too much for Julian; he left after two years, and Theodore of Philae made overtures to the Nobadae, perhaps with some success. In any case, the Nobadae were converted, and Silko served the empire well by chastising the Blemmyes and forcing Christianity upon them.

The fringes of the empire did not escape. In the Libyan interior, the two oases of Jalo and Awjila still preserved the worship of Ammon. Justinian closed the temples, disbanded their hierodules and built a church dedicated to the Virgin instead.[333] But in spite of Justinian's best efforts, paganism was persistent. In 578, after Justinian's death, the emperor Tiberius II hounded down the unbelievers at Heliopolis (*mod.* Ba'albek) in Phoenicia, which was still largely pagan, and the persecution revealed that pagan rites were still secretly practised in many cities round about, including Antioch and Edessa. At Tyndaris in Sicily, which is now, by the ironies of history, the site of an immensely popular cult of the Black Virgin, local notables in the 590s protected pagans from the bishop.[334]

Justinian had no time for religious dissent. His laws against heretics are couched in blunt, implacable prose. Their style is that of the literature of theological controversy: undiplomatic, intolerant and vituperative. Heretics were considered mad, stupid or sick. Nestorians were depraved. As in Soviet Russia, deviationism was attributed to insanity. The Manichaean heretics were deemed the most odious, and the Montanists ran them a close second. Penalties were harsh. Heretical sects had their churches and church properties confiscated and their meetings outlawed. For two types of heretical felons, capital punishment was prescribed: Manichees, and Catholics who lapsed into heresy.[335] Generally, however, the regime preferred to rely on banning heretics from the civil *militia* and denying them the right to bequeath or accept legacies.

Informants were encouraged. Clergy were to scrutinize their congregations and laymen to inform on each other. If any heretic was caught holding a meeting in his house, it was to be confiscated and transferred to the church.[336] But for all that, the heretics were tenacious. Many were rural villagers, and a stubborn lot: the Montanists of Phrygia, rather than submit to Justinian's crusade, shut themselves up in their churches and set them on fire.[337] The Manichaeans were persecuted into extinction in the eastern empire, though in North Africa the sect managed to survive the Byzantine regime.[338] But the major heresy, Monophysitism, if anything thrived with persecution. It forced the regime to negotiate. In the last months of his life, Justinian himself accepted the extreme Monophysite doctrine of Julian of Halicarnassus, which was a back-handed admission of defeat.

The aim of Justinian's policy was one empire, one church and one orthodoxy. He failed in his own lifetime, and it was not until the empire had lost its eastern provinces that such a policy was even possible. Yet in Justinian's reign, secular space grew narrower, the political and ecclesiastical sectors moved into closer union, and there was no safe place left for the outsider.

5

THE FINAL YEARS

THE LAST DECADE

The final decade of Justinian's reign reads like the transcript of the Last Judgement upon his administration. It is a recital of disasters and ominous portents for the future. In the midsummer of 556, there was the Samaritan revolt. It was swiftly suppressed but it was an embarrassment, for Justinian had considered the Samaritan problem solved. Court circles averted their eyes.[1] In the same year, a bread shortage sparked a demonstration in the Hippodrome which mortified the emperor, for there was a Persian ambassador in the imperial *loge* to witness it.[2] In 557, the Tzani rebelled. Justinian had been proud of their addition to the Roman Empire,[3] but now the difficult task of conquering them had to be done again. Finally about midnight, on 14 December, in the same year, Constantinople was shaken by a great earthquake. Earthquakes were common enough in the area, but this one was especially severe, and it drove residents into the streets where they shivered in the cold and sleet until morning came. Tremors continued for more than a week, though they grew less intense. In their terror the citizens turned to religion, but as Agathias noted, their piety did not endure for long. The quake was a test of Hagia Sophia's daring architecture, and it did not pass. On 7 May of the next year, the eastern semi-dome of the church, and probably part of the main dome, collapsed.[4]

It was about the same time as the dome fell that the bubonic plague returned to Constantinople. It had travelled over the empire since its first outbreak, and now it came back to the capital for a fresh crop of victims. But the following year, Constantinople faced a another terror. The Kutrigur Bulgars swept across the Danube again and threatened to take Constantinople. Seven years earlier, the Kutrigurs had crossed the Danube, ferried across by the Gepids, who wanted to rid themselves of embarrassing allies: the Gepid king had made a compact with them to counterbalance the Lombards, and the 12,000 Kutrigurs, eager for battle, arrived while the Gepids and Lombards were still at peace. Justinian's defence was balance-of-power diplomacy. He persuaded the Utigurs east of the Sea of Azov to attack Kutrigur territory, and, as he hoped, the Kutrigur khagan hurriedly made peace in order to deal with the Utigur threat. But by 558, the war between the Utigurs and Kutrigurs had ceased, and in March, 559, a new khagan, Zabergan, leading a Kutrigur horde which included Slavs, took advantage of sub-zero weather to cross the frozen Danube.

In Thrace the horde split into three spearheads. One advanced into Greece, but the fortifications at Thermopylae held, and it got no further. The garrison at Thermopylae consisted of regular troops; one of the sins which Procopius[5] attributed to the *logothetes* Alexander 'Scissors' had been to replace the garrison of local militia men at Thermopylae with regulars, annexing entertainment funds from the cities of Greece to pay their stipends. The invasion of 559 vindicated Alexander's reform. The Kutrigurs did not get past Thermopylae. A second spearhead made for the Thracian Chersonese, but the Long Wall across the isthmus (not to be confused with the Anastasian Long Wall west of Constantinople) was ably defended by a young officer from Justinian's native city bearing the same name as Justinian's cousin, Germanus, and possibly a relative: in any case, Justinian had brought him to Constantinople at the age of 8 and saw to his education. He defeated the Kutrigurs and forced them to retreat, though he was wounded himself in a sortie.

But Zabergan himself with a force of 7,000 horsemen advanced on the capital. The Master of the Soldiers in Thrace was the Sergius whom we have already encountered as an incompetent praetorian prefect in Africa. The passage of time had not improved his capacity. The Kutrigurs vanquished him and took him prisoner. Then, looting as they advanced, they made for the Long Wall where the damage inflicted by the earthquake of 557 was not yet repaired, and there they routed a force of conscripts and *scholares*, the decorative soldiers of the palace guard who were quite unfit for active service.[6] The way was open to Constantinople. Justinian manned the Theodosian Walls with senators, young recruits and *scholares*. They were all he had.

At this point, Justinian summoned Belisarius from retirement. The story is told by Agathias, and loses nothing in the telling. The frail old man put on his armour again. With a scratch force, the core of it made up of 300 of his veterans, he advanced to a village a few kilometres outside the Theodosian Wall, and made his camp there. His effective soldiers were few but he had a flock of peasants from the Thracian countryside who had fled before the Kutrigurs. 'Yet', wrote Agathias with a learned reference to the battle of Thermopylae where the Spartan king Leonidas and his Lacedaemonian troops died defending the pass against the Persians in 480 BC, 'the Romans with Belisarius to lead them employed the boldness of the Lacedaemonians, and utterly routed the enemy and slew all they laid their hands on, while they themselves suffered no harm worth mention.' Zabergan rode against the Romans with 2,000 horse in close order. Belisarius countered by hiding 200 cavalry in a valley where they could rake the Kutrigur flanks with arrows as they passed, and before the Kutrigurs could recover, Belisarius with his motley force charged them, making as much racket as they could. The Kutrigurs imagined they were facing a much larger army than they were, and fled in panic.[7]

The immediate danger over, Justinian recalled Belisarius, and Zabergan joined the remnants of the Kutrigur spearhead which had returned from its débâcle in the Chersonese. For four more months they plundered Thrace, while Justinian with his court moved to Selymbria on the Propontis where the Long Wall reached the sea and oversaw its rebuilding. Clearly he was aware that the public perception of him as the sustainer of the empire needed to be refurbished, and though he was seventy-seven years old, and for half a century had left his capital only for the occasional holiday at one of his palaces on the Asian side of the Bosporus, he believed that he must now present his subjects with the image of an active warrior as their emperor. But what induced the Kutrigurs to make peace was the news that Justinian was strengthening his Danube fleet. The treaty with the Kutrigurs gave them a subsidy and safe passage across the Danube. But their career was near its end. Justinian promised the khagan of the Utigurs the Kutrigur subsidy as well as his own if he would vanquish the Kutrigurs, and the war that resulted so weakened them both that they fell prey themselves to new invaders, though not before they made one more foray.

Having rid the Balkans of its enemies for the moment, Justinian returned to the capital. His entry was a formal *adventus*: the advent of a victor into his city. But there is a human touch to it: as Justinian passed the church of the Holy Apostles, he paused to light candles at the tomb of Theodora, who lay in her sarcophagus of 'Sardian stone' in the mausoleum which he had built for his empress and himself.[8]

Yet there was a sense of unease. In 560, a false rumour spread that the emperor had died. He had dropped out of sight, and the people, anticipating trouble, began to hoard bread. But it was only a migraine headache; Justinian reappeared, and the rumours were quashed. But violence in the streets was again on the increase. There were outbreaks in 553, 556, 559 and 560. In 556, Justinian was embarrassed by a demonstration in the Hippodrome against food shortages while the envoy of the Persian king was present.[9] In November, 561, the Greens attacked the Blues in the Hippodrome and the riot spread up and down the *Mese*, the city's main street, before it was repressed. In the spring of the next year, the Kutrigur Bulgars raided Thrace again and shoved aside an imperial army led by Justinian's nephew Marcellus.[10] In October there was another riot in Constantinople, and in the next month, a drought and clashes at the cisterns over water. And in the same month, there was a plot against Justinian which almost succeeded.

The conspirators were important men in the business world. One, named Ablabius, was perhaps a former moneyer (*monetarius*) and technically an imperial slave.[11] The second, Sergius,[12] was the nephew or cousin of Aetherius, the curator of one of the imperial palaces, who was later himself to take part in an abortive plot against Justin II, and lose his head. The third was an *argyroprates*: a goldsmith or a banker named Marcellus who had a workshop near Hagia Eirene, a short distance from the palace.[13] He paid Ablabius 50 gold pounds for his services. The plan was to kill the emperor as he sat in the palace dining-room, but it appears that although Ablabius had access to the dining-room, he had to give notice if he wanted to approach the sacred presence. Thus, when he notified a palatine official that he wanted to approach the emperor at the appointed hour, he inadvertently roused suspicion. Ablabius was caught, Marcellus killed himself and Sergius fled to the church of the Virgin at Blachernae.

A few weeks later, the dedication of the rebuilt church of Hagia Sophia took place, and Paul the Silentiary,[14] who delivered a long descriptive poem on the church, could hardly pass over the conspiracy in silence. The conspirators, he wrote, were already within the palace and were about to launch their attack when they were caught. The emperor put his trust in God, who granted him victory.

256

But the leader of the plot died by his own hand, for the spirit of Justice knew that if he were taken alive, Justinian would pity him and spare his life!

So Marcellus, money-changer and banker, was the prime mover of the plot. We can only guess his motives, but there were reasons for dissatisfaction among his guild members. Peace had been negotiated with Persia at the end of the pevious year, and it called for an annual subsidy to Persia of 30,000 *solidi per annum*, which was only slightly more than the sum paid under the truce of 545. However, the first seven years were to be paid in advance and thus some 2,900 gold pounds[15] had to be delivered forthwith. Justinian resorted to requisitions and forced loans. His successor, Justin II, found 'the treasury crushed by debts and reduced to the last degree of poverty', to quote a decree he promulgated the day after Justinian's death,[16] and Justin II had reason to know: on his accession he faced a great throng of people in the Hippodrome, who presented IOUs and demanded repayment.[17] But Justinian was too old to learn frugality. Only three months before the conspiracy, he had required the money-changers, and silver and jewel merchants, to present a costly display of lights for the dedication of the new church of the martyr Theodora, which may well have brought their dissatisfaction to the boiling point.[18] They were perhaps all the more unhappy because three years before the conspiracy, Justinian had dealt maladroitly with a problem of deflated currency in Alexandria caused by debased gold coins issued for use there. He withdrew them from circulation with a measure that must have hurt the money-changers and bankers, if it was enforced.[19] Were there repercussions in Constantinople?[20]

Sergius was dragged from his place of asylum, and under torture, he revealed other names: two more silversmiths, Belisarius' curator and Belisarius himself. They were arrested and brought before the urban prefect, Procopius. It would be one of the great ironies of history if this Procopius had been the historian whose works have given Belisarius his reputation, good and bad, and whose defamation of Justinian colours our judgement of him. But there is no sound testimony for the identification, and where coincidence is the only evidence, we can only make guesses. Belisarius had his attendants removed and was put under house arrest. Six months later, Justinian restored him to favour, and in March of 565, he died.

The emperor's last great triumph took place only a few weeks after the conspiracy. On the day before Christmas, Hagia Sophia was rededicated. The dome had been rebuilt under the direction of Isidore the Younger, and it had been made higher in order to reduce its outward thrust. The procession, with the emperor and the patriarch in the lead, wound its way from the church of St Plato to Hagia Sophia. A later and muddled author known as the 'Anonymous of Banduri' relates that Justinian advanced alone to the ambo of the rebuilt church, stretched out his hands and cried, 'Glory to God who has deemed me worthy to complete such a work! I have conquered you, Solomon!'[21] True or not, the story captures the psychology of the great emperor. The son of obscure parents in the equally obscure village of Tauresium, he had become the chosen of God to restore His empire and built Him a church that surpassed the Temple of the great royal builder, Solomon, with whom Justinian's coevals *did* compare him.[22] His energy and his sense of mission had brought him far, and now he was near the end.

On the eastern frontier, the truce which the Persian king's ambassador Izedh Gushnasp had negotiated in Constantinople in 557 had ended active hostilities for the moment. Khusro turned his attention to Persia's old enemy, the Ephthalites, and he wanted his hands free of war with the empire. There had been another convulsion on the Asian steppe. From the mid-fourth century, the Mongolian horde known to the Chinese as the Juan-juan had dominated a broad belt of land from Manchuria as far west as Lake Balkash or even further. But from 386 to 534 the Toba empire, a confederation of Turkish-speaking tribes known in Chinese sources as the northern Wei dynasty, ruled the plains of northern China, and as long as it lasted, it blocked Juan-juan penetration into China. There seems to have been a rapid shift in power after 534: the Toba empire fell to the Juan-juan, in China the Sui dynasty set out to reunite all China and in the north, the Turks who had fallen under Juan-juan subjection rose up against their overlords, and massacred them. The Turks were as great a potential menace to Sui dynasty China as were the Juan-juan, but the horde split into east and west halves, and the western Turks, led by a khagan named Sizabul or Silzabul in the Greek sources, joined the Persians against the Ephthalites.

Ephthalite power was in decline: in 549 they had evacuated northern India, where their domination had lasted some 60 years, and now they were crushed between the Turks and Sassanid Persia. In 561, Izedh Gushnap boasted to the imperial Master of Offices Peter the Patrician that his royal master Khusro had destroyed Ephthalite power,[23] but he was stretching the truth. Ephthalite resistance was not broken until ca. 567, and Khusro wanted to free his hands for a joint offensive with the Turks.

Late in 561 Peter the Patrician and Izedh Gushnap met at Dara and hammered out the terms of a fifty-year peace. The struggle had ended in a stand-off, though Justinian could claim a clear victory in Lazica. The Persians evacuated it, but the status of Suania was left open, for all that Peter argued that it was a client kingdom of Lazica. The subsidies which had been a condition of peace with Persia throughout the sixth century were continued. Peter asked for their cancellation but settled on an annual sum of under 420 gold pounds, which compares well enough with the 500 pounds that Anastasius had agreed to pay Kavadh in 507.[24] But for the prosperous empire of Anastasius, the payment had not been a burden. Now it was. Yet the remainder of the treaty should have given the Byzantines little cause for complaint. The Christians in Persia would be granted freedom of worship, there would be no compulsory conversions to the Persian state religion, and abhorrent though the custom might be to good Mazdeans, Christians would be allowed to inhume their dead. In return, the Christians were to abandon any effort to make conversions among the Mazdeans.

The commercial clauses reveal a common interest. All trade between the two empires was to pass through the 'treaty ports' of Nisibis and Dara. No merchants should try to avoid them. The smugglers whom Persia and Rome agreed to outlaw were probably Arabs for the most part, and this clause was directed against them. It was not that the customs duties at the Dara port of entry were substantial, for they averaged about 10 per cent *ad valorem*.[25] Rather it was unthinkable that the export–import trade should be uncontrolled. Another proviso stated that the Arab allies of both empires would be bound by the treaty. The Lakhmids, headed now by Mundhir's successor 'Amr (554–569/70), and the Ghassanids were henceforth to keep the peace: a clause soon honoured in the breach, for within two years, in October, 564, the Ghassanid phylarch Harith reported an attack by 'Amr.[26] The Byzantines promised not to station a large army at Dara or make it the headquarters of the Master of the Soldiers of the East, but in return the Persian king yielded the point that the fort's existence was contrary to a pledge made by Rome in 442.

On the Danube frontier, the Bulgar threat faded out after 562, and the Slavs, without the Bulgars to sweep them up into their hordes, were quiescent for the moment. Slavic attacks were to start again in 579, but by then, a new ethnic group, whom the Greeks called Avars, had appeared to orchestrate them. Constantinople laid eyes on the Avars for the first time in January, 558, when an Avar embassy appeared there. These mounted warriors from the steppe fought with sabres, long lances and an efficient reflex bow, and it is they who introduced into Europe the use of the stirrup, which they had borrowed from China. They were probably the remnant of the Juan-juan horde, who fled westwards before the Turks, sweeping up some fugitive Ephthalites, but apparently making no contact with Sassanid Persia.[27] When they reached the plains north of the Caucasus, they encountered the Alans and sought the protection of the Alan king, Sarosius. The Alans, who were Christians and part of the Byzantine commonwealth, referred the Avars to the imperial commander in Lazica.

The commander was Justin, the son of Germanus, and when the Avars asked him for land and an alliance, he recognized that this was a matter for the emperor himself. He forwarded the Avar envoys to Constantinople where their arrival made a vivid impression, for they were outlandish, frightening men with their hair hanging in long pony-tails down their backs. They wanted land within the empire and a subsidy in return for an alliance.[28] They got a subsidy but no land; instead Justinian directed them against the Sabir Huns in the Caucasus. The Avars vanquished them, and then, moving westwards, fell upon the Antai in the Western Ukraine and Bessarabia. They then meted out the same treatment to the other ethnic groups whom they encountered between the Caucasus and Carpathians, in particular the Kutrigurs and Utigurs, and in 561 or 562, they reached the north bank of the Danube, again asking for land, this time in Dobruja, where the Kutrigur invasion had left the frontier defences in ruins.

Justinian temporized. Avars in the Dobruja region would imperil Thrace. He offered the Avar khagan, Baian, the old Herulian territories in north-west Serbia between the Lombards and the Gepids, but Baian was too prudent for that. He might have crossed the Danube and taken what he wanted by force, but the Master of Soldiers in Thrace, who was once again Germanus' son, Justin, warned the emperor in time, and Baian's envoys were detained in Constantinople while the defences of the Danube were put in order. When at last the envoys rejoined their khagan, Justin saw to it that they did not cross the frontier before they gave up the arms they had purchased in the capital, presumably from the imperial ordnance factories, for they had a monopoly of arms manufacture.

For the moment, the Avar khagan swallowed his annoyance and continued to collect his subsidy. Next year, however, he set off to attack the Franks, perhaps with Constantinople's blessing, but the Franks proved too tough for him. Defeated in a battle beyond the Elbe, he had to settle for a treaty with the Merovingian king Sigebert and supplies sufficient for the journey back to the lands north of the Danube. Justin maintained a careful watch, and Baian could only bide his time.

In Africa, there was another outbreak of hostility with the Berbers. In 563, the praetorian prefect of Africa, John Rogathinus, had a friendly Berber sheikh, Coutsina, assassinated. The reason is obscure. Coutsina had been a loyal ally during John Troglita's prefecture, and in Corippus' *Johannid* he is portrayed as the good and faithful Moor in contrast with Antalas, the villainous renegade.[29] We can only guess what provoked the breach with Rogathinus. The execution set off a rebellion, and pillage and massacre spread over Numidia before Justinian's cousin Marcian, whom the old emperor dispatched to Africa, could bring the situation under control.[30] One victim of the rebellion may have been the poet-schoolmaster Corippus, whose epic on John Troglita's exploits, which he had drafted at great speed in 549, had presumably brought him some bounty, though whether he was robbed by the Berbers or by imperial officials who took advantage of the breakdown of authority, we cannot know. In any case, he came to Constantinople to appeal to the emperor, and there he found a post in the service of the quaestor of the imperial palace, Anastasius, where he still was when Justinian died.

The African insurgence outlasted Justinian, though he moved promptly enough to repress it. But the old emperor seems to have been troubled at heart, worried, perhaps, for the salvation of his soul. 'The old man no longer cared; he was altogether cold and only grew warm with love of another life', wrote Corippus.[31] In 563, he left the capital for a pilgrimage to the shrine of St Michael at Germia in western Galatia (*mod.* Yürme) where there was preserved a fragment of Christ's tunic.[32] What moved him to make this difficult journey at the age of 81 we cannot know. For half a century, he had not gone more than a few kilometres from his capital. But the pilgrimage betrays the mindset of his old age. Theology had become an obsession.

Justinian died suddenly on 14 November, 565, aged 83. But before his death, he made one last foray into the doctrinal battlefield. The condemnation of the 'Three Chapters' and all the turmoil surrounding it had done nothing to heal the split between the orthodox and the Monophysites. Among the Monophysites themselves there was a division between the disciples of Severus and Theodosius, of whom the most zealous was Jacob Baradaeus, and the followers of Julian of Halicarnassus, the Aphthartodocetists, who were now the strongest sect in Egypt. A third Monophysite splinter creed, 'Tritheism', arose there, too, towards the end of the 550s, and it won over John Philoponus in Alexandria, who equipped it with Aristotelian terminology. Theodora's grandson Athanasius was an enthusiast and it was not until after Justinian's death, in the 570s, that Tritheism declined. So also did Aphthartodocetism, but it was yet to have its most famous convert.

Theodore Askidas died early in 558. His place was taken by a bishop from Joppa whose name we do not know, but like Theodore, his sympathies were no doubt with the Origenists, though he was careful not to say so publicly. He reminded the old emperor that there was more than one Monophysite sect, and if he could not win over the followers of Severus, why not approach the Aphthartodocetists? The suggestion must have piqued the emperor's interest. In 557, he had convoked Jacob Baradaeus and a large selection of his monks in Constantinople in another effort to solve the Monophysite problem, but the meeting had been fruitless. On the eve of the rededication of Hagia Sophia, he issued an edict proclaiming the orthodoxy of Chalcedon.[33] But then, near the end of 564, he promulgated an edict affirming the incorruptibility of Christ's body.

We do not know what Pope John III's reaction was in Rome. He had the luxury of distance from Constantinople, and was not required to make an immediate comment. Eutychius of Constantinople was not so fortunate. He had no doubt that Justinian's edict was heretical, and having failed to convince the emperor, he flatly refused to sign. Justinian was in no mood to trifle. On 22 January, 565, while the patriarch was conducting the commemorative service for St Timothy in the church of Sts Sergius and Bacchus, a detachment of troops led by the two senators Aetherius and Addaeus seized him and took him to the monastery of Choracoudin. On the last day of the month, a synod of bishops who were the emperor's partisans, or were cowed by him, deposed the unfortunate patriarch, and he was soon on his way back to the monastery at Amaseia whence he had come. Justinian was determined to have a more malleable patriarch, and the closeness of death left him no time to dally.

THE FINAL YEARS

He found his man in the nuncio of the Antiochene patriarch at court, John Scholasticus, who came from the village of Sirimis near Antioch.³⁴ John had come to Constantinople with a goal. He was a lawyer; hence his name *Scholastikos*, and when the patriarch of Antioch had chosen to ordain him as a priest and make him his nuncio at court, John had consulted Saint Symeon Stylites the Younger, who foretold a brilliant career for him that would culminate with the patriarchate in Constantinople. Then John ventured a further question: who would the next emperor be? The saint was silent for a long time, and then swore John to secrecy, as well he might: such questions smacked of treason. The next emperor, the saint foretold, would be Justin, the emperor's nephew, the son of Justinian's sister Vigilantia.

On reaching Constantinople, John broke his promise to the saint at the first opportunity, and revealed the prophecy to Justin. As a result, he gained Justin's favour and support in his bid for the patriarchate. He was a skilful apparatchik. He seems to have convinced Justinian that he would support his Aphthartodocetist edict, but he would not be the first of the patriarchs to give his consent. The other patriarchs stood firm, as John no doubt suspected they would. Apollinarius, the Melkite patriarch of Alexandria, was a staunch old soldier who had been ordained a priest and elevated to the patriarchate all in July, 551.³⁵ Macarius of Jerusalem had just been appointed to his patriarchal throne, or rather reappointed, for he had already been deposed once on suspicion of Origenist leanings. But the best theologian of them all was Anastasius of Antioch, and it was he who took the lead. In 565 he convoked in Antioch a synod of the bishops of his patriarchate, which rejected Justinian's edict. Justinian was preparing tough action when he died. All the patriarchs must have heaved great sighs of relief, especially John Scholasticus, who had temporized as long he could, and now death removed the heretical old emperor and brought John's patron to the throne in the nick of time.

THE AFTERMATH

Justinian had designated no heir. He left behind him three nephews, as well as two sons of his cousin Germanus, and the choice lay between a pair of these, both named Justin. Justin, the son of Germanus, had inherited his father's military ability, and at Justinian's death he was Master of the Soldiers of Illyricum, guarding the

263

Danube frontier against Avar invasion. He was the better candidate and probably the old emperor knew it. But Theodora had detested Germanus and his family, and though more than a decade and a half had passed since her death, Justinian never quite freed himself of her influence. The other Justin was the son of Justinian's sister Vigilantia and married to Theodora's niece, Sophia. Sophia shared her aunt's theology and ambition, as well as some of her ability. Since her Monophysitism could have harmed her husband's progress to the throne, she abandoned it, but without cutting her contacts.[36] Justin's own career had been undistinguished, but he held the post of *cura palatii*, which kept him at the centre of imperial power. The patriarch John Scholasticus was his man, and so was the Count of the Excubitors, Tiberius, who was eventually to succeed him as emperor. Justin had secured the post for him the year before Justinian died.

The old emperor died without warning, on the night of 14 or 15 November, probably in his sleep. The aged eunuch, Callinicus, *praepositus* of the Sacred Bedchamber, was the only official present at his death-bed, and he claimed that with his dying breath, Justinian had designated Justin, Vigilantia's son, as his successor. Only Callinicus knew, and there is room for scepticism. But the court machinery began to function smoothly and efficiently. Callinicus with a group of senators who had been roused from their beds hurried to the Sophiae palace overlooking the Sea of Marmara. There Justin and Vigilantia met them. Justin made a show of reluctance which we should not assume was pure hypocrisy: emperors customarily showed reluctance when they were offered the throne, and occasionally it was sincere. In this case, however, Justin yielded speedily enough, and, escorted by the senators, Sophia and he made their way from their mansion through the night to the Great Palace. The Excubitors blocked the palace entrances, and early in the morning, before the capital knew of Justinian's death, the patriarch John Scholasticus crowned Justin in the palace, probably in the Triclinium of the Nineteen Couches where Justin I had crowned Justinian. Then the new emperor, wearing the crown, proceeded to the imperial *loge* in the Hippodrome to receive the acclamations of the people and to address them. The stage management worked well.

Justin II had taken over the levers of power, but he had yet to consolidate it. The Avars were told to expect no more subsidies. The move was popular, and for the moment, the Avars were in no position to insist, for they had just suffered a defeat at the hands of the

Franks.[37] A new praetorian prefect, Thomas, was sent to Africa to restore order.[38] The other Justin, the son of Germanus, was dispatched as Augustal duke to Alexandria, where he was assassinated on the empress Sophia's orders. His murder may have been the spark that ignited a conspiracy in Constantinople: on 3 October, 566, two senators, Addaeus and Aetherius who had helped bundle Eutychius off the patriarchal throne in Justinian's last days, were beheaded. The charge was an attempt to poison Justin.[39]

With Persia, the treaty of 562 was still in effect, and by its terms, Constantinople was to pay Khusro a yearly subsidy of 420 gold pounds. However, Suania remained an open sore. Khusro was determined to avoid its cession to the empire, and Justin considered his reluctance to give it up a breach of the treaty. Yet when the second instalment of the subsidy came due in 569, Justin paid. However the third instalment, which was due in 572, he refused to pay.

There were several reasons. One was that in the division of spoils after the Ephthalite overthrow, the western Turks had acquired sovereign rights over Transoxiana, and the merchants from Sogdiana who had plied the overland silk route to China before the Ephthalites choked off the trade saw a chance to reopen business. Khusro was not interested, for the Turks were potentially as great a menace to his kingdom as the Ephthalites had been. The envoys, led by a Sogdian merchant named Maniach who had come to the Persian court to negotiate the sale of raw silk, were given poison at a reception, and Maniach was lucky to escape alive with a few companions. So in 568, an embassy arrived in Constantinople, and Justin was offered the splendid prospect of a Turkish alliance against the Avars, and a route to China that bypassed Persia.[40] Eventually nothing was to come of it, but it increased Justin's overconfidence.

Second, there was the Sassanid interference in Himyar, which was to result in the conquest of that kingdom. But the final straw was a revolt in Persian-ruled Armenia. The Persian governor erected a Zoroastrian fire-temple at the Persarmenian capital of Dvin, in the midst of a Christian population, and killed a prince of one of the great Armenian feudal families. Persarmenia rose in revolt under the brother of the murdered prince. Refugees from Persarmenia streamed into imperial territory.[41] Justin was incensed. In any case, he believed that if war came, he would win.

He had little reason for confidence. In the Balkans, power had shifted to Byzantine disadvantage. Justinian had managed to maintain a balance of rancour between the Gepids in Pannonia Secunda and their neighbours to the north-east, the Lombards, and had recruited soldiers from them both. But within two years of Justinian's death, the Gepids secured an alliance with Justin, and to offset it, the Lombard king Alboin offered an alliance to the Avar khagan, Baian. In 567, the Avars and Lombards virtually annihilated the Gepids, who got little advantage from their pact with the empire.

The immediate results were to Constantinople's advantage. Justin seized the fortress of Sirmium on the Danube, which the Gepids had occupied in 536, and when the Avars demanded it as the spoils of war, Justin refused. He sent his henchman Tiberius against them as *strategos autokrator* (general with full powers), who inflicted a defeat on them. But the war with Persia was soon to drain the Danube frontier of troops, and in 573, Baian crossed the Danube and wiped out a weak Byzantine army under Tiberius' command. There was nothing for it but to make peace, and pay the Avars an annual tribute of 80,000 *solidi*, which made Justinian's subsidy seem small by comparison. The empire did, however, maintain its grip on the fortress of Sirmium until 582,[42] and the Avars kept the peace while Justin was alive: in 580, they even lent the empire assistance against the Slavs.

As for the Lombards, they speedily realized that the Avars would make uncomfortable neighbours, and in 568, their king Alboin led them into Italy, with thousands of Saxons, Gepids, Sarmatians and Bulgars in their train. The attack took the Byzantine general staff by surprise. Only a few months before, Justin had removed Narses from command and recalled him, though, in spite of orders, Narses preferred to remain in Italy. There, from his palace in Rome, he watched the Lombard advance. Without his leadership, the imperial defence was ineffectual. The Lombards had occupied most of the Po valley by 569. But their invasion was a disorderly one, and after Alboin's assassination in 573, there was no strong line of kings to coordinate it. Italy settled into stalemate, and the result of Justinian's costly reconquest was long, desultory warfare.[43]

The war with Persia turned out no better. The campaign of 573 started well. The Byzantines caught the Persians by surprise, and they advanced across the frontier and beleaguered Nisibis. The siege dragged on; the Master of the Soldiers, Justinian's nephew Marcian, abandoned it at one point and then resumed it with greater success. But Justin grew impatient, and as a result, managed to snatch defeat from the jaws of victory. He sent another commander to replace Marcian, whereupon the army mutinied. The Persians counterattacked; Khusro laid siege to Dara and another Persian expeditionary force advanced into Syria as far as Antioch before it swung back to join Khusro.[44]

It was during the siege of Dara that the Ghassanid phylarch, Mundhir, discovered a plot against his life: by mistake, a letter from Justin to Marcian was delivered into his hands. Mundhir read his own death sentence, whereupon he rode off with his Saracens into the desert.[45] Mundhir was the son and successor of the phylarch Harith ben Djabala, who in 541 had asked Theodora for Monophysite bishops, and thereby launched Jacob Baradaeus on his career. Mundhir's withdrawal left the frontier open for the *razzias* of Persia's Lakhmid allies, and it took three years before he could be wooed back into alliance. By coincidence, it was on the festival day of St Sergius, the saint *par excellence* of the Arabs, that the Persians captured Dara after a siege of more than five months.

It is foolish to attach especial significance to coincidences; nonetheless, Mundhir's defection was a straw in the wind. In 580–581, there was another quarrel with Mundhir, and in 582, the breach became permanent. The alienation of the Ghassanids and the eventual break-up of the Ghassanid federation was to contribute in no small degree to the Byzantine weakness in the face of the seventh-century Moslem invasion.

The news that the great fortress of Dara had fallen was more than Justin could bear. Faced with disaster on every side, his sanity gave way. He went mad.

It was the empress who took over, with the help of the loyal Count of the Excubitors, Tiberius. She bought a one-year truce in *Oriens*, excluding Armenia, for 45,000 *solidi*, and on 7 December, 574, in a brief period of coherence, Justin was persuaded to appoint Tiberius as Caesar. Justin himself lingered on until 578. In the spring of the next year, Khusro himself died before negotiations for peace were complete.

At the start of Justin's reign, when his portrait reached Aphrodito, the seat of the duke of the Thebaid in Egypt, the local poet and leading citizen Dioscorus took up his pen to write a panegyric. The result has not won him a place among the great poets of antiquity, but it is an interesting composition which expresses well the hopes for a new beginning. It hails Justin as a bringer of life and goodness, an emperor who loved Christ. With some delicacy, it goes on to say, 'You exalt the faith received from God that brings renown to mankind.'[46] It was an implied plea for theological peace, and Justin was willing to do his best. His wife's sympathies were with the Monophysites, and so perhaps were his own.

Justinian's Aphthartodocetist edict was quietly discarded. Justin received the aged Monophysite leader Theodosius with the honour due a patriarch, and when he died on 22 June, 566, Theodora's grandson, Athanasius, pronounced a funeral eulogy wherein he denounced Chalcedon. There followed a series of conferences in Constantinople which did make some headway: the Monophysites of *Oriens* went so far as to agree to desert their own patriarch and accept communion with Anastasius, the Chalcedonian patriarch of Antioch, provided that the *Henotikon* was accepted, Chalcedon condemned and the dead Severus rehabilitated. The outlook looked promising.

But in the end, it was the Syriac monks who kept the breach open. The emperor charged the patrician John, who was on his way to Persia with an embassy, to pause at Callinicum on the frontier and meet the Monophysites at the monastery of Mar Zakai. A great throng of clergy and monks attended. John brought with him from Constantinople an edict which set forth a new *Henotikon*, declaring the doctrine of Nicaea the sole faith, and confessing Christ 'out of two natures, one *hypostasis* and *persona*'. The bishops and archimandrites were impressed. But the monks who listened to John saw the ending of the cause which had staved off accidie in the long lonely hours, and lent them a sense of empowerment in the face of the ruling élite on the one hand, and their own bishops on the other. They raised a tumultuous cry, demanding to see the edict which John had brought. Riot broke out, the copy of the edict was torn to pieces and Jacob Baradaeus himself was threatened. The patrician John left with precipitate haste for Persia. The monks had had the final say. They could not bear to have the clock set back.

Justin did not give up; he continued to consult and in 571, he published a second *Henotikon*. It did not do. The Monophysites would have nothing less than an explicit condemnation of Chalcedon. Justin's patience snapped. He turned to persecution, and henceforth until the Moslem invasions made the quarrel irrelevant, except for a four-year interlude at the start of Tiberius II's reign, the persecution of the Monophysites continued, and in the eastern provinces the rage against Chalcedon smouldered on.[47]

Would the other Justin, the son of Germanus, have done better? The 'might-have-beens' of history are notoriously hard to measure. But if the correct answer is yes – and probably it *is* the correct answer – then the empire paid heavily for the empress Theodora's prejudice against the family of Germanus. Theodora's wisdom faltered when her family interests were at stake, and though she had been dead seventeen years when her husband died, her memory was still as a powerful patron for her kinsmen. Justin was a man of average ability thrust into a position that was beyond his competence, and he left the empire with its finances and defences precarious.

CONCLUSION AND ASSESSMENT

How, then, should we judge the great emperor? He presided over the end of the protobyzantine period, when the continuities from the past finally ceased to matter. The empire of 565 cannot have been the empire he had hoped to create when his uncle Justin became emperor in 518 and he had moved into a position of power. Any judgement is likely to be unjust. But first some general comments.

His power base was the eastern empire, from the Balkans to Mesopotamia, and it was his chief concern to defend it. He paid handsomely to secure the 'Endless Peace' of 533, and made the error of imagining that it was solid. Hence he was unprepared for Khusro's attack of 540. The result was a major blow to his prestige; how great we can gather from Procopius, who digresses briefly in his *History of the Wars* to express his own horrified reaction to the sack of Antioch. The plague made a riposte difficult; nevertheless, plague or not, the empire mustered some 30,000 troops for an offensive. Its complete failure spotlights one of the grave weaknesses of Justinian's regime. The ever-victorious emperor secluded in his palace might plan military campaigns, but success in the field depended upon the capacities of his generals, whom he could manipulate at will, but in the end, he was at their mercies. Yet there can be no doubt that the security of the eastern empire was Justinian's major concern. It absorbed the largest share of the defence budget, and the record of Justinian's building activity shows that it was in that sector that he was especially anxious to maintain his prestige.

In the West, Justinian's policy was opportunist, though behind it was the dream of renewing the empire. Justinian sent Belisarius to attack the Vandal kingdom because the time seemed ripe and the African Catholics urged him to act. But the expeditionary force that Belisarius led was meagre. Justinian was taking a very small risk. Once the Vandals had fallen, Theodoric's unfortunate daughter Amalasuintha offered him an opportunity in Italy. But when the

Ostrogothic kingdom proved a difficult conquest, Justinian was prepared to cut his losses and negotiate a peace which would have left the Goths in control of Italy north of the Po. It was Belisarius who was determined to capture Ravenna and got his way with a combination of perfidy to the Goths and insubordination to his emperor. We need hardly be surprised that in the grim 540s, Justinian neglected Italy and starved it of troops. His top priority was not there.

The foray into Visigothic Spain in 552 was pure opportunism. It did have a military excuse: it protected the African conquest. And there was the long shadow of the imperial past. But the real reason was that Justinian could not resist a good opportunity.

He left behind a reputation as a builder, which is in part due to his *chef d'œuvre*, Hagia Sophia in Constantinople, and in part to Procopius' *Buildings*. Had there been a Procopius to write an encomium on the emperor Anastasius' building programme, he too might have had an equal reputation. Anastasius concentrated on defence works, but his outlay was huge. However, he ruled in a period of increasing prosperity, and if he left a surplus of 320,000 pounds of gold in the treasury at his death, as Procopius[48] asserts, it was due more to an expanding taxation base than to imperial parsimony.

The family of Justin I was an upstart dynasty, and Justinian and Theodora tried to compensate. They used court ceremonial to offset their lack of background. Senators, including patricians, were for the first time made to prostrate themselves in the presence of the emperor and empress.[49] The new dynasty spent money lavishly. Four thousand pounds of gold were squandered on the wild-beast fights at the inaugural games for Justinian's consulship in 521,[50] and even before Theodosius II's Hagia Sophia burned down in the *Nika* revolt, Justinian was planning a church that would outshine the other churches in Constantinople, particularly St Polyeuktos, which embodied the vocabulary of disparagement by the *crème de la crème* of the old élite. His conquests in the west were governed by opportunism, but they were also his answer to the dispraise of the old ruling classes. Even now, we can feel the satisfaction with which this upstart emperor put on record in a *Novel*[51] that he, Justinian, had recovered the empire which had been lost through the neglect of previous emperors.

Then came the plague. Taxation revenues shrank dramatically, but expenses did not. Modern economists would have called for downsizing, but that was not an option. Money somehow continued to be raised. It is little wonder that Justinian left behind him a reputation for avarice.

The age of Justinian marks the last great flowering of classical culture. There is some irony to that: Justinian himself may have appreciated the classics as an honourable legacy of the past, but it is hard to believe that he cared much for them personally. He accepted the traditions of the Greek *paideia* so long as the teachers were themselves Christians and committed to Christian truth.[52] The Neoplatonic Academy at Athens was closed; the last pagan teacher we can identify at Alexandria, Olympiodorus, fades from history in the 560s. At Gaza in Palestine, there was a brilliant group of belle-lettrists who flourished under Anastasius and continued active well into Justinian's reign. They made the Greek classics their models and eschewed the theological controversies which dominated the age.[53] But the greatness of the Gaza school was past by the middle of the century.

In the capital, Paul the Silentiary and Agathias wrote epigrams that belong completely to a non-Christian world. Paul's erotic epigrams in particular represent the antithesis of Christian spirituality. But these men were no more than tiny islands of classical culture. The passion of the age was theology, and Justinian shared it. Book production declined during his reign, and the circulation of classical texts diminished.[54] The élite, who were grounded in the classics and could read a work such as Procopius' *History of the Wars of Justinian* with pleasure, became a small minority centred for the most part in Constantinople. The colours of the forest are most brilliant after the first frost. The same can be said of the secular writers of Justinian's reign who carried the great traditions of the classical age. Their winter was coming swiftly.

Justinian was himself a self-confident theologian, and the progression of his thinking is revealing. We encounter his theological mindset first when Justin I came to the throne. At that point, the pope in Rome was still, in his view, the keeper of orthodoxy. Justinian was a child of Latin Christianity. But he rapidly modified his views. The first influence upon him may have been his rival Vitalian, who championed the Theopaschite doctrine preached by the Scythian monks, but after Vitalian there was the much greater influence of his wife, Theodora. By the middle of the century, Justinian had Rome under his political control, and he was no longer prepared to endure papal intransigence. In the 'Three Chapters' controversy, Justinian the Caesaropapist stood revealed. Silverius was hustled off the papal throne, Pope Vigilius was made to yield and the recalcitrant African bishops were manoeuvred out of the way. Justinian's method called first for argument, then force. Finally, in his old age, Justinian lapsed into extreme Monophysitism himself. His religious views had travelled all the way from Pope Leo the Great to Julian of Halicarnassus.

What thoughts occupied the great emperor's mind in the last months of his life? Not matters of this world, or so contemporaries thought. He had bestirred himself from Constantinople and made a pilgrimage to the shrine of St Michael at Germia. He was a troubled man. Theodora slept in her sarcophagus in the imperial mausoleum beside the church of the Holy Apostles, secure in her Monophysite faith, but her influence did not die with her. How had God judged her soul? And how would He judge the soul of the emperor, her husband? What was important in Justinian's last months was not that he had extended Roman rule to the whole world, from the Caucasus in the east, westwards to Spain and 'Thule, the daughter of Ocean', to paraphrase a somewhat wooden encomium by Agathias which is preserved in the *Greek Anthology*.[55] What mattered was the terrible surmise with which Procopius concluded his *Secret History*: Justinian's death would reveal the truth: was he a man or the Antichrist sent to lead believers astray?[56] Time was pressing. The great emperor had served God, and God had requited his effort with plague, earthquakes, floods and invasions. Yet it was still the emperor's duty to lead his subjects to the right faith, and Justinian continued his search for it, with his memory travelling back to the conversations he had had with Theodora's confessors years before. Only weeks from his death, this great vicegerent of God made his final effort to make peace with Heaven and set his flock upon the path of truth, which he had divined at last.

NOTES

INTRODUCTION

1 Averil Cameron (1970); eadem (1985).
2 *Wars* 8.15.17.
3 Menander Rhetor 2.374.21–25, trans. D.A.Russell and N.G.Wilson, *Menander Rhetor*, Oxford, 1979. Saradi (1995), p. 41, refers to the *Buildings*, with some justification, as a 'purely rhetorical work'.
4 *Aed.* 4.1.37; cf. Lawrence (1983), pp. 193–194.
5 Evans (1972), pp. 43–44. Macrides and Magdalino (1988), p. 76, n. 104, state (surprisingly) that 'there seems to have been no attempt to pursue the possible compromise solution: that different parts of the *Buildings* were composed at different times.'
6 *Aed.* 1.1.67–78.
7 The arguments of Michael Whitby (1985b) on the date seem to me compelling. For an admirable account of the problems, see Averil Cameron (1985), pp. 9–18; 86. For a recent defence of Cameron's dates, see Greatrex (1994).
8 SH 18.33; 23.1; 24.29; 24.33.
9 See Scott (1987), pp. 217–220, who dates Justinian's ban on the celebration of Passover before Easter (SH 28.16–18) to 552. *Contra*: Greatrex (1994). However, Scott's attempt to relate Justinian's introduction of light-weight coinage (SH 25.11–12) to an incident reported in Malalas for 553 is probably ill-founded: see p. 300, nn. 243–244 below.
10 Baldwin (1978a), pp. 106–107, thinks he intended to go further into the reign of Maurice and may have done so, but there is no evidence for it.
11 See Croke (1990).
12 18.6 (p. 428).
13 Cf. Scott (1985).
14 Moderan (1986), pp. 207–211.
15 Ure (1951), p. 147.
16 From John Ciardi (trans.), *Dante Alighieri*, The Paradiso (New American Library, 1961), Canto VI.
17 Ibid. (n. 16), p. 77.

273

1 THE IMPERIAL ENVIRONMENT

1 Vict. Tun., *sub anno* 518; Mal. 16.22; cf. Stein, *Histoire* I, p. 217; Browning (1987), p. 17. Theoph. (A.M. 6010) has the emperor struck by lightning.
2 See pp. 36–40.
3 Ravegnani (1989), pp. 21–23; Vasiliev (1950), pp. 68–82; Browning (1987), pp. 19–21; Rubin (1960), pp. 55–60; Jones, *LRE*, pp. 266–268; cf. Boak (1919).
4 Mal. 17.2 (p. 411); Marc. Com. *sub anno* 519; SH 6.26; Zach. Myt. 8.1.
5 Cf. Barnes (1984b), pp. 50–51. For a sensible critique of Barnes' 'Constantine' see Averil Cameron (1983a).
6 Cf. Isaac (1986), pp. 228–231. This is Eusebius' date, which does not tally with Hdt. 4.144.2.
7 Mango (1981), p. 343.
8 Mal. 13.39 (p. 345); cf. Mango (1985), pp. 33–34.
9 Gilles (1988), p. 19.
10 Mango (1959), pp. 42–45; Cameron and Herrin (1984), pp. 262–263.
11 The term *factio* refers to the 'stables' or professional companies which fielded the teams. It does not refer to the fans, for which the word was *pars* or *populus*, in Greek, *meros* or *demos* (*demoi*). See Veyne (1990), pp. 472–473; Roueché (1993), pp. 44–47.
12 Holum (1982), pp. 65–73; Patlagean (1986), p. 94. Cf. *Wars* 7.37.4, where Totila holds chariot races in the Circus Maximus after capturing Rome.
13 Alan Cameron (1976a), pp. 180–183.
14 Pausanias 1.24.8; cf. Frantz (1988), pp. 75–76; Fowden (1991), pp. 119–131.
15 *Wars* 5.15.4; 9–14; cf. Cameron and Herrin (1984), pp. 198; 243–263; Janin (1964), pp. 77–80. Rome also had a Palladium which legend claimed that Diomedes had given Aeneas.
16 Mal. 13.7 (p. 320).
17 For 'God-fearers' in the synagogues, see Reynolds and Tannenbaum (1987), pp. 45–65.
18 Amm. Marc. 25.5.4 'tumultuantibus paucis'.
19 Segal (1955), pp. 122–124; id. (1970), pp. 110–111.
20 Amm. Marc. 25.7.9; 9.1–13; 10.12–13.
21 Socrates, *Hist. Eccl.* 4.34; cf. Johnson and West (1949), pp. 217–218; 304. Local recruiting did not stop completely by any means, but it was voluntary.
22 Jones, *LRE* I, pp. 173–182; Barnwell (1992), pp. 11–19.
23 Stein, *Histoire* I, pp. 353–364.
24 *Wars* 5.1.6–8; cf. Goffart (1980), p. 100.
25 *Wars* 5.1.6–8; *Jones*, LRE I, pp. 240–248; Burns (1980), pp. 64–78; Barnwell (1992), pp. 135–139. The official translation of *imperator*, however, was *autokrator*, cf. Bury (1910), p. 19.
26 Jones, *LRE* II, p. 698; Browning (1987), p. 32; Averil Cameron (1993), p.13; cf. Russell (1972), who thinks a population of 300,000 possible at this time, and MacMullen (1974), pp. 62–63; 168–169, who esti-

mates Roman urban densities at 200 per acre (495 per hectare). Jacoby (1961) estimates 360,000 for the city and 15,000 for Sycae ca. 541. Cf. Charanis (1966), p. 17; Mango (1986), pp. 119–120; Kazhdan and Constable (1982), pp. 54–55. See also p. 276, n. 60.

27 Hitherto it had been the thirteenth region of the city: Janin (1964), pp. 43–58; Mango (1986), p. 118.
28 Hdt. 1.153.
29 4.11; cf. Oppenheim (1964), pp. 125–142.
30 Mango (1972), p. 193.
31 Kahler (1967), p. 14; Mainstone (1988), pp. 129–143. Hagia Eirene and Hagia Sophia together were enclosed by a wall and served by the same clergy: Socrates, *Hist. Eccl.* 2.16; George (1912), pp. 1–2.
32 *Aed.* 1.2.1–12; cf. Croke (1980). On the use of a bronze alloy to imitate gold, see Adelson (1957), p. 67.
33 Janin (1964), pp. 59–86; See also Mango (1985), *passim*.
34 Alan Cameron (1976b), pp. 269–270; Browning (1975b), pp. 38–39. Agathias 3.1–4 mentions working at his desk in the Basilica. The *Yerebatan* cistern was under this building.
35 *Cod. Just.* 8.10.12.6.
36 Frantz (1988), pp. 76–77. The date of removal is uncertain.
37 Foss (1976), pp. 42–43.
38 Lopez (1945), p. 11.
39 See pp. 52–54.
40 *Cod. Theod.* 14.9.3; 15.1.53; 6.21.1; Jones, *LRE* I, pp. 549; 707–708; Mango (1980), pp. 129–131; id. (1985), p. 30; id. *ODB*, I, pp. 516–518, s.v. 'Public Monuments'. The Capitolium lay half-way between the *Milion* and the Golden Gate.
41 Cf. Liebeschuetz (1989); id. (1990), pp. 111–125.
42 Cf. Epstein (1982).
43 Harrison (1983); id. (1989); Mainstone (1988), pp. 147–148.
44 The reference to 'demarchs' sounds anachronistic: cf. Alan Cameron (1976a), pp. 258–261; Geanakoplos (1984), pp. 256–257.
45 Marc. Com. *sub anno* 447; cf. Tsangadas (1980), pp. 7–15; Rice (1958), pp. 66–68; Dagron (1974), pp. 11–12; 356–357; Miller (1969), pp. 12–13.
46 4.43–35.
47 Tsangadas (1980), pp. 33–35.
48 Cf. Croke (1982a), who argues for construction under Anastasius, and Michael Whitby (1985b), who backs a fifth-century date. The wall has never been properly surveyed, and the date of its construction, or reconstruction, is insecure: see Crow (1995), esp. pp. 109–112, and 118.
49 Lemerle (1954), pp. 282–286; Popović (1978), pp. 607–611; Moorhead (1994), pp. 145–152.
50 Theoph. A.M. 6051.
51 Seventy-two *solidi* made up one gold pound.
52 *Nov.* xxvi (May 15, 535); Jones, *LRE*, pp. 231, 656; Bury, *LRE* II, pp. 339–340; Obolensky (1971), pp. 67–68. *Aed.* 4.9.6–13 refers to Justinian's rebuilding of the Anastasian Walls.
53 Mango (1986), pp. 121–123; id. (1985), pp. 19–20. See also

Duncan-Jones (1977–78), p. 51, who points out that the Vitruvian 'rule' (8.6.1–2) of one-third an aqueduct's capacity for private consumption is an unreliable guide.

54 *AnthGr* I, pp. 61–79.

55 Ward (1992).

56 Jones, *LRE*, pp. 976–977.

57 Nine, if we count one in the fourteenth region: Mango (1981), pp. 339–341.

58 Michael Whitby (1985b), pp. 576–578.

59 Mango (1986), pp. 121–123; id. (1985) pp. 41–42; id. (1981), pp. 339–341; Janin (1964), pp. 198–224; Jones, *LRE*, pp. 695–696; 705. The latest discussion of Constantinople's water supply is Mango (1995).

60 *Edict XIII*. The common *artaba* was 38.78 litres, and 38.78 litres of wheat weighs slightly more than 30 kgs (Bagnall [1993]), p. 332, *pace* Durliat (1990), pp. 257–260 who uses an *artaba* of ca. 20 kgs. For a rehearsal of the arguments on the size of the *artaba*, see Müller (1993) pp. 3–5. It is impossible to attempt to reckon the size of Constantinople's population from this figure, because, first, bread consumption varied from about 5 pounds a day for a soldier to half a pound for an underfed ascetic, and second, spoilage and loss to rodents must have accounted for a variable proportion, but was always large. Justinian's requisition was probably set well above the bare minimum. For the date of *Edict XIII*, which was addressed to John the Cappadocian, see Rémondon (1955), pp. 120–121. Malz (1942–43) argues cogently for 553/4, after John's fall, but to accept her date we must imagine another unattested 'John' who served as prefect.

61 *Cod. Theod.* 14.16.3; *Cod. Just.* 11.24.2.

62 Alexandria had an annual allowance of 2 million *medimnoi* (SH 16.43), which would supply one-third of a million people annually: Johnson and West (1949), pp. 250–251.

63 Even after the Vandal conquest, African grain continued to reach Rome under the terms of a treaty between Aetius and Gaiseric: *Wars* 3.4.13.

64 Cf. Hendy (1985), p. 170, who uses the adaeration rate of 1 *solidus* = 10 *artabai*. For the term *annona* in the sixth century, see A. J. Cappel, *ODB*, I, pp. 105–106, s.v. 'annona'. The *annona civica* should be distinguished from the *annona militaris*, which was a ration unit for the army: see Segrè (1942–43), pp. 406–411.

65 Socrates, *Hist. Eccl.* 2.13; cf. Johnson and West (1949), pp. 233–234. Alexandria, Antioch and Carthage also had bread doles, and there is enough evidence to suggest that Sardis had one too: Foss (1976), p. 18.

66 However, *Cod. Theod.* 14.17.5 (AD 369) does make it clear that bread (*panis gradilis*) obtained from these distribution centres was intended for the poor with no other resources.

67 *Cod. Just.* XI, 24.1 (392).

68 Jones, *LRE*, pp. 696–705; Janin (1964), pp. 44–45; Patlagean (1977), pp. 58; 185–186; ead. (1986), pp. 70–71; Karpolizos and Kazhdan, *ODB* I, p. 321, s.v. 'Bread'; Nesbitt, *ODB* III, p. 2091, s.v. 'Tokens'. Heraclius suppressed the bread dole in August, 618. On inheritance and sale of *tesserae* in Roman law, see Veyne (1990), pp. 245; 282–283.

69 *Aed.* 5.1.8–16; cf. Müller (1993), pp. 6–7. Cf. Mango (1985), pp. 39–40, 53–54; MacCoull, *ODB* I, pp. 679–681, s.v. 'Egypt'; Durliat (1995), pp. 28–30.
70 Theoph. A.M. 6055.
71 For the regulations, see *Cod. Just.* XI, 1–5.
72 For Constantine's tariff, I follow Cracco Ruggini (1971), p. 157, n. 194, against Johnson and West (1949), p. 160; cf. Jones (1974), pp. 81–83.
73 Kazhdan and Constable (1982), pp. 55–56.
74 Rémondon (1972), p. 273; Gascou, *CE* V, pp. 1608–1611, s.v. 'Metanoia'; Johnson and West (1949), pp. 160–161.
75 Jones, *LRE* pp. 56; 22; 613–614; 1272, n. 114; Diehl (1901), p. 96.
76 *Cod. Just.* I.14.8 (446).
77 SH 14.8.
78 Ravegnani (1989), pp. 29–32. Mango (1959), p. 56, suggests that the Magnaura (= *magna aula*) was identical with the senate house east of the Augustaeum that, according to *Aed.* 1.10.6–9, was rebuilt by Justinian after its destruction in 532, but we hear no more of it. De'Maffei (1988), p. 24, n. 46, rejects the identification. The senate house seems to have shared a basilical plan with the Magnaura. The university of Constantinople used it after its revival in the Middle Byzantine period.
79 Laslett (1971), pp. 10–12; 261.
80 Cf. Stambaugh (1988), pp. 225–226 who estimates ca. 250,000.
81 Mango (1981), pp. 341–344.
82 Spieser (1984), p. 318.
83 *Nov.* 105.1 (AD 536)
84 Cf. Roueché (1993), pp. 47–30; 61–80 and no. 44 (p. 73).
85 Roueché (1989), p. 223.
86 Roueché (1984), pp. 181–188.
87 Roueché (1989), pp. 218–220.
88 Mango (1981), p. 345 (quoting Baynes); Spyridakis (1967).
89 *P. Oxy.* XXXIV, 2707.
90 Jones (1983), pp. 36–38; Alan Cameron (1973) pp. 252–258; id. (1976a), pp. 9–10; Roueché (1993), pp. 7–11.
91 Forbes (1933), *passim*; Jullian, *D-S*, III:1, pp. 782–785, s.v. 'Juvenes, Juventus'.
92 Frantz (1988), pp. 17–18.
93 Foss (1976), p. 21.
94 Baldwin (1978a), p. 102.
95 Roueché (1993), pp. 137–140.
96 Cf. Alan Cameron (1983), pp. 83–84.
97 Cf. *Cod. Theod.* 1.16.6, where Constantine I recognized spontaneous applause for public officials in the circus as measures of their performance, and warned against attempts to orchestrate it.
98 Mal. 16.2 (p. 392).
99 Patlagean (1977), pp. 216–231; Alan Cameron (1973), pp. 232–239. For Justinian's support of the Blues, see SH 7.1–38; Evag. 4.32; John of Nikiu 90.16. Cf. Veyne (1990), pp. 392–396, for imperial Rome.

100 D-F IV, p. 235. For Bury's comment, see pp. 567–568.
101 Alan Cameron (1974b) pp. 92–120. Cf. Baldwin (1978b); Carile (1978), pp. 54–56. For urban mass demonstrations from the fifth to the seventh century, see Patlagean (1986), pp. 93–107, who points out that they took place as well in public spaces other than the hippodromes, e.g. theatres, porticoes, baths and taverns.
102 Vasiliev (1964), I, pp. 155–156. The theory of 'upper-class Blues' was worked out in detail by Jarry (1968). Cf. Fotiou (1978); Baldwin (1978b); Patlagean (1986), pp. 96–97.
103 D-F, IV, pp. 567–68. The theory that the *demoi* were militia was first put forward by Manojlović in 1904: see Manojlović (1936).
104 *Wars* 2.8.28–29. For youth groups within the circus parties, see Patlagean (1986), pp. 123–124.
105 Romanos 47, str. 16 (SC 283, p. 111); *Nov.* 13.1.1.
106 Alan Cameron (1974a); id. (1976a), pp. 11–44.
107 Mango (1981), pp. 348–349; Kazdhan and Constable (1982), pp. 129–130.
108 *Wars* 1.24.2; SH 7.1–38; cf. Carile (1978), pp. 49–50; Patlagean (1986), pp. 121–123.
109 Karlin-Hayter (1981a), p. 2.
110 SH 9.35–46; cf. Vasiliev (1950), pp. 117–119.
111 Mal. 17.18.
112 Alexander (1967), p. 14.
113 *De Mag.* 2.12; 3.42.
114 Cf. Mary Whitby (1985b) on Paul the Silentiary's debt to Claudian.
115 Jones, *LRE*, pp. 834–836.
116 See Lee (1993), pp. 40–48.
117 *Cod. Theod.* 6.27.2; *De Mag.* 3.12.24.
118 The tag comes from Honoré (1978), p. xi.
119 See Kazhdan, *ODB* III, p. 1709, s.v. *'praepositus sacri cubiculi'*; id., *ODB* III, pp. 1765–66, s.v. *'quaestor'*. The imperial estates in Cappadocia by the *sixth* century took up much of the province and were administered by the *comes domorum*, subordinate to the *praepositus*: Jones, *LRE*, pp. 426–427; Jones (1983), pp. 187–190.
120 The *praefectus praetorio per Illyricum* moved his headquarters from Sirmium to Thessaloniki in the mid-fifth century: Cormack (1981b), p. 104.
121 Diehl (1896), pp. 97–107.
122 *Nov.* 80 (539); SH 20.9–10.
123 See, in general, Ostrogorsky (1956), pp. 32–40; Haussig (1971), pp. 50–55; Diehl (1901), pp. 90–100; Jones, *LRE*, pp. 370–372; 563–606; Ensslin, *CMH* IV, ii, pp. 1–54; Guilland (1980); Kazhdan, *ODB* III, p. 2144, s.v. 'Urban Prefect'.
124 *De Mag.* 2.6.
125 *Nov.* 8 (535). Less than two months after *Nov.* 8, Justinian relented to the extent that he allowed special clerks in the *quaestor's* office to sell their posts to suitable successors for 100 *solidi*: *Nov.* 35. Cf. Veyne (1981), pp. 351–53.
126 *Nov.* 56 (537).

127 Carney (1971), II, pp. 3–19; Bandy (1983), pp. ix–xxvi; Ure (1951), pp. 102–120.
128 Hendy (1985), pp. 169–170.
129 Jones, *LRE*, p. 397; Mango (1980), p. 40.
130 *Cod. Theod.* 1.16.7.; cf. Jones (1968), pp. 170–172.
131 Mal. 18.67 (pp. 470–471).
132 *Nov.* 80.6 (539).
133 See Bagnall (1993), pp. 66, 136–137, who points out that Egypt in Late Antiquity *may* have had one bureaucrat per 5,000 population. Modern New York has a ratio of one to thirty for city employees alone.
134 Jones, *LRE* I, pp. 592–596.
135 *Cod. Theod.* 190.
136 Norman (1958); Jones, *LRE* I, pp. 543–552; Dagron (1974), pp. 119–171; Saradi-Mendelovici (1988), pp. 372–376; De Ste Croix (1981), pp. 467–474.
137 Jones, *LRE*, pp. 525–530; 542–545; cf. Barnish (1988).
138 *De Mag.* 1.28 (trans. Bandy); cf. Jones, *LRE* I, pp. 759–760.
139 Cf. Whittow (1990), pp. 9–10.
140 *Nov.* 101 (539). See further Roueché (1989), pp. 62–63.
141 Roueché (1979).
142 Cf. Liebeschuetz (1992), pp. 27–28. *Vindices* were not found in every city.
143 3.42. See Whittow (1990), pp. 4–12.
144 Cf. Ravegnani (1989), pp. 33–34; Hopkins (1963). Hopkins lists the chief positions held by eunuchs as 1) Grand Chamberlain, 2) Superintendent of the Bedchamber (*primicerius sacri cubiculi*), 3) Chief Steward of the Palace (*castrensis sacri palatii*), 4) Count of the Imperial Estate in Cappadocia (*comes domorum per Cappadociam*), 5) Count of the Imperial Wardrobe (*comes sacrae vestis*), 6) Captain of the Bodyguard (*spatharius*), 7) Keeper of the Purse (*sacellarius*).
145 *Nov.* 142 (558).
146 Haldon (1979), pp. 20–27.
147 SH 23.24; *Nov.* 130 (545) regulates billeting of soldiers, which is evidence that abuses *did* occur.
148 Pringle (1981) I, pp. 55–57.
149 *Wars* 5.14.2–3.
150 Maurice, *Strategikon* 1.2; Hannestad (1960), p. 175.
151 Gascou (1976), pp. 143–156; cf. Averil Cameron (1993), p. 50, Jones, *LRE* I, pp. 666–667.
152 Isaac (1992), pp. 208–213; id. (1988).
153 *Cod. Just.* I, 27, 2, 4 (534); cf. Pringle (1981) I, p. 97.
154 SH 24.12–14; Jones, *LRE* I, p. 284; Kennedy (1985), p. 167. However, at Nessana in Third Palestine, a cavalry corps of *limitanei* lasted until ca. 590: Gutwein (1981), pp. 324–325.
155 Parker (1990), pp. 107–109; id. (1991), pp. 141–142.
156 Scorpan (1980), p. 3.
157 *Cod. Just.* I.27 (ii) 7–9 (534); cf. Pringle (1981) I, p. 67.
158 Keenan (1990).
159 Cf. Bowersock (1976), pp. 219–29; Mayerson (1986); id., (1989). On customs dues, see De Laet (1949), pp. 455–482, esp. pp. 472–473.

160 Cf. Segrè (1942–43), pp. 432–433; Bury, *LRE* II, p. 78.
161 *De Mensibus* 1.27; cf. Hendy (1985), pp. 176–177.
162 5.13; cf. MacMullen (1980).
163 *Wars*, 3.2–4; 5.14.2–3.
164 Turtledove (1983), pp. 220–222.
165 *Cod. Just.* 12.33.7; cf. Haldon (1979), p. 26.
166 *Nov.* 116.
167 *Wars* 1.1532; cf. Fauber (1990), pp. 3–4.
168 Teall (1965); Fotiou (1988).
169 Cf. Jones, *LRE* II, pp. 858–860; Patlagean (1986), pp. 55–57.
170 For a translation and commentary, see Boak (1928–29); cf. Vryonis (1963), pp. 296–299.
171 Bogaert (1973), pp. 260–266.
172 *Cod. Just.* 12.54.1; cf. Barnish (1985), pp. 5–9; Stöckle (1911); Jones, *LRE* pp. 858–864; Andreadès in Baynes and Moss (1948).
173 *PLRE* IIIB, pp. 999–1002, s.v. 'Petrus 9'.
174 Norman (1958); Cracco Ruggini (1971), pp. 152–159. Members of the shippers' guild (*navicularii*) might even belong to the senatorial order, but they were a special case.
175 *De Mag.* 1.50. See Janin (1964), pp. 95–100 for the Constantinople guilds.
176 Roueché (1993), pp. 119–128; Vryonis (1963).
177 Cf. Jones, *LRE*, p. 860; Jones (1974), pp. 48–49.
178 *MAMA* III, 197–788; Patlagean (1977), pp. 158–170; ead. (1986), pp. 35–50; Trombley (1987).
179 *Nov.* 3.i.(1) (535); cf. *Nov.* 6.vii.
180 Jones (1974), pp. 342; 348.
181 *Nov.* 5.2 (535).
182 *DHGE* I, cols. 274–282; *DACL* I, cols. 307–321.
183 Bury, *LRE* II, p. 362.
184 Cf. Jones (1983), pp. 25; 90–91. The law was not strictly enforced.
185 *BGU* 669.
186 Cf. *Nov.* 43.1 (536).
187 Jones, *LRE* p. 934; cf. De Ste Croix (1981), pp. 495–497.
188 Cf. Boojamra (1975), pp. 356–358 for the role of the church in institutionalized charity.
189 Monks (1953).
190 Patlagean (1977), p. 82.
191 Cf. Avi-Yonah (1958), pp. 48–49.
192 Rémondon (1972), pp. 265–266.
193 Alföldy (1974), pp. 216–222.
194 For Scetis: Chitty (1966), pp. 60–61; 64. Monasteries: Barison (1938), pp. 29–148; Tchalenko, *Villages* I, pp. 19–21, 162–173; Rémondon (1972); also Talbot, *ODB* II, pp. 1392–94; *CE* III, pp. 954–958: s.v. 'Enaton'; *CE* V, pp. 1608–1611: s.v. 'Metanoia'; *CE* V, pp.1639–1645: s.v. 'Monasteries, Economic Activities of'. Cf. Diehl (1901), pp. 505–531 Chitty (1966).
195 *Vie de S. Sabas*, 56–57.
196 Chitty (1966), p. 91.

197 *DACL* XV, cols. 1697–1718: s.v. 'Stylites'.
198 Cf. Averil Cameron (1983b), pp. 71–82.
199 *Or.* 2.101A.
200 Cranz (1952); Dvornik (1966) I, pp. 611–626; Baynes (1955), pp. 13–18; cf. Fotiou (1985). See also in general Downey (1963), pp. 73–81.
201 Cf. Fowden (1993), pp. 92–93.
202 Johnson and West (1949), p. 36.
203 Topping (1978), p. 31, n. 67.
204 Cf. Moss, *CMH* IV, pp. 3–4; cf. Julian *Or.* 2.101B–C.
205 Worp (1982), p. 220. This was not true before Constantine I.
206 McCormick (1986), pp. 124–129.
207 *Nov.* 6, trans. Barker (1957), pp. 75–76.
208 *Deo auctore* (Watson 1985): 15 Dec. 530.
209 *Nov.* 98.2.2.
210 Cf. *Aed.* 2.6.6.
211 Runciman (1977), pp. 26–50; Geanakoplos (1966a), pp. 55–83.
212 *Nov.* 105.4; cf. Hunger (1965), pp. 354–355; Downey (1968), pp. 7, 11; Bagnani (1949).
213 Cf. De Ste Croix (1982), pp. 384–392; Charlesworth (1937).
214 Herrin (1991), pp. 219–220; Guilland (1948), pp. 676–678. In emergencies, the emperor could summon the people to the Hippodrome by hoisting a flag.
215 Cf. Aufhauser (1959); Charanis (1940–41); M. McCormick, *ODB*, pp. 533–534 s.v. 'Coronation'; Ravegnani (1989), pp. 21–25.
216 Bury (1910), pp. 12–13.
217 As his name 'Justinianus' indicates.
218 Vasiliev (1950), pp. 95–96; Ravegnani (1989), p.23. SH 9.53 claims that the ceremony took place three days before Easter, that is, in the Lenten season.
219 Barker (1957), pp. 54–61; cf. Henry (1967).
220 Behr (1974); Fotiou (1981); id. (1985); Piccinini (1991), pp. 169–170. For the dialogue, see Mai (1827), pp. 571–609.
221 Cf. *Cod. Just.* 10. 31; *Nov.* 38; *Nov.* 101.
222 Romanos 53, str. 3 (SC 283)
223 Christensen (1944), pp. 342–347; Guidi, *EI*² VI, pp. 949–952, s.v. 'Mazdak', esp. p. 951.
224 90.54–60; cf. Magoulias (1967), p. 231; Lieu (1992), p. 214.
225 Mal. 17.21 (p. 423).
226 *Cod. Just.* I.5.5 (428).
227 *Aed.* 2.6.6.
228 *Aed.* 1.4.24.
229 Romanos 54 (SC 283); cf. Topping (1978), pp. 22–27.
230 Croke (1981), pp. 145–147; cf. *Nov.* 77.
231 Evag. 5.1.
232 Cf. Averil Cameron (1977), pp. 16–17.
233 Downey (1960), pp. 114–135; Herrin (1991), pp. 225–230.
234 *Cod. Theod.* 16.10.2; cf. Kaegi (1965b), pp. 243–244.
235 Trombley (1985); Fowden (1993), pp. 62–63; Maas (1992), pp. 67–70.

236 Fowden (1988), pp. 56–57.
237 Frantz (1965); Gregory (1986), p. 238.
238 *Cod. Theod.* 16.10.2 (341); cf. Barnes (1984a). Errington (1988), pp. 314–318, argues that Constantine's law against sacrifice was followed by a change of policy in 325.
239 *Cod. Theod.* 16.10.10 (391); 16.10.11 (391).
240 *Cod. Just.* I.11.7.
241 *Cod. Just.* I.11.8
242 *Cod. Just.* I.4.15; I.11.9; cf. Michael Whitby (1991), pp.115–116.
243 Cf. Constantelos (1964–65), p. 372. For Judaism, see Cohen (1976); cf. Geanakoplos (1966b), pp. 179–180.
244 Alan Cameron (1969b), pp. 106–110.
245 Chuvin (1990), pp. 131–141; Maas (1992), pp. 48–52; Holmes (1912), pp. 420–439.
246 Athanassiadi (1993), p. 12.
247 Frantz (1965).
248 *Cod. Just.* I.5.12 (527).
249 *Cod. Just.* I.5.18.10 (529).
250 *Cod. Just.* I.5.19 (529).
251 *Cod. Just.* I.5.22 (531).
252 *Cod. Just.* I.11.10.1 (529).
253 *Cod. Just.* I.11.10.4 (529).
254 *Cod. Just.* I.11.10.2; I.11.10.3. Justinian was untroubled by the teaching of pagan philosophy by *Christian* teachers, which continued at Alexandria and Gaza: Downey (1958b).
255 On the closure of the Academy, see Gerostergios (1974), pp. 169–79; Irmscher (1981); Alan Cameron (1969a); Blumenthal (1978); id. (1993); Frantz (1965); ead. (1988), pp. 86–92; Herrin (1987), pp. 77–79; Chuvin (1990), pp. 135–141; Averil Cameron (1993), pp. 132–136; Hällström (1994).
256 18.47 (p. 451). Honoré (1978), pp. 46–47 points out that such a law may have existed in the *Codex Vetus*, which we do not have.
257 18.38 (p. 448). This is our only evidence for legal training at Athens in Late Antiquity, but it should not be dismissed: see Hällström (1994), pp. 146–147.
258 Cf. Downey (1958b).
259 *PLRE* IIIA, p. 134: 'Asclepiodotus 1'.
260 Frantz (1988), pp. 42–44. The 'House of Proclus' is now under Dionysius the Areopagite Street. For a recent treatment of the evidence, see Karivieri (1994).
261 Cf. Potter (1994), pp. 203–204.
262 Eitrem (1942).
263 *PLRE* II: 'Proclus 4'.
264 Charlton (1991), pp. 20–22.
265 (1969), p. 103.
266 Alan Cameron (1969), p. 9: Olympiodorus, though openly pagan, continued to teach philosophy at Alexandria three decades after the Academy at Athens was closed. Hällström (1994), pp. 157–160 suggests, no doubt rightly, that the closure of the Academy was part

of Justinian's programme to centralize higher education, but this need not have been his sole, or even his dominant, motive.

267 Blumenthal (1993), pp. 318–320. On Alexandria, see Wilson (1983), pp. 42–49.

268 Agathias 2.30.1; Tardieu (1986); Athanassiadi (1993), pp. 24–29; Averil Cameron (1993), pp. 132–136.

269 Wilson (1983), pp. 37–38. Procopius, too, drew the parallel between Justinian and Domitian, who was a well-established paradigm of a 'bad emperor': SH 8.13–14.

270 Frantz (1988), pp. 90–92.

271 Cf. Jeauneau (1991), pp. 3–7. Dionysius was first cited, to our knowledge, in 532 in discussions with the Monophysites in Constantinople: Wilson (1983), pp. 54–55.

272 Cf. Frend (1972b), p. 115.

273 Grégoire, in Baynes and Moss (1948), pp. 94–100; Fowden (1993), pp. 121–124; Segal (1970), pp. 150–151; Nichols (1992), pp. 27–38; Kazhdan, ODB II, pp. 1459–1460.

274 According to Michael the Syrian, who was probably following John of Ephesus, Dioscorus, thinking (perhaps rightly) that Leo's language in the Tome overstated his true position, suppressed it to avoid a quarrel with Rome: Every (1979), p. 258.

275 Meyendorff (1968), pp. 52–53; Gray (1979), pp. 71–74.

276 Chitty (1966), pp. 86–91; Honigmann (1950); cf. Frend (1972b), p. 14; Holum (1982), p. 67.

277 For the sensitivity of Palestine's economy to the inflow, see Avi-Yonah (1958), pp. 40–48.

278 28 July 482. For the text: Coleman-Norton (1966) III, no. 527.

279 Frend (1972b), pp. 137–183; Wigram (1923), pp. 12–37; Gray (1979), pp. 28–34.

280 Coleman-Norton (1966) III, nos. 549; 550.

281 Coleman-Norton (1966) III, no. 636; Cod. Just. I.1.6. (533); cf. Gray (1979), pp. 48–50.

282 Hussey (1986), pp. 10–13.

283 As suggested by Bark (1944), pp. 410–426.

284 Cf. Lemerle (1954); Browning (1975a), pp. 33–34.

285 Mal. 18.46; cf. Croke (1980). The Gepids occupied Sirmium in 526, and the Lombards appeared in Pannonia perhaps as early as 527. Neither was a serious threat during Justinian's reign.

286 Nov. 11, pref.; cf. Popović (1978), pp. 600–601; Barnea (1991).

287 Aed. 4.5–6; see also pp. 222–224.

288 SH 18.20.

289 Obolensky (1971), pp. 66–72; Evans (1960), pp. 25–28.

290 Pringle (1981) I, p. 12.

291 Humphrey (1980), p. 116.

292 Vict. Vit. 1.3–5.

293 Cf. Evans (1973), pp. 256–257.

294 Barnish (1986), p. 192.

295 Cf. Shaw (1982), pp. 44–47; Lewin (1989); Warmington (1954), pp. 69–75; Mattingly (1987), pp. 83–88. In Numidia, most of the

Romano-Berber churches probably adhered to the Donatist heresy: Frend (1984).
296 Lassus, *PECS*, pp. 899–902, s.v. 'Thamugadi'.
297 *Wars* 4.12.28–13.1; cf. Janon (1980).
298 So called by Corippus (*Ioh.* 3.294); they are called the Leuathai by Procopius (*Wars* 4.21.2; 4.21.20; 4.22.20; 4.28.47). Cf. Mattingly (1987), pp. 91–93; Roques (1994), p. 263.
299 *Wars* 3.8.14.
300 *Aed.* 6.5.2–3.
301 Hitchner (1990), pp. 246–247.
302 Cf. Fulford (1980), p. 71; id. (1987), p. 60.
303 *Wars* 4.6.5–10.
304 Pringle (1981) I, pp. 1–24; Diehl (1896), pp. 8–15.
305 Cf. Goffart (1980), pp. 58–102, who interprets the *sortes* which the Goths were given as income from shares of the taxes on Roman property and not actual real estate. *Contra*: Burns (1980), pp. 78–90 and Barnish (1986) maintain the older view that the *sortes* were land allotments. They were not, however, tax-free.
306 The other was appointed in Constantinople.
307 *Wars* 5.1.26–27.
308 *Consolation of Philosophy*, 1.4 (Penguin trans.); cf. Bury, *LRE* II, pp. 153–155.
309 Wickham (1981), pp. 22–24; Thompson (1982), pp. 92–93.
310 Cf. De Ste Croix (1981), p. 383.
311 *Wars* 5.1.26–27.
312 Burns (1980), pp. 99–100.
313 Oman (1962), p. 32.
314 Hodgkin (1880–89) III, pp. 519–553; Stein, *Histoire* II, p. 262.
315 On the use of these terms in Procopius, see Arrignon and Duneau (1981).
316 Bowersock (1976), pp. 219–229; Mayerson (1986); id. (1989).
317 Sartre (1982), p. 157.
318 *Wars* 1.19.3–4; cf. Rubin (1989), pp. 388–389; 407, n. 28, who argues that Iotabe was the northern outpost of a trade route controlled by Jewish merchants which followed the east coast of the Red Sea to Yemen. On the island there was an autonomous Jewish colony until Justinian annexed it. Sartre (1982), pp. 154–155, believes that the sheikh Amorcesos was not a Kindite but an Arab newcomer from Persian territory who settled his clan in the northern coastal region of the Hedjaz. Cf. Avi-Yonah (1984), p. 237; Shahîd, *ODB* I, p. 80, s.v. 'Amorkesos' surmises that Amorcesos was a Ghassanid who had been in Persian service.
319 Mal. 18.16 (p. 434); cf. Shahîd (1960), p. 60; Trimingham (1979), pp. 192–195. Harith drove Mundhir from Hira, but died in Mundhir's counterattack: see Christensen (1944), pp. 358–359.
320 *Wars* 1.19.8–14.
321 *Wars* 1.17.47–48; Gutwein (1981), pp. 313–320; Trimingham (1979), pp. 113–114; Kawar (1956), pp. 181–192; cf. Sartre (1982), pp. 168–170.

322 At least after ca. 531: Kawar (1956), p. 194. See also Smith (1954), pp. 442–443.
323 *Wars* 1.17.42–43.
324 Zach. Myt. 8.5. Doubt is allowable: cf. Trimingham (1979), pp. 193–194. Mundhir's mother was a Christian and so was his wife Hind, daughter of Harith of Kinda.
325 *Wars* 1.17.45–48; 2.28.13–14; Hitti (1956), pp. 78–83; Shahîd (1989), pp. 120–133; 405–458.
326 Lieu (1979), pp. 14–15; id. (1992), pp. 221–222; cf. Miyakawa and Kollantz (1989), pp. 89–118. Probably both the Ephthalites and the 'Black Huns' of Attila's horde were displaced from their homelands on the Asian steppe directly or indirectly by the rise of the Juan-juan confederacy in Outer Mongolia in the mid-fourth century: cf. McNeill (1963), pp. 385–386.
327 Vasiliev (1950), p. 256 puts the date in 523, but it was more likely 528 or 529: Mal. 18.30 (p. 444), followed by Christensen (1944), pp. 359–60; Guidi, *EI²*, p. 951.
328 Frye (1984), p. 322–323.
329 Christensen (1944), pp. 316–362.
330 Frye (1984), pp. 320–325.
331 Josh. Styl. 53; *Wars* 1.7.21–32; Zach. Myt. 7.4; cf. Harvey (1990), pp. 59–61; Stein, *Histoire* II, pp. 92–101.
332 Cf. Segal (1970), pp. 157–158.
333 Gordon (1959), pp. 25–26.
334 Zach. Myt. 7.6; De'Maffei (1986).
335 Crow (1981), pp. 12–14.
336 *Wars* 1.2.15; *Aed.* 2.1.4–5.
337 Cf. Brown (1969), p. 103.
338 Toumaroff (1963), p. 133.
339 Obolensky (1971), p. 88.
340 Mal. 18.14; cf. Obolensky (1971), pp. 87–88. On the silk route, see J. I. Miller (1969), pp. 140–141.
341 *Wars* 8.4.2.
342 *Nov.* 28, Pref. refers to them as forts rather than cities.
343 Cf. Vasiliev (1950), pp. 257–264. On the Caucasus monarchies: Lang (1966), pp. 81–101.
344 Men. Prot. 6.1: see Blockley, pp. 79–87.
345 *Wars* 1.12.3; cf. Lang (1966), pp. 95–99; Fowden (1993), p. 93. Christianity came to Iberia late in Constantine I's reign or early in that of Constantius II.
346 *Wars* 2.29.15. Their descendants are the Ossetians in the northern Caucasus: Vernadsky (1942–43).
347 *Wars* 8.2–3; 1.12.2–3; 15.20–25; Agathias 4.13.7; 5.2–3; Chrysos (1978); Bury, *LRE* II, pp. 79–80; Obolensky (1963); id. (1971), pp. 42–53.
348 Cf. *Nov.* 1, Pref.; *Nov.* 28, Pref.
349 Bowman (1978), p. 30.
350 Updegraff (1988), pp. 45–89; Adams (1977), pp. 383–390; id. (1991), p. 257.

351 Adams (1977), pp. 336–338. On the suppression, see p. 250.
352 Chitty (1966), pp. 60–61; 144–145; Wagner (1987), pp. 394–400.
353 Axum (*mod.* Ethiopia) was Christianized in the mid-fourth century and was a suffragan bishopric of the patriarch of Alexandria.
354 See pp. 112–114; cf. Rubin (1989). On Himyar's trade, see J. I. Miller (1969), pp. 178–179.
355 On the frontier of *Romania* as conceived by the élite in Constantinople in Justinian's day, see Arrignon and Duneau (1981), pp. 23–24.

2 THE NEW DYNASTS: THEIR EARLY YEARS OF POWER

1 Evans (1972), pp. 23–25; Vasiliev (1950), pp. 52–68; Bury, *LRE* II, pp. 18–20.
2 The sole source for Justinian's full name, 'Fl(avius) Petr(us) Sabba(tius) Iustin(ianus)', is his consular diptychs made for his consulship in 521. Thus the adoption had taken place before 521, and Alan Cameron (1976b), pp. 282–283 adduces evidence for 520. See Cutler (1984), pp. 75–115.
3 *Nov.* 13, Pref.; see also *Nov.* 13.1.1.
4 *Aed.*, 4.1.24; Claude (1969), pp. 243–44; Markus (1979), pp. 289–292.
5 *Wars*, 3.9.5; *Aed.* 1.3.3; SH 6.19; 11.5; 12.29.
6 PO I, pp. 452–453.
7 Coleman-Norton (1966) III, pp. 964–968.
8 Marc. Com. *sub anno* 521; cf. Cutler (1984), p. 103; Hendy (1985), pp. 192–193. A good portion of the cost was paid by the treasury.
9 SH 6.26.27; Zach. Myt. 8.1; cf. Vasiliev (1950), pp. 105–108.
10 SH 6.26.27–28.
11 Charanis (1939), pp. 63–65; Vasiliev (1950), pp. 190–205; Stein, *Histoire* II, pp. 228–230.
12 The daughter could not have been born much later than 515, and SH 9.30 implies that Justinian met Theodora *after* Justin's accession. If we can trust SH, Justinian could not have been the father of Theodora's daughter: cf. Alan Cameron (1978), p. 270.
13 *Cod. Theod.* 15.7.1 (371); cf. Roueché (1993), p. 27.
14 SH 9.16 (trans. Richard Atwater, Ann Arbor, 1961). See Diehl (1901), pp. 35–71; id. (1904), pp. 5–62; Averil Cameron (1985), pp. 67–83.
15 PO XVII i, pp. 188–189.
16 Cf. Fisher (1978), pp. 272–273. SH 6.17 uses Euphemia as a foil for Theodora in order to stress the latter's disrepute, and hence we should treat his report with caution. Ex-slaves were barred from marrying senators, and if the marriage took place before the husband reached senatorial rank, it would come to an end when he did. Somehow Justin got around this law. Daube (1967), p. 386, thinks that Lupicina was made freeborn retroactively.
17 *Cod. Just.* 5.4.23 (520–523).
18 SH 9.47–54; cf. Diehl (1901), p. 8. Daube (1967), p. 392 points out that the law covered only ex-actresses, not prostitutes. However, contem-

porary opinion made no distinction between the two, nor does *Nov.* 51 (536).

19 *Nov.* 8.1 (535).
20 *Cod. Theod.* 15.5.4 (380); 8 (381); 9 (381). On performers, see Rouché (1993), pp. 25–28.
21 Hardy (1968), p. 31.
22 *Nov.* 22.3 (535).
23 Cf. Rubin (1960), pp. 107–110.
24 SH 17.32–37.
25 Harrison (1983); cf. Palmer (1988), pp. 145–146.
26 SH 30.21–26.
27 SH 15.24–35; 17.7–14.
28 *HE* 2.11; cf. Alan Cameron (1978), pp. 269–271; Diehl (1901), p. 62; Stein, *Histoire* II, p. 628.
29 SH 4.37; 5.18; 9.2–54; 17.16–23.
30 SH 16.11.
31 PO XVII, p. 529.
32 Diehl (1904), pp. 65–67.
33 *Vie de S. Sabas*, 71.
34 SH 10.15.
35 Cf. Evag. 4.10. Evagrius could hardly have read the SH, and yet he also speculates that Justinian and Theodora operated by mutual understanding. See also Hardy (1969), pp. 31–32, for the argument that Justinian intentionally tolerated Theodora's pro-Monophysite activity.
36 Mango (1972), p. 190.
37 *Nov.* 51 (536); cf. *Nov.* 14 (535) outlawing persons who exploit young girls for prostitution.
38 *Aed.* 1.9.1–10; SH 17.5–6; cf. Mal. 18.24 (pp. 440–441); John of Nikiu 93.3.
39 Evag. 4.30.
40 *Wars* 7.31.2–18.
41 SH 9.8; 10.11; cf. *Aed.* 1.11.8.
42 *Wars* 8.13.14; SH 15.12–18; cf. Mal. 18.22 (p. 438).
43 Cf. Cront (1982).
44 Stein, *Histoire* II, pp. 20–27; 31–39; Frend (1972b), pp. 163–4; 173–182; 192–193; Wigram (1923), pp. 38–50.
45 Chitty (1966), p. 110. In the protobyzantine period, 'archimandrite' was a synonym of '*abbas*' or '*hegoumenos*': the superior of one or more monasteries: cf. *Nov.* 123. 24. After Justinian, the term was reserved for the superiors of monasteries that were particularly old and/or important: Hanton (1927–28), p. 67.
46 CSCO II, p. 238.
47 *Vie de S. Sabas*, 66–67.
48 Vasiliev (1950), p. 160.
49 Tchalenko, *Villages*, pp. 19–21.
50 Segal (1970), p. 116; Frend (1972b), pp. 201–234.
51 Wigram (1923), p. 95.
52 This was a year of earthquakes at both Constantinople and Antioch. Antioch had also had a severe earthquake the preceding year.

53 Segal (1970), pp. 95–98.
54 PO XVII; cf. Harvey (1981) pp. 37–40; ead. (1990), *passim*.
55 Evag. 4.6; Frend (1972b), p. 249.
56 Brock (1973), pp. 13–19; Baker (1968); cf. *DACL* XV, cols. 1697–1718, s.v. 'Stylites'.
57 John of Eph. *Lives*, PO XVII, ii, pp. 607–623; Frend (1972b), p. 263, n. 3.
58 PO XVII, i, p. 300.
59 Mango (1972); id. (1975); cf. Cormack (1981b), p. 134.
60 Brock (1981), pp. 87–90.
61 John of Eph. *Lives* (PO XVII, i, pp. 24–35); cf. Frend (1972a), pp. 20–21.
62 John of Nikiu 92.7; cf. Wigram (1923), p. 125; Stein, *Histoire* II, pp. 389–391. John identifies Zoilus' successor as Melkite patriarch, Apollinaris, as a Monophysite, but his popular reputation seems to have been Chalcedonian: Frend (1972b), p. 325.
63 Rémondon, *DictSpir* 4/1, cols. 532–548, s.v. 'Égypte chrétienne', esp. cols. 539–540.
64 The joint reign lasted long enough to produce a series of gold coins showing the two emperors enthroned on the obverse: Hahn and Metcalf (1988), pp. 19–27.
65 Shahid (1971), see also Vasiliev (1950), pp. 274–302; Brock and Harvey (1987), pp. 100–121; Möberg (1924), pp. xxiv–lxxii; J. Dousse, *DHGE* XV, cols. 210–227, s.v. 'Elesboan'. On the date, see Shahid (1971), pp. 235–242; Brock and Harvey (1987), pp. 103–104; cf. Smith (1954), p. 452; Rubin (1989), pp. 392–393.
66 Zach. Myt. 8.3.
67 Rubin (1989), p. 393 dates the persecution of Najran to 518.
68 Smith (1954), pp. 463–468; Whitehouse and Williamson (1973), p. 44; cf. Groh (1889), p. 97.
69 Cf. *Wars* 1.20.1–13.
70 *Wars* 1.11.11–12.
71 His baptismal name was Ursicinus: Adontz (1970), p. 111.
72 *Wars* 1.12.20–22; 1.15.31–33.
73 Hart (1941), pp. 50–56; 63.
74 At the modern village of Durak Basi (Turkish) or Kasr Sergey-Han (Syrian): De'Maffei (1988), p. 51.
75 *PLRE* IIIA s.v. 'Hermogenes I', pp. 590–593.
76 *Vie de S. Sabas*, 71.
77 Mal. 18.35 (pp. 446–447); 18.54 (p. 455); SH 11.21–30; cf. Schur (1989), pp. 87–89.
78 Cf. Agathias 2.22.5.
79 Cf. Evans (1972), pp. 56–58.
80 Scott (1985).
81 Mal. 18.60 (p. 464); cf. Moorhead (1994), p. 23.
82 Lee (1993), pp. 15–20. Hitherto, except for the king's personal bodyguard of 10,000 mounted troops, the Persian army was based on a levy system, with the nobility serving as cavalry and their tenants as infantry. Khusro's standing army, paid from the royal treasury, modified but did not replace this system.

83 *Wars* 1.22.2–6; 11–19; cf. Stein, *Histoire* II, pp. 294–296; cf.
Moorhead (1994), pp. 23–24, who notes Khusro's need for peace.
84 *Wars* 1.26.1–4.
85 Mal. 18.71 (p. 476). See *PLRE* IIIA s.v. 'Calopodius 1' pp. 267–268;
'Edermas' pp. 434–435. Karlin-Hayter (1973) identifies Narses with
Kalopodios, but a more likely explanation is that Justinian appointed
Narses to replace Kalopodios during the riots. Still the best account
of the revolt is Bury (1897). I have also benefited from an unpublished paper by G. Greatrex.
86 Theoph. 181.32–184.2. For a full translation, see Bury, *LRE* II, 71–74;
Diehl (1901), pp. 458–461.
87 *Chron. Pasch.* R776 (p. 620) [Whitby and Whitby, p. 114].
88 See Mal. 17.18 (p. 422).
89 Cf. SH 11.43–46.
90 Cf. Davis (1975), p. 187.
91 *PLRE* IIIB, pp. 1343, s.v. 'Tryphon 1'. For his brother: *PLRE* II, p.
1096, s.v. 'Theodorus 57'.
92 Lamma (1947), pp. 89–90.
93 Cf. Bury, *LRE* II, pp. 39–48; Bury (1897); Stein *Histoire* II, pp. 449–456.
94 *Wars* 1.24.54; cf. Mal. 18.71 (p. 476): 'about 35,000'.
95 SH 10.19; *Chron. Pasch.* R732 (p. 625) [Whitby and Whitby, p.
123]; Theoph. 185.6–8. The 'Young Greens' were a subgroup of the
Greens: Patlagean (1986), pp. 123–124. We find them also in the
theatre at Alexandria: cf. Alan Cameron (1983), p. 83.
96 Marc. Com. *sub anno* 532.
97 Isocrates, *Archidamus*, 45; Diodorus 14.8.5; Aelian, *Var. Hist.* 4.8; cf.
Evans (1984), pp. 380–382; Averil Cameron (1985), pp. 166–167. Ure
(1951), pp. 202–203 compares Clytaemnestra in Aesch. *Agamemnon*.
98 Zach. Myt. 9.14.
99 SH 12.12; 19.12, cf. Honoré (1978), p. 18.
100 Cf. SH 12.12.
101 Stein, *Histoire* II, pp. 402–417.
102 Cf. Patlagean (1974), pp. 68–69.

3 THE RESTORATION OF THE EMPIRE: THE WARS OF JUSTINIAN

1 *Nov.* 30.11.2. For the Byzantine offensive, see Pringle (1981) I, pp.
16–22; Diehl (1896), pp. 3–93.
2 Vict.Tun. a. 534.
3 Vict. Vit. 1.23; 3.19; cf. Barnish (1987), p. 181.
4 For the timetable of the expedition, see Pringle (1981) II, p. 351, n. 20.
5 Cf. Kaegi (1965a), pp. 23–36.
6 Clover (1982), pp. 19–20.
7 *Wars* 4.9; McCormick (1986), pp. 125–129.
8 Cf. Gurevich (1982), p. 123: 'Behaviour in the face of death, the words
uttered in the hour of death, this is what concerns the Germanic people
when they think about heroes.'

NOTES

9 *Cod. Just.* 1.27.1–2.
10 We have, however, no reference to the actual creation of the post of Master of the Soldiers of Africa (*Magister Militum Africae*) until after Justinian's death: Pringle (1981) I, pp. 55–56.
11 Cf. Janon (1980), pp. 346–347.
12 Cf. Kaegi (1965a), pp. 37–47.
13 *Wars* 4.16.3.
14 Cass. *Variae* 11.1.6–8.
15 Cf. Burns (1980), pp. 64–66.
16 Cass. *Variae* 10.3.7.
17 Lilybaeum had been transferred to the Vandal kingdom as part of Amalafrida's dowry.
18 *PLRE* II s.v. 'Opilio 4' p. 808.
19 Cass. *Variae* 10.21.2; 10.20.4; cf. Bury, *LRE* II, 164–167.
20 *PLRE* IIIB s.v. 'Petrus 6', pp. 994–998.
21 Cf. Browning (1987), pp. 105–106; Stein, *Histoire* II, p. 343. On Agapetus' mission, see Sotinel (1992), p. 444.
22 Cf. Moorhead (1986), pp. 120–121.
23 *Wars* 5.16.11.
24 *Wars* 5.23.26, claiming a Gothic source, puts them at 30,000, but the estimate is high.
25 *Wars* 6.6.1.
26 This was true for the war generally: Thompson (1982), pp. 104–109; Moorhead (1983). On the other hand, army desertions were almost entirely from the Byzantines to the Goths, and not vice versa.
27 *Wars,* 5.14.4; 5.25.13.
28 1.14; cf. Sotinel (1992), pp. 444–449, who examines the sources for this incident and concludes that there may have been grounds for suspecting Silverius.
29 Stein, *Histoire* II, p. 330–331.
30 Cf. *Lib. Pont.* 101; Bury, *LRE* II, pp. 377–380; Stein, *Histoire* II, pp. 386–387.
31 Moorhead (1994), pp. 81–82, following Liberatus of Carthage, an intensely hostile source: cf. Sotinel (1992), pp. 447–448.
32 See p. 183.
33 *Wars* 6.16.17.
34 *Wars* 6.28.25–26.
35 In 539, Justinian was trying by diplomacy to persuade Khusro to keep the 'Endless Peace' treaty: *Wars* 2.4.17–26.
36 Cf. Moorhead (1994), pp. 85–86, esp. n. 20.
37 *Wars* 2.4.1–12; Popović (1978), pp. 607–608.
38 *Wars* 1.25.11–12.
39 Hahn and Metcalf (1988), p. 12.
40 His name appears on his coins as 'Baduila'.
41 *Wars* 6.7.15: Antonina's son-in-law brought a strong company of horse from Libya.
42 De'Maffei (1988), pp. 55–56.
43 The exact sites of Iaudas' strongholds are unknown: Janon (1980), pp. 347–348.

44 Janon (1980), pp. 350–351; Pringle (1981) I, pp. 27–29.
45 *Wars* 4.21.1–15; cf. Mattingly (1987), p. 92. It may have been as a result of this incident that the Byzantines abandoned part of the wall that they had just built at Lepcis and built a shorter circuit, taking in only the easternmost sector of the city: see Goodchild and Ward Perkins (1953), pp. 72–73.
46 Marc. Com. a. 537; *Wars* 1.26.5–12.
47 Cf. Kawar (1956), pp. 186; 208.
48 *Nov.* 31 (18 March, 536). 'Other Armenia' became Armenia IV, governed by a *consularis* whose seat was Martyropolis. Cf. *Aed.* 3.1.16–29.
49 *Nov.* 21 (18 March 536): Adontz (1970), pp. 143–144; cf. Toumanoff (1963), pp. 172–175; Stein, *Histoire*, II, pp. 470–472.
50 Mal. 18.87 (p. 480) states that Germanus was sent as Master of the Soldiers to Antioch with his son Justin, consul for 540, but did nothing but exchange silver for gold at a profit. Cf. Downey (1953), who discredits Procopius (*Wars* 2.6.9–15; 8.8–16) on the weakness of Antioch's circuit wall.
51 Christensen (1944), p. 386; Stein, *Histoire* II, p. 490. John of Ephesus puts the population of Khusro's new city at 30,000: see Claude (1969), p. 164.
52 Evag. 4.26.
53 SH 2.26–27; cf. *Wars* 8.7.3–5.
54 SH 2.30.
55 D-F V, p. 369.
56 SH 2.1–25.
57 SH 3.29.
58 For its symptoms, see *Wars* 2.22.1–23.19; Evag. 4.29; John of Eph. *HE* frgs. II E–H; Agathias 5.10.1–7 (on the plague of 558).
59 Marc. Com. *sub anno* 543; *pace* Stein, *Histoire* II, p. 841. The dates are still *sub iudice*.
60 *Wars* 2.24.8–12.
61 *History of the Franks* 4.5.
62 Russell (1958), pp. 118–119; cf. Allen (1979), p. 15.
63 Russell (1958), p. 48.
64 Boccaccio mentions similar spots in his description of the Black Death: see Nohl (1961), pp. 10–17. Zinsser (1960), p. 109, takes this as evidence that a severe type of smallpox participated.
65 Cf. Thuc. 2.51.5 and *Wars* 2.22.23.
66 Zach. Myt. 10. 9.
67 Conrad (1986), p. 146.
68 *Vie de S. Syméon*, 69–70.
69 Conrad (1986), pp. 151–157.
70 Mollaret (1989), pp. 101–106; Bratton (1981), pp. 117–119.
71 Conrad (1986), p. 147, is probably right to claim that bubonic, septicaemic and pneumonic forms of the plague all occurred. However, the bubonic form must have predominated.
72 Cf. Bury (1910), pp. 25–27.
73 John of Eph. *HE*, frgs. E–G.

74 Mal. 18.92 (p. 286); Zach. Myt. 9.9 (pp. 312–313); Agathias 5.10.6; Evag. 2.13; 4.8; 4.29; cf. Nohl (1961), pp. 78–79.
75 Downey (1955); Vercleyen (1988).
76 2.16.1–6.
77 Mich. Syr. 9. 29.
78 18.36–44.
79 SH 23.15–22.
80 *Nov.* 128; cf. Bury, *LRE* II, p. 350.
81 Janin (1952), pp. 149–150.
82 Poos (1991), pp. 181–82; 209.
83 *Nov.* 122; cf. Patlagean (1986), p. 52.
84 Kennedy and Liebeschuetz (1988), pp. 67–71; cf. Liebeschuetz (1992), pp. 5–6. The plague ended a period of prosperity: Russell (1968).
85 SH 4.1–31.
86 *Ioh.* 1.68–109; Stein, *Histoire* II, pp. 501–502.
87 *Wars* 2.28.9–10; 8.10.10–16; Zach. Myt. 12; Bury, *LRE* II, pp. 112–113; cf. Blockley (1980), pp. 89–96, who, however, does not mention Tribunus.
88 Agathias 2.22.3–5.
89 *PLRE* IIIB s.v. 'Rusticus 4', pp. 1103–1104.
90 Agathias 3.3.5–6.
91 Probably the prefect of Africa at the time of Guntarith's revolt: see *PLRE* IIIA s.v. 'Athanasius I'; 'Athanasius II', pp. 142–145.
92 He bore the title *nakhverghan*, but we do not know his name: Stein, *Histoire* II, p. 514, n. 2.
93 Agathias 3.14.4–5; 4.1.2–6; 4.11.2; 4.21.1–3; 4.23.2–3.
94 Cf. Lewis (1969), p. 138.
95 Vict.Tun. *a.* 543.
96 *Wars* 4.22.1–4; cf. Diehl (1896), pp. 339–340.
97 Isidore 42–43; cf. Diehl (1896), pp. 343–344. For discussion of the date, see Pringle (1981) II, p. 368, n. 33.
98 *Ioh.* 4.232–237 makes Athanasius the leader in the plot whereas his role in Procopius' account is a passive one.
99 *Ioh.* 3.302; 7.277; 8.126; cf. Janon (1980), p. 351.
100 *Wars* 8.27.22.
101 Pringle (1981) I, p, 114; cf. Averil Cameron (1989), pp. 176–178.
102 *Wars* 7.12.4.
103 Thompson (1982), pp. 98–100.
104 *Wars* 7.10.19–23; 11.12–16.
105 Cf. Adshead (1990), pp. 105–106.
106 *Wars* 7.22.26.
107 *Bury,* LRE II, p. 249.
108 *Wars* 8.21.1–3; cf. Stein, *Histoire* II, p. 592.
109 Procopius (*Wars* 7.29.9) calls the whale a *ketos* (sea-monster), and its appetite for dolphins and the name the Byzantines gave it, *Porphyrios*, which suggests a dark purplish colour, may indicate a large killer whale. One would not expect to find a true whale in the waters around the Dardanelles.
110 *Get.* 316.

111 *Wars* 8.32.12.
112 In autumn, 553: Averil Cameron (1970), p. 143.
113 See Thompson (1969), pp. 15–16; 155–156; 320–334; Hillgarth (1966), pp. 495–496.
114 *Get.* 303; cf. Isidore 47.
115 *CIC* III, App. vii; cf. O'Donnell (1979), pp. 135–136.
116 Mal. 18.140 (p. 492); cf. Fauber (1990), pp. 161–164.
117 Pringle (1981) I, p. 115.

4 THE HOME FRONT: DOMESTIC PROBLEMS

1 *Hist. Pat.* p. 459.
2 See p. 138.
3 Zach. Myt. 9.19.
4 Theodosius' successor, Paul, established the custom for the Melkite (so called after the Syriac word for 'imperial') patriarchs of Alexandria, who were henceforth ordained in Constantinople and maintained in Alexandria with the muscle of the Augustal prefect.
5 Frend (1972b), p. 288.
6 Segal (1970), pp. 151–152.
7 John of Eph. *Lives*, PO XVII, p. 525. The second 'John' was John of Hephaestopolis: PO XVII, pp. 526–540.
8 Cf. *Wars* 2.19.15–49; Trimingham (1979), pp. 166–167.
9 Frend (1972b), pp. 283–292; Wigram (1923), pp. 132–146; Trimingham (1979), pp. 119; 165–168; Roueché (1989), p. 144.
10 See pp. 145–146.
11 Meyendorff (1968), pp. 54–60; Gray (1979), pp. 61–68; Bury, *LRE* II, pp. 383–391; Stein, *Histoire* II, pp. 634–638. Justinian's edict of 544 was couched in three chapters; hence the title of the controversy.
12 Meyendorff (1983), pp. 25–27.
13 The present monastery of Mar Saba in the Kidron valley occupies part of the site of the Great Laura. The New Laura was south of Teko'a at Khirbet bir-e-Wa'ar: Tsafrir (1989), p. 1746.
14 *Vie de S. Sabas*, 84; cf. Stein, *Histoire* II, pp. 392–395.
15 The Origenist monks were not ousted from First Palestine until late 554: Stein, *Histoire* II, p. 656.
16 On the African reaction, see Diehl (1896), pp. 434–449; cf. Sotinel (1992), p. 456.
17 Mal. 18.115 (p. 486).
18 See Every (1979).
19 Averil Cameron (1988), p. 225: 'a rather shabby affair'.
20 No bishops from Italy, Spain, Gaul, Dalmatia or Illyricum attended the Council. The western church was represented only by eight or nine prelates from Africa.
21 Cf. *Wars* 8.26.7–10.
22 See Devreesse, *DTC* XII, cols. 660–669, s.v. 'Pelagius I'.
23 Evag. 5.1.
24 See Amann, *DTC* VIII, col. 597, s.v. 'Jean III'.

25 *Hist. Pat.* p. 466 states that the Monophysites in Alexandria secretly built two churches for themselves, one near the site of the Serapeum and the other east of the amphitheatre, but Justinian, learning this, put all the city churches under Chalcedonian authority.

26 Frend (1972), pp. 282–295.

27 *Nov.* 8, pref. (535).

28 *De. Mag.* 2.15.3.

29 SH 11.2; cf. 7.7.

30 Evag. 4.30.

31 *Wars* 1.24.11–16. See, in general, Honoré (1978).

32 Theoph. A.M. 6022; Mal. 18.42 (p. 449).

33 *De Mag.* 3. 57.1–60.4.

34 *Wars* 1.24.11–16; 3.10.7–8; 3.13.12; cf. Lamma (1947), p. 89.

35 *PLRE* IIIA s.v. 'Iulianus 4', pp. 729–730; cf. Mal. 18.61 (p. 465).

36 Cf. Mal. 18.67 (p. 470).

37 *De Mag.* 3.49; *PLRE* II s.v. 'Marinus 7', pp. 726–728; Jones, *LRE* I, p. 236.

38 SH 30.1–11.

39 *Cod. Just.* 12.50 (51).22; 23.

40 *Wars* 3.13.12–20.

41 *De Mag.* 3.70.1–6.

42 *Nov.* 8, pref. (15 April, 535) ; cf. Diehl (1901), pp. 270–274; Stein, *Histoire* II, p. 464.

43 SH 4.1–4.

44 He died in Constantinople, still a deacon, at least nominally: cf. Mal. 19.89 (p. 481). On John's fall, see now Greatrex (1995), pp. 6–9.

45 Cf. Stein, *Histoire* II, p. 483: 'le plus grand homme que l'Empire ait eu dans le domaine de la politique intérieure'.

46 *PLRE* II, s.v. 'Phocas 5', p. 881; *PLRE* III, s.v. 'Phocas', p. 1029; cf. Maas (1992), pp. 78–82.

47 Bury, *LRE* II, p. 368.

48 SH 22.2; *PLRE* IIIB, s.v. 'Theodotus 3', p. 1301.

49 SH 22.1–11, 14–38; *PLRE* IIIB, s.v. 'Petrus 9', pp. 999–1002.

50 SH 22.38. See pp. 236–237.

51 Cf. Diehl (1919). Merchants and money-changers in Egypt valued 81 of these adulterated gold *solidi* to the pound rather than the ususal 72 for pure gold coins. Justinian (*Edict* 11) had to intervene in 559 to withdraw the adulterated gold.

52 Mal. 18.135 (p. 491).

53 *PLRE* IIIA, s.v. 'Basilides', pp. 172–173.

54 A *discussor* or *logothetes*: see Jones, *LRE* I 589; cf. *Wars* 7.1.31–33; *PLRE* IIIA s.v. 'Alexander 5', pp. 43–44.

55 SH 27.3–19; 29.1–11; cf. *PLRE* IIIB s.v. 'Rhodon', pp. 1085–1086.

56 Agathias 16.1; *PLRE* IIIB s.v. 'Narses 1', pp. 912–928; Stein, *Histoire* II, pp. 612–622; A. Lippold, *RE* Suppl. XII s.v. 'Narses', cols. 870–889; Fauber (1990), *passim*.

57 Cf. De'Maffei (1988), pp. 89–94.

58 Brown (1984), pp. 21–24.

59 Probably in 573–574: *PLRE* IIIB, p. 926.

60 *PLRE* IIIB s.v. 'Petrus 6', pp. 994–998; SH 24.22–23; cf. Stein, *Histoire* II, pp. 723–729; Blockley (1985a), pp. 11–12.

61 *PLRE* II s.v. 'Bessas', pp. 226–229.

62 *PLRE* IIIA s.v. 'Ioannes 46', pp. 652–661; 'Ioannes 71', pp. 669–671; 'Ioannes 72', p. 670.

63 *Wars* 8.13.14; cf. SH 22.35.

64 Honoré (1978), pp. 28–30.

65 *Nov.* 111.

66 *C(onstitutio). Haec quae necessario* (13 Feb., 528).

67 Cf. Turpin (1987), pp. 626–630.

68 Cf. Honoré (1971), pp. 9–10; Kunkel (1966), p. 141.

69 This is the theory which Friedrich Bluhme formulated in 1818, and it may be taken as proven: Bluhme (1820); Kunkel (1966), pp. 258–259; Schulz (1946), p. 319. Honoré and Rodger (1970), also Honoré (1978), pp. 139–186, have attempted to take a further step and demonstrate who read each book, and what volume of extracts he made from it, but their results should be used with caution: see Osler (1985).

70 Honoré (1981), p. xv.

71 *C(onstitutio). Imperatoriam* (21 Nov., 533).

72 Honoré (1971), pp. 4–13; id. (1978), pp. 16–19, 48–52; Kunkel (1966), pp. 153–158; Thomas (1975), pp. vii–xi; Stein, *Histoire* pp. 402–417. Some fragments of the *Codex Vetus*, Bk. 1, survive in *P. Oxy.* 1814.

73 C. *Cordi* 4.

74 Hence the name, the 'Greek Collection'. It is sometimes also known as the 'Marcian Collection', from the Marcian library in Venice which preserves the best manuscript: see Bonini (1977), pp. 76–78.

75 C. *Omnem* 7.

76 Buckland (1963), pp. 49–50; Jolowicz and Nicholas (1972), pp. 506–509.

77 3.1.3, trans. Carney (1971), III, p. 63; cf. Archi (1978), pp. 142–149.

78 Pringsheim (1940), p. 241.

79 Cf. Stolte (1994), pp. 50–51.

80 Cf. Schiller (1971), pp. 495–502.

81 Synesius, *Letters*, 148 (trans. A. Fitzgerald, London, 1926).

82 Breen (1944–45), pp. 259–266. The *Digest* was cited in a legal decision as early as 1076.

83 *Nov.* 54, pref. (537). The term *adscripticius* (Greek *enapographos*) for a *colonus* tied to an estate appears in the East in about the mid-fifth century. It was not used in the Western empire: Jones (1974), pp. 302–303.

84 Gaius, *Institutes* I.1: 8–55.

85 *Nov.* 58.2.1 (539).

86 *Dig.* 37.14; cf. *Cod. Just.* V.4.3 (529).

87 *Dig.* 38.1.17; 38.1.19.

88 *Nov.* 119.2 (544).

89 *Nov.* 22 (535).

90 *Nov.* 123.17 (546).

91 *Nov.* 153 (541).

92 Suet. *Claudius* 25.2.
93 Cf. *Nov.* 22.8.
94 That is the implication of *Nov.* 62.2, which allows a peasant who has sunk to adscript status to win freedom by acquiring enough land to make leasing any more unnecessary. See, in general, Lemerle (1979), pp. 21–26.
95 *Nov.* 123.4 (546). An adscript who became a priest might have free status, but on condition that he continued to work his leased farm: *Nov.* 123.17.1 (546).
96 *Cod. Just.* XI.48.21 was the original measure; *Nov.* 54 (537) ruled that it was not retroactive and *Nov.* 162.2 (539) ruled further that children emancipated as a result of the law should remain on their farms as free persons. *Cod. Just.* XI.48.24 allowed a master to dissolve the marriage of an adscript and a free woman in order to deny their offspring free status. Cf. Jones (1974), pp. 305–307; Lemerle (1979), pp. 23–24.
97 *Nov.* 157 (542).
98 *Nov.* 14.1 (535).
99 *Cod. Just.* 5.4.23.
100 SH 9.51.
101 *Nov.* 5.2 (535). On Justinian's regard for the position of women, see Fisher (1978), pp. 256–257.
102 Thomas (1976), p. 431.
103 *Nov.* 61.1.2 (537). In the preface to this law, Justinian notes his preference for the term *donatio propter nuptias*.
104 *Nov.* 22.3 (535).
105 *Nov.* 134.9 (556).
106 *Nov.* 140 (566).
107 *Nov.* 22 (535); 117.9 (542).
108 *Nov.* 36 (535)
109 *Nov.* 21 (536).
110 *Nov.* 16, pref.
111 *Nov.* 16.1; 16.7.1.
112 *Nov.* 38, pref. (535).
113 *Nov.* 38.1.
114 *Nov.* 38.1; 2; 3; 6; *Nov.* 89 (539); *Nov.* 101 (539).
115 *Cod. Just.* 10.67 (66) (529). Appointment to *honorary* urban or praetorian prefectures did not release a decurion from curial duties: *Nov.* 70 (538).
116 *Nov.* 123.15 (546).
117 For the same tendency at work in the theological controversies of the period, see Gray (1988), p. 288.
118 *Nov.* 24; 25; 26; 27; 28; 29; Edict 13. Cf. Maas (1986).
119 *Nov.* 24 (535); *Nov.* 25 (535).
120 Cf. *Nov.* 145 (553) for the rise in civil disorder in Pisidia and Phrygia, which Justinian connects with the abolition of civil administration.
121 *Nov.* 105 (536).
122 *Nov.* 13 (535).
123 Jones, *LRE*, p. 294; Foss (1976), pp. 12–13; cf. Foss (1972), pp. 57–58.

124 *Nov.* 145.1.
125 Cf. Bury, *LRE* II, pp. 360–361; Velkov (1977), pp. 62–63.
126 *Edict* 13. For the date: Rémondon (1955).
127 The common *artaba* was 38.78 litres (Bagnall [1993]), p. 332), but we do not know if the common *artaba* is meant here. See pp. 31–32.
128 Bury, *LRE* II, pp. 342–343; Jones, *LRE* I, pp. 280–282; Hardy (1968), pp. 33–35.
129 *Nov.* 10.
130 Cf. Jones (1974), pp. 347–349.
131 *Nov.* 3 (535); *Nov.* 16 (535).
132 *Nov.* 67 (538).
133 *Nov.* 7 (535). In the same year, Justinian ruled that after a monk with property entered a monastery, the property was to remain with the monastery, thereby disallowing an ascetic's right, which he had possessed earlier, to will his property to heirs of his choice. The rule was later relaxed, but full freedom was never restored to monks or nuns after they entered a monastery to dispose of their property as they saw fit: Orestano (1956).
134 *Nov.* 40 (535).
135 *Nov.* 57 (537).
136 *Nov.* 123.6; 7 (546).
137 *Nov.* 79 (539); *Nov.* 83 (539).
138 *Nov.* 83.1.
139 *Nov.* 86.4 (539).
140 *Nov.* 8 (535).
141 SH 21.16–19.
142 SH 23.22; cf. *Nov.* 130.9 (545).
143 SH 11.31–36 (cf. Mal. 18.18 [p. 436]); 16.19; 16.23–25; 9.11; 20.9; cf. *Nov.* 141 (559).
144 Cf. Ure (1951), pp. 165–167, whose remarks are worth reading.
145 See pp. 3–4.
146 Averil Cameron (1985), p. 86.
147 *Nov.* 67.2 (538).
148 Cf. Geanakoplos (1966b).
149 Harrison (1986), pp. 5–10; id. (1983); cf. Moorhead (1994), pp. 49–52; 58–59.
150 Cf. Downey (1950), pp. 262–264; Grabar (1967), pp. 92–96. Excavations suggest that Justinian's church took over the length of the nave and the small apse from the Theodosian church.
151 Emerson and Van Nice (1951a), pp. 102–103. See, in general, Mainstone (1988).
152 Cf. Harrison (1989), pp. 137–144.
153 Emerson and Van Nice (1951b), pp. 163–169.
154 Krautheimer (1983), p. 47; George (1912), pp. 1–5; 69–70.
155 *Nov.* 59.3 (537); cf. Miller (1990).
156 Downey (1950), p. 263. See also Downey (1957).
157 Foss (1977a), pp. 472–475.
158 *Aed.* 5.6.1–26; Avigad (1970), pp. 137–138; id. (1993); Tsafrir (1989), p. 1744; De'Maffei (1988), pp. 26–30.

NOTES

159 John Moschus, *Pratum Spirituale* (PG lxxxvii, col. 2857A)
160 *Aed.* 5.9.1–22.
161 Kuhnel (1993), p. 198; cf. Tsafrir (1993a), pp. 8–10, and De'Maffei (1988), pp. 30–31, who accept the tradition that Justinian restored the church after it suffered in the Samaritan revolt of 529.
162 Tsafrir (1993c), p. 327.
163 Forsyth (1968), pp. 1–9.
164 Evag. 4.18.
165 See Pringle (1981) I, pp. 109–111; 122–125; Claude (1969), pp. 11–12. However, not every bishop resided in a city.
166 Lawrence (1983), pp. 188–189; De'Maffei (1988), pp. 87–88.
167 PO XVII, pp. 18–35.
168 Cf. Liebeschuetz (1977), p. 494: 'It is thus likely . . . that Procopius fails to mention a garrison in connection with the great majority of fortifications in the De Aedificiis because they were, in fact, not garrisoned.'
169 Alföldy (1974), pp. 213–227.
170 Sauvaget (1939), pp. 121–126; Sartre (1982), pp. 177–188.
171 *Wars* 1.13.2; cf. De'Maffei (1986), pp. 238–242.
172 Cf. Liebeschuetz (1977), pp. 490–493.
173 *Aed.* 2.1.11–21; cf. *Wars* 2.13.17–18. See Crow (1981); Croke and Crow (1983); Lawrence (1983), pp. 197–199; De'Maffei (1986), pp. 242–248; ead. (1988), p. 54.
174 *Aed.* 3.2.11–14; De'Maffei (1986), pp. 250–253; ead. (1988), pp. 56–57.
175 De'Maffei (1988), pp. 57–58.
176 Scorpan (1980), pp. 50–74. Scorpan, pp. 83–85, puts the completion of the Danube line ca. 543.
177 Poulter (1988), p. 87; De'Maffei (1988), p. 79. Kondić (1984), pp. 133–135 reports that eight Justinianic fortifications have been identified within a 55 kilometre area in the Iron Gate region.
178 D–F ch. 40 (IV, p. 268).
179 Lawrence (1983), pp. 190–192.
180 *Aed.* 4.1.15–33; cf. Bavant (1984), pp. 272–285. For Interior Illyricum, see Wozniak (1982). Excavations at Nicopolis on the Danube reveal that the rebuilt protobyzantine 'city' was merely a *castellum* which provided refuge to the population outside the walls in time of danger: Poulter (1990).
181 Scorpan (1980), pp. 50–74.
182 *Aed.* 4.2.2–15; SH 26.31–33; cf. Cherf (1992).
183 SH 26.31–34.
184 *Aed.* 4.2.27–28.
185 *IG* IV, 204; cf. Gregory (1993), pp. 12–13; 80–83.
186 Barnish (1985), pp. 5–6.
187 Christie and Rushworth (1988), pp. 79–81; 86–87. The walls at Ardea, which are considered Justinianic, need further work before their date is secure.
188 *CIL* 6, 1199.
189 See Geremek (1990); Whittow (1990), pp. 4–12.

298

190 Saradi-Mendelovici (1988), pp. 377–396; Kennedy (1985a); Russell (1986), pp. 144–154.
191 Kennedy (1985b), pp. 6–7.
192 For Gerasa, see Ostrasz (1989), pp. 72–74; for Thessaloniki see Evans (1977).
193 *Aed.* 2.10.22; 4.1.24; 5.3.1; 5.2.4; 5.3.7.
194 Kennedy (1985b), pp. 8–9.
195 *Aed.* 2.10.23.
196 Lassus (1972), p. 149, correcting Downey (1961), pp. 547–548, and id. (1963), pp. 253–254, who claimed that the rebuilt street was only the width of the sidewalk of the older colonnaded street.
197 *Aed.* 4.1.23.
198 *Aed.* 6.5.8–11; 6.6.8–16. The extent to which the *topos* of the beautiful city, adorned with splendid public buildings, still dominated the rhetorical tradition is well documented by Saradi (1995), pp. 40–42.
199 Kennedy and Liebeschuetz (1988), pp. 65–66; Humphrey (1980), pp. 113–114; Saradi-Mendelovici (1988), pp. 384–388.
200 Popović (1975), pp. 497–502.
201 Cf. Spieser (1984), pp. 323–324.
202 *Cod. Theod.* 9.17.6.
203 Snively (1984), pp. 120–121.
204 Kenrich (1982), p. 56.
205 See Mitchell (1993), p. 120, for this development in Anatolia.
206 *Wars* 2.6.17; 7.1; 7.14; 7.19–37.
207 *Wars* 2.6.16.
208 *Vita* 52–53; cf. Foss (1991), pp. 306–307.
209 *Nov.* 80 (539); cf. Dagron (1979), pp. 51–52.
210 Mitchell (1993), p. 128; cf. Whittow (1990), who argues that the vitality of the councils persisted despite their change of composition.
211 Cf. Spieser (1984), pp. 336–338, and Dagron (1984), p. 339.
212 *Nov.* 118.15. Security may have been the motive for the change: cf. Saradi-Mendelovici (1988), p. 393.
213 Cf. Conrad (1986), pp. 155–157.
214 Russell (1986), pp. 144–150; id. (1987).
215 Cf. Croke (1981), pp. 145–147.
216 Brown (1987), p. 290.
217 Durliat (1990), p. 3.
218 Foss (1991), pp. 306–310.
219 *Hist. Pat.* p. 485.
220 *Nov.* 24.1.
221 Cf. Magoulias (1990), pp. 69–70; Fowden (1990), p. 366. On commerce in general in Late Antiquity, see Jones, *LRE*, pp. 844–872.
222 See MacMullen (1970); W. Kroll, 'Nundinae', RE 17/2, cols. 1467–1472; Vryonis (1981).
223 Amm. Marc. 14.3.3. Batnae (*mod.* Tell Butnan) was made into a fortified garrison point by Justinian: *Aed.* 2.7.18.
224 Jones (1974), p. 148.
225 Sauvaget (1939).
226 Sozomen 2.4.1–8; cf. Vryonis (1981), pp. 212–214.

227 Glucker (1987), pp. 93–98.
228 Wars 3.14.7–8; cf. Fulford (1980), p. 71; id. in Fulford and Peacock (1984), pp. 113–114.
229 PO XVII, pp. 576–585.
230 An *emporos* in Greek, as distinct from a *kapelos*, who was a retail dealer or shopkeeper: J. I. Miller (1969), p. 173.
231 Jones, *LRE*, pp. 861–862; Lopez (1945); Oikonomides (1986); Jacoby (1991/92); Muthesius (1993).
232 Cf. Oikonomides (1986), p. 34; Jones, *LRE*, pp. 295–296.
233 Wars 1.20. 9–12; cf. Rubin (1989), p. 401.
234 Wars 8.17.1–8; Theophanes of Byzantium, *FHG* IV, p. 270.
235 Whitehouse and Williamson (1973), p. 29. Muthesius (1993), p. 66 cites Chinese sources as evidence for sericulture in Syria in the fifth century.
236 Lopez (1945), pp. 9–10; Jones, *LRE*, p. 826.
237 SH 20.1–5; 26.18–20; cf. Bury, *LRE* II, p. 356; Jones, *LRE* p. 296.
238 Nov. 85 (539).
239 SH 12.6–10.
240 30.32–33. See, in general, Runciman, *CEH* II, pp. 87–88; cf. Vryonis (1962).
241 As argued by Adelson (1957) and Lewis (1969).
242 Kent (1959), p. 238; cf. Bellinger, *DOC* I, pp. 72–73.
243 22.38; cf. 25.12, where the SH reports that the *solidus* was tariffed at 180 *folles* (the common bronze coin) rather than 210, as a result of imperial innovation. This resulted in a lowering of the value of the *solidus*. Probably both entries report the same thing: see Adelson (1957), pp. 104–108.
244 18.117 (p. 486).
245 Fulford (1980) pp. 75–76; Fulford and Peacock (1984), p. 114; Humphrey (1980) p. 117.
246 Phocaea appears to be the source of the good Late Roman C ware, which has now been renamed Phocaean Red Slip ware. Other sites in the area of Phocaea, and in Cyprus and Egypt, produced similar *terra sigillata* for local markets: Sodini (1993), p. 174.
247 SH 18.5–9.
248 SH 18.13–19; cf. Brown (1984), pp. 114–117.
249 Cf. Brown (1984), p. 33.
250 Markus (1979), pp. 292–302. See also Brown (1988).
251 Jones, *LRE*, p. 295.
252 Nov. 32; 33; 34 (535); cf. Jones, *LRE*, p. 775.
253 Tchalenko, *Villages*, I, p. 81.
254 Sodini *et al.* (1980), pp. 9; 292–301; cf. Kennedy (1987), p. 247.
255 Kennedy and Liebeschuetz (1988), pp. 68–73.
256 SH 11.29; cf. Avi-Yonah (1958), pp. 41–51.
257 Cf. Kennedy (1987), pp. 250–251
258 Dagron (1979), p. 43; Gutwein (1981), pp. 272–274.
259 Aed. 1.1.9.
260 Cf. Goldenberg (1979).
261 Rabello (1987) I, p. 25.

262 Reynolds and Tannenbaum (1987); Avi-Yonah (1984), pp. 44–45.
263 *Cod. Theod.* 16.8.2 (330).
264 *Cod. Theod.* 16.8.3 (321). This was a dubious privilege, and the same law allowed two or three persons from each Jewish community the privilege of immunity from nomination.
265 *Cod. Theod.* 16.8.8. (392).
266 *Cod. Theod.* 16.8.9 (393); 16.8.11 (396).
267 *Cod. Theod.* 2.8.26 (409; 412); 16.8.20.1 (412), cf. *Cod. Just.* I.9.12.
268 *Cod. Theod.* 16.8.13 (397).
269 *Cod. Theod.* 12.1.157 (398); 158 (398); 159 (398).
270 *Cod. Theod.* 7.8.2 (368; 370; 373); *Cod. Just.* I.9.4.
271 *Cod. Theod.* 16.8.9 (393); 16.8.12 (397); 16.8.21 (412); 16.8.25 (423).
272 *Cod. Theod.* 16.8.25.1 (15 Feb., 423). On 8 June of the same year, we have a ruling that if Christians plunder Jews or pagans who are living at peace, they should be compelled to restore triple or quadruple the amount robbed: *Cod. Theod.* 16.10.24.
273 *Nov.* of Theodosius 3 (dealing also with Samaritans, pagans and heretics); cf. Avi-Yonah (1984), p. 216.
274 Cf. Avi-Yonah (1984), pp. 238–240.
275 Jacoby (1967), pp. 168–169.
276 *Cod. Theod.* 3.7.2; 9.7.5 (388).
277 *Cod. Theod.* 16.8.5 (336).
278 *Cod. Theod.* 16.8.7 (352).
279 *Cod. Theod.* 16.8.28 (426).
280 *Cod. Theod.* 16.9.1 (336); 16.9.3 (415).
281 *Cod. Theod.* 16.9.3 (415); 16.9.4 (417).
282 Lewis (1969), pp. 11–14.
283 *Leviticus* 25.40. *Exodus* 21.2 limits a Jewish slave's servitude to a Jewish master to seven years.
284 Groh (1988), pp. 86–89; cf. Wilken (1980), pp. 460–462. Hachlili (1989), p. 4, states that the sixth century was 'the most prolific period of synagogue construction' in Israel.
285 *Cod. Theod.* 16.8.15.
286 *Cod. Theod.* 16.8.22.
287 *Cod. Theod.* 16.9.29 (429).
288 Jones, *LRE* II, pp. 944–950; Avi-Yonah (1984), pp. 237–238.
289 Cf. Hobson (1993) for Egyptian villages.
290 John of Eph. *Lives*, PO XVII, pp. 89–95.
291 Foss (1976), pp. 29–30.
292 Rey-Coquais, *PECS*, pp. 66–67 s.v. 'Apamea'.
293 Kraabel (1979), pp. 483–497; Wiseman (1984), pp. 296–301. Wiseman suggests a connection between the action against the Stobi synagogue and *Cod. Theod.* 16.4.2; 16.5.15, both issued at Stobi by Theodosius I in 388, and both, especially the latter, restricting religious freedom, though neither singles out the Jews for mention.
294 Rubin (1989), p. 402, suspects that the rabbinical school at Tiberias may have had some involvement in Yusuf's revolt, but if so, it seems not to have disturbed the imperial authorities.

NOTES

295 *Cod. Just.* I.5.12 (527). Jews, however, are not specifically included in *Cod. Just.* I.5.18 or I.5.19 (529), which restrict rights of inheritance and veto entry into the public service.
296 *Nov.* 37.
297 *Wars* 5.8.41; 5.10.24–26.
298 *Nov.* 131.15 (545).
299 *Nov.* 45 (537). The honours were difficult to identify: pp. 46; 229.
300 *Nov.* 146 (553); cf. Gray (1993), pp. 264–268.
301 SH 28.16–18; cf. Avi-Yonah (1984), p. 249; JE VII, p. 397.
302 Scott (1987), pp. 217–220.
303 For a comprehensive overview, see Gerostergios (1974), pp. 180–191.
304 *Nov.* 139.
305 Gray (1993), pp. 262–264; Chen (1987). The synagogue was, however, built on a synagogue site, where there had been two earlier synagogues, and though it was larger than its predecessor by some 21 per cent, it did not break the laws against the construction of *new* synagogues.
306 Groh (1988).
307 Avi-Yonah (1984), p. 247.
308 *Nov.* 16.1 (535) rules that no one, not even an *illustris*, might refuse the office. The *defensor* registered wills, assisted in collecting taxes and ran a 'small claims court', for cases with claims under 300 *solidi*.
309 *Nov.* 86 (539).
310 Fowden (1993), pp. 69–72.
311 Chitty (1966), pp. 157–158; Vasiliev (1952), pp. 194–195; cf. Jones, *LRE*, p. 950. For the fear of a pro-Persian Jewish 'Fifth Column', see Patlagean (1986), pp. 115–117.
312 Cf. Sulpicius Severus, *Dialogue* 1.3–5; *Aed.* 6.2.21–23. For Boreum, see Goodchild (1951); Roques (1994), pp. 261–263; Lawrence (1983), p. 192. Cf. Rabello (1987) I, pp. 234–235.
313 Procopius, our only source, calls it a 'temple' but this is probably only an example of his classicizing vocabulary. Still, a 'temple' attributed to Solomon suggests something more than an ordinary synagogue and reminds us of the Jewish colony at Elephantine, or the Jewish temple at Leontopolis in Egypt, which was closed by the emperor Vespasian.
314 Cf. Holum (1982), pp. 67; 72, n. 19. Zeno excluded Samaritans from the army after the revolt of 484.
315 Mal. 15.8 (p. 382).
316 SH 11.24–30.
317 This excerpt is preserved in Constantine Porphyrogenitus' *De insidiis*. See Jeffreys, Jeffreys and Scott (1986), p. 260.
318 *Cod. Just.* I.5.17 (undated; however *Nov.* 129, pref., dates it to the aftermath of the revolt). For the revolt, see Schur (1989), pp. 87–89.
319 *Nov.* 129.
320 Theoph. A.M. 6048.
321 Cf. Schur (1989), p. 89; Rabello (1987) I, pp. 427–432.
322 *Nov.* 144, pref.
323 *Cod. Just.* I.5.
324 *Cod. Just.* I.11.
325 18.42 (p. 449).

326 Chitty (1966), pp. 132–138.
327 Mal. 18.136 (p. 491); cf. Michael Whitby (1991), p. 123, who points out that these may have been pagan pictures and statues that were city ornaments, now destroyed so that they might not seduce the imprudent. If so, the protobyzantine period was turning on its artistic heritage from the classical past.
328 Michael Whitby (1991), pp. 111–112; cf. Jones, *LRE*, p. 939.
329 Foss (1976), pp. 28–29; 116, source 21.
330 Cf. Nautin (1967), pp. 4–6; Fauber (1990), p. 3. The closure of the Isis temple dates between mid-535 and the end of 537, while Narses the eunuch was in command in Alexandria.
331 *Wars* 1.19.37; cf. Trombley (1985), p. 342. For the inscription, Nautin (1967), pp. 14–15.
332 Bury, *LRE* II, pp. 328–330.
333 Roques (1994), p. 263.
334 Michael Whitby (1991), p. 128.
335 *Cod. Just.* I.5.12.3; 16.2; cf. SH 11. See Thurman (1968), pp. 22–27; Jones, *LRE*, pp. 954–955.
336 *Nov.* 132 (544).
337 SH 11.23.
338 See Lieu (1992), pp. 210–215.

5 THE FINAL YEARS

1 *Aed.* does not mention the revolt. I think the omission was intentional, and does not show that the work was written before the revolt: cf. Averil Cameron (1985), pp. 14; 92.
2 Mal. 18.121 (p. 488); Theoph. A.M. 6048.
3 See *Nov.* 1, pref.; *Nov.* 28, pref.; cf. Stein, *Histoire* II, pp. 516–517.
4 Agathias 5.3.1–5.6; Downey (1955); cf. Vercleyen (1988), pp. 158–159.
5 SH 26.31–34; cf. *PLRE* IIIA s.v. 'Alexander 5', pp. 43–44.
6 See SH 24.15–23; cf. Agathias 5.15.2.
7 Agathias 5.19.1–12.
8 Mesarites 40.1–10 (Downey 1957).
9 Theoph. A.M. 6048.
10 Theoph. A.M. 6054; Lemerle (1954), pp. 286–287.
11 Barnish (1985), pp. 35–36; Jones (1974), p. 83. On the other hand, he may have been a musician attached to one of the factions: see *PLRE* IIIA, s.v. 'Ablabius 1', pp. 2–3.
12 See *PLRE* IIIB, s.v. 'Sergius 6', p. 1128.
13 Four of the conspirators were *argyropratai*, and the word can mean jeweller as well as banker: Bogaert (1973), p. 262.
14 I.22–32; cf. Theoph. A.M. 6055; Mal. 18.141 (pp. 493–495).
15 30,000 *nomismata* (*solidi*) p.a. = 416.6 gold pounds, which over 7 years = 2,916.6 pounds. At the end of seven years, the total for the next three years would fall due, and thereafter payment would be on a yearly basis: Men. Prot. frg. 6.1 (Blockley [1985] pp. 62–63); cf.

Diehl, *CMH* II, p. 30.
16 Diehl, *CMH* II, p. 51.
17 *Laud. Iust.* 2.361–387, cf. Averil Cameron (1976), pp. 176–177.
18 Mal. 18.137 (p. 492); cf. Macrides and Magdalino (1988), p. 72.
19 Cf. Diehl (1919), pp. 158–166.
20 Both SH 25.12 and Mal. 18.117 (p. 486) record attempts to debase the coinage.
21 *Anonymi Narratio* (ed. Preger), c. 27.
22 Cf. *Laud. Iust.* 4.283–284.
23 Men. Prot. frg. 6.1 (Blockley, pp. 203–211); cf. Stein, *Histoire* II, p. 518, n. 1; McNeill (1963), pp. 385–393; Lieu (1992), pp. 225–226.
24 Gordon (1959), pp. 24–26.
25 Muthesius (1993) pp. 28–29.
26 Cf. Shahid (1956), pp. 192–202; Smith (1954), p. 430. The Lakhmids continued to draw a Byzantine subsidy of 100 gold pounds a year: Trimingham (1979), p. 198.
27 Bivar (1972), pp. 286–287.
28 Mal. 18.125 (p. 489); Theoph. A.M. 6050; Lemerle (1954), p. 288; Browning (1987), pp. 160–162; cf. Hauptmann (1927–28), pp. 147–156; Bury, *LRE* II, pp. 314–316.
29 Cf. Corippus, *Ioh.* 8.465; cf. Moderan (1986). Coutsina had, in fact, been in rebellion in 534–535 and in 546, had been in temporary alliance with Antalas.
30 Theoph. A.M. 6055.
31 *Laud. Iust.* 2.265–266.
32 Theoph. A.M. 6056; cf. Browning (1987), p. 163; Mitchell (1993), pp. 117; 129. Yürme has recently been renamed Gümüşkonak.
33 Mal. 18.142 (p. 495).
34 On John, see Van den Ven (1965).
35 Stein, *Histoire* II, p. 629.
36 Averil Cameron (1975).
37 *Laud. Iust.* 3.230–401; cf. Hauptmann (1927–28), p. 150.
38 *Laud. Iust.* 1.18–21.
39 Cf. Averil Cameron (1976), p. 131.
40 This must have been the so-called 'Scythian' route (see J. I. Miller [1969], p. 122, map 2), which was now under Turkish control.
41 Turtledove (1983); Barker (1966), pp. 216–218; Gourbert (1951), pp. 65–67; Groh (1889), pp. 97–100.
42 On Sirmium, see Bavant (1984), pp. 250–264.
43 Hauptmann (1927–28), pp. 151–155.
44 Evag. 5.8–10.
45 John of Eph. *HE* 6.4; cf. Groh (1889), pp. 103–104.
46 *P. Cair. Masp.* II 67183; cf. MacCoull (1988), pp. 72–76.
47 Frend (1972b), pp. 316–323.
48 SH 19.7.
49 SH 30.21–24.
50 Marc. Com. *sub anno* 521.
51 *Nov.* 30.11.2.

52 Cf. Downey (1958b).
53 Michael Whitby (1991), pp. 121–122; Downey (1958a).
54 Cavallo (1978), pp. 235–236.
55 *Anth. Gr.* 4 (3b).
56 SH 30.34.

SOURCES

Aed. = Procopius, *Buildings*, ed. and trans. H. B. Dewing, with the collaboration of Glanville Downey. *LCL*. London/Cambridge, Mass., 1940.

Agathias = *Agathiae Myrinaei Historiarum Libri Quinque*, ed. R. Keydell. Berlin, 1976. (Trans. Joseph D. Frendo, Berlin, 1975).

Amm. Marc. = *Ammianus Marcellinus*, I–III, ed. J. C. Rolfe. *LCL*. London/Cambridge, Mass. 1935–1939.

AnthGr = *Anthologie Grecque*[2] ed. Pierre Waltz, I–IX. Paris, 1960–.

Cass. *Variae* = Cassiodorus, *Variae*, trans. S. J. B. Barnish. Translated Texts for Historians XII. Liverpool, 1992.

Chron. Pasch. = *Chronicon Paschale*, ed. L. Dindorf, 2 vols. Bonn, 1832. CSHB XVI–XVII. (Trans. Michael Whitby and Mary Whitby. Translated Texts for Historians VII. Liverpool, 1989).

CIC = Rudolfus Schoell, ed., *Corpus Iuris Civilis*[6]. 3 vols. Berlin, 1954.

Cos. Ind.= *Topographie chrétienne*, ed. and trans. Wanda Wolska-Conus. Paris, I (1968); II (1970); III (1973).

De Mag. = Ioannes Lydus, *On Powers*, or *The Magistracies of the Roman State*, ed. and trans. Anastasius C. Bandy. Philadelphia, 1983.

Evag. = Evagrius, *Ecclesiastical History*, ed. J. Bidez and L. Parmentier, London, 1898, repr. Amsterdam, 1964. (Trans. A.-J. Festugière: Évagre, *Histoire Ecclésiastique*, *Byzantion* 45 (1975), pp. 187–488.)

Get. = Jordanes, *Getica*, ed. T. Mommsen, MGH *AuctAnt* 5.1. (Trans. C. C. Mierow, *The Gothic History of Jordanes*[2]. Princeton, 1915, repr. New York, 1960.)

Hdt. = Herodoti, *Historiae*, ed. C. Hude. Oxford, 1927.

Hist. Pat. = *History of the Patriarchs of the Coptic Church of Alexandria* II (PO I).

Ioh. = Flavii Cresconii Corippi, *Iohannidos seu De Bellis Libycis*. Libri VIII. Cambridge, 1970.

Isidore = Isidori Episcopi Hispalensis, *Historia Gothorum Wandalorum Sueborum*, ed. T. Mommsen. MGH *AuctAnt* 11.2.

John of Eph. *HE* = John of Ephesus, *Historiae Ecclesiasticae Pars Tertia*, 2 vols. Paris, 1936, repr. Louvain, 1952. (Trans: (Latin): W. J. Van Douwen and J. P. N. Land, *Verhandelingen der Koninklijke Akademie van Wetenschappen, Afdeeling Letterkunde* XVIII. Amsterdam, 1889; (German): Dr J. M. Schonfelder, *Die Kirchengeschichte des Johannes von Ephesus*. Munich, 1962.)

John of Eph. *Lives* = John of Ephesus, *Lives of the Eastern Saints*, PO XVII (1923), pp. 1–307; XVIII (1924), pp. 513–698; XIX (1926), pp. 153–285.

John of Nikiu = John of Nikiu, *The Chronicle of John, (c. 690 AD) Coptic Bishop of Nikiu*, trans. Robert Henry Charles. London, 1916, repr. Amsterdam.

Josh. Styl. = *The Chronicle of Joshua the Stylite*, composed in Syriac, AD 507, with translation and notes by William Wright. Cambridge, 1882.

Laud. Iust. = Flavius Cresconius Corippus, *In laudem Iustini Augusti minoris*, ed. Averil Cameron. London, 1976.

LibPont. = *Liber Pontificalis*. MGH, *Gestarum Pontificum Romanorum*, I. Berlin, 1898.

Mal. = John Malalas, *Chronographia*, ed. L. Dindorf. Bonn, 1831. (Trans. Elizabeth Jeffreys, Michael Jeffreys and Roger Scott, with Brian Croke, Jenny Ferber, Simon Franklin, Alan James, Douglas Kelly, Ann Moffatt, Ann Nixon, *The Chronicle of John Malalas, Byzantina Australiensia* IV. Melbourne, 1986.)

Marc. Com. = Marcellinus Comes, *Chronicon*. MGH XI. *Auct.Ant., Chronica minora* II, ed. Theodore Mommsen, pp. 37–109.

Men. Prot. = *The History of Menander the Guardsman*, ed. and trans. Roger Blockley. Liverpool, 1985.

Mich. Syr. = Michael the Syrian, *Chronique de Michel le Syrien, 1166–1199*, ed. and trans. J.-B. Chabot, t. II.1. Paris, 1902.

Pausanias = Pausaniae, *Graeciae descripto*, ed. Maria Helena Rocha-Pereira. Leipzig, 1973–.

Romanos = Romanos le Mélode, *Hymnes*, ed. J. Grosdidier de Matons, I–V. Paris, 1964–81.

SH = Procopius, *The Anecdota or Secret History*, ed. and trans. H. B. Dewing. *LCL*. London/Cambridge, Mass., 1935.

Socrates, *Hist. Eccl.* = *The Ecclesiastical History of Socrates surnamed Scholasticus or the Advocate*, translated from the Greek. Bohn's Ecclesiastical Library. London, 1904.

Theoph. = Theophanes the Confessor, *Chronographia*, ed. C. de Boor. 2 vols. Leipzig, 1883–85, repr. Hildesheim, 1963.

Vict.Tun. = Victoris Tunnensis *episcopi, Chronica*, ed. Th. Mommsen. MGH *Auct. Ant.* II, Berlin, 1894.

Vict. Vit. = Victor of Vita, *Historia Persecutionis Africanae Provinciae sub Geiserico et Hunirico Regibus Wandalorum*, ed. C. Halm. MGH. *Auct. Ant.* III.1.

Vie de S. Sabas = Cyrille de Scythopolis, *Vie de Saint Sabas*, trans. A.-J. Festugière. *Les Moines d'Orient* III/2. Paris, 1961.

Vie de S. Syméon = *La Vie Ancienne de S. Syméon Stylite le Jeune* I–II, ed. and trans. Paul van den Ven. Brussels, 1962.

Vie de Théodore = *La Vie de Théodore de Sykéon* I–II, ed. and trans. A.-J. Festugière. *Subs. Hag.* 48. 1970.

Wars = Procopius of Caesarea, *History of the Wars*, ed. and trans. H. B. Dewing. I–V. *LCL*. London/Cambridge, Mass., 1914–28.

Zach. Myt. = Ps. Zachariah of Mytilene, *The Syriac Chronicle*, trans. F. J. Hamilton, D. D. and E. W. Brooks. London, 1899, repr. New York, 1979.

BIBLIOGRAPHY

Bibliographic abbreviations follow the practice of *The Oxford Dictionary of Byzantium*, with the following additions:

AHB = *Ancient History Bulletin*

CE = *The Coptic Encyclopedia*, ed. Aziz S. Atiya. New York, 1991, 8 vols.

Chron.d'Ég. = *Chronique d'Égypte*

D-F = Gibbon, Edward (1909), ed. J. B. Bury, *The Decline and Fall of the Roman Empire*, I–VII. London

D-S = Ch. Daremberg et Edm. Saglio, *Dictionnaire des antiquités grecques et romaines*. Paris, 1900, repr. Graz, 1963

IG = *Inscriptiones Graecae*

JE = *The Jewish Encyclopaedia*, ed. L. Adler. I. Singer *et al.* New York, 1901–6.

JJP = *Journal of Juristic Papyrology*

ODB = *Oxford Dictionary of Byzantium*

PasPres = *Past and Present*

PECS = *Princeton Encyclopaedia of Classical Sites*, ed. Richard Stillwell. Priceton, 1976.

PMasp = Jean Maspéro, *Papyrus grecs de l'époque byzantine*, in *Catalogue générale des antiquités égyptiennes du Musée du Caire* 3 vols. Cairo, 1911–16.

P. Oxy. = *The Oxyrhynchus Papyri* I. London 1898; repr. 1966

SMRH = *Studies in Medieval and Renaissance History*

Villes et peuplement = *Villes et peuplement dans l'Illyricum protobyzantin. Actes du colloque organisé par l'école française de Rome, 12–14 mai, 1982*. Rome, 1984

Adams, William Y. (1977), *Nubia, Corridor to Africa*. London.

—— (1991), 'The United Kingdom of Makouria and Nobadia. A Medieval Nubian Anomaly', in W. V. Davies, ed., *Egypt and Africa. Nubia from Prehistory to Islam*. London, pp. 257–263.

Adelson, Howard L. (1957), *Light Weight Solidi and Byzantine Trade during the Sixth and Seventh Centuries*. New York.

Adontz, N. (1970), *Armenia in the Period of Justinian. The Political Conditions based on the NAXARAR System*, trans. Nina G. Garsoian. Lisbon.

Adshead, K. (1990), 'Procopius' *Poliorcetica*: Continuities and Discontinuities', in Clarke (1990), pp. 93–119.

Ahrweiler, H. (1961), 'Fonctionnaires et bureaux maritimes à Byzance', *RÉB* 19, pp. 239–252.

Alexander, Paul (1967), *The Oracle of Baalbek: The Tiburtine Sibyl in Greek Dress*. Washington, D.C.

Alfoldy, Geza (1974), *Noricum*, trans. Anthony Birley. London.

—— (1985), *The Social History of Rome*, trans. David Braund and Frank Pollack. London/Sydney.

Allen, P. (1979), 'The "Justinianic" Plague', *Byzantion* 49, pp. 5–20.

Andreadès, A. (1934/37), 'The Jews in the Byzantine Empire', *Economic History* 3, pp. 1–23.

Archi, G. G., ed. (1978), *L'Imperatore Giustiniano. Storia e Mito*. Giornate di Studio a Ravenna, 14–16 Ottobre, 1976. Milan.

Arrignon, J.-P. and Duneau, J.-F. (1981), 'La Frontière chez deux auteurs byzantins: Procope de Césarée et Constantine VII Porphyrogénète', in Ahrweiler, H., ed., *Geographica Byzantina*. Serie Byzantina Sorbonensia 3. Paris.

Athanassiadi, Polymnia (1993), 'Persecution and Response in Late Paganism', *JHS* 113, pp. 1–29.

Aufhauser, J. B. (1959), 'Die sakrale Kaiseridee in Byzanz', *Numen* Suppl. 4 (8th International Congress for the History of Religions), pp. 531–542.

Avi-Yonah, M. (1958), 'The Economics of Byzantine Palestine', *IEJ* 8, pp. 39–51.

—— (1984), *The Jews under Roman and Byzantine Rule. A Political History of Palestine from the Bar Kokba War to the Arab Conquest*. Oxford, 1976, repr. Jerusalem.

Avigad, N. (1970), 'Excavations in the Jewish Quarter of the Old City of Jerusalem, 1970. (Second Preliminary Report)', *IEJ* 20, pp. 129–140.

—— (1993), 'The *Nea*: Justinian's Church of St. Mary, Mother of God, Discovered in the Old City of Jerusalem', in Tsafrir (1993a), pp. 128–135.

Bagnall, Roger S. (1993), *Egypt in Late Antiquity*. Princeton, N.J.

Bagnani, G. (1949), 'Divine Right and Roman Law', *Phoenix* 3, pp. 51–59.

Baker, Dom Aelred (1968), 'Syriac and the Origins of Monasticism', *Downside Review* 86, pp. 342–353.

Baldwin, Barry (1978a), 'Menander Protector', *DOP* 32, pp. 99–125.

—— (1978b), 'A Note on the Religious Sympathies of Circus Factions', *Byzantion* 48, pp. 275–276.

Bandy, Anastasius C. (1983), *Ioannes Lydus, On Powers*, or *The Magistracies of the Roman State*. Introduction, Critical Text, Translation, Commentary, and Indices. Philadelphia.

Barison, Paola (1938), 'Ricerche sui monasteri dell'Egitto bizantino ed arabo secondo documenti dei papiri greci', *Aegyptus* 18, pp. 29–148.

Bark, William (1944), 'Theodoric vs. Boethius: Vindication and Apology', *AHR* 49, pp. 410–426.

Barker, E. (1957), *Social and Political Thought in Byzantium from Justinian I to the last Palaeologos. Passages from Byzantine Writers and Documents*. Oxford.

Barker, John W. (1966), *Justinian and the Later Roman Empire*. Madison, Wisc.

Barnea, Ioan (1991), 'Sur les rapports avec Byzance du Territoire situé au Nord du Bas-Danube durant le période Anastase 1er–Justinien 1er', *Études Byzantines et Post-Byzantines* 2, pp. 47–57.

Barnes, T. D. (1984a), 'Constantine's Prohibition of Pagan Sacrifices', *AJPh* 105, pp. 68–72.

—— (1984b), 'The Constantinian Reformation', *The Crake Lectures, 1984*. Sackville, New Brunswick, pp. 39–57.

Barnish, S. J. B. (1985), 'The Wealth of Julius Argentarius: Late Antique Banking and the Mediterranean Economy', *Byzantion* 55, pp. 5–38.

—— (1986), 'Taxation, Land and Barbarian Settlements in the Western Empire', *BSR* 54, pp. 170–195.

—— (1987), 'Pigs, Plebeians and *Potentes*: Rome's Economic Hinterland', *BSR* 55, pp. 157–185.

—— (1988), 'Transformation and Survival in the Western Senatorial Aristocracy, c. AD 400–700', *BSR* 56, pp. 120–155.

—— (1989), 'The Transformation of Classical Cities and the Pirenne Debate', *JRA* 2, pp. 385–400.

Barnwell, P. S. (1992), *Emperors, Prefects and Kings. The Roman West, 395–565*. Chapel Hill.

Bassett, S. G. (1991), 'The Antiquities of the Hippodrome in Constantinople', *DOP* 45, pp. 87–96.

Bavant, Bernard (1984), 'La Ville dans la Nord de l'Illyricum (Pannonie, Mésie I, Dacie et Dardanie)', in *Villes et peuplement*, pp. 245–288.

Baynes, N. H. and Moss, H. St.L. B. (1948), *Byzantium. An Introduction to East Roman Civilization*. Oxford.

—— (1955), 'Eusebius and the Christian Empire', *Annuaire de l'Institut de Philologie et d'Histoire Orientale* 2 (1933–34), 13–18, repr. *Byzantine Studies and Other Essays*. Oxford.

Beck, H.-G. (1965), 'Konstantinopel', *BZ* 58, pp. 115–139.

Behr, C. A. (1974), 'A New Fragment of Cicero's *De Republica*', *AJPh* 95, pp. 141–149.

Besevliev, Veselin (1980), 'Bulgaren als Söldner in der italienischen Kriegen Justinians I' *JÖB* 29, pp. 21–26.

Beskow, Per (1988), 'The Theodosian Laws against Manichaeism', in *Manichaean Studies*, ed. Peter Bryden (Lund Studies in African and Asian Religions, I). Lund, pp. 1–11.

Bivar, A. D. V. (1972), 'Cavalry Equipment and Tactics on the Euphrates Frontier', *DOP* 39, pp. 271–291.

Blockley, R. C. (1980), 'Doctors as Diplomats in the Sixth Century AD', *Florilegium* 2, pp. 89–100.

—— (1985), *Rome and Persia. International Relations in Late Antiquity*. The 1985 Davidson Dunton Lecture. Ottawa.

Bluhme, F. (1820), 'Die Ordnung der Fragmente in den Pandektentiteln', *Zeitschrift für geschichtliche Rechtswissenschaft* 4, pp. 257–472; repr. *Labeo* 6 (1960) pp. 50–96; 235–277; 368–404.

Blumenthal, H. (1978), '529 and After: What Happened to the Academy?' *Byzantion* 48, pp. 369–85.

—— (1993), 'Alexandria as a Centre of Greek Philosophy in Later Classical Antiquity', *ICS* 18, pp. 307–325.

Boak, A. E. R. (1919), 'Imperial Coronation Ceremonies of the Fifth and Sixth Centuries', *HSCP* 30, pp. 37–47.

—— (1928/29), 'The Book of the Prefect', *Journal of Economic and Business History* 1, pp. 597–619.

Bogaert, Raymond (1973), 'Changeurs et banquiers chez les pères de l'Église', *Ancient Society* 4, pp. 239–270.

Bonini, Roberto (1977), *Introduzione allo studio dell'età Giustineanea.* Bologna.

Boojamra, John L. (1975), 'Christian *Philanthropia*. A Study of Justinian's Welfare Policy and the Church', *Vyzantina* (Thessaloniki) 7, pp. 347–373.

Bowersock, G. W. (1976), '*Limes Arabicus*', *HStClPhil* 80, pp. 210–229.

Bowman, Alan K. (1978), 'The Military Occupation of Upper Egypt in the Reign of Diocletian', *BASP* 15, pp. 25–38.

Bratton, Timothy L. (1981), 'The Identity of the Plague of Justinian', *Transactions and Studies of the College of Physicians of Philadelphia* Ser. 5, 3, pp. 113–124; 174–180.

Breen, Quirinus (1944–45), 'The Twelfth-Century Revival of Roman Law', *Oregon Law Review* 24, pp. 244–287.

Brock, Sebastian (1973), 'Early Syrian Asceticism', *Numen* 20, pp. 1–19.

—— (1981), 'The Conversations with the Syrian Orthodox under Justinian', *OrChrP* 47, pp. 87–121.

—— and Harvey, Susan Ashbrook (1987), *Holy Women of the Syrian Orient.* Berkeley.

Brown, Peter (1967), 'The Later Roman Empire', *Economic History Review*, Ser. 2, 20, pp. 327–343.

—— (1969), 'The Diffusion of Manichaeism in the Roman Empire', *JRS* 59, pp. 92–103.

—— (1987), 'Late Antiquity', in Paul Veyne, ed., *A History of Private Life* I. Cambridge, Mass., pp. 235–311.

Brown, T. S. (1984), *Gentlemen and Officers. Imperial Administration and Aristocratic Power in Byzantine Italy AD 554–800.* Rome.

—— (1988), 'The Interplay between Roman and Byzantine Traditions and Local Sentiment in the Exarchate of Ravenna', *Settimane di Studio del Centro Italiano di Studi del Centro Italiano sull'alto Mediaevo* 36, pp. 127–160.

Browning, Robert (1975a), *Byzantium and Bulgaria.* London.

—— (1975b), *The Emperor Julian.* London.

—— (1987), *Justinian and Theodora².* London.

Buckland, W. W. (1963), *A Text-book of Roman Law from Augustus to Justinian³*, revised by Peter Stein. Cambridge.

Burns, Thomas S. (1980), *The Ostrogoths. Kingship and Society. Historia* Einzelschrift 36. Wiesbaden.

Bury, J. B. (1897), 'The Nika Riot', *JHS* 17, pp. 92–119.

—— (1910), *The Constitution of the Later Roman Empire.* Cambridge.

Cameron, Alan (1969), 'The Last Days of the Academy at Athens', *PCPhS* 195 (n.s. 15), pp. 7–29.

—— (1973), *Porphyrius the Charioteer.* Oxford.

—— (1974a), 'Demes and Factions', *BZ* 76, pp. 74–91.
—— (1974b), 'Heresies and Factions', *Byzantion* 44, pp. 92–120.
—— (1976a), *Circus Factions. Blues and Greens at Rome and Byzantium.* Oxford.
—— (1976b), 'Theodorus *triseparchos*', *GRBS* 17, pp. 269–286.
—— (1978), 'The House of Anastasius', *GRBS* 19, pp. 259–276.
—— (1983), Review of Z. Borkowski, *Alexandrie II. Inscriptions des factions à Alexandrie*, *BASP* 20, pp. 75–84.
—— and Schauer, Diane (1982), 'The Last Consul: Basilius and his Diptych', *JRS* 72, pp. 126–143.
Cameron, Averil (1970), *Agathias.* Oxford.
—— (1975), 'The Empress Sophia', *Byzantion* 45, pp. 5–21.
—— (1977), 'Early Byzantine *Kaiserkritik*: Two Case Histories', *BMGS* 3, pp. 1–17.
—— (1979) 'Images of Authority: Elites and Icons in Late Sixth-Century Byzantium', *PasPres* 84, pp. 3–35, repr. in Mullet and Scott (1981), pp. 205–234.
—— (1982), 'Byzantine Africa – The Literary Evidence', in J. H. Humphrey, ed., *Excavations at Carthage 1978 Conducted by the University of Michigan*, VII. Ann Arbor, Mich., pp. 29–62.
—— (1983a), 'Constantinus Christianus', *JRS* 73, pp. 184–190.
—— (1983b), 'Eusebius of Caesarea and the Rethinking of History', in E. Gabba, ed., *Tria Corda. Scritti in onore di Arnaldo Momigliano.* Como, pp. 71–88.
—— (1983c), 'The History of the Image of Edessa: The Telling of a Story', in Mango and Pritsak (1983), pp. 80–94.
—— (1984) '"Sports fans" of Rome and Byzantium', *LCM* 9.4, pp. 50–51.
—— (1985), *Procopius and the Sixth Century.* Berkeley.
—— (1986), 'History as Text: Coping with Procopius', in Christopher Holdsworth and T. P. Wiseman, eds, *The Inheritance of Historiography, 350–900.* Exeter, pp. 53–66.
—— (1988), 'Eustratius' *Life* of the Patriarch Eutychius and the Fifth Ecumenical Council', *KATHEGETRIA. Essays presented to Joan Hussey on her 80th Birthday.* Camberly, pp. 225–247.
—— (1989) 'Gelimer's Laughter: The Case of Byzantine Africa', in Clover and Humphreys (1989), pp. 171–190.
—— (1993), *The Mediterranean World in Late Antiquity.* London.
—— and Herrin, Judith, eds and trans. (1984), *Constantinople in the Early Eighth Century: The 'Parataseis Syntomoi Chronikai'.* Leiden.
Carile, Antonio (1978), 'Consenso e dissenso fra propaganda e fronda nelle fonti narrative dell'età Giustinianea', in Archi (1978), pp. 39–93.
Carney, T. F. (1971), *Bureaucracy in Traditional Society. Roman and Byzantine Bureaucracies Viewed from Within.* 3 vols. Lawrence, Kan.
Casson, Lionel (1982), 'Belisarius' Expedition against Carthage', in J. H. Humphrey, ed., *Excavations at Carthage, 1978, Conducted by the University of Michigan*, VII. Ann Arbor, Mich., pp. 23–28.
Castrén, Paavo, ed. (1994), *Post-Herulian Athens. Aspects of Life and Culture in Athens AD 267–529.* Helsinki.
Cavallo, Guglielmo (1978), 'La circolazione libraria nell'età di Giustiniano', in Archi (1978), pp. 203–236.

Charanis, Peter (1939), *Church and State in the Later Roman Empire. The Religious Policy of Anastasius the First, 491–518*. Madison, Wis.

—— (1940–41), 'Coronation and its Constitutional Significance in the Later Roman Empire', *Byzantion* 15, pp. 49–66.

—— (1966), 'Observations on the Demography of the Byzantine Empire', *CEB 13: Major Papers*. Oxford, pp. 1–19.

Charlesworth, M. P. (1937), 'The Virtues of a Roman Emperor: Propaganda and the Creation of Belief', *ProcBrAc 23*, pp. 105–133.

Charlton, William, trans. (1991), *Philoponus: 'On Aristotle on the Intellect (de Anima 3.4–8)'*. Ithaca.

Chen, Doron (1987), 'The Ancient Synagogues at Nabratein: Design and Chronology', *PEQ* 109, pp. 44–49.

Cherf, W. J. (1992), 'Carbon-14 Chronology for the Late-Roman Fortifications of the Thermopylai Frontier', *JRA* 5, pp. 261–264.

Chitty, Derwas J. (1966), *The Desert a City*. Oxford.

Christensen, Arthur (1944), *L'Iran sous les Sassanides²*. Copenhagen.

Christie, N. and Rushworth, A. (1988), 'Urban Fortification and Defensive Strategy in Fifth and Sixth Century Italy: The Case of Terracina', *JRA* 1, pp. 73–87.

—— (1990), 'Byzantine Liguria; An Imperial Province against the Longobards, AD 568–643', *BSR* 58, pp. 229–271.

Chrysos, Evangelos K. (1978), 'The Title *Basileus* in Early Byzantine International Relations', *DOP* 32, pp. 29–75.

Chuvin, Pierre (1990), *A Chronicle of the Last Pagans*, trans. B. A. Archer. Cambridge, Mass.

Clarke, Graeme, ed. (1990), with Brian Croke, Alanna Emmett Nobbs and Raoul Mortley, *Reading the Past in Late Antiquity*. Canberra.

Claude, Dietrich (1969), *Die byzantinische Stadt im 6. Jahrhundert*. Munich.

Clover, Frank M. (1982), 'Carthage and the Vandals', in J. H. Humphrey, ed., *Excavations at Carthage 1978, Conducted by the University of Michigan*, VII. Ann Arbor, Mich., pp. 1–22.

—— and Humphreys, R. S., eds (1989), *Tradition and Innovation in Late Antiquity*. Madison.

Cohen, Jeremy (1976), 'Roman Imperial Policy towards the Jews from Constantine until the End of the Palestinian Patriarchate (ca. 429)', *BS/EB* 3/1, pp. 1–29.

Coleman-Norton, P. R. (1966), *Roman State and Christian Church. A Collection of Legal Documents to AD 535*. 3 vols. London.

Conrad, Lawrence (1986), 'The Plague in Bilad al-Sham in Pre-Islamic Times', *The IVth International Conference on Bilad al-Sham (1983)*, Amman, pp. 143–163.

Constantelos, Demetrios J. (1964–65), 'Paganism and the State in the Age of Justinian', *Catholic Historical Review* 50, pp. 372–380.

Cormack, Robin (1981a), 'The Classical Tradition and the Byzantine Provincial City: the Evidence of Thessalonike and Aphrodisias', in Mullett and Scott (1981), pp. 103–119.

—— (1981b), 'Interpreting the Mosaics of S. Sophia at Istanbul', *Art History* 4, pp. 131–149.

Cracco Ruggini, Lellia (1971), *Le associazioni professionali nel mondo Romano-Bizantino.* Spoleto.

Cranz, F. Edward (1952), 'Kingdom and Polity in Eusebius of Caesarea', *HThR* 45, pp. 47–66.

Croke, Brian (1980), 'Justinian's Bulgar Victory Celebration', *Byzantinoslavica* 41, pp. 188–195.

—— (1981), 'Two Early Byzantine Earthquakes and their Liturgical Commemoration', *Byzantion* 51, pp. 122–147.

—— (1982a), 'The Date of the "Anastasian Long Walls" in Thrace', *GRBS* 23, pp. 59–78.

—— (1982b), 'Mundo the Gepid: From Freebooter to Roman General', *Chiron* 12, pp. 125–135.

—— (1990), 'City Chronicles of Late Antiquity', in Clarke (1990), pp. 165–203.

—— and Crow, James (1983), 'Procopius and Dara', *JRS* 73, pp. 143–159.

Cront, Gheorghe (1982), 'La Repression de l'homme au Bas-Empire pendant le règne de Justinien 1er (527–565)', *Byzantiaka* 2, pp. 37–51.

Crow, J. (1981), 'Dara: A Late Roman Fortress in Mesopotamia', *Yayla* 4, pp. 12–20.

—— (1995), 'The Long Walls of Thrace', in Mango and Dagron (1995), pp. 109–124.

Cutler, A. (1984), 'The Making of the Justinian Diptychs', *Byzantion* 54, pp. 75–115.

Dagron, Gilbert (1970), 'Les Moines et la Ville. Le Monachisme à Constantinople jusqu'au concile de Chalcédoine (451)', *Travaux et Mémoires* 4, pp. 229–276.

—— (1974), *Naissance d'une capitale. Constantinople et ses institutions de 330 à 451.* Paris.

—— (1979), 'Entre village et cité: la bourgade rurale des IV–VII siècles en Orient', *Koinonia* 3, pp. 29–52.

Daube, David (1967), 'The Marriage of Justinian and Theodora. Logical and Theological Reflections', *The Catholic University of America Law Review* 16, pp. 380–399.

Davis, Natalie Zemon (1975), *Society and Culture in Early Modern France.* Stanford.

De Laet, Siegfried J. (1949), *Portorium. Étude sur l'organisation douanière chez les Romains surtout à l'époque du Haut-Empire.* Bruges.

De Ste Croix, G. E. M. (1981), *The Class Struggle in the Ancient Greek World, from the Archaic Age to the Arab Conquests.* London/Ithaca, N.Y.

De'Maffei, Fernanda (1986), 'Fortificazione di Giustiniano sul limes orientale: monumenti e fonti', *CEB* 17: *Major Papers.* New Rochelle, N.Y., pp. 237–263.

—— (1988), *Edifici di Giustiniano nell'ambito dell'Impero.* Spoleto.

Diehl, Charles (1896), *L'Afrique byzantine. Histoire de la domination byzantine en Afrique (533–709).* Paris.

—— (1901), *Justinien et la civilisation byzantine au VIe siècle.* 2 vols. Paris.

—— (1904), *Theodora, impératrice de Byzance.* Paris.

—— (1919), 'Une crise monétaire au VIe siècle', *REGr* 32, pp. 156–166.

Donner, Fred M. (1989), 'The Role of Nomads in the Near East in Late

Antiquity (400–800 CE)', in Clover and Humphreys (1989), pp. 73–85.

Downey, Glanville (1939), 'Procopius on Antioch', *Byzantion* 14, pp. 361–378.

—— (1950), 'Justinian as Builder', *ArtB* 32, pp. 262–266.

—— (1953), 'The Persian Campaign in Syria in AD 540', *Speculum* 28, pp. 340–348.

—— (1955), 'Earthquakes at Constantinople and Vicinity, 342–1454', *Speculum* 30, pp. 596–600.

—— (1957), 'Education in the Christian Roman Empire: Christian and Pagan Theories under Constantine and his Successors', *Speculum* 32, pp. 48–61.

—— (1958a), 'The Christian Schools in Palestine: A Chapter in Literary History', *Harvard Library Bulletin* 12, pp. 297–319.

—— (1958b), 'Justinian's View of Christianity and the Greek Classics', *Anglican Theological Review* 40, pp. 13–22.

—— (1960), *Constantinople in the Age of Justinian*. Norman, Okla.

—— (1961), *A History of Antioch in Syria from Seleucus to the Arab Conquest*. Princeton.

—— (1963), *Gaza in the Sixth Century*. Norman, Okla.

—— (1968), *Justinian and the Imperial Office. Lectures in Memory of Louise Taft Semple*. Cincinnati.

Duncan-Jones, R. P. (1977–78), 'Aqueduct Capacity and City Population', *Ninth Annual Report, Society for Libyan Studies*, p. 51.

Durliat, Jean (1990), *De la ville antique à la ville byzantine. Le Problème des subsistances*. Collection de l'École française de Rome 136. Rome.

—— (1995), 'L'Approvisionnement de Constantinople', in Mango and Dagron (1995), pp. 19–33.

Dvornik, Francis (1966), *Early Christian and Byzantine Political Philosophy: Origin and Background* I–II. Washington, D.C.

Eitrem, S. (1942), 'La Théurgie chez les neoplatoniciennes et dans les papyrus magiques', *Symbolae Osloenses* 22, pp. 49–79.

Emerson, William and Van Nice, Robert L. (1951a), 'Hagia Sophia. The Collapse of the First Dome', *Archaeology* 4/2, pp. 94–103.

—— (1951b), 'Hagia Sophia: The Construction of the Second Dome and its Later Repairs', *Archaeology* 4/3, pp. 162–171.

Epstein, Ann Wharton (1982), 'The Rebuilding and Redecoration of the Holy Apostles in Constantinople: A Reconsideration', *GRBS* 23, pp. 79–92.

Errington, R. Malcolm (1988) 'Constantine and the Pagans', *GRBS* 29, pp. 309–318.

Evans, J. A. S. (1968), 'Procopius and the Emperor Justinian', *The Canadian Historical Association: Historical Papers*, pp. 126–39.

—— (1972), *Procopius*. New York.

—— (1973), 'The Shadow of Edward Gibbon', in Paul Fritz and David Williams, eds, *City and Society in the Eighteenth Century*. Toronto, pp. 247–257.

—— (1977), 'The Walls of Thessalonica', *Byzantion* 47, pp. 361–362.

—— (1984) 'The "Nika" Rebellion and the Empress Theodora', *Byzantion* 54, pp. 380–382.

Evans, Stanley G. (1960), *A Short History of Bulgaria*. London.
Every, George (1979), 'Was Vigilius a Victim or an Ally of Justinian?', *Heythrop Journal* 20, pp. 257–266.
Fauber, Lawrence (1990), *Narses, Hammer of the Goths. The Life and Times of Narses the Eunuch*. New York.
Fisher, Elizabeth A. (1978), 'Theodora and Antonina in the *Historia Arcana*: Fact and/or Fiction?' *Arethusa* 11, pp. 253–279.
Fitton, James (1976), 'The Death of Theodora', *Byzantion* 46, p. 119.
Forbes, Clarence Allan (1933), *NEOI. A Contribution to the Study of Greek Associations*. APA Philological Monographs II. Middletown, CT.
Forsyth, George H. (1968), 'The Monastery of St. Catherine at Mt Sinai: The Church and Fortress of Justinian', *DOP* 22, pp. 1–19.
Foss, Clive (1972), 'Byzantine Cities of Western Asia Minor'. Diss. Harvard University.
—— (1976), *Byzantine and Turkish Sardis*. Cambridge/London.
—— (1977a), 'Archaeology and the "Twenty Cities" of Byzantine Asia', *AJA* 81, pp. 469–486.
—— (1977b), 'Late Antique and Byzantine Ankara', *DOP* 31, pp. 27–87.
—— (1979), *Ephesus after Antiquity: A Late Antique, Byzantine and Turkish City*. Cambridge.
—— (1991), 'Cities and Villages of Lycia in the Life of Saint Nicholas of Zion', *GOrThR* 36, pp. 303–339.
Fotiou, A. (1978), 'Byzantine Circus Factions and their Riots', *JÖB* 27, pp. 1–10.
—— (1981), 'Dicearchus and the Mixed Constitution in Sixth-Century Byzantium', *Byzantion* 51, pp. 533–547.
—— (1985), 'Plato's Philosopher King in the Political Thought of Sixth-Century Byzantium', *Florilegium* 7, pp. 17–29.
—— (1988), 'Recruitment Shortages in the VIth Century', *Byzantion* 58, pp. 65–77.
Fowden, Garth (1988), 'City and Countryside in Late Roman Athens', *JHS* 108, pp. 48–59.
—— (1990), 'Religious Developments in Late Roman Lycia. Topographical Preliminaries', *Poikila* (*Meletemata* 10), pp. 343–370.
—— (1991), 'Constantine's Porphyry Column: The Earliest Literary Allusion', *JRS* 81, pp. 119–131.
—— (1993), *Empire to Commonwealth. Consequences of Monotheism in Late Antiquity*. Princeton.
Frantz, Alison (1965), 'From Paganism to Christianity in the Temples of Athens', *DOP* 19, pp. 185–205.
—— (1988), *The Athenian Agora XXIV. Late Antiquity AD 67–700*. Princeton, N.J.
Freeman, Philip, and Kennedy, David, eds (1986), *The Defence of the Roman and Byzantine East. Proceedings of a Colloquium held at the University of Sheffield in April, 1986*. BAR Int.Ser. 297. Oxford.
Frend, W. H. C. (1972a), 'The Monks and the Survival of the East Roman Empire in the Fifth Century', *PasPres* 54, p. 3–24.
—— (1972b), *The Rise of the Monophysite Movement. Chapters in the History of the Church in the Fifth and Sixth Centuries*. Cambridge.

—— (1978), 'The Christian Period in Mediterranean Africa, ca. 200–700', *CHAfr* II, pp. 410–489.

—— (1984a), 'A Note on Religion and Life in a Numidian Village in the Later Roman Empire', *Bulletin archéologique du Comité des travaux historiques et scientifiques* n.s. 17B, pp. 261–171. (*106ᵉ Congrès national des sociétés savantes de France*, Rousillon, 1982.)

—— (1984b), *The Rise of Christianity*. Philadelphia.

Frye, Richard N. (1972), 'Byzantine and Sasanian Trade Relations with Northeastern Russia', *DOP* 26, pp. 263–269.

—— (1984), *The History of Ancient Iran*. Munich.

Fulford, M. G. (1980), 'Carthage: Overseas Trade and Political Economy, ca. AD 400–700', *Reading Medieval Studies* 6, pp. 68–80.

—— (1987), 'Economic Interdependence Among Urban Communities of the Roman Mediterranean', *World Archaeology* 19/1, pp. 58–75.

—— and Peacock, D. P. S. (1984), *Excavations at Carthage: The British Mission* I, 2. Sheffield.

Gascou, J. (1976), 'Les Institutions de l'hippodrome en Égypte byzantine', *BIFAO* 76, pp. 185–212.

Geanakoplos, Deno J. 1966a), *Byzantine East and Latin West: Two Worlds of Christendom in the Middle Ages and Renaissance*. Oxford.

—— (1966b), 'Church Building and "Caesaropapism": AD 312–565', *GRBS* 7, pp. 167–186.

—— (1984), *Byzantium. Church, Society and Civilization Seen Through Contemporary Eyes*. Chicago.

Geffcken, Johannes (1978), *The Last Days of Greco-Roman Paganism*, trans. Sabine MacCormack. Europe in the Middle Ages Series VIII. Amsterdam/New York/Oxford.

George, Walter (1912), *The Church of Saint Eirene at Constantinople*. Oxford.

Geremek, Hanna (1990), 'Sur la question des *boulai* dans les villes égyptiennes aux Vᵉ–VIIᵉ siècles', *JJP* 20, pp. 47–54.

Gerostergios, Asterios N. (1974), 'The Religious Policy of Justinian I and his Religious Beliefs'. Diss. Boston School of Theology.

Gilles, Pierre (1988), *The Antiquities of Constantinople²*, trans. John Ball. Introd. Ronald G. Musto. New York. (First published in 1729.)

Glucker, Carol A. M. (1987), *The City of Gaza in the Roman and Byzantine Periods*. BAR Int. Ser. 325. Oxford.

Goffart, Walter (1980), *Barbarians and Romans, AD 418–584*. Princeton, N. J.

Goldenberg, Robert (1979), 'The Jewish Sabbath in the Roman World up to the Time of Constantine the Great', *ANRW* II.19.1, pp. 414–447.

Goodchild, R. G. (1951), 'Boreum of Cyrenaica', *JRS* 41, pp. 11–16.

—— and Ward Perkins, J. B. (1953), 'The Roman and Byzantine Defences of Lepcis Magna', *BSR* 21, pp. 42–73.

Gordon, C. D. (1959), 'Procopius and Justinian's Financial Policies', *Phoenix* 13, pp. 23–30.

Goubert, Paul (1951), *Byzance avant l'Islam* I. Paris.

Grabar, André (1967), *The Golden Age of Justinian, from the Death of Theodosius to the Rise of Islam*. New York.

Gray, E. W. (1973), 'The Roman Eastern *Limes* from Constantine to Justinian', *Proceedings of the African Classical Association* 12, pp. 24–40.

Gray, Patrick T. R. (1979), *The Defense of Chalcedon in the East (451–553)*. Leiden.

—— (1988), 'Forgery as an Instrument of Progress: Reconstructing the Theological Tradition in the Sixth Century', *BZ* 81, pp. 284–289.

—— (1993), 'Palestine and Justinian's Legislation on Non-Christian Religions', in Halpern and Hobson (1993), pp. 241–270.

Greatrex, Geoffrey (1994), 'The Dates of Procopius' Works', *BMGS* 18, pp. 101–114.

—— (1995), 'The Composition of Procopius' *Persian Wars* and John the Cappadocian', *Prudentia* 27, pp. 1–13.

Gregory, Timothy (1982a), 'The Fortified Cities of Byzantine Greece', *Archaeology* 35, pp. 14–21.

—— (1982b), 'Fortification and Urban Design in Early Byzantine Greece', in Hohlfelder (1982), pp. 43–64.

—— (1986), 'The Survival of Paganism in Christian Greece: A Critical Survey', *AJPh* 107, pp. 224–242.

—— (1993), *Isthmia V: The Hexamilion and the Fortress*. Princeton, N.J.

Groh, Dennis E. (1988), 'Jews and Christians in Late Roman Palestine: Towards a New Chronology', *Biblical Archaeologist* 51, pp. 80–96.

Groh, Kurt (1889), *Geschichte des oströmischen Kaisers Justin II*. Leipzig, repr. Aalen 1985.

Guilland, R. (1948), 'The Hippodrome at Byzantium', *Speculum* 33, pp. 676–682.

—— (1980), 'Études sur l'histoire administrative de l'empire byzantin – L'Éparque', *BS* 41, pp. 17–32.

Gurevich, Aron Ja. (1982), 'On Heroes, Things, Gods and Laughter in Germanic Poetry', *SMRH*, n.s. 5, pp. 105–172.

Gutwein, Kenneth C. (1981), *Third Palestine. A Regional Study of Byzantine Urbanization*. Washington, D.C.

Hachlili, Rachel (1989), 'The State of Ancient Synagogue Research', in Hachlili, Rachel, ed., *Ancient Synagogues in Israel, Third–Seventh Century C.E.. BAR* Int. Ser. 499. Oxford, pp. 1–6.

Hackel, S., ed. (1981), *The Byzantine Saint*. Sobornost Suppl. 5. London.

Hahn, Wolfgang and Metcalf, William E., eds (1988), *Studies in Early Byzantine Gold Coinage*. Numismatic Studies XVII. New York.

Haldon, John F. (1979), *Recruitment and Conscription in the Byzantine Army, c. 550–950. A Study in the Origins of the Stratiotika Ktemata*. Österreichische Akademie der Wissenschaften, Phil-Hist. Klasse. Sitzungsberichte 357. Band. Vienna.

Hällström, Gunnar af (1994), 'The Closing of the Neoplatonic School in AD 529: An Additional Aspect', in Castrén (1994), pp. 141–160.

Halpern, Baruch and Hobson, Deborah H., eds (1993), *Law, Politics and Society in the Ancient Mediterranean World*. Sheffield.

Hannestad, Knud (1960), 'Les Forces militaires d'après la guerre gothique de Procope', *ClassMed* 21, pp. 136–183.

Hanton, E. (1927–28), 'Lexique explicatif du recueil des inscriptions grecques chrétiennes d'Asie Mineure', *Byzantion* 4, pp. 53–136.

Hardy, Edward R. (1968), 'The Egyptian Policy of Justinian', *DOP* 22, pp. 21–41.

Harrison, R. M. (1983), 'The Church of St. Polyeuktos in Istanbul and the Temple of Solomon', in Mango and Pritsak (1983), pp. 276–279.

—— (1986), *Excavations at Saraçhane in Istanbul* I. *The Excavations, Small Finds, Coins, Bones and Molluscs.* Princeton.

—— (1989), *A Temple for Byzantium.* London.

Hart, Liddell (1941), *The Way to Win Wars. The Strategy of Indirect Approach.* London.

Harvey, Susan Ashbrook (1980), 'Asceticism in Adversity: An Early Byzantine Experience', *BMGS* 6, pp. 1–11.

—— (1981) 'The Politicization of the Byzantine Saint', in Hackel (1981), pp. 37–42.

—— (1988), 'Remembering Pain: Syriac Historiography and the Separation of the Churches', *Byzantion* 58, pp. 295–308.

—— (1990), *Asceticism and Society in Crisis. John of Ephesus and 'The Lives of the Eastern Saints'.* Berkeley.

Hauptmann, L. (1927–28), 'Les Rapports des Byzantins avec les Slaves et les Avares pendant la seconde moitié du VIᵉ siècle', *Byzantion* 4, pp. 137–170.

Haussig, H. W. (1971), *A History of Byzantine Civilization*, trans. J. M. Hussey. London.

Hendy, Michael F. (1985), *Studies in the Byzantine Monetary Economy, c. 300–1450.* Cambridge.

Henry III, Patrick (1967), 'A Mirror for Justinian. The *Ekthesis* of Apapetus Diaconus', *GRBS* 8, pp. 281–308.

Herrin, Judith (1987), *The Formation of Christendom.* Oxford.

—— (1991), 'Byzance: le palais et la ville', *Byzantion* 61, pp. 213–230.

Hillgarth, J. N. (1966), 'Goths and Chronicles: Propaganda in Sixth-Century Spain and the Byzantine Background', *Historia* 15, pp. 483–508.

Hitchner, R. Bruce (1990), 'The Kasserine Archaeological Survey – 1987', *AntAfr* 26, pp. 231–260.

Hitti, Philip K. (1956), *History of the Arabs from the Earliest Times to the Present.*⁶ London.

Hobson, Deborah (1993), 'The Impact of Law on Village Life in Roman Egypt', in Halpern and Hobson (1993), pp. 193–217.

Hodgkin, Thomas (1880–89), *Italy and Her Invaders*, III–IV, repr. New York, 1967.

Hohlfelder, Robert (1977), 'Trans-Isthmian Walls in the Age of Justinian', 18, *GRBS*, pp. 173–179.

—— ed. (1982), *City, Town and Countryside in the Early Byzantine Era.* New York.

Holmes, William Gordon (1912), *The Age of Justinian and Theodora*², I–II. London.

Holum, Kenneth G. (1982), 'Caesarea and the Samaritans', in Hohlfelder (1982), pp. 65–73.

Honigmann, Ernest (1950), 'Juvenal of Jerusalem', *DOP* 5, pp. 209–279.

Honoré, A. M. (1971), *Justinian's Digest. Work in Progress.* Inaugural Lecture, University of Oxford. Oxford.

—— (1978), *Tribonian*. London/Ithaca.

—— and Rodger, Alan (1970), 'How the Digest Commissioners Worked', *ZSavRom* 87, pp. 246–313.

Hopkins, M. K. (1963), 'Eunuchs in Politics in the Later Roman Empire', *PCPhS* 189, n.s. 9, pp. 62–80.

Humphrey, John C. (1986), *Roman Circuses. Arenas for Chariot Racing.* Berkeley/Los Angeles.

Humphrey, John H. (1980), 'Vandal and Byzantine Carthage: Some New Archaeological Evidence', in John Griffiths Pedley, ed., *New Light on Ancient Carthage*. Ann Arbor.

Hunger, H. (1965), 'Kaiser Justinian I (527–565)', *Anzeiger der Österreichen Akademie der Wissenschaften*, Phil.-Hist. Klasse 102, pp. 339–356.

—— (1986), 'Der Kaiserpalast zu Konstantinopel. Seine Funktionen in der byzantinischen Aussen- und Innenpolitik', *JÖB* 36, pp. 1–11.

Hussey, J. M. (1986), *The Orthodox Church in the Byzantine Empire.* Oxford.

Irmscher, Johannes (1981), 'Paganismus im Justinianischen Reich', *Klio* 63, pp. 683–688.

Isaac, Benjamin (1986), *The Greek Settlements in Thrace until the Macedonian Conquest.* Leiden.

—— (1988), 'The Meaning of the Terms *Limes* and *Limitanei*', *JRS* 78, pp. 125–147.

—— (1992), *The Limits of Empire. The Roman Army in the East*². Oxford.

Jacoby, D. (1961), 'La Population de Constantinople à l'époque byzantine: un problème de démographie urbaine', *Byzantion* 31, pp. 81–109.

—— (1967), 'Les Quartiers juifs de Constantinople à l'époque byzantine', *Byzantion* 37, pp. 167–221.

—— (1991/92), 'Silk in Western Byzantium before the Fourth Crusade', *BZ* 84/85, pp. 452–500.

Janin, R. (1952), 'Les églises et les monastères de Constantinople byzantin', *RÉB* 9, pp. 143–153.

—— (1964), *Constantinople byzantin. Développement urbain et répertoire topographique*.² Paris.

Janon, Michel (1980), 'L'Aurès au VIᵉ siècle. Note sur le récit de Procope', *AntAfr* 15, pp. 345–351.

Jarry, J. (1968), *Hérésies et factions dans l'empire byzantine au VIIe siècle.* Cairo.

Jeauneau, Édouard (1991), 'The Neoplatonic Themes of *Processio* and *Reditus* in Eriugena', *Dionysius* 15, pp. 3–29.

Johnson, Allan Chester and West, Louis C. (1949), *Byzantine Egypt: Economic Studies.* Princeton.

Jolowicz, H. F. (1952), *Historical Introduction to Roman Law*². Cambridge.

—— and Nicholas, Barry (1972), *Historical Introduction to the Study of Roman Law*³. Cambridge.

Jones, A. H. M. (1968), *Studies in Roman Government and Law.* New York.

—— (1974), *The Roman Economy. Studies in Ancient Economic and Administrative History*, ed. P. A. Brunt. Oxford.

—— (1983), *The Cities of the Eastern Roman Provinces*². Oxford, 1971, repr. Amsterdam.

Kaegi, Walter E. (1965a), 'Arianism and the Byzantine Army in Africa, 533–546', *Traditio* 21, pp. 23–53.
—— (1965b), 'The Fifth-Century Twilight of Byzantine Paganism', *ClassMed* 26, pp. 243–275.
Kahler, Heinz (1967), *Hagia Sophia*. London.
Karivieri, Arja (1994), 'The "House of Proclus" on the Southern Slope of the Acropolis: A Contribution', in Castrén (1994), pp. 115–139.
Karlin-Hayter, Patricia (1973), 'Les *Akta dia Kalapodion*. Le contexte religieux et politique', *Byzantion* 43, pp. 84–107.
—— (1981a), 'Factions, Riots and Acclamations', *Variorum Reprints*. London.
—— (1981b), 'La Forme primitive des *Akta dia Kalapodion*', *Variorum Reprints*. London.
Kawar, I, (1956), 'The Arabs in the Peace Treaty of AD 561', *Arabica* 3, pp. 181–213; repr. in Irfan Shahîd, *Byzantium and the Semitic Orient before the Rise of Islam*. London, 1988.
Kazhdan, Alexander and Constable, Giles (1982), *People and Power in Byzantium*. Washington, D.C.
—— and Cutler, A. (1982), 'Continuity and Discontinuity in Byzantine History', *Byzantion* 52, pp. 429–478.
Keenan, James G. (1990), 'Evidence for the Byzantine Army in the Syene Papyri', *BASP* 27, pp. 139–150.
Kennedy, Hugh (1985a), 'From *Polis* to Madina: Urban Change in Late Antique and Early Islamic Syria', *PasPres* 106, pp. 3–27.
—— (1985b), 'The Last Century of Byzantine Syria: A Reinterpretation', *ByzF* 10, pp. 141–183.
—— (1987), 'Recent French Archaeological Work in Syria and Jordan', *BMGS* 11, pp. 245–252.
—— and Liebeschuetz, J. H. W. G. (1988), 'Antioch and the Villages of Northern Syria in the Fifth and Sixth Centuries AD: Trends and Problems', *Nottingham Medieval Studies*, 32, pp. 65–90.
Kenrich, P. M. (1982), 'Excavations at Sabratha 1948–1951', *Libyan Studies* 13, pp. 51–60.
Kent, J. P. C. (1959), Review of H. L. Anderson, *Light Weight Solidi and Byzantine Trade during the Sixth and Seventh Centuries*, *NChron* 19, pp. 237–240.
Kollantz, Miyakawa A. (1989) 'Die Hephthaliten, ihr Volkstum und Geschichte nach den chinesischen, orientalischer und byzantinischer Berichten', *Byzantiaka* 9, pp. 89–118.
Kondič, Vladimir (1984), 'Les Formes des fortifications protobyzantines dans la région des Portes de Fer', in *Villes et peuplement*, pp. 131–161.
Kraabel, Alf Thomas (1979), 'The Diaspora Synagogue: Archaeological and Epigraphic Evidence since Sukenik', *ANRW* II.19.1, pp. 477–510.
Krautheimer, Richard (1983), *Three Christian Capitals*. Berkeley, Calif.
Kuhnel, Gustav (1993), 'The Twelfth-Century Decoration of the Church of the Nativity: Eastern and Western Concord', in Tsafrir (1993a), pp. 197–203.
Kunkel, Wolfgang (1966), *An Introduction to Roman Legal and Constitutional History*, trans. J. M. Kelly. Oxford.

Lamma, Paolo (1947), 'Giovanni di Cappadocia', *Aevum. Rassegna di Scienze Storiche Linguistiche e Filologiche* 21, pp. 80–100.

Lang, David Marshall (1966), *The Georgians*. London.

Laslett, Peter (1971), *The World We Have Lost*[2]. London.

Lassus, Jean (1972), *Antioch-on-the-Orontes* V. *Les Portiques d'Antioche*. Princeton.

Lawrence, A. W. (1983), 'A Skeletal History of Byzantine Fortification', *BSA* 78, pp. 171–227.

Lee, A. D. (1993), *Information and Frontiers. Roman Foreign Relations in Late Antiquity*. Cambridge.

Lemerle, Paul (1954), 'Invasions et migrations dans les Balkans depuis la fin de l'époque romaine jusqu'au VIIIe siècle', *Revue Historique* 211, pp. 265–308.

—— (1979), *The Agrarian History of Byzantium from the Origins to the Twelfth Century*. Galway.

Levine, Lee I. (1979), 'The Jewish Patriarch (Nasi) in Third Century Palestine', *ANRW* II.19.2, pp. 649–688.

Lewin, Ariel (1989), 'La difesa dal deserto', *L'Africa romana. Atti del VI convegno di studio Assari, 16–18 dicembre 1988*. Sassari, pp. 197–209.

Lewis, Archibald R. (1969), 'Byzantine Light-Weight Solidi and Trade to the North Sea and the Baltic', in E. B. Atwood and Archibald Hill, eds, *Studies in Language, Literature and Culture of the Middle Ages and Later*. Austin, Texas.

Liebeschuetz, J. W. H. G. (1977), 'The Defences of Syria in the Sixth Century', *Studien zu den Militärgrenzen Roms* II: *Vorträge des 10. Internationalen Limeskongresses in der Germania Inferior*. Cologne/Bonn.

—— (1986), 'Generals, Federates and *Bucellarii* in Roman Armies around AD 400', in Freeman and Kennedy (1986), pp. 463–474.

—— (1989), 'The Gainas Crisis at Constantinople in 399', in D. H. French and C. S. Lightfoot, eds, *The Eastern Frontier of the Roman Empire. BAR* Int. Ser. 553, I. Oxford, pp. 277–284.

—— (1990), *Barbarians and Bishops: Army, Church and State in the Age of Arcadius and Chrysostom*. Oxford.

—— (1992), 'The End of the Ancient City', in Rich (1992), pp. 1–49.

Lieu, Samuel N. C. (1979), *The Religion of Light. An Introduction to the History of Manichaeism in China*. Hong Kong.

—— (1992), *Manichaeism in the Later Roman Empire and Medieval China*[2]. Tübingen.

Lopez, Robert Sabatino (1945), 'The Silk Industry in the Byzantine Empire', *Speculum* 20, pp. 1–42.

Maas, Michael (1986), 'Roman History and Christian Ideology in Justinianic Reform Legislation', *DOP* 40, pp. 17–31.

—— (1992), *John Lydus and the Roman Past. Antiquarianism and Politics in the Age of Justinian*. London/New York.

McCormick, Michael (1986), *Eternal Victory. Triumphal Rulership in Late Antiquity, Byzantium, and the Early Medieval West*. Cambridge/Paris.

MacCoull, Leslie S. B. (1988), *Dioscurus of Aphrodito*. Berkeley.

Maclagan, Michael (1968), *The City of Constantinople*. London.

MacMullen, Ramsay (1970), 'Market-Days in the Roman Empire', *Phoenix*

24, pp. 333–341.

—— (1974), *Roman Social Relations, 50 BC to AD 284*. New Haven.

—— (1980), 'How Big was the Roman Imperial Army?', *Klio* 62, pp. 451–460.

McNeill, William H. (1963) *The Rise of the West. A History of the Human Community*. Chicago.

Macrides, Ruth and Magdalino, Paul (1988), 'The Architecture of *ekphrasis*: Construction and Context of Paul the Silentiary's *ekphrasis* of Hagia Sophia', *BMGS* 12, pp. 47–82.

Magoulias, Harry J. (1967), 'The Lives of Byzantine Saints as Sources of Data for the History of Magic in the Sixth and Seventh Centuries AD', *Byzantion* 37, pp. 228–269.

—— (1990), 'The Lives of Saints as Sources for Byzantine Agrarian Life in the Sixth and Seventh Centuries', *GOrThR* 35, pp. 59–70.

Mai, Angelo (1827), *Scriptorum Veterum Nova Collectio a Vaticanis Codicibus Edita* II.

Mainstone, Rowland J. (1988), *Hagia Sophia. Architecture, Structure and Liturgy of Justinian's Great Church*. London.

Mallet, C. E. (1887), 'The Empress Theodora', *EHR* 2, pp. 1–20.

Malz, Gertrude (1942–43), 'The Date of Justinian's Edict XIII', *Byzantion* 16, pp. 135–141.

Mango, Cyril (1959), *The Brazen House. A Study of the Vestibule of the Imperial Palace of Constantinople*. Copenhagen.

—— (1972), 'The Church of Saints Sergius and Bacchus at Constantinople and the Alleged Tradition of Octagonal Palatine Churches', *JÖB* 21, pp. 189–193.

—— (1975), 'The Church of Sts. Sergius and Bacchus Again', *BZ* 68, pp. 385–392.

—— (1980), *Byzantium. The Empire of New Rome*. London.

—— (1981), 'Daily Life in Byzantium', *CEB* 16 = *JÖB* 31/1, pp. 337–353.

—— (1985), *Le Développement urbain de Constantinople (IVe–VIIe siècles)*. Travaux et Mémoires du centre de recherche d'histoire et civilisation de Byzance. Collège de France, Monographies 2. Paris.

—— (1995), 'The Water Supply', in Mango and Dagron (1995), pp. 9–18.

—— (1986), 'The Development of Constantinople as an Urban Centre', *CEB 17: Major Papers*. New Rochelle, N.Y., pp. 117–136.

—— and Dagron, Gilbert, eds (1995), *Constantinople and its Hinterland*. Papers from the twenty-seventh Spring Symposium of Byzantine Studies, Oxford, April 1993. Aldershot.

—— and Pritsak, Omeljan (1983), *Okeanos. Essays Presented to Ihor Ševčenko on his Sixtieth Birthday. Harvard Ukrainian Studies* VII. Cambridge, Mass.

Manojlović, G. M. (1936), 'Le Peuple de Constantinople', trans. H. Grégoire, *Byzantion* 11, pp. 617–716; first published in Serbo-Croat in *Nastavni Vjesnik* 12 (1904), pp. 1–91.

Markus, R. A. (1979), 'Carthage – Prima Justiniana – Ravenna: An Aspect of Justinian's *Kirchenpolitik*', *Byzantion* 49, pp. 277–302.

Mattingly, David J. (1987), 'Libyans and the "Limes": Culture and Society in Roman Tripolitania', *AntAfr* 23, pp. 71–74.

Mayerson, Philip (1986), 'The Saracens and the *Limes*', *BASOR* 262, pp. 35–47.
—— (1989), 'Saracens and Romans: Micro–Macro Relationships', *BASOR* 274, pp. 71–79.
Metcalf, William E. (1988), 'The Joint Reign Gold of Justin I and Justinian I', in Hahn and Metcalf (1988), pp. 19–27.
Meyendorff, John (1968), 'Justinian, the Empire and the Church', *DOP* 2, pp. 43–60.
—— (1983), *Byzantine Theology. Historical Trends and Doctrinal Themes²*. New York.
Miller, Dean A. (1969), *Imperial Constantinople*. New York.
Miller, J. Innes (1969), *The Spice Trade of the Roman Empire, 29 BC to AD 641*. Oxford.
Miller, Timothy S. (1990), 'The Sampson Hospital at Constantinople', *ByzF* 15, pp. 101–135.
Mitchell, Stephen (1993), *Anatolia: Land, Men and Gods in Asia Minor* II. Oxford.
Miyakawa, H. and Kollantz, A. (1989), 'Die Hephthaliten, ihr Volkstum und Geschichte nach dem chinesischen, orientalischen und byzantinischen Berichte', *Byzantiaka* 9, pp. 89–118.
Möberg, Axel, ed. and trans. (1924), *The Book of the Himyarites. Fragments of a Hitherto Unknown Syriac Work*. Lund.
Moderan, Yves (1986), 'Corippe et l'occupation byzantine de l'Afrique: pour une nouvelle lecture de la *Johannide*', *AntAfr* 22, pp. 195–212.
Mollaret, Henri H. (1989), 'Le Cas de la Peste', *Annales de démographie historique*, pp. 101–110.
Momigliano, Arnaldo (1955), 'Cassiodorus and Italian Culture of his Time', *ProcBrAc* 41, pp. 207–225.
Monks, George R. (1953), 'The Church at Alexandria and the City's Economic Life in the Sixth Century', *Speculum* 28, pp. 349–362.
Moorhead, J. (1983), 'Italian Loyalties during Justinian's Gothic War', *Byzantion* 53, pp. 575–596.
—— (1986), 'Culture and Power among the Ostrogoths', *Klio* 68, pp. 112–122.
—— (1994), *Justinian*. London.
Müller, Andreas E. (1993), 'Getreide für Konstantinopel', *JÖB* 43, pp. 1–20.
Mullet, Margaret and Scott, Roger, eds (1981), *Byzantium and the Classical Tradition*. Birmingham.
Muthesius, Anna (1993), 'The Byzantine Silk Industry: Lopez and Beyond', *JMedHist* 19, pp. 1–67.
Nautin, Pierre (1967), 'La Conversion du temple de Philae en église chrétienne', *CahArch* 17, pp. 1–43.
Nichols, Aidan (1992), *Rome and the Eastern Churches. A Study in Schism*. Edinburgh.
Nohl, Johannes (1961), *The Black Death. A Chronicle of the Plague*. London, 1926; repr. London.
Norman, A. F. (1958), 'Gradations in Later Municipal Society', *JRS* 48, pp. 79–85.

Ober, Josiah (1987), 'Pottery and Miscellaneous Artifacts from Fortified Sites in Northern and Western Attica', *Hesperia* 56, pp. 197–227.

Obolensky, Dimitri (1963), 'The Principles and Methods of Byzantine Diplomacy', *CEB* 12, I. Belgrade, pp. 45–61.

—— (1971), *The Byzantine Commonwealth: Eastern Europe, 500–1453.* London; repr. London, 1974.

O'Donnell, James J. (1979), *Cassiodorus.* Berkeley, Calif.

Oikonomides, Nicolas (1986), 'Silk Trade and Production in Byzantium from the Sixth to the Ninth Century: The Seals of the *Kommerkiarioi*', *DOP* 40, pp. 33–53.

Oman, Sir Charles (1962), *The Dark Ages, 476–918[7].* London.

Oppenheim, A. Leo (1964), *Ancient Mesopotamia. Portrait of a Dead Civilization.* Chicago.

Orestano, Riccardo (1956), 'Beni dei monaci et monasteri nella legislazione Giustinianea', in Giuffrè, A., ed., *Studi in onore di Pietro de Francisci*, III. Milan, pp. 560–593.

Osler, Douglas J. (1985), 'The Compilation of Justinian's Digest', *ZSavRom* 102, pp. 129–184.

Ostrasz, A. A. (1989), 'The Hippodrome of Gerasa: A Report on Excavations and Research, 1982-1987', *Syria* 66, pp. 51–77.

Ostrogorsky, George (1956), *History of the Byzantine State*, trans. Joan Hussey. Oxford.

Palmer, Andrew (1988), 'The Inauguration Anthem of Hagia Sophia in Edessa: A New Edition and Translation with Historical and Architectural Notes and a Comparison with a Contemporary Constantinopolitan *kontakion*', *BMGS* 12, pp. 117–167.

Parker, S. Thomas (1990), 'Preliminary Report on the 1987 Season of the *Limes Arabicus* Project', *BASOR* Suppl. 26, pp. 89–136.

—— (1991), 'Preliminary Report on the 1989 Season of the *Limes Arabicus* Project', *BASOR* Suppl. 27, pp. 117–154.

Patlagean, Evelyne (1974), 'La Pauvreté à Byzance au temps de Justinien: les origines d'un modèle politique', *Éudes sur l'histoire de la pauvreté (Moyen Age–XVIème siècle)*, I, sous la direction de Michel Mollat. Paris.

—— (1977), *Pauvreté économique et pauvreté sociale à Byzance, 4e–7e siècle.* Paris/La Haye.

—— (1986), *Povertà ed emarginazione in Bisanzio IV–VII Secolo.* Roma/Bari.

Pertusi, Agostino (1978), 'Giustiniano e la cultura del suo tempo', in Archi (1978), pp. 181–199.

Piccinini, P. (1991), 'L'ideologia politica bizantina', *Rivista di Bizantinistica* 1, pp. 163–180.

Poos, L. R. (1991), *A Rural Society after the Black Death: Essex 1350–1525.* Cambridge.

Popovič, Vladislav (1975), 'Les Témoins archéologiques des invasions avaro-slaves dans l'Illyricum byzantine', *MEFRA* 87, pp. 445–504.

—— (1978), 'La Descente des Kutrigurs, des Slaves et des Avars vers la mer Égée: Le Témoinage de l'archéologie', *CRAI*, pp. 596–648.

Potter, David (1994), *Prophets and Emperors. Human and Divine Authority from Augustus to Theodosius.* Cambridge, Mass.

Poulter, Andrew (1988), 'Nicopolis ad Istrum, Bulgaria: An Interim Report and the Excavation, 1985–7', *The Antiquarian Journal* 68, pp. 69–89.

—— (1990), 'Nicopolis', *Current Archaeology* 121, pp. 37–42.

Pringle, Denys (1981), *The Defence of Byzantine Africa from Justinian to the Arab Conquest.* 2 vols. BAR Int. Ser. 99 (i-ii). Oxford.

Pringsheim, F. (1940), 'The Character of Justinian's Legislation', *Law Quarterly Review* 56, pp. 229–246.

Rabello, Alfredo M. (1987), *Giustiniano, Ebrei e Samaritani alla luce delle fonti storico-letterarie, ecclesiastiche e giuridiche.* 2 vols. Milan.

Ravegnani, Giorgio (1989), *La corte di Giustiniano.* Rome.

Rémondon, Roger (1955), 'L'Édit XIII de Justinien, a-t-il été promulgué en 539?', *Chron.d'Ég.* 30, pp. 112–121.

—— (1972), 'L'église dans la société égyptienne à l'époque byzantine', *Chron.d'Ég.* 42, pp. 254–277.

Reynolds, Joyce and Tannenbaum, Robert (1987), *Jews and God-Fearers at Aphrodisias. Greek Inscriptions with Commentary.* PCPhS Suppl. XII. Cambridge.

Rice, David Talbot, ed. (1958), *The Great Palace of the Byzantine Emperors.* Edinburgh.

Rich, John, ed. (1992), *The City in Late Antiquity.* London.

Roueché, Charlotte (1979), 'A New Inscription from Aphrodisias and the Title *Pater Poleos*', *GRBS* 20, pp. 173–185.

—— (1984), 'Acclamations in the Later Roman Empire: New Evidence from Aphrodisias', *JRS* 84, pp. 181–199.

—— (1989), with contributions by J. M. Reynolds, *Aphrodisias in Late Antiquity. JRS* Monographs V. London.

—— (1993), *Performers and Partisans at Aphrodisias in the Roman and Late Roman Periods. JRS* Monographs VI. London.

Roques, D. (1994), 'Procope de Césarée et la Cyrénaique de 6ᵉ s. ap. J.C.', *Libyan Studies* 25, pp. 259–264.

Rubin, Berthold (1960), *Das Zeitalter Iustinians* I. Berlin.

Rubin, Z. (1989), 'Byzantium and Southern Arabia – the Policy of Anastasius', in D. H. French and C. S. Lightfoot, eds, *The Eastern Frontier of the Roman Empire. Proceedings of a Colloquium held at Ankara in September, 1988.* BAR Int. Ser. 553. Oxford, pp. 383–420.

Runciman, Steven (1977), *The Byzantine Theocracy.* Cambridge.

Ruprechtsberger, Erwin M. (1989), 'Byzantinische Befestigungen in Algerien und Tunisien', *Antike Welt* 20, pp. 2–21.

Russell, James (1986), 'Transformation in Early Byzantine Urban Life: The Contribution and Limitations of Archaeological Evidence', *CEB* 17, *Major Papers.* New Rochelle, N.Y., pp. 137–154.

—— (1987), 'Excavation and Restoration at Roman Anemurium (Turkey)', *Transactions of the Royal Society of Canada* 5/2, pp. 145–162.

Russell, Josiah Cox (1958), *Late Ancient and Medieval Population Control.* Transactions of the American Philosophical Society, n.s. 48, pt. 3. Philadelphia.

—— (1968), 'That Earlier Plague', *Demography* 5, pp. 174–184.

—— (1972), 'Population in Europe 500–1500', in Carlo M. Cipolla, ed., *The Fontana Economic History of Europe.* London, pp. 25–70.

Saradi-Mendelovici, H. (1988), 'The Demise of the Ancient City and the Emergence of the Mediaeval City in the Eastern Roman Empire', *Échos du Monde Classique/Classical Views* 32, n.s. 7, pp. 365–401.

—— (1995), 'The *Kallos* of the Byzantine City: The Development of the Rhetorical *Topos* and Historical Reality', *Gesta* 34, pp. 37–56.

Sartre, Maurice (1982), *Trois études sur l'Arabie romaine et byzantine*. Collection Latomus 178. Brussels.

Sauvaget, J. (1939), 'Les Ghassanids et Sergiopolis', *Byzantion* 14, pp. 115–130.

Schiller, A. Arthur (1971), 'The Courts are No More', *Studi in onore di Edoardo Volterra*. Milan, pp. 469–502.

Schulz, F. (1946), *History of Roman Legal Science*. Oxford.

Schur, Nathan (1989), *History of the Samaritans*. Beiträge zur Erforschung des Alten Testamentes und des Antiken Judentums 18. Frankfurt am Main.

Scorpan, C. (1980), *Limes Scythiae. Topographical and Stratigraphical Research on Late Roman Fortifications on the Lower Danube*. BAR Int. Ser.

Scott, Roger (1981), 'The Classical Tradition in Byzantine Historiography', in Mullett and Scott (1981), pp. 61–74.

—— (1985), 'Malalas, the *Secret History* and Justinian's Propaganda', *DOP* 39, pp. 99–109.

—— (1987), 'Justinian's Coinage and Easter reforms and the Date of the *Secret History*', *BMGS* 11, pp. 215–221.

Segal, J. B. (1955), 'Mesopotamian Communities from Julian to the Rise of Islam', *ProcBrAc* 41, pp. 109–39.

—— (1970), *Edessa, 'The Blessed City'*. Oxford.

Segrè, Angelo (1942–43), 'Essays on Byzantine Economic History I. The *Annona Civica* and the *Annona Militaris*', *Byzantion* 16, pp. 393–444.

Shahîd, Irfan (1960), 'Byzantium and Kinda', *BZ* 53, pp. 57–73.

—— (1971), *The Martyrs of Najran. New Documents*. Brussels.

—— (1979), 'Byzantium in South Arabia', *DOP* 33, pp. 23–94.

—— (1989), *Byzantium and the Arabs in the Fifth Century*. Washington, D.C.

Shaw, Brent D. (1982), 'Fear and Loathing: The Nomad Menace and Roman Africa', *L'Afrique Romaine/Roman Africa*. The Vanier Lectures for 1980. Ottawa, pp. 29–50.

Smith, Morton (1983), 'How Magic was Changed by the Triumph of Christianity', *Graeco-Arabica* 2, pp. 51–58.

Smith, Sidney (1954), 'Events in Arabia in the 6th Century AD', *BSOAS* 16, pp. 425–468.

Snively, Carolyn S. (1984), 'Cemetery Churches of the Early Byzantine Period in Eastern Illyricum', *GOrThR* 29, pp. 117–124.

Sodini, Jean-Pierre (1993), 'La Contribution de l'archéologie à la connaissance du monde byzantin (IVᵉ–VIIᵉ siècles)', *DOP* 47, pp. 139–184.

—— Tate, G., Bavant, B. and S.; Biscop, J.-L.; Orssaud, D. (1980), 'Déhès (Syrie du Nord), Campagnes I–III (1976–1978)', *Syria* 57, pp. 1–304.

Sotinel, Claire (1992), 'Autorité pontificale et pouvoir impérial sous le règne de Justinien: Le pape Vigile', *MEFRA* 104/1, pp. 439–463.

Spieser, Jean-Michel (1984), 'La Ville en Grèce du IIIᵉ au VIIᵉ siècle', in *Villes et peuplement*, pp. 315–340.

Spyridakis, Stylianos (1967), 'Circus Factions in Sixth-Century Crete', *GRBS* 8, pp. 249–250.

Stambaugh, John E. (1988), *The Ancient Roman City*. Baltimore.

Stöckle, Albert (1911), *Spatrömische und byzantinische Zunfte. Klio*, Beiheft IX; repr. Wiesbaden, 1963.
Stolte, Bernard (1994), 'Justinian *Bifrons*', in Paul Magdalino, ed., *New Constantines. The Rhythm of Imperial Renewal in Byzantium, 4th–13th Centuries*. Aldershot.
Tardieu, M. (1986), 'Sabiens coraniques et "Sabiens" de Harran', *Journal Asiatique* 274, pp. 1–44.
Teall, J. L. (1965), 'The Barbarians in Justinian's Armies', *Speculum* 40, pp. 294–322.
Thomas, J. A. C. (1975), *The Institutes of Justinian. Text, Translation and Commentary*. Cape Town.
—— (1976), *Textbook of Roman Law*. Amsterdam.
Thompson, E. A. (1969), *The Goths in Spain*. Oxford.
—— (1980), 'Barbarian Invaders and Roman Collaborators', *Florilegium* 2, pp. 71–88.
—— (1982), *Romans and Barbarians. The Decline of the Western Empire*. Madison.
Thurman, W. S. (1968), 'How Justinian I sought to handle the Problem of Religious Dissent', *GOrThR* 13, pp. 15–40.
—— (1971), 'A Juridical and Theological Concept of Nature in the Sixth Century AD', *Byzantinoslavica* 32, pp. 77–85.
Topping, Eva (1976), 'The Apostle Peter, Justinian and Romanos the Melode', *BMGS* 2, pp. 1–15.
—— (1978), 'On Earthquakes and Fires: Romanos' Encomium to Justinian', *BZ* 71, pp. 22–35.
Toumanoff, Cyril (1963), *Studies in Christian Caucasian History*. Georgetown.
Trimingham, J. Spencer (1979), *Christianity Among the Arabs in Pre-Islamic Times*. London/New York.
Trombley, Frank (1985), 'Paganism in the Greek World at the End of Antiquity', *HThR* 78, pp. 327–352.
—— (1987), 'Korykos in Cilicia Trachis: The Economy of a Small Coastal City in Late Antiquity (*Saec.* V–VI) – A Precis', *AHB* 1.1, pp. 16–23.
—— (1993–94), *Hellenic Religion and Christianization, c. 370–529*. I (1993); II (1994). Leiden.
Tsafrir, Yoram (1989), 'Christian Archaeology in Israel in Recent Years', *Actes du XI' Congrès international d'archéologie chrétienne* II. Collection de l'École Française de Rome 123, pp. 1737–1770.
—— (ed.) (1993a), *Ancient Churches Revealed*. Jerusalem.
—— (1993b), 'The Development of Ecclesiastical Architecture in Palestine', in Tsafrir (1993a), pp. 1–16.
—— (1993c), 'Monks and Monasteries in Southern Sinai', in Tsafrir (1993a), pp. 315–333.
Tsangadas, Byron C. (1980), *The Fortification and Defense of Constantinople*. East European Monographs LXXI. Boulder, Colo.
Tsirpanlis, C. N. (1974), 'John Lydos on the Imperial Administration', *Byzantion* 44, pp. 479–501.
Turpin, W. (1987), 'The Purpose of Roman Law Codes', *ZSavRom* 104, pp. 620–630.

Turtledove, Harry (1983), 'The True Size of the Post-Justinianic Army', *BS/ÉB* 10/2, pp. 216–222.

Updegraff, R. T. (1988), with additional remarks by L. Török, 'The Blemmyes I. The Rise of the Blemmyes and the Roman Withdrawal under Diocletian', *ANRW* II.10.1, pp. 44–106.

Ure, Percy Neville (1951), *Justinian and his Age*. Harmondsworth.

Van den Ven, P. (1965), 'L'Accession de Jean le Scholastique en siège patriarchal de Constantinople en 565', *Byzantion* 35, pp. 320–352.

Vasiliev, A. A. (1950), *Justin the First*. Dumbarton Oaks Studies I. Cambridge, Mass.

—— (1964), *The History of the Byzantine Empire*². Madison, Wisc.

Velkov, Velizar (1977), *Cities in Thrace and Dacia in Late Antiquity*². Amsterdam.

Vercleyen, Frank (1988), 'Tremblements de terre à Constantinople: L'Impôt sur la population', *Byzantion* 58, pp. 155–173.

Vernadsky, George (1942–43), 'Sur l'origine des Alains', *Byzantion* 16, pp. 81–86.

Veyne, Paul (1981), 'Clientèle et corruption au service de l'état: La Venalité des offices dans le Bas-Empire romain', *Annales E.S.C.* 36, pp. 339–360.

—— (1990), *Bread and Circuses*, trans. Brian Pearce. London.

Vryonis, Speros Jr. (1962), 'The Question of Byzantine Mines', *Speculum* 37, pp. 1–17.

—— (1963), 'Byzantine *Demokratia* and the Guilds in the Eleventh Century', *DOP* 17, pp. 289–314.

—— (1981), 'The *Panegyris* of the Byzantine Saint: A Study in the Nature of a Medieval Institution, its Origins and Fate', in Hackel (1981), pp. 196–226.

Wagner, Guy (1987), *Les Oasis d'Égypte à l'époque grecque, romaine et byzantine d'après les documents grecs*. Cairo.

Waltz, Pierre, ed. (1960), *Anthologie Grecque*², I (Livres I–IV), Paris.

Ward, Roy Bowen (1992), 'Women in Roman Baths', *HThR* 85, pp. 125–147.

Warmington, B. H. (1954), *The North African Provinces from Diocletian to the Vandal Conquest*. Cambridge.

Watson, Alan, trans. (1985), *The Digest of Justinian*. 4 vols. Philadelphia.

Whitby, Mary (1985a), 'The Occasion of Paul the Silentiary's *Ekphrasis* of S. Sophia', *CQ* 35, pp. 215–228.

—— (1985b), 'Paul the Silentiary and Claudian', *CQ* 31, pp. 507–516.

Whitby, Michael (1985a), 'Justinian's Bridge over the Sangarios and the Date of Procopius' *De Aedificiis*', *JHS* 105, pp. 129–148.

—— (1985b), 'The Long Walls of Constantinople', *Byzantion* 55, pp. 560–583.

—— (1986a), 'Procopius and the Development of Roman Defences in Upper Mesopotamia', in Freeman and Kennedy (1986), pp. 717–735.

—— (1986b), 'Procopius' Description of Dara (*Buildings* II.1–3)', in Freeman and Kennedy (1986), pp. 737–783.

—— (1991), 'John of Ephesus and the Pagans: Pagan Survivals in the Sixth Century', in M. Salamon, ed., *Paganism in the Later Roman Empire and in Byzantium*. Cracow, pp. 111–131.

Whitehouse, David and Williamson, Andrew (1973), 'Sasanian Maritime Trade', *Iran* 11, pp. 24–49.

Whittow, Mark (1990), 'Ruling the Late Roman and Early Byzantine City: A Continuous History', *Past and Present* 129, pp. 3–29.

Wickham, Chris (1981), *Early Medieval Italy. Central Powers and Local Society*. London/Basingstoke.

Wigram, W. A. (1923), *The Separation of the Monophysites*. London; repr. New York, 1978.

Wilken, Robert L. (1980), 'The Jews and Christian Apologetics after Theodosius I *Cunctos Populos*', *HThR* 73, pp. 451–471.

Wilson, N. G. (1983), *Scholars of Byzantium*. London.

Wiseman, James R. (1984), 'The City in Macedonia Secunda', in *Villes et peuplement*, pp. 289–314.

Worp, K. (1982), 'Byzantine Imperial Titulature in the Greek Documentary Papyri', *ZPapEpig* 45, pp. 199–223.

Wozniak, Frank E. (1982), 'The Justinianic Fortification of Interior Illyricum', in Hohlfelder (1982), pp. 119–209.

Yannopoulos, Panayotis (1991), 'Le Couronnement de l'empereur à Byzance: ritual et fond institutionnel', *Byzantion* 61, pp. 71–92.

Zinsser, Hans (1960), *Rats, Lice and History*. Boston, 1935; repr. New York.

INDEX

Anastasius 11, 23, 26, 29–31, 35–6, 38, 42–3, 47, 50, 55, 66, 76–7, 82, 90, 97, 103, 105–7, 125, 178, 195, 197, 211, 222, 234, 247, 259, 270; his family 40, 102, 122, 124; his coronation oath 61; builds fortress of Dara 90–1, 221

Anastasius, grandson of Theodora 102

Anastasius, patriarch of Antioch 263

Anatolius, patriarch, crowns Marcian 61

Anatolius, member of law commission 203

Anchialos in Scythia Minor 77

Anicia Juliana, builder of St Polyeuktos 28, 101, 216–17

Ankara 16

annona civica 31–3

Anonymous of Banduri 258

Anonymous Valesianus 86

Antalas, son of Guefan, sheikh of the Frexes 83, 134, 169–71, 261

Antlas, Hippodrome claqueur 119

Anthemius of Tralles, architect of Hagia Sophia 217

Anthimius, praetorian prefect 28

Anthimus, patriarch of Constantinople 111, 184

Antioch 7, 11, 17–18, 38–9, 45, 106, 149, 161, 221, 233, 237–8; circus at 36; Olympia closed down 37; headquarters of Master of Soldiers of the East 43; sack by Persians 156–7; rebuilt by Justinian 226–7

Antiochus, victim of John the Cappadocian 194

Antonina, wife of Belisarius 98, 102, 116, 127, 143, 159, 173, 175, 186; her natural son Photius 159; her lover Theodosius 159; plots the fall of John the Cappadocian 196–7

Antony and Cleopatra 3

Apamea, circus at 36

Aper, praetorian prefect 13–14

Aphrodite, Greek goddess 16

Aphthartodocetists, Aphthartodocetism 106, 183, 192, 213, 262–3, 268

Apion family 49

Apollinaris, Apollinarianism 71, 73

Apollinarius, Melkite patriarch of Alexandria 263

Arcadius, emperor 25, 27

Archelaos, patrician 133

Archimedes 217

Areobindus, officer assigned to Africa 169–70

Areobindus, steward of Theodora 102

Argos (Greece), theatre 35

Ariadne, Zeno the Isaurian's widow 11, 21

Arians 105, 171; Arianism 71; among the Vandals 81–2, 126, 130, 134–5; among the Goths 85; *see also* Ravenna

Aristotle 24, 70; *Politics* 24

Armenia 20, 48, 91, 110, 155, 210, 267; Persarmenia 48, 91, 115, 165, 265; its capital Dvin 265; conversion to Christianity 91

army 48–52; its size 51; *comitatenses* 49, 220; *limitanei* 49–51, 220

Arsaces, Armenian commander of garrison at Sura 155

Arsaces, conspirator against Justinian 176

Artabanes 104; prevented from marrying Preiecta 104

Artabanes, army officer, member of Arsacid house 170, 176, 179

Artemis, Greek goddess 16; Artemision 16

Aspar, leader of Gothic federates 21

Athalaric 86, 136–7, 181

Athanagild 180, 200

Athanasius, archbishop of Alexandria 72

Athanasius, monk, grandson of Theodora 102, 192, 262, 268

Fifth Ecumenical Council 74, 188,
190, 193
Fifty Decisions 204
Firmus of Numidia 189
Flavian, patriarch of
Constantinople 73
Flavian, patriarch of Antioch 106
Fliehburgen 220, 222–3, 227
Forbidden City of Beijing 24
Forum of Arcadius 27
Forum of the Ox 27
Forum Tauri (Forum of
Theodosius) 26–7, 52

Gaianus 183, 200; Gaianists, *see*
Aphthartodocetists
Gainas, leader of Gothic laeti 27
Gaiseric, Vandal king 80–2, 84,
126–7
Gaius Pescennius Niger 16
Gaius, jurist 202, his *Institutes* 204
Galba, Roman emperor 14
Galerius 14; his Caesar, Severus 14
Galla Placidia 80
Gallienus, emperor 13
Gamaliel VI, last *Nasi* 242
Gaza 233; school 27, 271
Gelimer, last Vandal king 81,
126–7, 129–33, 233
Gerasa, 255; circus at 37
Germanus, Justin's nephew 79, 97,
104, 152, 228, 263; suppresses
rebellion of Stotzas 135–6;
retreats from Antioch 156;
marries Matasuintha 176–7;
disliked by Theodora 201, 269
Germanus, defends Long Wall
across Chersonese 254
Ghassanids 50, 86–9, 117, 221,
223; Harith, Ghassanid sheikh
50, 87, 118, 154, 159, 166, 259;
asks for Monophysite bishop
185; Harith's brother, Abu-Karib,
phylarch of Third Palestine
87–8; his son Mundhir 267
Gibbon, Edward 1, 2, 38–9, 55,
159, 222
Godas 127
God-fearers 19, 240

Golden Gate 27–8
Golden Milestone (Constantinople)
17, 25
Gortyna, metropolis of Crete,
circus at 37
Grand Chamberlain, *see praepositus
sacri cubiculi*
Gratian, emperor 20
Greek Anthology 30, 272
Greens, Hippodrome faction 18,
28, 36–40, 100; in Nika revolt
119–21, 123–5; Green party of
Cyzicus 197
Gregory of Nazianzus 68
Gregory the Great 201
Gregory of Tours 160
Grod, king of 'Huns' of Bosporus
92
Gubazes, Laz king 158, 166–9
Gubba Barraya monastery 192
Guefan, Berber sheikh 83
guilds 52–4
Guntarith, *bucellarius* of Solomon
152; leads putsch 170, 189

Habib, holy man 109, 220
Hadrian, emperor 30; prohibits
circumcision 240
Hagia Eirene 24, 54, 217, 256
Hagia Sophia 1, 3–4, 8, 12, 16,
18, 24–5, 31, 40, 54, 56, 61,
64, 77, 101, 189, 213, 216–18,
241, 256, 258, 262, 270;
destroyed in Nika revolt 121,
125; collapse of dome 253
Harpocrates 72
Harran (Carrhae) 70, site of cult
of Moon Goddess 66
Hart, Liddell 116
Helena, Constantine's mother 18;
her statue 24; St Helena church
54
Helios, sun god 16
Heraclius, emperor, first to use
term *basileus* officially 58
Hermogenes, Master of Offices
116, 118
Hero of Alexandria, author of *On
Vaulting* 217

Herodotus 2, 24, 79
Heruls, barbarian tribe 13, 122;
sack Athens 37, 68; revolt of
Herul mercenaries under Sindual
181
Hilderic, Vandal king 85–6,
126–7, 128–9
Himyar (*mod.* Yemen) 95, 234–5,
265; Himyarite affair 112–14,
244; royal city Zafar 113
Hippodrome 11–12, 16–18, 20,
24, 33, 35, 53, 60–1, 65, 100,
119–25, 194, 253, 256–7, 264;
chariot races 36–7; demes
36–40; parties dress like Huns
40
*History of the Patriarchs of
Alexandria* 97, 111
History of the Wars of Justinian, see
Procopius
Hodgkin, Thomas 86
Holy Apostles church 3, 27, 65,
216, 218, 255
Horapollo 70
Hormisdas Palace 35, 62, 110;
shelters Anthimus 184
Hormisdas, pope 77–8, 98; 107,
186
Huneric, Vandal king 82
Hypatius, nephew of Anastasius
11, 103, 107, 122–5

Iamblichus 69
Iaudas, Berber sheikh 134, 152–3,
171
Ibas, bishop of Edessa 71–2, 75,
186
Iberians 93; Peter the Iberian 93;
Iberian royal house flees to
Constantinople 115
Ildibad, Witigis' successor 151
Ildiger, army officer 146–7
imperial office 58–65; emperor
compared with David, Solomon
and Moses 60, 258
Institutes 41, 204–5, 207
Irnerius of Bologna 207
Isidore of Miletus 217
Isidore the Younger 217, 258

Isis 72
Istanbul 1, 217
Iunillus 199
Izedh Gushnasp, Persian diplomat,
167, 258–9

Jacob Baradaeus 185–6, 192, 262,
267–8
Jews 45, 95, 120, 140, 233,
240–7; Jewish academy at
Nisibis 20; Jewish synagogues
19; putsch in Himyar 112–13;
the patriarch or *Nasi* 242; the
archipherecite 243; conversion
of Jews at Boreum 246–7; Bar
Kokhba revolt 247
John, successor of Elias as
patriarch of Jerusalem 107
John, archimandrite of
Beith-Apthonia 106
John, brother of Rusticus 168
John, member of Arsacid house
170
John, son of Sisiniolus 170
John, son(?) of Theodora 102
John of Tella 185
John II, pope 77, 85, 184
John III, pope 192, 200, 262
John Chrysostom 24
John Malalas, chronicler 7, 12, 68,
118, 237, 248–9
John, nephew of Vitalian 143–7,
149, 154, 172–3, 201
John of Asia (John of Ephesus) 6,
102, 161, 185, 198, 249–50;
his *Lives of the Eastern Saints* 6,
99, 108, 220, 233; life saved by
Maro 109
John of Nikiu 7, 63
John Laxarion 199
John Philoponus 8, 70, 262
John the Cappadocian, praetorian
prefect 44, 49, 125, 151, 153,
159, 194–9, 245; dismissed in
Nika revolt 121, 194; opposes
Vandal expedition 127; his fall
196–7; chairs commission to
update law code 203; suppresses
most dioceses 212

Master of Soldiers 49; in the East
43; of Illyricum 43; of Africa
49; of Thrace 49
Matasuintha, daughter of
Amalasuintha 140, 145, 149,
176–7
Maurice, emperor 181
Maxentius, son of Maximian 14
Maximian, archbishop of Ravenna
238
Maximian, colleague of Diocletian
14
Maximin Daia, Caesar 14–15
Mazdak 63, 89; Mazdakites 63,
89–90
Mazikes 94
Megara, Greek city state 16
Megas, bishop of Beroea 156, 228
Mehmed II Fatih, mosque in
Istanbul 218
Menander Protector 5, 37
Menas, director of Hospice of
Sampson, consecrated patriarch
184, 188, 217; his death 189
merchants 52–53
Mese, main street of
Constantinople 17, 25, 27, 52
Mesopotamia, province 6, 20
Metanoia monastery at Canopus
34, 75–6, 105, 111
Michael the Syrian 6
Mihr-Mihroe, Persian general
117; captured by John
Troglita 166–7; campaigns in
Lazica 167
Milan 14–15, 17
Mohammed, prophet 114
monasteries 56–57, 164; at Scetis
94
Monophysitism 38, 71, 73, 75–8,
86, 91, 231, 250–1, 268, 272;
Monophysites 103, 105, 125,
183–92; their persecution
105–12, 234
Montanists 105, 245, 251
Monte Cassino, founded by St
Benedict 71
Moscow Kremlin 24
Moses 8

Mundilas, one of Belisarius'
bodyguards 146–7
Mundo, Gepid prince 25, 52, 79,
118, 122, 139; his son Maurice
139
municipal councils 47–8, 211,
225, 228

Najran, Yemenite city 113
Narses Kamsarakan 52, 250; his
brother Aratius 52; his brother
Isaac 52, 172–3; Kamsarakan
feudal family 115
Narses, eunuch 43, 119, 124,
147–8, 183, 191, 199–201,
224–5, 266; his victory in Italy
177–81, 196–7; his death 201
Nea Ekklesia (Theotokos) in
Jerusalem 3, 218; *hegoumenos*
Constantine 218
Negus of Ethiopia 23
Nero, Roman emperor 14
Nestorius 71–3, 75–6, 107, 186;
Nestorians, Nestorianism 8,
185–6, 251
Nicaea, council of 93; Nicene
Creed 76, 268
Nicomedia 16–17; circus at 36
Nika riots 7, 24–5, 30, 34, 40,
44, 63–4, 104, 119–25, 193–5,
200, 204
Nisibis, city 20, 72, 259, 266
Nobadia, Nubian kingdom 94
nomos empsychos 58, 61
Nonnus, abbot of the New Laura
187
Numerian, son of Carus, Roman
emperor 14

Odoacer 22–3, 78, 81, 84, 151,
176, 199
Olympic Games 21, 37
Oman, Sir Charles 85
Opilio, Roman senator 138
Origen, Origenism 187–8
Othman, caliph 181
Ottoman Turks 18, 28
Oxyrhynchus in Egypt, circus at
37

Theodoric, king of the Ostrogoths 22–3, 77–8, 82, 84–6, 115, 136–7, 153, 171, 174, 176
Theodosian Code 46
Theodosian Walls of Constantinople 18, 28–9
Theodosius I, emperor 20–1, 25–6, 32, 60, 66, 86, 222; Theodosian house 40, 101
Theodosius II, emperor 21, 24, 27, 29, 41, 46, 65, 73–4, 202, 241–2, 270; his consort Eudocia 239
Theodosius, archimandrite of the Judaean cenobitic monasteries 107
Theodosius, Monophysite patriarch of Alexandria, 111, 183–5, 192, 250, 262; his death 269
Theodotus 198
Theopaschite doctrine 77–8, 98, 271
Theophanes the Confessor 7, his *Chronographia* 7
Theophilus, jurist 203–4
Theophilus, suppresses Samaritans 249
Thermopylae 28, 79, 223–4, 254
Thessaloniki 16–18, 28, 35, 43, 97, 137, 150, 223, 238; circus at 36; seat of prefecture of Illyricum 43, 227
Theudobald, Merovingian king 178–9
Third World 1
Thomas, bishop of Apamea 157, 228
Thrasamund, Vandal king 82, 85
Three Chapters dispute 7, 175, 186–92, 271
Thucydides 2, 160–1
Tiber river 16–17
Tiberius II 5, 51, 237, 264, 266–8
Tigris river 20
Timothy 'the Cat' 76
Timothy III, patriarch of Alexandria 101, 113
Timothy Salofaciolus 76, 105
Titus, Roman emperor 132
Topkapi palace 16

Totila (Baduila) 151, 154, 171–8, 199, 201; defeated at *Busta Gallorum* 177–7, 200
trade and commerce 232–9; traders Elijah and Theodore 233–4; silk 26, 234–5; olive oil 233, 238; *see also* Axum
Trajan, Roman emperor 13, 142; founded Nicopolis on the Danube 222
Trajan's Forum in Rome 26
Trdat the Great of Armenia 91
Trdat, Armenian architect 217
Tribonian, 121, 125, 193–4, 199, 210–11; chairs commission to draw up the *Digest* 203–4
Tribunus, Greek doctor 166
Triclinium of the Nineteen Couches in the Great Palace 34, 62
Trier 17
Tritheists, Monophysite splinter group 102, 192, 262
Tryphon 122
Tsars of Kievan and Muscovite Russia 62
Tyre, circus at 37
Tzani 93–4
Tzath, chosen king of Lazica 168

Ulitheus, uncle of Witigis 144
Ulpian, jurist 202
University of Constantinople 27
University of Istanbul 27
Uraias, Witigis' nephew 147, 149, 151
urban prefect 43
Ure, Percy 8

Valens, emperor 20, 31, 45; abandons conscription 49
Valentinian I, emperor 20
Valentinian III, emperor 22, 80–1, 126, 202; Eudoxia, his wife 81
Valerian, Master of Soldiers 159
Varsanuphius, monk 249
Vatican Library 4
Verina, empress, builds church of the Virgin 54

Vespasian, Roman emperor 132
Via Egnatia 28
Victor of Vita 80
Victor Tunnenis, bishop of
Tunnena 7, 191
Victoria Augusti 18
Victorinus, builder of *Hexamilion*
wall at Isthmus of Corinth
224
Vigilius, deacon 186; pope 145–6,
174, 181, 188–90, 238, 272
Virgin Diaconissa, church 65
Vitalian, Master of Soldiers in
Thrace 76–7, 97–8, 107–8, 271
Vitalius, Master of Soliders of
Illyricum 171–2

Whites, Hippodrome faction 18,
36, 39
Witigis 140–2, 144–6; 149–51,
155, 175; marries Matasuintha
140

women, laws protecting their
rights 209–10

Yusuf As'ar Yat'an a.k.a. Masruq
a.k.a. Dhu Nuwas 112–13; *see
also* Himyar

Z'ura, holy man 111, 220
Zachariah of Mytilene 161
Zeno the Isaurian 11, 21–3, 25,
31, 55, 76–8, 105, 235; his
Henotikon 76, 81, 105, 107;
a new *Henotikon* 268
Zeuxippus Baths 17, 25–6, 30;
destroyed in Nika revolt 121
Zhamasp, brother of Kavadh 90
Zichia 92
Zimarchus 96
Zoilus, Palestinian monk chosen
patriarch of Alexandria 111
Zosimus, author of *New History*
67